Moving Environments

ENVIRONMENTAL
HUMANITIES

Moving Environments

Affect, Emotion, Ecology, and Film

Alexa Weik von Mossner, editor

WILFRID LAURIER UNIVERSITY PRESS

Wilfrid Laurier University Press acknowledges the financial support of the Government of Canada through the Canada Book Fund for our publishing activities.

LAURIER
Inspiring Lives.

Library and Archives Canada Cataloguing in Publication

Moving environments : affect, emotion, ecology, and film / edited by Alexa Weik von Mossner.
(Environmental humanities series)
Includes bibliographical references and index.
Issued in print and electronic formats.
ISBN 978-1-77112-002-9 (pbk.).—ISBN 978-1-77112-004-3 (epub).—
ISBN 978-1-77112-003-6 (pdf)

1. Motion pictures—Psychological aspects. 2. Motion pictures—Social aspects. 3. Human ecology in motion pictures. 4. Ecocriticism. I. Weik von Mossner, Alexa, author, editor II. Series: Environmental humanities series

PN1995.M73 2014   791.43'66   C2014-902718-4
                                                                 C2014-902719-2

Front-cover image: *Being* Caribou © 2005 National Film Board of Canada. Cover design and text design by Angela Booth Malleau.

© 2014 Wilfrid Laurier University Press
Waterloo, Ontario, Canada
www.wlupress.wlu.ca

RECYCLED
Paper made from
recycled material
FSC   FSC® C103567
www.fsc.org

This book is printed on FSC recycled paper and is certified Ecologo. It is made from 100% post-consumer fibre, processed chlorine free, and manufactured using biogas energy.

Printed in Canada

Every reasonable effort has been made to acquire permission for copyright material used in this text, and to acknowledge all such indebtedness accurately. Any errors and omissions called to the publisher's attention will be corrected in future printings.

Contents

Acknowledgements

My great thanks go out to everyone who contributed to making this collection possible, which grew out of a highly successful and inspiring workshop I had the pleasure of organizing at the Rachel Carson Center for Environment and Society at the University of Munich during my time as Carson Fellow. The book owes its existence, foremost, to the community of colleagues who participated in this workshop and whose fine work is represented here. To all my contributors, thank you for the many rich and thought-provoking exchanges and conversations about the interrelations of affect, emotion, ecology, and film that took place before, during, and after the workshop and for your enthusiasm, dedication, and great patience. I also wish to thank the two directors of the Rachel Carson Center, Christof Mauch and Helmuth Trischler, for their extremely generous support of the project, both during the workshop phase and later on when it began to transform itself into a book.

I am indebted to Lisa Quinn, Acquisitions Editor at Wilfrid Laurier University Press, and to the series editor, Cheryl Lousley, who immediately saw the timeliness and worth of the project and supported it from the earliest moment of its gestation. My thanks also go to the two anonymous readers for their insightful comments and suggestions for revisions.

I am grateful to Elsevier for granting permission to reprint portions of my article "Troubling Spaces: Ecological Risk, Narrative Framing, and Emotional Engagement in Franny Armstrong's *The Age of Stupid*," which originally appeared in *Emotion, Space and Society* 6.1 (2013), in Chapter 2 of the volume.

Introduction

Ecocritical Film Studies and the Effects of Affect, Emotion, and Cognition

Alexa Weik von Mossner

Moving Environments explores the role played by affect and emotion in the production and reception of films that centrally feature natural environments and nonhuman actors, both real and animated. Affect—our automatic, visceral response to a given film or sequence—and emotion—our cognitive awareness of such a response—are, in the words of Carl Plantinga, "fundamental to what makes film artistically successful, rhetorically powerful, and culturally influential."[1] Without doubt this is also true for films that are implicitly or explicitly concerned with environmental issues and themes. However, the exploration of affect and emotion and their relevance to human experience of and attitudes toward nonhuman nature has occupied, at best, a marginal place within ecocritical film studies. This is why I initiated a workshop on the topic in the summer of 2011, hosted by the Rachel Carson Center for Environment and Society at the University of Munich and bringing together some of the leading ecocritical film scholars. Participants were asked to respond to the following questions: How do films represent human emotion and affect in relation to different environments? How do these films influence our emotions while seeing them and after seeing them, and how do they generate meanings? How do they affect our relationship to the human and more-than-human world and what can we say about their affective or "passionate" politics? The essays assembled in this volume are our partial and preliminary answers to these questions and the result of a two-day intensive workshop of presenting and discussing early drafts, with much deliberation and revision in the aftermath of the meeting.

The volume deliberately covers a wide range of films, not all of which would qualify for Paula Willoquet-Maricondi's definition of "ecocinema," which, in her understanding, has "consciousness-raising and activist intentions, as well as responsibility to heighten awareness about contemporary issues and practices affecting planetary health."[2] While many of the films under consideration in the individual chapters do have activist intentions, others are primarily interested in entertainment value and box office results. Whether such commercial interests automatically turn the latter group into "environmentalist films," defined by David Ingram as "ideological agglomerations that draw on and perpetuate a range of contradictory discourses concerning the relationship between human beings and the environment,"[3] is an intriguing question that isn't easily answered. As the contributions to this volume by Nicole Seymour, David Whitley, Adrian Ivakhiv, and Pat Brereton demonstrate, the commercialism and sentimentalism of popular films does not necessarily stop them from being effective eco-films; their affective appeal may in fact give rise to both enjoyment *and* reflection. Choosing a wide scope of film texts for its investigations, including popular fiction film, documentaries, animation, and experimental film, *Moving Environments* seeks to open a new discursive space at the disciplinary intersection of film studies, theories of affect and emotion, and a growing body of ecocritical scholarship that studies the complex relationship between imaginative texts and the physical environment.[4] Once opened, that space should invite further inquiry into the relationship between film, emotion, and ecology in various contexts.

To date, relatively few scholars have studied cinema and media texts from an ecocritical perspective, and many of those who have published books within the field are among the contributors to this volume. Gregg Mitman's *Reel Nature* (1999) and Derek Bousé's *Wildlife Films* (2000) both consider our mediated encounters with wildlife in nature documentaries, examining how such films shape our perception of nature and how commercial considerations have led to what Mitman has called the "genre of sugar-coated educational nature films initiated by Walt Disney in the late 1940s."[5] If "emotional drama had to be made part of filmed nature" in much of wildlife film, as Mitman has argued,[6] the same is true for Hollywood blockbusters that focus on human–nature relationships. David Ingram's *Green Screen* (2000) was the first study to explore environmental Hollywood films from an ecocritical perspective, suggesting that such films bring together a range of contradictory discourses around environmental issues while largely perpetuating romantic attitudes to nature. Sean Cubitt's *EcoMedia* (2005), Pat Brereton's *Hollywood Utopia* (2005), Robin Murray and Joseph Heumann's *Ecology and Popular Film*

(2009), and Deborah Carmichael's edited volume *The Landscape of Hollywood Westerns* (2006) similarly examine representations of nature in popular film. Murray and Heumann have recently enlarged our knowledge with two additional ecocritical books, both of which focus on specific film genres: *"That's All Folks"? Ecocritical Readings of American Animated Features* (2011) and *Gunfight at the Eco-Corral: Western Cinema and the Environment* (2012). Recent years have also seen the publication of Paula Willoquet-Maricondi's *Framing the World* (2010) and Stephen Rust, Salma Monani, and Sean Cubitt's *Ecocinema Theory and Practice* (2013). Both of these essay collections offer wide-ranging introductions to ecocritical film studies, providing readers with in-depth analyses of a broad range of films and mapping the various theoretical approaches within the emerging field.

While our affective engagements with environmental film are an implicit concern in most of these studies, Adrian Ivakhiv's *Ecologies of the Moving Image* (2013) is more directly concerned with the way in which "images move us."[7] Proposing a "process-relational" model of cinema, Ivakhiv reminds us of "the thick immediacy of cinematic spectacle, the shimmering texture of image and sound as it strikes us and resounds in us viscerally and affectively."[8] This visceral experience of the moving image, he writes, is what "moves us most immediately and directly" when we are watching film. Together with the sequential unfolding of narrative, the affective spectacle of the moving image is what engages us in a film during and after the viewing experience.[9] In his contribution to this volume, Ivakhiv demonstrates how his process-relational model of film can be employed to analyze the "global affects" of James Cameron's *Avatar* (2009), a film that has been both lauded and heavily criticized for its melodramatic framing of an eco-social resistance narrative. David Whitley's *The Idea of Nature in Disney Animation* (2012) also makes an important contribution to the study of affect in environmental film as it challenges the notion that the sentimentality of mainstream Hollywood movies necessarily prevents viewers from developing a critical awareness of environmental issues. "The enhanced role of sentiment within dramatic narratives," argues Whitley, "could provide audiences ... with a cultural arena within which heightened emotions and humour, rather than operating as a barrier to thought and critical engagment, might offer a relatively safe space within which crucial issues could be rehearsed and even—in light forms—explored."[10]

Moving Environments builds on the important work done in these earlier studies while also expanding it by investigating our affective engagements with environmental film from a range of theoretical perspectives. It thereby breaks new ground not only in ecocriticism, but also more generally in film studies as well as in the emerging interdisciplinary fields of affect studies and cognitive cultural studies. While film scholars outside of ecocriticism have produced an impressive body of work on the emotional aspects of film viewing using psychoanalytic, phenomenological, Deleuzian, and cognitivist frameworks, there has been relatively little interest in these studies in the affective and emotional impact of cinematic representations of natural environments, which are often understood as a metaphor for interior psychic worlds or as backdrop for the development of character and narrative. Ecocritics, however, are trained to pay attention to the role that environments and ecological concerns play *in* the development of character and narrative. The essays collected in this volume offer insight not only into the intricacies of human–nature interactions on film, but also into the interplay between films and viewers as well as the larger cultural ramifications of such interaction. In addition, this should make them interesting beyond the relatively narrow disciplinary boundaries of ecocritical film studies, not least because many of them explicitly or implicitly draw on the important insights of previous work on affect and emotion in psychology, philosophy, anthropology, geography, sociology, and film and cultural studies. Rather than presenting a single, cohesive theoretical approach, the collection aims at opening up multiple paths for further exploration.

AFFECT, EMOTION, AND THE ENVIRONMENT

Our emotional engagement with different environments and the world as such has only recently come back into the focus of scholarly attention. Clinical evidence collected by leading neurologists during the 1990s supported the notion of ecological psychologists, such as James Gibson, that human behavior is radically situated.[11] However, this path-breaking research also pointed to the central role played by emotions in an individual's relation to a given environment. In *Descartes' Error: Emotion, Reason and the Human Brain* (1994), neuroscientist Antonio Damasio explains that an "organism interacts directly with the environment as an ensemble: the interaction is neither of the body alone nor of the brain alone," which is why "mental phenomena can be fully understood only in the context of an organism's interacting in an environment."[12] Because cognition, in Damasio's understanding, cannot be separated from emotion, and emotion is linked to the feelings of the body, it is inevitable that our physical environment influences how we feel and consequently how we think. At the same time, how we feel and think at any given moment also changes our subjective perception of our environment. Damasio's correction of "Descartes' error," and the resulting rehabilitation of affective and emotional processes as not the irrational *opposite* of reason but rather an integral *part* of it, has been vastly influential over the past two decades, informing not only the work of cognitive psychologists but also that of scholars in a variety of humanities and social science disciplines who are now exploring the complex role played by emotions in the relationship between humans and their environments.

In *Loving Nature: Towards an Ecology of Emotion* (2002), social anthropologist Kay Milton draws on Damasio's clinical research in order to develop a better understanding of "how people relate to nature and natural beings."[13] Emotions, she explains, "operate in the relationship between an individual organism and its environment; they are induced when an organism interacts with objects in that environment."[14] Milton's anthropological work is interesting for ecocritical film and cultural studies scholars because it integrates the findings of neuropsychological research in a sustained discussion of "how human beings, as individual organisms, come to think and feel as they do, not only about nature and natural things, but about whatever they encounter in their environment."[15] She thus demonstrates how the insights of neuroscience can be made useful for explicitly environmentalist endeavors and, by extension, also for ecocritical analyses of film. After all, the built space of a movie theater is an environment as well, with the added complication that part of what we encounter there is not actually present in any material sense but projected on the screen. I will return to the specific emotional repercussions of this fact, but first mention two other recent examples for the renewed interest in the role played by emotional processes in human relationships to specific ecological spaces, one of them in the field of cultural geography, and the other in sociology.

Already in 1974, geographer Yi-Fu Tuan's *Topophilia* explored "the human being's affective ties with the material environment." Tuan asserted that "topophilia is not the strongest of human emotions," and believed that "when it is compelling we can be sure that the place or environment has become the carrier of emotionally charged events or is perceived as a symbol."[16] Today, this understanding of topophilia as a phenomenon that predominantly points to other, stronger emotional engagements has been replaced by a focus on a wide variety of emotional attachments to geographical space. In their introduction to *Emotion, Place and Culture* (2009), editors Mick Smith, Joyce Davidson, Laura Cameron, and Liz Bondi observe that "emotions are amongst the most important ways in which … humans are both connected with and disconnected from their world."[17] Emotions, they suggest, "might need to be understood as events that take place in, and reverberate through, the real world and real beings."[18] Emotions, here, are understood as a material, bodily force that arises in response to certain places and environmental conditions. They are indeed the basic mechanism that connects us to our environment, shapes our knowledge, and motivates our actions. If we want to understand human attachment to place as well as many other complex relationships between (human) animals and their environments, Smith et al. suggest that we need to pay attention to emotional processes, regardless of the fact that these tend to be extremely complex and often transitory and elusive.[19]

Increased attention to affect and emotion is also relevant for sociologists who have an interest in the environment, as demonstrated by Tonya K. Davidson, Ondine Park, and Rob Shields's recent edited volume *Ecologies of Affect: Placing Nostalgia, Desire, and Hope* (2011), which features essays that capture the significance of virtuality and affect in forming human relationships to material places and social spaces. Their attention to virtuality is of particular interest, because it reminds us that our attachments to various environments are shaped not only by our physical interaction with the material places and their inhabitants themselves, but also by mediated and imagined representations of these places. "Recognizing the virtual," the editors explain, "enables us to designate elements that allow a place to maintain its ethos or for a picture to maintain its power even as both decay over time."[20] Relying on the theoretical frameworks of affect studies, rather than on cognitive psychology, Davidson, Park, and Shields stress a point that has also been considered vital by ecocritical film scholars such as Sean Cubitt (2005), namely, that our affective relationships to various environments as well as human and non-human entities today are developed to a substantial degree and mediated by our engagement with virtual technologies, such as film.

FILM EMOTION AND THE ENVIRONMENT

Today, scholars who investigate the role of affect and emotion in our enjoyment of film tend either to draw on psychoanalytical theories and semiotics or to rely on the more recent insights of neuroscience and cognitive psychology. However, as Belinda Smaill's chapter on *Darwin's Nightmare* and *The Cove* and Janet Walker's essay on Hurricane Katrina documentaries demonstrate, some strands of what has become labelled as "affect theory" (Massumi 1995, 2002; Carter and McCormack 2006; Duff 2010) can also productively be applied to environmental film in order to gain a better understanding of cinematic mediations of human attachment to place.[21] In addition, we have to take into consideration phenomenological approaches to film emotion (for example, Sobchack 1992, 2004; Rosch 1996; Marks 2000; and Rutherford 2003), which understand film viewing principally as an embodied experience and emphasize full-fledged corporeal rather than purely intellectual or visual engagements with film. As David Ingram argues in his contribution to this volume, phenomenological approaches to film often begin from first-person responses and extrapolate from the theorist's personal reaction to individual films. Because of their somewhat "unscientific" methodology, such approaches have been criticized for their inevitable subjectivity and bias, but, as Ingram convincingly shows, they can nevertheless be helpful for ecocritical readings of film when combined with more scientific, cognitivist approaches.

Cognitivist approaches to film openly reject the combination of psycho-analysis and semiotics—often labelled "screen theory"—that came to dominate film studies during the last decades of the twentieth century, and instead build their approaches directly on the clinical research of neuroscience and cognitive psychology.[22] If they give particular attention to the role of *emotion* in the film-viewing experience, then they often also integrate the work of philosophers (among them, de Sousa 1990; Roberts 2003; and Robinson 2005) who have developed comprehensive theories of emotion.[23] In their introduction to *Passionate Views* (1999), Carl Plantinga and Greg Smith remind us that movie theatres occupy a central place "in the emotional landscape of the modern world as one of the predominant spaces where societies gather to express and experience feelings."[24] Plantinga and Smith are part of an international group of scholars who have produced an impressive body of work on the emotional aspects of film viewing, among them Noël Carroll (1996, 2003), Ed Tan (1996), Murray Smith (1995), and Torben Grodal (2009).[25] All of these scholars are keenly interested in the role of emotions in film viewing, and their work as a whole—individual specializations and inevitable theoretical disagreements aside—offers an intriguing exploration of the ways in which films engage their viewers' "real" and pre-existing emotion systems, relying not only on storytelling, but also on various filmic techniques such as lighting, editing, and music. Cognitivist theories of film emotion are productively utilized for ecocritical readings in several chapters of the present volume, among them those of David Ingram, Bart Welling, and Salma Monani, as well as my own contribution.

While some of us thus find cognitive film theory highly productive for an ecocritical analysis of film emotion, others look critically at its somewhat limited (and limiting) concentration on the interaction between an individual film and an abstract, ideal spectator. Smaill, for example, explains in *The Documentary* (2011) that cognitive approaches "do not differentiate between broader social contexts of representation and reception" and thus do not pay enough attention to "the sociality of emotions."[26] Because of her interest in the latter, Smaill turns to the work of affect theorists such as Sara Ahmed (2004) and Lauren Berlant (2008) who understand public spheres as affect worlds, reminding us that the emotions that films elicit in audiences "circulate in the public sphere where they are fashioned across histories of signification, different media forms and other technologies of social life."[27] In her contribution to this volume, Smaill draws on this theoretical archive in order to scrutinize the ways in which politically engaged marine-life documentaries can advocate for environmental or ecological politics. Because such films continue to affect their audiences long after the viewing process is over, she makes clear, the emotions they produce are not only private matters, but also have important cultural ramifications that need to be addressed.

Smaill makes an important point that is of interest especially for ecocritics who investigate the larger social and political repercussions of individual film texts. However, as Pat Brereton argues in his contribution, any theories regarding these larger dimensions of environmental film reception, and the role of affect and emotion within them, should be substantiated by empirical research. A small step toward such substantiation was recently made when five audience-response studies were conducted independently in the United States, Britain, Germany, and Japan on the influence of Roland Emmerich's science-fiction disaster blockbuster *The Day After Tomorrow* (2004) (Leiserowitz 2004; Lowe et al. 2005; Balmford et al. 2004; Reusswig, Schwarzkopf, and Pohlenz 2004; Aoyagi-Usui 2004). While there were important cross-cultural differences, the five studies also demonstrated that the film had significant impacts on viewers' attitudes toward climate change.[28] The recent success of a number of theatre-released documentary films underscores that this is true not only for popular fiction films, but also for non-fiction films. As I explain in more detail in my chapter on the emotional impact of eco-documentaries, empirical evidence suggests that Davis Guggenheim's *An Inconvenient Truth* (2006), starring Al Gore, and Franny Armstrong's *The Age of Stupid* (2009), have both had considerable influence on their audiences' perceptions and attitudes. Unfortunately, empirical audience-response studies are still very limited, and there is no doubt that we urgently need more of them in order to gain a better understanding of how film viewing influences the attitudes of *real* audiences toward environmental concerns. Although we will hopefully see more of these studies in the future, they still need to be complemented by theoretical work. This is where ecocritical film scholars can contribute their share of expertise by tackling the elusive subject of the relationship between affect, emotion, ecology, and film.

OVERVIEW OF CHAPTERS

The twelve essays in this collection are grouped into four parts that discuss different aspects of our emotional engagement with various kinds of film texts. Part I, "General and Theoretical Considerations," explores the relevance and utility of various theoretical approaches to cinematic affect and emotion in the context of ecocritical film analysis, many of which are discussed in later chapters. In "Emotion and Affect in Eco-films: Cognitive and Phenomenological Approaches," David Ingram argues that a combination of cognitivist and phenomenological approaches is most fruitful for an exploration of the role played by affect, emotion, and cognition in our engagement with ecocinema, insisting at the same time that not all versions of cognitivism and phenomenology are equally useful for ecocriticism. Among the scholars whose work Ingram finds most productive for cine-ecocriticism are Greg Smith and Laura Marks. In Ingram's view, Smith's "associative" model of emotions takes the full spectrum of cognitive, emotional, and affective dimensions in film spectatorship into consideration more fully than other cognitivist approaches; Marks's version of phenomenological film theory is particularly useful because it "opens the way for a biocultural synthesis of phenomenological and cognitivist approaches to film that could be of use to eco-film criticism."[29] By way of example, the essay then employs a combination of cognitivist and phenomenological methods in its ecocritical analysis of Bill Forsythe's *Local Hero* (1983) and Andrew Kötting's *This Filthy Earth* (2001), considering the complex ways in which these two eco-films work on their audiences.

In "Emotions of Consequence? Viewing Eco-documentaries from a Cognitive Perspective," I am concerned with the question of whether eco-documentaries engage our emotions in ways that are in any way different from those we experience during the watching of a fiction film. As non-fiction films that "document reality," documentaries are often thought to be categorically different from fictional feature films. The cognitive film scholar Dirk Eitzen has argued that one of the things that give the documentary genre its emotional power is viewers' belief in its non-fictional nature and their understanding of the *consequential nature* of what is presented on the screen.[30] While agreeing with Eitzen that there is something qualitatively different in our emotional reactions to documentary film, the essay argues that things are actually more complicated than he makes them out to be. In order to understand the "peculiar appeal" of eco-documentaries such as *An Inconvenient Truth* and *The Age of Stupid* we must consider the emotionalizing power of cinematic techniques that work *across* film modes and genres.

The importance of more light-hearted approaches in our emotional engagement with ecocinema is demonstrated in the third essay, by Nicole Seymour, entitled "Irony and Contemporary Ecocinema: Theorizing a New Affective Paradigm." Seymour starts from the observation that politically engaged ecocinema, and environmentalism more broadly, tend to be dominated by more serious affective modes, such as earnestness and sanctimony. Playful modes such as irony, Seymour attests, are largely absent, or limited to brief interludes. She takes up Bronislaw Szerszynski's claim that "the most appropriate philosophical foundation for ecological politics is ... a generalised irony"[31] in order to explore how such irony can inform the ecological politics of cinema, and illustrates her claims through an in-depth look at Mike Judge's *Idiocracy* (2006). Judge's film, Seymour demonstrates, mines a serious genre, dystopian science fiction, for comic effect while offering the same kind of anti-capitalist ecological critique found in more serious films such as *Food, Inc.* (2009). Through these readings, Seymour's essay demonstrates how films can make use of irony to push environmentalist agendas, while at same time looking ironically at their own status as ecocinema.

The second part of the volume, "Anthropomorphism and the Non-human in Documentary Film," is concerned with more serious modes of affect, as it addresses the crucial issue of anthropomorphism and the ways in which documentary filmmakers rely on strategic "othering" or "saming" to engage their audiences emotionally and push arguments for human and/or animal rights. Bart Welling's essay, "On the 'Inexplicable Magic of Cinema': Critical Anthropomorphism, Emotion, and the Wildness of Wildlife Films," starts from the fact that anthropomorphism, traditionally defined as the projection of human emotions onto non-human beings, has often been attacked as problematic or even dangerous by natural scientists and humanities scholars alike. However, Welling argues, as important as it is to be aware of the problems caused by *superficially* anthropomorphic representations, there are good reasons for doubting that a completely "*non*-anthropomorphic relationality" between humans and animals is possible. Welling maintains that if it is true that anthropomorphism is in fact the default condition of the human mind, then the real challenge is to develop theories from within an inherently anthropomorphic framework that explain what happens between viewers and wildlife documentaries on an emotional level. Taking a cue from cognitive and biocultural film scholars, Welling's essay examines the emotions evoked by wildlife films such as *Winged Migration* (2001) and *Being Caribou* (2004) in evolutionary as well as cultural contexts.

The second and third chapters in Part II both focus on eco-documentaries that explore the socio-cultural, industrial, and environmental issues emerging from the harvesting of a particular marine species. Belinda Smaill's essay, "Emotion, Argumentation, and Documentary Traditions: *Darwin's Nightmare* and *The Cove*," is interested in the ways in which the two documentaries engage viewers in an unfolding narrative that focuses on the spectacle of non-human life within a specific geo-cultural location. Smaill argues that despite many similarities, the two films function in very different ways as advocacies for environmental or ecological politics. Underpinning her discussion is the understanding that documentary cinema relies as much on emotions as it does on rationalization. Her essay explores how non-human life, such as the fish in *Darwin's Nightmare* and the dolphin in *The Cove*, is made available to the viewer and how in both cases the image of the non-human is central to the formulation of an emotional political address to the viewer.

Smaill's essay is complemented in intriguing ways by Robin Murray and Joseph K. Heumann's "Documenting Animal Rights and Environmental Ethics at Sea," which is the third essay in this section. Murray and Heumann offer a different angle of analysis on documentary films that are concerned with fisheries. Their essay contrasts the principles of organismic environmentalism with those of the animal rights movement, arguing that the former's reliance on logical arguments rather than emotional appeals weakens the rhetorical strength of its arguments, especially when applied in environmental documentaries, including *Darwin's Nightmare* (2004) and *The End of the Line* (2009). Reminding us of Peter Singer's claim that "human equality ... requires us to extend equal consideration to animals too,"[32] Murray and Heumann single out *The Cove* as a film that successfully draws on the emotional appeal of animal rights arguments in its strong advocacy for the dolphins of Taiji by reminding viewers that, like humans, animals can feel pain.

Part III, "The Effects and Affects of Animation," explores the powerful potentialities of animated film and the genre's cognitive and affective impacts. In his contribution, "Animation, Realism, and the Genre of Nature," David Whitley explores some of the ways in which the makers of popular animated film have shaped concerns within what Leo Braudy has called the "genre of nature."[33] Taking up Braudy's proposition that the 1980s produced a new film genre because of a perceived crisis in human relationships with the natural world, Whitley explores the question of whether such a "genre of nature" has been developed in distinctive forms within the medium of animation. Comparing the Academy Award–winning French nature documentary *March of the Penguins* (2005) with the animated feature *Happy Feet* (2006), Whitley argues that while the realism of the documentary lends a degree of moral authority to the environmental fable around which the narrative is structured, the unrealistic elements of *Happy Feet*, although not entirely convincing aesthetically, constitute a successful harnessing of realist and non-realist strategies in an attempt to engage viewers' empathy with a natural world in crisis.

The second essay in Part III, Adrian Ivakhiv's "What Can a Film *Do*? Analyzing *Avatar's* Global Affects," scrutinizes the peculiar affective appeal of James Cameron's mega-blockbuster with the aid of the process-relational model of cinema that Ivakhiv develops in his *Ecologies of the Moving Image* (2013). The model understands the film experience as "an affective-cognitive journey into a film-world that comes to interact, in variable ways, with the cognitive-affective potencies of the real, extra-filmic world."[34] Seen in this framework, Ivakhiv argues, the wide variety of viewers' responses to *Avatar* can be made sense of, whether it is the irate criticism the film has received from some ecocritics, the enthusiastic forms of identification it elicited among many younger viewers, or the often surprisingly positive commentaries it received from many indigenous groups. Ivakhiv explains that these divergent responses are results of different modes of viewing, which in turn trigger different affective and cognitive responses. The very strength of Cameron's environmentalist science fiction epos, he maintains, is that it makes available a wide range of affects that remain with viewers long after they have left the theatre, and that these affects are nevertheless comprehensive enough to work successfully in cross-cultural audiences.

Pat Brereton's "Animated Ecocinema and Affect: A Case Study of Pixar's *UP*" is similarly concerned with the affective appeal of animated 3-D blockbusters, in this case with Pete Docter's *UP* (2009). Brereton argues that Pixar's success is due not only to their superior skills and craftsmanship across scripting and animation, but also to its careful and effective eco-branding and marketing. He further maintains that we must look beyond the film text itself and include in our analysis DVD bonus features, which often successfully function as a bridge between the text and the creative makers of a film. In the case of *UP*, he demonstrates, the filmmakers use the bonus features to speak directly to individual consumers. The uses and benefits of DVD bonus features, in Brereton's view, is that they can frame creative intentionality and speak more directly to audience affect, thus adding to the range of affects proffered by the film text itself. His essay demonstrates how such affective connections are made, through a close reading of *UP*.

The fourth and final section of the volume, "The Affect of Place and Time," examines filmic portrayals of human relationships to specific ecological spaces as well as the effects of vanguard reorganizations of cinematic time. Janet Walker's "Moving Home: Documentary Film and Other Remediations of Post-Katrina New Orleans" explores the ways in which "post-Katrina" documentaries locate emotional expressions of loss and longing to return in relation to ruined neighborhoods. Her essay draws on affect theory developed by several scholars, including Brian Massumi and Nigel Thrift, in order to analyze how documentaries such as Spike Lee's *When the Levees Broke* (2006) and Jonathan Demme's *Right to Return* (2007) contemplate and honour the voices of the dispossessed, the lure of home and community, and the cause of social justice. However, Walker is also critical of the affective appeal of these testimonial documentaries, because they may actually *inhibit* recognition of significant environmental considerations and change. The second part of her chapter therefore looks at alternative Katrina films that are marked by a more optimistic affective tone—most centrally Luisa Dantas's *Land of Opportunity* (2011)—and explores how space and community are productively reimagined and remediated in such films.

Salma Monani's "Evoking Sympathy and Empathy: The Ecological Indian and Indigenous Eco-activism" starts from the observation that emotion and affect are the very basis of the stereotypical image of what Shepard Krech III has called the "Ecological Indian."[35] Monani reminds us of the controversies that have surrounded the affective connotations of the Ecological Indian image and argues that ecocritical film scholars have not yet paid enough attention to the ways in which Native co-optation of the icon has complicated its emotive and affective possibilities. Her chapter explores such Native co-optation and its complexities by focusing on the films showcased at a Native American Film and Video Festival themed "Mother Earth in Crisis," which was hosted by the Smithsonian's National Museum of the American Indian in 2011. In doing so, she highlights the "vexing Faustian contract" involved in the co-optation of trope: that, on the one hand, it is an important symbol of how some Indian communities actually see themselves, and that, on the other hand, it threatens to become a sell-out to colonial marketing iconography. Monani suggests that the festival serves as a site to move beyond this dilemma, because it allows the presentation of a wide variety of indigenous films and thus makes room for other types of eco-activism that suggest alternatives to the constrained eco-imaginary of the Ecological Indian.

In the concluding chapter, "Affect and Environment in Two Artists' Films and a Video," Sean Cubitt reflects on the impossibility of reducing cinematic affect to the relatively narrow canon of stimuli known from narrative cinema, be it documentary films, independent cinema, or blockbuster movies.

Concentrating on three experimental films that share landscape as a motif— Stan Brakhage's *Dog Star Man* (1961–64), Chris Welsby's *Sky Light* (1986), and Robert Cahen's *Voyage d'hiver* (1993)—Cubitt highlights the intricacies of these films' intriguing experiments with incommensurable temporalities, and argues that they allow or even force viewers to become aware of the passing of time. By leaving aside the mechanisms that feature films normally use in order to avoid viewers' awareness of the passage of time, Cubitt maintains, and by staying away from what he considers mainstream cinema's tendency "to steal the time from us while substituting its action for our thoughts,"[36] experimental films, such as the ones that are at the centre of his chapter, allow viewers to become aware of the passage of time and thus literally *give* them time to experience moments of affect proffered by the films. Such an awareness of time, Cubitt suggests, is also essential to an emotional understanding of ecology, and the reception of experimental films therefore may well facilitate pro-environmental action.

The essays collected here are not pretending to offer definite or comprehensive answers to the difficult questions that opened our discussion on the relationship between affect, emotion, ecology, and film. The aim of this volume is to showcase a variety of different approaches to the topic, and to demonstrate that affect and emotion *do* play an important role in our enjoyment of and engagement in not only ecocinema in the more narrow sense, but also in films that, for various reasons, lend themselves to an ecocritical reading. Of course, much of the work presented here is initiatory, and it is meant to be exactly that. We all hope that the essays collected in *Moving Environments* will help instigate continued research within the burgeoning field of ecomedia studies.

NOTES

1   Carl Plantinga, *Moving Viewers: American Film and the Spectator Experience* (Berkeley: University of California Press, 2009), 5.

2   Paula Willoquet-Maricondi, "Shifting Paradigms: From Environmentalist Films to Ecocinema," in *Framing the World: Explorations in Ecocriticism and Film*, ed. Paula Willoquet-Maricondi (Charlottesville: University of Virginia Press, 2010), 45.

3   David Ingram, *Green Screen: Environmentalism and Hollywood Cinema* (Exeter: University of Exeter Press, 2000), viii.

4   My definition here is an even broader version of the refreshingly broad and inclusive working definition suggested by Cheryll Glotfelty in *The Ecocriticism Reader* (1996). Glotfelty wrote that "ecocriticism is the study of the relationship between literature and the physical environment," thus limiting ecocriticism to the study of literary texts. Cheryll Glotfelty, "Introduction: Literary Studies in an Age of Environmental Crisis," in *The Ecocriticism Reader: Landmarks in Literary Ecology*, ed. Cheryll Glotfelty and Harold Fromm (Athens: University of Georgia, 1996), xviii.

5   Gregg Mitman, *Reel Nature: America's Romance with Wildlife on Film* (Seattle: University of Washington Press, 2009), 3.

6   Mitman, *Reel Nature*, 4.

7   Adrian Ivakhiv, *Ecologies of the Moving Image: Cinema, Affect, Nature* (Waterloo, ON: Wilfrid Laurier University Press, 2013), 2.

8   Ivakhiv, *Ecologies of the Moving Image*, ix.

9   Ivakhiv, *Ecologies of the Moving Image*, ix.

10 David Whitley, *The Idea of Nature in Disney Animation* (Farnham, UK: Ashgate, 2012), 2–3.

11 James J. Gibson, *The Ecological Approach to Visual Perception* (Boston: Houghton Mifflin, 1979).

12 Antonio Damasio, *Descartes' Error: Emotion, Reason, and the Human Brain* (London: Vintage, 1994), xxvii.

13 Kay Milton, *Loving Nature: Towards an Ecology of Emotion* (London; New York: Routledge, 2002), 2.

14 Milton, *Loving Nature*, 4.

15 Milton, *Loving Nature*, 6.

16 Yi-Fu Tuan, *Topophilia: A Study of Environmental Perception, Attitudes, and Values* (Englewood Cliffs, NJ: Prentice-Hall, 1974), 93.

17 Mick Smith, Joyce Davidson, Laura Cameron, and Liz Bondi, "Introduction: Geography and Emotion—Emerging Constellations," in *Emotion, Place and Culture*, ed. Mick Smith, Joyce Davidson, Laura Cameron, and Liz Bondi (Farnham, UK: Ashgate, 2009), 2.

18 Smith et al., "Introduction," 2.

19 Liz Bondi, Joyce Davidson, and Mick Smith are also the general editors of the interdisciplinary journal *Emotion, Space, and Society*. Smith has recently edited a special issue of the journal on "Ecology and Emotion," Mick Smith, ed. "Ecology and Emotion," Special issue, *Emotion, Space and Society* 6, no. 1 (2013).

20 Tonya K. Davidson, Odine Park, and Rob Shields, eds. *Ecologies of Affect: Placing Nostalgia, Desire, and Hope* (Waterloo, ON: Wilfrid Laurier University Press, 2011), 8.

21 For a good overview of affect theory, see Melissa Gregg and Gregory J. Seigworth, eds., *The Affect Theory Reader* (Durham, NC: Duke University Press, 2010).

22 For a detailed analysis of the differences between psychoanalytical and cognitivist approaches to film emotion, see Noël Carroll, "Prospects for Film Theory: A Personal Assessment," and Stephen Prince, "Psychoanalytic Film Theory and the Problem of the Missing Spectator," both in *Post-Theory: Reconstructing Film Studies*, ed. David Bordwell and Noël Carroll (Madison: University of Wisconsin Press, 1996).

23 For a good overview of recent philosophical theories of emotion, see Robert C. Solomon, ed., *Thinking about Feeling: Contemporary Philosophers on Emotions* (New York: Oxford University Press, 2004).

24 Carl Plantinga and Greg M. Smith, eds. *Passionate Views: Film, Cognition, and Emotion* (Baltimore, MD: Johns Hopkins University Press, 1999), 1.

25 For a good introduction into cognitive approaches to film emotion, see Plantinga and Smith, *Passionate Views* (1999).

26 Belinda Smaill, *The Documentary* (New York: Palgrave Macmillan, 2011), 8.

27 Smaill, *The Documentary*, 1.

28 See my recent essay on the topic for a detailed discussion of the five studies in combination with a cognitive approach to film emotion: "Facing *The Day after Tomorrow*: Filmed Disaster, Emotional Engagement, and Climate Risk Perception," in *American Environments: Climate—Culture—Catastrophe*, eds. Christof Mauch and Sylvia Mayer (Heidelberg: Universitätsverlag Winter, 2012), 97–115.

29 David Ingram, this volume, 29.

30 Dirk Eitzen, "Documentary's Peculiar Appeals," in *Moving Image Theory*, ed. Joseph D. Anderson and Barbara Fisher Anderson (Carbondale: Southern Illinois University Press, 2005), 186.

31 Bronislaw Szerszynski, "The Post-Ecologist Condition: Irony as Symptom and Cure," *Environmental Politics* 16, no. 2 (April 2007): 340.

32 Peter Singer, *Animal Liberation* (New York: Avon Books, 1975), 1.

33 Leo Braudy, "The Genre of Nature: Ceremonies of Innocence," in *Refiguring American Film Genres: Theory and History*, ed. Nick Browne (Berkeley: University of California Press, 1988), 279.

34 Adrian Ivakhiv, this volume, 159.

35 Shepard Krech III, *The Ecological Indian: Myth and History* (New York: W.W. Norton, 1999).

36 Sean Cubitt, this volume, 263.

BIBLIOGRAPHY

The Age of Stupid. Directed by Franny Armstrong. London: Spanner Film, 2009. DVD.

Ahmed, Sara. *The Cultural Politics of Emotion*. New York: Routledge, 2004.

Aoyagi-Usui, Midori. "*The Day after Tomorrow*: A Study on the Impact of a Global Warming Movie on the Japanese Public." National Institute for Environmental Studies (NIES) Working Paper, Tsukuba, Japan, October 2004.

Avatar. Directed by James Cameron. Los Angeles: Twentieth Century Fox, 2009. DVD.

Balmford, Andrew, Percy FitzPatrick, Andrea Manica, Lesley Airey, Linda Birkin, Amy Oliver, and Judith Schleicher. "Hollywood, Climate Change, and the Public." *Science* 17 (September 2004): 1713.

Being Caribou. Directed by Leanne Allison and Diana Wilson. Montreal: National Film Board of Canada, 2004. DVD.

Berlant, Lauren. *The Female Complaint: The Unfinished Business of Sentimentality in American Culture*. Durham, NC: Duke University Press, 2008.

Bousé, Derek. *Wildlife Films*. Philadelphia: University of Pennsylvania Press, 2000.

Braudy, Leo. "The Genre of Nature: Ceremonies of Innocence." In *Refiguring American Film Genres: Theory and History*, edited by Nick Browne, 278–309. Berkeley: University of California Press, 1988.

Brereton, Pat. *Hollywood Utopia: Ecology in Contemporary American Cinema*. Bristol, UK: Intellect, 2005.

Carmichael, Deborah A., ed. *The Landscape of Hollywood Westerns: Ecocriticism in an American Film Genre*. Salt Lake City: University of Utah Press, 2006.

Carroll, Noël. *Engaging the Moving Image*. New Haven, CT: Yale University Press, 2003.

———. "Prospects for Film Theory: A Personal Assessment." In *Post-Theory: Reconstructing Film Studies*, edited by David Bordwell and Noël Carroll, 37–68. Madison: University of Wisconsin Press, 1996.

Carter, Sean, and Derek P. McCormack. "Film, Geopolitics and the Affective Logics of Intervention." *Political Geography* 25 (2006): 228–45.

The Cove. Directed by Louie Psihoyos. Santa Monica, CA: Lions Gate, 2009. DVD.

Cubitt, Sean. *EcoMedia*. Amsterdam: Rodopi, 2005.

Damasio, Antonio. *Descartes' Error: Emotion, Reason, and the Human Brain*. London: Vintage, 1994.

Darwin's Nightmare. Directed by Hubert Sauper. New York: Homevision, 2004. DVD.

Davidson, Tonya K., Odine Park, and Rob Shields, eds. *Ecologies of Affect: Placing Nostalgia, Desire, and Hope*. Waterloo, ON: Wilfrid Laurier University Press, 2011.

The Day after Tomorrow. Directed by Roland Emmerich. Los Angeles: Twentieth Century Fox, 2004. DVD.

De Sousa, Ronald. *The Rationality of Emotion*. Cambridge, MA: MIT Press, 1990.

Dog Star Man. Directed by Stan Brakhage. 1961–64. *By Brakhage: Anthology*. New York: Criterion, 2001. DVD.

Duff, Cameron. "On the Role of Affect and Practice in the Production of Place." *Environment and Planning D: Society and Space* 28 (2010): 881–95.

Eitzen, Dirk. "Documentary's Peculiar Appeals." In *Moving Image Theory*, edited by Joseph D. Anderson and Barbara Fisher Anderson, 183–99. Carbondale: Southern Illinois University Press, 2005.

The End of the Line. Directed by Rupert Murray. London: Dogwoof Pictures, 2009. DVD.

Food, Inc. Directed by Robert Kenner. New York: Magnolia Home Entertainment, 2009. DVD.

Gibson, James J. *The Ecological Approach to Visual Perception*. Boston: Houghton Mifflin, 1979.

Glotfelty, Cheryll. "Introduction: Literary Studies in an Age of Environmental Crisis." In *The Ecocriticism Reader: Landmarks in Literary Ecology*, edited by Cheryll Glotfelty and Harold Fromm, xv–xxxvii. Athens: University of Georgia, 1996.

Gregg, Melissa, and Gregory J. Seigworth, eds. *The Affect Theory Reader*. Durham, NC: Duke University Press, 2010.

Grodal, Torben. *Embodied Visions: Evolution, Emotion, Culture, and Film*. Oxford: Oxford University Press, 2009.

Happy Feet. Directed by George Miller, Warren Coleman, and Judy Morris. Burbank, CA: Warner Bros, 2006. DVD.

Idiocracy. Directed by Mike Judge. Los Angeles: Twentieth Century Fox, 2007. DVD.

An Inconvenient Truth. Directed by Davis Guggenheim. Los Angeles: Paramount Classics, 2006. DVD.

Ingram, David. *Green Screen: Environmentalism and Hollywood Cinema*. Exeter: University of Exeter Press, 2000.

Ivakhiv, Adrian. *Ecologies of the Moving Image: Cinema, Affect, Nature*. Waterloo, ON: Wilfrid Laurier University Press, 2013.

Krech III, Shepard. *The Ecological Indian: Myth and History*. New York: W.W. Norton, 1999.

Land of Opportunity. Directed by Luisa Dantas. New Orleans: JoLu Productions, 2011. DVD.

Leiserowitz, Anthony A. "Before and After *The Day After Tomorrow*: A U.S. Study of Climate Risk Perception." *Environment* 46, no. 9 (2004): 23–37.

Local Hero. Directed by Bill Forsythe. 1983. London: Channel 4, 2008. DVD.

Lowe, Thomas, Katrina Brown, Suraje Dessai, Miguel de Franca Doria, Kat Haynes, and Katharine Vincent, "Does Tomorrow Ever Come? Disaster Narrative and Public Perceptions of Climate Change." *Tyndall Centre for Climate Change Research Working Paper 72*. Norwich, UK: University of East Anglia, 2005.

March of the Penguins. Directed by Luc Jacquet. Burbank, CA: Warner Bros, 2005. DVD.

Marks, Laura M. *The Skin of the Film: Intercultural Cinema, Embodiment, and the Senses.* Durham, NC: Duke University Press, 2000.

Massumi, Brian. "The Autonomy of Affect." *Cultural Critique* 31 (Autumn 1995): 83–109.

———. *Parables for the Virtual: Movement, Affect, Sensation.* Durham, NC: Duke University Press, 2002.

Milton, Kay. *Loving Nature: Towards an Ecology of Emotion.* London: Routledge, 2002.

Mitman, Gregg. *Reel Nature: America's Romance with Wildlife on Film.* Seattle: University of Washington Press, 1999.

Murray, Robin L., and Joseph K. Heumann. *Ecology and Popluar Film: Cinema on the Edge.* Albany: State University of New York Press, 2009.

———. *Gunfight at the Eco-Corral: Western Cinema and the Environment.* Norman: University of Oklahoma Press, 2012.

———. *"That's All Folks"? Ecocritical Readings of American Animated Features.* Lincoln: University of Nebraska Press, 2011.

Plantinga, Carl. *Moving Viewers: American Film and the Spectator Experience.* Berkeley: University of California Press, 2009.

Plantinga, Carl, and Greg M. Smith, eds. *Passionate Views: Film, Cognition, and Emotion.* Baltimore, MD: Johns Hopkins University Press, 1999.

Prince, Stephen. "Psychoanalytic Film Theory and the Problem of the Missing Spectator." In *Post-Theory: Reconstructing Film Studies,* edited by David Bordwell and Noël Carroll, 71–85. Madison: University of Wisconsin Press, 1996.

Reusswig, Fritz, Julia Schwarzkopf, and Philipp Pohlenz. "Double Impact: The Climate Blockbuster *The Day after Tomorrow* and Its Impacts on the German Cinema Public." *PIK Report* 92 (October 2004): 1–65.

Right to Return: New Home Movies from the Lower Ninth Ward. Directed by Jonathan Demme. Arlington, VA: Public Broadcasting Service, 2007. DVD.

Roberts, Robert C. *Emotions: An Essay in Aid of Moral Psychology.* Cambridge: Cambridge University Press, 2003.

Robinson, Jenefer. *Deeper Than Reason: Emotion and Its Role in Literature, Music, and Art.* Oxford: Oxford University Press, 2005.

Rosch, Eleanor. "The Environment of Minds: Toward a Noetic and Hedonic Ecology." In *Cognitive Ecology,* edited by Morton P. Friedman and Edward C. Carterette, 5–27. London: Academic Press, 1996.

Rust, Stephen, Salma Monani, and Sean Cubitt, eds. *Ecocinema Theory and Practice.* New York: Routledge, 2013.

Rutherford, Anne. "Cinema and Embodied Affect." *Senses of Cinema* 25 (2003): 1–15.

Singer, Peter. *Animal Liberation.* New York: Avon Books, 1975.

Sky Light. Directed by Chris Welsby. UK, 1986.

Smaill, Belinda. *The Documentary.* New York: Palgrave Macmillan, 2011.

Smith, Mick, ed. "Ecology and Emotion." Special issue, *Emotion, Space, and Society* 6 (2013): 1–116.

Smith, Mick, Joyce Davidson, Laura Cameron, and Liz Bondi, eds. "Introduction: Geography and Emotion—Emerging Constellations." In *Emotion, Place and Culture*, edited by Mick Smith, Joyce Davidson, Laura Cameron, and Liz Bondi, 5–20. Farnham, UK: Ashgate, 2009.

Smith, Murray. *Engaging Characters: Fiction, Emotion, and the Cinema*. New York: Oxford University Press. 1995.

Sobchack, Vivian. *The Address of the Eye: A Phenomenology of Film Experience*. Princeton, NJ: Princeton University Press, 1992.

———. *Carnal Thoughts: Embodiment and Moving Image Culture*. Berkeley: University of California Press, 2004.

Solomon, Robert C., ed. *Thinking about Feeling: Contemporary Philosophers on Emotions*. New York: Oxford University Press, 2004.

Szerszynski, Bronislaw. "The Post-Ecologist Condition: Irony as Symptom and Cure." *Environmental Politics* 16, no. 2 (April 2007): 337–55.

Tan, Ed S. *Emotion and the Structure of Narrative Film: Film as an Emotion Machine*. London: Routledge, 1996.

This Filthy Earth. Directed by Andrew Kötting. London: FilmFour, 2001. DVD.

Trouble the Water. Directed by Carl Deal and Tia Lessin. New York: Zeitgeist Films, 2008. DVD.

Tuan, Yi-Fu. *Topophilia: A Study of Environmental Perception, Attitudes, and Values*. Englewood Cliffs, NJ: Prentice-Hall, 1974.

UP. Directed by Pete Docter. Emeryville, CA: Pixar, 2009. DVD.

Voyage d'hiver. Directed by Robert Cahen. France, 1993.

Weik von Mossner, Alexa. "Facing *The Day After Tomorrow*: Filmed Disaster, Emotional Engagement, and Climate Risk Perception." In *American Environments: Climate—Culture—Catastrophe*, edited by Christof Mauch and Sylvia Mayer, 97–115. Heidelberg: Universitätsverlag Winter, 2012.

When the Levees Broke: A Requiem in Four Acts. Directed by Spike Lee. New York: HBO, 2006. DVD.

Whitley, David. *The Idea of Nature in Disney Animation*. Farnham, UK: Ashgate, 2012.

Willoquet-Maricondi, Paula. "Shifting Paradigms: From Environmentalist Films to Ecocinema." In *Framing the World: Explorations in Ecocriticism and Film*, edited by Paula Willoquet-Maricondi, 43–61. Charlottesville: University of Virginia Press, 2010.

Winged Migration. Directed by Jacques Perrin, Jacques Cluzaud, and Michel Debats. Paris: BAC Films, 2001.

PART I

General and Theoretical Considerations

1

Emotion and Affect in Eco-films
Cognitive and Phenomenological Approaches

David Ingram

In this chapter, I present a theoretical framework for analyzing "eco-films" in terms of the cognitive, emotional, and affective responses they elicit in their viewers. I define an "eco-film" broadly as any film that can be interpreted as addressing ecological or environmental issues, whether more or less explicitly, and go on to analyze Bill Forsyth's *Local Hero* (1983) and Andrew Kötting's *This Filthy Earth* (2001) as eco-films, in that they construct their narratives around images of the British landscape that reflect differing conceptions of the relationship between human beings and the environment in which they live. At a theoretical level, I argue that a combination of cognitivist and phenomenological approaches can articulate the aesthetic means by which these films work as eco-films.

COGNITIVISM, PHENOMENOLOGY, AND ECO-FILM STUDIES

Although some film theorists consider "affect" to be synonymous with "emotion," I follow both cognitivists and phenomenologists in distinguishing between the two, taking "affect" to mean a viewer's automatic, visceral response to a film, whereas "emotion" includes a cognitive element in addition to this bodily feeling. Cognitivist Greg Smith describes affect as "a developmental antecedent of emotion that exists at birth and that cannot be taught to respond in any other way besides its hardwired response."[1] Similarly drawing on cognitive psychology, Noël Carroll writes that "certain affects—like the churning stomach sensations that viewers reported resulted from watching the cars chases in *Bullitt*—are not examples of emotions proper. Emotions proper require a

cognitive component."[2] He explains that emotion is made up of two components: "a cognitive component, such as a belief or a thought about some person,
place, or thing, real or imagined; and a feeling component (a bodily change
and/or a phenomenological experience), where, additionally, the feeling state
has been caused by the relevant cognitive state, such as a belief or a belief-like
state."[3] According to Carroll's version of cognitivist theory, filmmakers "criterially prefocus" their film texts in order to "encourage spectators to assess or to
subsume the events onscreen under certain categories, namely the categories
pertinent to the excitation of the relevant emotional states."[4] These emotional
cues may be more or less "recessive" or "subtle," according both to the stylistic
preferences of individual filmmakers and to the genre or mode of film they are
working in.[5]

A good film theory will be based on defensible philosophical principles,
will account for all relevant aspects of film spectatorship, and, if possible, generate informative textual interpretations of individual films. An important
criterion in the first regard, particularly for eco-film studies, is that it should
be compatible with the latest findings in the natural sciences. In this respect,
although cognitive approaches vary amongst themselves, they all draw on, and
gain plausibility from, important scientific research in fields such as neuroscience and evolutionary biology. Cognitivist film theory, as developed by Greg
Smith and Noël Carroll, is thus attractive for eco-film criticism because it is
part of an emerging "biocultural" model of culture that is scientifically complex
and plausible, albeit open to ongoing contestation. Torben Grodal extends this
paradigm into "evolutionary bioculturalism," a nuanced ecological approach to
cinema which attempts to account for film spectatorship in a scientifically convincing way, and should not be dismissed as mere "scientism."[6] Although the
evolutionary functionalism of Grodal's approach may be challenged by theories
which favour less deterministic, more open and creative theories of adaptation,
the biocultural paradigm nevertheless promises much for future research in the
intersections of ecology and culture. His use of science is neither dogmatic nor
reductive, nor merely metaphorical or obscurantist.

Not all versions of cognitivism and phenomenology are equally useful for
ecocriticism, however, in that some are more self-limiting in their scope than
others. Carroll's version of cognitivist theory, for example, is more interested
in emotion than in affect, in that he excludes what he calls "cognitively impene-
trable effect" from his analysis.[7] In contrast, phenomenologist Anne Rutherford argues for the primacy of affect in film studies, asserting that film theory
needs to move from "the concern with sensation or with emotion understood
as sentiment organised along the axis of narrative identification, or with desire,
to an understanding of embodied affect, in the theorisation of spectatorship."[8]

Both Carroll and Rutherford thus tend to be overly exclusive in their respective approaches, though from opposite directions. In contrast, a robust film theory will attempt to account for all relevant manifestations of cognition, emotion, and affect in cinema, rather than narrow its concerns to just one of these factors, as Rutherford and Carroll both do in their different ways. A film theory that is concerned with spectatorship in terms of both emotional identification and embodied affect will thus be richer than one that focuses exclusively on one or other of these factors.[9]

Within cognitivist theory, Greg Smith achieves this degree of comprehensiveness with his "associative" model of emotions, which fully takes into consideration cognitive, emotional, and affective dimensions in film spectatorship. His "mood-cue" approach to film analysis is concerned with the multiple ways in which films cue particular emotions. "Filmic cues that can provide emotional information," he writes, "include facial expression, figure movement, dialogue, vocal expression and tone, costume, sound, music, lighting, mise-en-scène, set design, editing, camera (angle, distance, movement), depth of field, character qualities and histories, and narrative situation. Each of these cues can play a part in creating a mood orientation or a stronger emotion."[10] As we shall see in this essay, this method can be combined with phenomenological perspectives to produce a well-rounded and nuanced approach to film analysis useful for eco-film studies.

Before examining how these different methods apply to particular case studies, however, the main philosophical differences between cognitivism and phenomenology need to be explored. These derive from their different starting points: phenomenology begins from a first-person approach to film spectatorship, whereas cognitivism is more concerned with third-person approaches. Cognitivist theorists such as Carroll and Greg Smith thus formulate generalized assumptions about a "normal" film viewer. Carroll is concerned with the "normatively correct address of the text—the emotive effect that the text is supposed to have, or is designed to have on the normal audience."[11] A notion of intentionality is thus central to his theory, as he explains: "Some people may find beheadings humorous; but that is not the emotional response that *A Man for All Seasons* is designed to promote."[12] Viewers who depart from the normative response display what Murray Smith calls "apparently perverse allegiances," whereby "individual spectators" may take "perverse pleasure in representations that were not designed for that purpose—think of a pedophile watching *Home Alone* (1990), for example, or a necrophiliac watching documentary footage of the aftermath of a massacre."[13] Such responses may be accounted for without detriment to cognitive theory as a whole.

In contrast to cognitivism, phenomenology begins from first-person responses to a film by linking the individual perceiving body with its wider environment through the concept of "embodiment." When applied to film studies, this concept has the positive role of taking into consideration subjective responses to films, including personal variations within those responses. Phenomenology also tends to put affect, or the viewer's own bodily responses to a film, at the centre of film analysis and appreciation. Vivian Sobchack avoids the danger of lapsing into egocentrism that this approach may encourage by asking whether her response to a film is personal and idiosyncratic or is shared by others. She writes that "grounding broader social claims in autobiographical and anecdotal experience is not merely a fuzzy and subjective substitute for rigorous and objective analysis but purposefully provides the phenomenological—and embodied—premises for a more processual, expansive, and resonant materialist logic through which we, as subjects, can understand (and perhaps guide) what passes as our objective historical and cultural existence."[14] Sobchack's critical interest in her own bodily responses to a film thus does not exclude the social, historical, and cultural contexts within which such responses are formed, nor the response of other spectators to the film in question.

Laura Marks's version of phenomenological film theory similarly suggests the possibility of moving between first-person and third-person responses in film criticism. She writes that the close-ups of magnolia flowers in Shani Mootoo's short film *Her Sweetness Lingers* (1994) "remind me of how they feel and how they smell," adding that each viewer will have his or her own response to a film, based on personal memories and experiences, and that these associations "are probably somewhat different from the artist's and other viewers' associations with them."[15] This extension of film studies beyond personal response to the social construction of such responses makes phenomenological film theory potentially useful for eco-film studies, particularly when combined with cognitivist approaches. Indeed, Marks comes close to an eco-phenomenology of cinema in her advocacy of what she sees as multi-sensory films that evoke the senses of touch and smell as well as sight and hearing. Such films, she argues, may help to sharpen the audience's sensory awareness, and thereby contribute to a growing acuity for ecological awareness.

These claims are based on a post-structuralist critique of "ocularcentrism," according to which the primacy of vision and visuality in Anglo-American societies is assumed to be culturally rather than biologically determined. Ocularcentrism is considered by its critics to be a central factor in dominant notions of both rationality and capitalist economics, and to have produced a dangerous sense of detachment from the environment. Marks thus cites the

Frankfurt School approvingly because it advocated an aesthetics of "mimesis" as "a form of yielding to one's environment, rather than dominating it, and thus offers a radical alternative to the controlling distance from the environment so well served by vision."[16] It is in this that her approach comes close to an explicitly ecological theory of cinema. She argues that ocularcentrism can be countered in cinema by a "tactile epistemology" according to which "one calls up the presence of the other materially."[17] The essay-films which Marks champions thus challenge ocularcentrism by exploring a "haptic" or "tactile" visuality which invokes senses other than sight, particularly touch and smell. Marks acknowledges that this haptic or tactile visuality "is still not touch";[18] indeed, she adds that the mournful quality of the films she writes about is a recognition of the impossibility of achieving full tactility in an audio-visual medium. Nevertheless, she argues that such works constitute a "critique of visual mastery" that "speaks from an awareness about the destructive and literally imperialist potential of vision."[19]

Marks's version of phenomenology carefully avoids an extreme form of social constructionism which rejects the existence of pre-cultural bodily factors in cinema spectatorship. Rutherford, on the other hand, asserts more unequivocally that the dominance of vision over the other senses in human beings is primarily a culturally determined phenomenon. She argues rightly that the "insistence on scientific models of the body derived from biomedical discourse and the concomitant occlusion of phenomenological concepts of embodiment, have persistently thwarted the articulation of an aesthetics of embodiment which recognizes the full resonance of embodied affect in the experience of cinema spectatorship."[20] However, she then goes on to criticize the influence of biomedical discourse, including anatomy, physiology, and clinical practice, on film studies, not because of its limited or misleading focus, but because of its "assumptions of a structural, empirically measurable body."[21] When she writes critically that "traditional models of sense perception have been empirically-based, and have understood visual perception as pre-cultural," she appears to conflate the epistemological limitations of biomedical discourse with a total rejection of empirical science in general.[22] Yet this extreme anti-empiricism is unwarranted, in that the practical success of medical science suggests that the body is empirically measurable, within epistemological limits, and therefore that a major component of human vision is "pre-cultural." What cognitive theorist David Bordwell calls "good naturalization" is thus crucial in examining such biological factors.[23] Lacking this empirical basis, phenomenological theories of embodiment can be vague and implausibly idealist.

Indeed, Rutherford's extreme social constructionism exposes the tendency towards idealism in phenomenology, a flaw that has been criticized recently by speculative realist philosophers. Quentin Meillassoux criticizes what he calls the "correlationism" at the heart of phenomenology, according to which reality is assumed to be the product of a necessary inter-relationship between subject and object. The universalist claims of correlationism are undermined by the findings of science, which reveal what Meillassoux calls the "ancestrality" of the world: the fact that the world existed before the evolution of human beings, and therefore cannot be dependent on them for its existence.[24] The metaphysical realism argued for by Meillassoux thus assumes that reality is largely mind-independent, or what he calls a "great outdoors": "that outside which was not relative to us, and which was given as indifferent to its own givenness to be what it is, existing in itself regardless of whether we are thinking of it or not; that outside which thought could explore with the legitimate feeling of being on foreign territory—of being entirely elsewhere."[25] Graham Harman similarly takes issue with the idealist tendencies in phenomenology when he argues that by treating "things" as "phenomena" rather than as "objects," phenomenology implies "that they are not allowed to interact with each other except when chaperoned by a 'thinking human subject.'"[26] Ray Brassier observes that human consciousness "harbours an underlying but sub-linguistic reality which is simply not accessible to first-person phenomenological description or linguistic articulation. Ironically, and contrary to phenomenology's guiding intuition, the *reality* of consciousness is independent of the subject's consciousness. Only the objective, third-person perspective is equipped with conceptual resources sensitive enough to map consciousness' opaque, sub-linguistic reality."[27] It is "incumbent on philosophy," he writes, "to rehabilitate the notion of a non-correlational reality the better to explicate the speculative implications of its scientific exploration—rather than continually reigning in the latter by tightening the correlationist leash."[28]

However, not all versions of phenomenology are idealist in the sense criticized by the speculative realist philosophers quoted above. For example, Don Ihde usefully distinguishes between "body one" and "body two," the biological and the culturally constructed body, arguing that both need to be taken into consideration in a comprehensive and plausible theory of phenomenological embodiment.[29] Moreover, recent research into the intersection of phenomenology and the cognitive sciences is looking for productive ways of combining the two approaches. If the dangers of cognitivism lie in an excessive reductionism, the emergence of a non-reductionist cognitive science, such as the "enactive" approach to cognition explored by Francisco Varela, Eleanor Rosch, and Evan Thompson, promises a nuanced and complex understanding of how human cognition works in relation both to film spectatorship and to the wider environment.[30] Rosch writes that "the ecological environment of goal-directed, acting minds is not a neutral world describable by physics but a noetic and hedonic environment consisting of affordances, normative reference points, counterfactual possible worlds, and a continual emotively toned process of comparison. The ecological environment is always defined and judged with respect to a goal-directed mind."[31] Although this "cognitive ecology," derived from the work of psychologist James Gibson, is correlationist in the sense criticized by speculative realists, phenomenological approaches of this kind may nevertheless be reconciled with speculative or metaphysical realism if one accepts the more limited idea that mind and environment are, as Rosch puts it, "analytically inseparable,"[32] and that whenever minds exist in an environment, the interaction between the two is crucial.

Laura Marks cites Varela's theory of embodied action as the basis for her speculations on film, noting for example, that "our perception of colour categories" is "both based on apparently physiological universals and culturally specific."[33] Marks thus presents a nuanced theory of visuality whose project "is not to condemn all vision as bent on mastery, nor indeed to condemn all mastery."[34] Rather, she is concerned with "the visuality typical of capitalism, consumerism, surveillance, and ethnography: a sort of instrumental vision that uses the thing seen as an object for knowledge and control."[35] She argues instead that "a form of visuality that yields to the thing seen, a vision that is not merely cognitive but acknowledges its location in the body, seems to escape the attribution of mastery."[36] Marks's version of phenomenological film theory thus opens the way for a biocultural synthesis of phenomenological and cognitivist approaches to film that could be of use to eco-film criticism. In the next section, a combination of the cognitivist and phenomenological methods outlined above will provide a way of exploring how two contrasting films work as eco-films.

INTERPRETING ECO-FILM: *LOCAL HERO* AND *THIS FILTHY EARTH*

Greg Smith's cognitive model allows for close readings of both *Local Hero* and *This Filthy Earth* to illustrate how they communicate their ecological and environmental meanings through a combination of cognition, emotion, and affect. As he notes, the narrative of *Local Hero* mostly focuses on the moral "conversion" of the protagonist, American oil executive "Mac" MacIntyre, to a "less driven person" who decides not to promote the building of a new oil refinery on an unspoiled Scottish island.[37] Berys Gaut clarifies the concept of audience "identification" central to cognitivist interpretations of this sort. The "question to ask whenever someone talks of identifying with a character," he writes, "is *in what respects* does she identify with the character; the act of identification is aspectual. To identify perceptually with a character is to imagine seeing what he sees; to identify affectively with him is to imagine feeling what he feels; to identify motivationally is to imagine wanting what he wants; to identify epistemically with him is to imagine believing what he believes; to identify practically with him is to imagine doing what he does; and so on."[38] Audience identification can take place on each of these levels, while different film techniques may foster each form of identification in a particular way. Reaction shots, for example, are useful vehicles for affective identification, in that they provide information for the viewer about a character's emotions and state of mind. In Gaut's terms, *Local Hero* puts across its ecological meanings mainly through the viewer's affective identification with MacIntyre. In Carroll's terms, the film is criterially prefocused so that the viewer may empathize imaginatively with the ethical dilemma MacIntyre faces regarding the development of the Scottish island, and may also approve of the way he comes to change his mind in response to the beauty of the island and the sense of community he discovers there. Although this normative response may not necessarily be shared by all viewers, who may potentially react in different ways to this narrative content, the prefocusing of the film's meaning is nevertheless clear. Tracing the dynamics of character identification, or what phenomenologist Rutherford dismisses as "emotion understood as sentiment organised along the axis of narrative identification," is thus a productive way of looking at *Local Hero* ecocritically, and does not deserve to be considered an inferior method of analysis.[39]

Local Hero also signifies ecological meanings through its landscape images, which work through a combination of cognitive, emotional, and affective means. Director Bill Forsyth spoke of wanting the film "to present a cosmic viewpoint to people, but through the most ordinary things."[40] A good example of this viewpoint comes when MacIntyre and his colleague Danny Oldsen are filmed in long shot discussing the oil business while walking on the beach. Without oil, they say, there would be no automobiles, no paint, no ink or nylon. As the two men engage in this dialogue, there is a cut to a longer shot which reveals the wider landscape in which they are walking. This cut works both affectively, emotionally, and cognitively, in that revealing the visual beauty of the Scottish landscape at sunset may evoke both affect, or a "gut" feeling beyond words, and an emotional response which may include, as Carroll puts it, "a belief or thought" about a particular "place, or thing, real or imagined."[41] The shot also works cognitively, in that it becomes an ironic commentary on the men's words and therefore a reason for the viewer not to support development on the island. When MacIntyre's mobile telephone bleeps to remind him that the business day is starting in Houston, the incongruousness of the sound also reinforces the meaning of the scene by working on all three levels.

The landscape imagery in *Local Hero* may be placed within Scott MacDonald's theorizing of landscape in ecocinema. He emphasizes the cognitive potential of images of beautiful landscapes to retrain perception along ecological lines. "Obviously," he writes,

> conventionally beautiful imagery *can* be used not only to confirm the status quo, but to promote activities that do long-term damage to places a good many of us recognize as worth preserving. We see this all the time in television advertising; indeed, it seems to be one of the central strategies of Madison Avenue. But beautiful imagery of beautiful places can also be a confrontation of the status quo, and particularly of the media status quo; it can model fundamental changes in perception not only in terms of what we see in movie theatres, on television, or on-line, but how we function in the 'real world'. And it can do so without announcing any polemical goal.[42]

In addition to the cognitive function of landscape imagery described here by MacDonald, anthropologist Kay Milton brings out the role of our emotional engagement with such images. She observes that an aesthetic appreciation of natural beauty can play an important role in motivating people to act in defence of their environment. "As we engage with our environment," she writes,

> we perceive meanings in it; this is how it becomes known to us. It is the meanings which give things their value. In other worlds, we value things by perceiving meanings in them. These meanings become known to us through the emotions they induce, which we then experience as feelings.... Thus the process of valuing things in the world is inseparable from the emotions and feelings they induce in us; without these emotions and feelings there would be no value.[43]

Milton and MacDonald thus make a case for the importance of landscape aesthetics in promoting ecological awareness. In *Local Hero*, the Scottish landscape signifies ecological meanings at both the cognitive and emotional levels described above. Its beauty is signified visually through such details as the repeated use of the twilight "golden hour" in filming on the beach, and aurally through such sounds as the ambient call of curlews on the soundtrack. The emotional appeal of these images and sounds is also linked to the plot of the film, in that the beauty of the landscape provides the reason for MacIntyre's decision to save the endangered environment.

At a conceptual level, *Local Hero* thus celebrates the environmentalist values of place attachment and ecological connectedness, as love of nature and of place triumph over narrow economic motives. These environmentalist meanings are communicated through the cognitive, affective, and emotional effects of the film's landscape imagery, as well as through other forms of textual redundancy that create both mood and cognitive meaning in the film. For example, when Ben Knox, who owns the beach and wants to protect it from development, refuses MacIntyre's offer to buy him any other beach in the world, he says that the beach is his "living" and "has to be worked." This sentiment is reinforced by the boss of Knox Oil and Gas, Felix Happer, when he says, "I could grow to love this place." When Happer finally decides to locate the oil refinery off-shore and to build a research institute on the island instead, this is given as a win-win scenario: the locals get much-needed jobs apparently without destroying the health of the environment. This compromise solution endorses moderate development and is the feel-good ending the comedy requires.

When watching *Local Hero*, then, the viewer's emotional, cognitive, and affective responses all work together and are difficult to separate. For example, sentimentality towards nature is both an emotional response to the film and a theme within the film itself, in which ironic humour prevents excessive senti-mentality. The narrative makes the point that it is the outsiders who tend to be ecologically minded, whereas the locals are pragmatically interested in money and jobs. After MacIntyre and Oldsen are concerned about a rabbit they run over in their car, hotel manager Gordon Urquhart kills it and serves it to them in a casserole. The harsh economics of the Scottish rural environment are further illustrated when one fisherman comments that the lobsters they export to London and Paris are too expensive for them to eat themselves. A further level of cognitive meaning in the film involves the ambiguous effects of globalization on the Scottish landscape, also reinforced through textual redun-dancy: though military jets practise bombing over the beach, the African vicar has been accepted by the local community, and, equally positively, the Russian fishing fleet, making its annual visit, is also accepted in a friendly way. The final shot of the film is of the red telephone box ringing with MacIntyre's unanswered call from America, signifying at a cognitive level the interconnec-tion between the local and the global, and at an emotional one the pathos of separation to which this condition can lead.

This Filthy Earth, like *Local Hero*, also signifies ecological meanings pri-marily through the affective identification that the viewer establishes with its central characters. The film is set in a harsh rural village in the North of England, and focuses on the relationship between two sisters, Francine and Kath, and two men, their brutal cousin Buto and a more gentle Polish immigrant, Lek. Whereas *Local Hero* does not offer an unambiguously moral character for the audience to identify with, the viewer of *This Filthy Earth* is likely to sympathize with Francine and Lek because they are innocent victims of the cruelty of the other characters. Francine is a sympathetic figure because she is morally virtuous, lonely, and unhappy: in Murray Smith's terms, she is the focus both of audience "alignment" in that she is given the most screen time in the film, and also of audience "allegiance," or what Gaut calls affective identification, particularly because of the preponderance of reaction shots given to her.[44] Lek is a sympathetic figure because he displays a tender side to his character, in contrast to Buto, who is domineering and violent.

Unlike in *Local Hero*, none of the characters in *This Filthy Earth* displays an ecological consciousness, and the film perhaps makes the former look naive in its reassuring Romantic ecological vision and optimistic, win-win environmental politics. "The film," writes Kötting, "should show signs of the berserk or slightly psychotic, an attempt to reflect the human condition."[45] If *Local Hero* is a "complex pastoral" in Leo Marx's terms, in that its pastoral idyll is under threat from development, *This Filthy Earth* is an anti-pastoral, in which the rural Northern English landscape is harsh, dirty, and cruel.[46] In both films, people struggle to survive through hard labour. However, whereas in *Local Hero* the Scottish landscape is a benign protagonist, in Kötting's film the natural world is an antagonist to be struggled against and in which human beings cannot live in a state of harmonious coexistence. The narrative turns on a catastrophic storm that floods the village and has dire consequences for both Francine and Lek. Moreover, in *This Filthy Earth*, unlike in *Local Hero*, adherence to place leads not to sentimental attachment and environmental resistance but to xenophobia and violence. The country folk are superstitious and ignorant, blaming the flood on Lek and eventually torturing him as a scapegoat. At the end of the film, when Francine has the chance to leave the farm with Lek, she decides to stay, telling him that it is "all I've got." When Lek leaves the village against a long shot of the fell-side, he is neither a figure of resistance nor a triumphal hero, local or otherwise; rather, landscape finally dominates human being in an image of dislocation and disharmony.

Kötting intended the look of his film to be a "poetic reality with roots in an eastern European landscape. A brutal, unforgiving world of inbreed [*sic*], where tenderness and decorum is [*sic*] a luxury that the inhabitants can ill afford."[47] Yet there is a vibrant energy both in the country folk's transgressions of bourgeois decorum and in the representation of the natural world in the film. Cinematic affect is an important factor in putting this across. Kötting wrote of wanting *This Filthy Earth* "to be experienced as a meditative and artistic medium, a place to experiment with dislocated moments in time, where plot and characters are often sacrificed in a desire to create cinematic devices and textures. A right muddle-up."[48] To this end he deploys many of the audio-visual techniques of experimental film, including contrasting film stocks, flare outs, halations, overexposures, blurred pans, and other slow and fast motion effects. As a result, the landscape imagery in the film does not allow for an easy immersion into familiar forms of natural beauty, as in *Local Hero*. *This Filthy Earth* refuses this Romantic aesthetic. Instead, the film's sudden, unpredictable changes in stylistic register work both cognitively and affectively to disrupt the stability of the diegetic world, thereby suggesting that the natural world is dynamic, violent, and chaotic. In this way, the landscape imagery has some of the autonomy described by film theorist Martin Lefebvre, who notes that, in some films, the "contemplation of the setting frees it briefly from its narrative function (but perhaps, in some cases, only for the length of a thought); for one instant, the natural, outdoor setting for the action is considered in its own right, as a landscape."[49] The two main formal techniques for achieving this sense of autonomy for landscape images are transition shots and *temps morts*, as in the art cinema of Antonioni and Pasolini.[50] As Lefebvre notes, "the more the landscape's spectacle is legitimized or recuperated by the unfolding of the action—the less violent the interruption of the story feels."[51] In this regard, *This Filthy Earth* includes, for example, a close-up of a leek being pulled from the soil that functions as a transition shot between dramatic scenes but, in its extended duration, also has a relative autonomy from the narrative flow, and thus emphasizes cinematic affect for its own sake.

Kötting's interest in cinematic affect also makes his film a candidate for Laura Marks's notion of "haptic" cinema, mentioned earlier in this essay: the film's opening moments include shots of a bull's ejaculating penis and of pus squirting out of a sore on a farmer's foot; Francine wipes bull sperm off her hands and later Buto smells his fingers after he has tested a female goose for its moistness. These images are strong in affect: the viewer may physically recoil in a way of interest to phenomenological theorists such as Marks and Sobchack. However, Kötting's treatment of the body, both human and animal, as obscene and abject works as much at a cognitive as at an affective level. When the film blurs ontological distinctions between human and animal, it evokes moods both of horror and of black humour and also cognitive meanings, reinforced by textual redundancy, in which the natural world is represented as a struggle between forces of life and death. For example, the close-up of the leek being pulled out of the ground signifies life by visually matching the bull's penis seen earlier in the film, while at the end of the film, death is signified when Francine's cow dies giving birth to her stillborn calf. As Grodal observes, art films work simultaneously at the level of cognition and affect; they "use visual means to indicate abstract meanings, including stylistic devices aimed at making visual phenomena special and suggestive of higher meaning."[52]

Phenomenological analysis also recognizes that moments of cinematic affect may work cognitively on the viewer. Indeed, in her analysis of "haptic" films, Marks tends to emphasize cognitive as well as affective factors in their reception. Such films, she writes, "achieve sensuous effects" and also "raise ontological questions."[53] For Sobchack, affective responses to a film can prompt ethical judgment in the viewer. Writing of the scene in which a rabbit is shot dead in Jean Renoir's *Rules of the Game* (1939), she argues that this narrative event contains within it the "charge of the real" which is also an "ethical charge"; that is, "one that calls forth not only response but also responsibility—not only aesthetic valuation but also ethical judgment.... It remands us reflexively to ourselves as embodied, culturally knowledgeable, and socially invested viewers."[54] For a critic who considers affective responses to films to be primary, then, the cognitive element in spectatorship is nevertheless significant as well.

CONCLUSION

A combination of cognitivist and phenomenological approaches to film criticism, outlined in the above analysis of *Local Hero* and *This Filthy Earth*, may articulate the complex ways in which eco-films work on their audiences. In general terms, eco-film studies will benefit from a combination of scientific and humanistic approaches, which should be considered potentially complementary, rather than antagonistic, forms of knowledge. Cognitivist philosopher Shaun Gallagher writes of the need for the first-person, introspective methods of phenomenology to be put on a rigorous, systematic basis for testing and verification by scientific experiment.[55] However, Sobchack's use of personal anecdote in film analysis can nevertheless be productive for film studies, even if it cannot be put on the rigorous methodological grounding required by experimental cognitive sciences. The empirical scientific methods that inform cognitivism are useful in accounting for the natural phenomena involved in film spectatorship, such as the role of the human eye in depth perception. Yet, as Malcolm Turvey argues, scientific theorizing cannot explain everything that needs to be accounted for in film spectatorship. Science, he writes, can explain

the natural constraints on the use of stylistic conventions, not why a specific group of filmmakers actually uses, or does not use, these conventions
in a specific situation. To understand the latter, the film scholar has to
undertake a traditional humanistic investigation into the *intentions* of the
group of filmmakers—into the specific historical context in which they are
using these conventions, how they understand their use, and the reasons
they have for using the stylistic conventions that they do. Such a humanistic investigation has no place, of course, in the natural sciences—there are
no *reasons* for the blind movements of matter in space to be investigated.[56]

Eco-film criticism will thus benefit from humanistic approaches which are
compatible with, and informed by, the natural sciences. The cognitive-phenom-
enological approaches outlined in this essay point in such a direction.

Cognitive philosopher Ronald de Sousa's notion of "paradigm scenarios"
provides a useful way of summarizing the role that the arts, including cinema,
can play in producing ecological knowledge. We learn paradigm scenarios as
children and have them further reinforced in adulthood by art and culture.
They involve two aspects: "first, a situation type providing the characteristic
objects of the specific emotion-type … and second, a set of characteristic or
'normal' *responses* to the situation, where normality is first a biological matter
and then very quickly becomes a cultural one."[57] For de Sousa, art (including,
for our purposes, cinema) plays an important role in shaping paradigm scenarios by creating stories through which we may account for our emotional
responses to objective situations. As he puts it, "at least one component of the
need for art is the desire to experience the emotions called forth by death, by
sexual thrill, by revenge, or by painful or ridiculous alienation, by evoking the
relevant paradigm scenarios without needing to live through the actual events
that are their natural causes."[58] We may add environmental crisis to this list of
experiences for which paradigm scenarios provide a valuable cultural function.
Moreover, as Gaut observes, photographic images are particularly emotive in
this respect. "Our emotional reactions to generalities," he writes, "such as sta-
tistics recording mortality in developing countries, are often muted: but our
emotions are triggered, other things equal, much more powerfully by specif-
ics, and the density of the photographic image is thus a powerful elicitor of
emotions."[59] According to the cognitivist approach to culture explored in this
essay, an eco-film can be any film which creates an environmental paradigm
scenario about potential ways of reacting to the natural or built environment.
In narrative cinema, fictional identification involves entertaining such virtual
scenarios. A broadly defined ecocinema can raise the kind of issues and debates
concerning ecology and the environment implied by *Local Hero* and *This Filthy
Earth* without being overly prescriptive or narrowly ideological.

NOTES

1 Greg M. Smith, *Film Structure and the Emotion System* (Cambridge: Cambridge University Press, 2003), 31.

2 Noël Carroll, "Film, Emotion, and Genre," in *Passionate Views: Film, Cognition, and Emotion*, ed. Carl Plantinga and Greg M. Smith (Baltimore, MD: Johns Hopkins University Press, 1999), 26.

3 Noël Carroll, *Beyond Aesthetics: Philosophical Essays* (Cambridge: Cambridge University Press, 2001), 221.

4 Carroll, "Film, Emotion, and Genre," 47.

5 Carroll, *Beyond Aesthetics*, 227.

6 Torben Grodal, *Embodied Visions: Evolution, Emotion, Culture, and Film* (Oxford: Oxford University Press, 2009), 17–18.

7 Carroll, "Film, Emotion, and Genre," 26.

8 Anne Rutherford, "Cinema and Embodied Affect," *Senses of Cinema* 25 (March 2003): 9, http://sensesofcinema.com/2003/feature-articles/embodied_affect.

9 The role of "desire" in film spectatorship, mentioned by Rutherford, takes us into important questions concerning the validity of psychoanalytical film theory which are beyond the scope of this essay.

10 G. Smith, *Film Structure*, 42.

11 Carroll, *Beyond Aesthetics*, 233.

12 Carroll, *Beyond Aesthetics*, 233.

13 Murray Smith, "Gangsters, Cannibals, Aesthetes, or Apparently Perverse Allegiances," in *Passionate Views: Film, Cognition, and Emotion*, ed. Carl Plantinga and Greg M. Smith (Baltimore, MD: Johns Hopkins University Press, 1999), 222.

14 Vivian Sobchack, *Carnal Thoughts: Embodiment and Moving Image Culture* (Berkeley: University of California Press, 2004), 6.

15 Laura Marks, *The Skin of the Film: Intercultural Cinema, Embodiment, and the Senses* (Durham, NC: Duke University Press, 2000), 148.

16 Marks, *The Skin*, 140.

17 Marks, *The Skin*, 138.

18 Marks, *The Skin*, 192.

19 Marks, *The Skin*, 193.

20 Rutherford, "Cinema," 1.

21 Rutherford, "Cinema," 2.

22 Rutherford, "Cinema," 6.

23 David Bordwell, "A Case for Cognitivism," *Iris* 9 (Spring 1989): 14, http://www.davidbordwell.net/articles/Bordwell_Iris_no9_spring1989_11.pdf.

24 Quentin Meillassoux, *After Finitude: An Essay on the Necessity of Contingency* (London: Continuum, 2008), 5.

25 Meillassoux, *After Finitude*, 7.

26 Graham Harman, *Guerilla Metaphysics: Phenomenology and the Carpentry of Things* (Chicago: Open Court, 2005), 330.

27 Ray Brassier, *Nihil Unbound: Enlightenment and Extinction* (London: Palgrave Macmillan, 2007), 29.

28 Brassier, *Nihil Unbound*, 63.

29 Don Ihde, *Bodies in Technology* (Minneapolis: University of Minnesota Press, 2002), xi.

30 Francesco J. Varela, Eleanor Rosch, and Evan Thompson, *The Embodied Mind: Cognitive Science and Human Experience* (Cambridge, MA: MIT Press, 1991).

31 Eleanor Rosch, "The Environment of Minds: Toward a Noetic and Hedonic Ecology," in *Cognitive Ecology*, ed. Morton P. Friedman and Edward C. Carterette (London: Academic Press, 1996), 19.

32 Rosch, "The Environment," 10.

33 Marks, *The Skin*, 203.

34 Marks, *The Skin*, 132.

35 Marks, *The Skin*, 131.

36 Marks, *The Skin*, 132.

37 G. Smith, *Film Structure*, 55.

38 Berys Gaut, *A Philosophy of Cinematic Art* (Cambridge: Cambridge University Press, 2010), 258.

39 Rutherford, "Cinema and Embodied Affect," 9.

40 Bill Forsyth, quoted in Ian Goode, "Mediating the Rural: *Local Hero* and the Location of Scottish Cinema," in *Cinematic Countrysides*, ed. Robert Fish (Manchester: Manchester University Press, 2007), 121–22.

41 Carroll, *Beyond Aesthetics*, 221.

42 Scott MacDonald, "Towards an Eco-Cinema," *Interdisciplinary Studies of Literature and Environment* 11, no. 2 (Summer 2004): 112–13.

43 Kay Milton, *Loving Nature: Towards an Ecology of Emotion* (London: Routledge, 2002), 100.

44 M. Smith, "Gangsters," 220.

45 Andrew Kötting, "It's a Dirty Job," *This Filthy Earth*. Film Four. 2001. DVD booklet, 12.

46 Leo Marx, *The Machine in the Garden: Technology and the Pastoral Ideal in America* (Oxford: Oxford University Press, 1964), 25.

47 Kötting, "It's a Dirty Job," 12.

48 Kötting, "It's a Dirty Job," 11.

49 Martin Lefebvre, "Between Setting and Landscape in the Cinema," in *Landscape and Film*, ed. Martin Lefebvre (New York: Routledge, 2006), 29.

50 Lefebvre, "Between Setting," 38.

51 Lefebvre, "Between Setting," 33.

52 Grodal, *Embodied Visions*, 228.

53 Marks, *The Skin*, 172.

54 Sobchack, *Carnal Thoughts*, 284.

55 Shaun Gallagher, "Phenomenology and Non-reductionist Cognitive Science," in *Handbook of Phenomenology and Cognitive Science*, ed. Shaun Gallagher and Daniel Schmicking (London: Springer, 2010), 21.

56 Malcolm Turvey, "Can Scientific Models of Theorizing Help Film Theory?" in *The Philosophy of Film: Introductory Texts and Readings*, ed. Thomas E. Wartenberg and Angela Curran (Oxford: Blackwell, 2005), 29.

57 Ronald de Sousa, *The Rationality of Emotion* (Cambridge, MA: MIT Press, 1987), 182.

58 De Sousa, *The Rationality*, 320–21.

59 Gaut, *A Philosophy*, 249.

BIBLIOGRAPHY

Bordwell, David. "A Case for Cognitivism." *Iris* 9 (Spring 1989): 11–40. http://www.davidbordwell.net/articles/Bordwell_Iris_no9_spring1989_11.pdf.

Brassier, Ray. *Nihil Unbound: Enlightenment and Extinction*. London: Palgrave Macmillan, 2007.

Carroll, Noël. *Beyond Aesthetics: Philosophical Essays*. Cambridge: Cambridge University Press, 2001.

———. "Film, Emotion, and Genre." In *Passionate Views: Film, Cognition, and Emotion*, edited by Carl Plantinga and Greg M. Smith, 21–47. Baltimore, MD: Johns Hopkins University Press, 1999.

De Sousa, Ronald. *The Rationality of Emotion*. Cambridge, MA: MIT Press, 1987.

Gallagher, Shaun. "Phenomenology and Non-reductionist Cognitive Science." In *Handbook of Phenomenology and Cognitive Science*, edited by Shaun Gallagher and Daniel Schmicking, 21–34. London: Springer, 2010.

Gaut, Berys. *A Philosophy of Cinematic Art*. Cambridge: Cambridge University Press, 2010.

Goode, Ian. "Mediating the Rural: *Local Hero* and the Location of Scottish Cinema." In *Cinematic Countrysides*, edited by Robert Fish, 109–26. Manchester: Manchester University Press, 2007.

Grodal, Torben. *Embodied Visions: Evolution, Emotion, Culture, and Film*. Oxford: Oxford University Press, 2009.

Harman, Graham. *Guerilla Metaphysics: Phenomenology and the Carpentry of Things*. Chicago: Open Court, 2005.

Ihde, Don. *Bodies in Technology*. Minneapolis: University of Minnesota Press, 2002.

Kötting, Andrew. "It's a Dirty Job." *This Filthy Earth*. Film Four. 2001. DVD booklet, 10–13.

Lefebvre, Martin. "Between Setting and Landscape in the Cinema." In *Landscape and Film*, edited by Martin Lefebvre, 19–59. New York: Routledge, 2006.

Local Hero. Directed by Bill Forsythe. 1983. London: Channel 4, 2008. DVD.

MacDonald, Scott. "Towards an Eco-Cinema." *Interdisciplinary Studies of Literature and Environment* 11, no. 2 (Summer 2004): 107–32.

Marks, Laura M. *The Skin of the Film: Intercultural Cinema, Embodiment, and the Senses*. Durham, NC: Duke University Press, 2000.

Marx, Leo. *The Machine in the Garden: Technology and the Pastoral Ideal in America*. Oxford: Oxford University Press, 1964.

Meillassoux, Quentin. *After Finitude: An Essay on the Necessity of Contingency*. London: Continuum, 2008.

Milton, Kay. *Loving Nature: Towards an Ecology of Emotion*. London: Routledge, 2002.

Rosch, Eleanor. "The Environment of Minds: Toward a Noetic and Hedonic Ecology." In *Cognitive Ecology*, edited by Morton P. Friedman and Edward C. Carterette, 5–27. London: Academic Press, 1996.

Rutherford, Anne. "Cinema and Embodied Affect." *Senses of Cinema* 25 (March 2003): 1–15. http://sensesofcinema.com/2003/feature-articles/embodied_affect/.

Smith, Greg M. *Film Structure and the Emotion System*. Cambridge: Cambridge University Press, 2003.

Smith, Murray. "Gangsters, Cannibals, Aesthetes, or Apparently Perverse Allegiances." In *Passionate Views: Film, Cognition, and Emotion*, edited by Carl Plantinga and Greg M. Smith, 217–38. Baltimore, MD: Johns Hopkins University Press, 1999.

Sobchack, Vivian. *Carnal Thoughts: Embodiment and Moving Image Culture*. Berkeley: University of California Press, 2004.

This Filthy Earth. Directed by Andrew Kötting. Film Four, 2001. DVD.

Turvey, Malcolm. "Can Scientific Models of Theorizing Help Film Theory?" In *The Philosophy of Film: Introductory Texts and Readings*, edited by Thomas E. Wartenberg and Angela Curran, 21–37. Oxford: Blackwell, 2005.

Varela, Francesco J., Eleanor Rosch, and Evan Thompson. *The Embodied Mind: Cognitive Science and Human Experience*. Cambridge, MA: MIT Press, 1991.

2

Emotions of Consequence?
Viewing Eco-documentaries from a Cognitive Perspective

Alexa Weik von Mossner

In this chapter, I will investigate the emotional appeal of eco-documentaries and ask whether they engage our emotions in ways that are different from those we experience during the watching of a fiction film with an environmentalist theme. Documentaries are often thought to be categorically different from fiction films, in part because of the general assumption that, as nonfiction films, they somehow "document reality." However, while most viewers feel that they simply "know" when they are watching a documentary rather than a fiction film, it has been surprisingly difficult for critics and theorists to come up with a rigid definition that would clearly separate the two. Distinctions must nevertheless be made, since there is broad agreement among film scholars that audiences *do* respond differently to fiction and documentary films. The work of cognitive film theorist Dirk Eitzen is particularly helpful for a better understanding of what he has called "documentary's peculiar appeals."[1] Eitzen has suggested that the difference between fiction and non-fiction lies not least in the ways in which viewers *feel* about the two, and that one of the things that gives the documentary mode emotional power is precisely the viewer's belief in its non-fictional nature and the resulting understanding that what she sees on the screen is *consequential.*[2] Since a great many eco-documentaries foreground the consequential nature of the issues they present, Eitzen's argument is well worth considering in an ecocritical context.

The relatively young genre of climate change documentaries is a particularly fruitful site for investigating these issues, both because of the filmmakers' belief in the urgency of their subject matter and the fact that the enormity and futurity of climate change pose representational problems that have implications for viewers' emotional engagement. As Julie Doyle points out in "Seeing the Climate?" (2010) documentary photography "as a discourse of evidence and truth within the context of the history of climate change campaigning" faces severe limitations because climate change campaigning necessitates "action to prevent climate change *before its effects [can] be seen*."[3] This obviously poses an enormous challenge not only to environmental groups such as Greenpeace, which strongly rely on visual evidence, but also to the makers of climate change documentaries. Over the past decade, documentary filmmakers have chosen very different narrative and visual strategies to deal with this representational problem in order to engage their audiences affectively and cognitively in the stories they tell. I have selected two films—Davis Guggenheim's Academy Award–winning *An Inconvenient Truth* (2006) and Franny Armstrong's drama-documentary hybrid *The Age of Stupid* (2009)— first because of their highly successful records and second because of their quite unusual emotionalizing strategies. My analysis of these films will show that the distinction between our emotional responses to fiction and non-fiction isn't always as clear-cut as Eitzen makes it out to be. In order to understand the "peculiar appeal" of these eco-documentaries we must in fact consider the emotionalizing power of cinematic techniques that work *across* film modes and genres. However, viewers' belief in the *consequential nature* of what is presented on the screen remains crucial for their emotional and cognitive responses.

A COGNITIVE APPROACH TO ECO-DOCUMENTARIES

Film scholars with a special interest in documentary film have debated the differences between fiction and non-fiction film—and the latter's exact relationship to reality. In his introduction to *Theorizing Documentary* (1993), Michael Renov argues that it is difficult to draw an exact line between feature films and documentaries because "nonfiction contains any number of 'fictive' elements, moments at which a presumably objective representation of the world encounters the necessity of creative intervention."[4] Bill Nichols turns the argument on its head in his *Introduction to Documentary* (2001) by claiming that "every film is a documentary" because "even the most whimsical of fictions gives *evidence* of the culture that produced it and reproduces the likenesses of the people who perform within it."[5] In Nichols's view, "there are only two kinds of film: (1) documentaries of wish-fulfillment and (2) documentaries of social representation."[6] Type one is what we tend to call *fiction*, because it is an expression of dreams and wishes, but also of more negative emotions such as fear. Type two is what we typically call *documentary*, because it gives "tangible representation to aspects of the world we already inhabit and share."[7] The fact that documentaries can give such tangible representation to "timely issues in need of attention" is, in Nichols's view, what gives them their peculiar appeal and a political power that extends beyond the immediate viewing experience.[8]

Although Nichols takes pains to keep his definition of documentary open and flexible, problems arise almost immediately. Clearly, not all fiction films are concerned with wish-fulfillment, and in the past several of them have attempted to give "tangible representation to aspects of the world we already inhabit and share." John Singleton's *Boyz n the Hood* (1991) is a pertinent example, concerned as it is with the social problems and dangers of black life in South Central Los Angeles, but environmentalist "biopics" such as Michael Apted's *Gorillas in the Mist* (1988) and Mike Nichols's *Silkwood* (1983) also meet this criterion. It is, in fact, almost impossible to draw a clear line between the two modes of filmmaking, since fiction films often have some non-fictional elements in them and makers of non-fiction films often deliberately use techniques we tend to associate with fiction films. The cognitive film scholar Noël Carroll even states that "the distinction between nonfiction and fiction was never really based on differences in formal techniques" because "when it comes to technique, fiction and nonfiction filmmakers can and do imitate each other, just as fiction and nonfiction writers can and do."[9]

In what way, then, *is* a documentary different from a fiction film? Carroll suggests that "films come labeled or indexed" either as fiction or non-fiction film, and that as viewers we thus expect a certain kind of film when we buy a ticket to see it.[10] Other scholars have argued that it is really up to the viewer to decide which film she understands as documentary and which one as fiction film, regardless of how the films are intended or labelled.[11] Dai Vaughan similarly claims that what makes a film "documentary" is the way it is looked at by the viewer and that "the history of documentary has been the succession of strategies by which film-makers have tried to make viewers look at films this way."[12] According to such an understanding, the special appeal of the documentary form lies in its actual or perceived relationship to the world outside of the movie theatre or television screen. As Carl Plantinga puts it, a non-fiction film "asserts, or is taken by the spectator to assert, that the states of affairs it presents occur or occurred in the actual world."[13] It is this assertion of actuality that Dirk Eitzen sees at the heart of our emotional response to non-fiction film. "Instead of calling nonfiction a mode," he suggests, "we might just as well say that, like teaching, arguing, and flirting, it is simply a *discourse of consequence*."[14]

Their consequential nature, however, does not change the fact that documentaries are *movies*, which, Eitzen reminds us, means that "they are contrived, just like fiction films."[15] And just like fiction films, they may use a number of techniques to get viewers emotionally invested in what is presented to them. There are many different ways in which such emotional appeals can be made. We may react emotionally to something we see (like a beautiful landscape, a tortured animal, or a dead person), or something we hear (like death cries or stimulating music), or our emotional response may be the result of our cognitive understanding of something we learn through either sounds or images (like a dialogue that reveals a plot against the main character of a film or a graph that indicates the predicted and actual melting rate of the polar ice caps, as seen in *An Inconvenient Truth*). In the first two cases, our emotional response is immediate and direct; in the third instance, it is the result of our cognitive processing of information we consider relevant and consequential. In all cases, however, cognitive and emotional processes complement one another, just as they do when we react to real-life experiences. The main difference is that through the use of cinematic components such as plot, character (including actor performance), setting, lighting, editing, sound, and music, filmmakers are able to *guide* our emotions during the viewing experience; as Greg Smith puts it, they continually "offer [us] invitations to feel" in certain ways.[16]

Such invitations are offered by fiction and non-fiction filmmakers alike, using many of the same cinematic components. Eitzen nevertheless insists that documentary films have *peculiar* means to tap into their audiences' emotions, means that are not shared by fiction films. His central example is Robert Gardner's *Forest of Bliss* (1985), a documentary about India that at one point shows a dog in distress: "An extremely emaciated and very bedraggled-looking mongrel is set upon by a pack of more-robust dogs. The lone mongrel tries to run away, but the pack catches it and brings it down. The mongrel whimpers and cowers submissively, but the pack attacks it relentlessly. Finally, the poor brute rolls over on its back in what is pretty obviously a plea for mercy. Still, the other dogs bite and tear at the hapless creature, evidently meaning to kill it."[17] Eitzen's description of the scene demonstrates his empathy for the beleaguered dog as well as his resulting feelings of pain and compassion, his anger at the attackers, and his sense of horror at witnessing the event. He explains: "Even in a fiction film, seeing an event like this would be profoundly disturbing. Seeing it in a documentary, I found it practically unbearable. I was literally nauseated. I wanted to turn away. And yet, because this was a documentary, I felt an even stronger compulsion to watch. Even more than that, I wanted to intervene. I wanted to pick up a rock and throw it at the dogs that were so viciously attacking one of their own kind."[18] Eitzen takes this observation of his own reaction to an emotionally powerful moment in a documentary film as the starting point for his deliberations about the peculiar power of this filmmaking mode. "When documentaries ... produce strong responses," he explains, "there is something special, something uniquely compelling and affecting, in their impact,"[19] something that is directly related to our cognitive understanding that what we see has real consequences in the real world. Building his argument on the insights of both ecological psychology and cognitive science, Eitzen explains that what he experienced during the viewing of *Forest of Bliss* was "an awareness of an inclination to intervene, had that been possible. In other words, it was an *emotion*—a recognition of my body's disposition toward what I was seeing.... This disposition is part of the distinctive impact of documentaries."[20] Documentary filmmakers may take advantage of this characteristic by inviting their viewers to take action, tying their "power to arouse a pleasurable or engaged response ... to an implied entreaty for special attention and concern."[21]

Such implied entreaties can indeed be found in most documentaries, but they are especially prevalent in films that use what David Bordwell and Kristin Thompson have called *rhetorical* form. According to Bordwell and Thompson, this form is marked by four attributes: (1) it addresses the viewer openly, trying to move him or her to a new intellectual conviction, to a new emotional attitude, or to action; (2) the subject of the film is a matter of opinion; (3) the filmmaker appeals to viewer emotions; (4) the film attempts to persuade the viewer to make a choice that will have an effect on his or her everyday life.[22] The makers of eco-documentaries have quite often used rhetorical form and relied on the "peculiar" emotional appeals described by Eitzen. Guggenheim's *An Inconvenient Truth* and Armstrong's *The Age of Stupid* are typical examples, but the same is true for other climate change documentaries such as Judith Helfand and Daniel Gold's *Everything's Cool* (2007) and Nadia Conners and Leila Conners Petersen's *The 11th Hour* (2008), as well as for documentary films on other ecological issues, including Louis Psihoyos's *The Cove* (2009) and Rupert Murray's *The End of the Line* (2009). All of these films try to move their viewers to a new intellectual conviction, to a new emotional attitude, or to action, and they all do so with the help of emotional appeals that are closely linked "to an implied entreaty for special attention and concern."

Research in cognitive psychology and decision-making suggests that these filmmakers do well to engage the emotions of their viewers if they want to change their rational thinking about the ecological issues they present and encourage them to become active. As Paul Slovic and other psychologists working in the field of decision research have found out, emotions matter at least as much as analytical thinking in both risk perception and decision-making. Building on the work of neuroscientist Antonio Damasio, Slovic explains in *The Perception of Risk* (2000) that over time he and his colleagues "have come to recognize just how highly dependent [risk perception] is upon intuitive and experimental thinking, guided by emotional and affective processes."[23] Although deliberation and analysis are important factors in many decision-making circumstances, writes Slovic, "reliance on affect and emotion is a quicker, easier and more efficient way to navigate in a complex, uncertain and sometimes dangerous world."[24] If affect is central to the perception of risk, rational thinking, and decision-making in our everyday lives, then there are good reasons for the makers of eco-documentaries to rely not only on rational appeals but also on visual and narrative strategies that have an emotional effect on viewers. The two rhetorical climate change documentaries I will now consider are both good examples of this approach, even as they deal in very different ways with the representational problems that are posed by their subject matter.

INTERTWINING EMOTIONAL AND RATIONAL APPEALS: *AN INCONVENIENT TRUTH*

In his contribution to Paula Willoquet-Maricondi's *Framing the World* (2010), Mark Minster singles out Helfand and Gold's *Everything's Cool* (2007) and Guggenheim's *An Inconvenient Truth* as two documentaries whose use of rhetorical devices he considers particularly effective. Both films, Minster explains, use all three rhetorical modes of persuasion—logos, ethos, and pathos—to get their arguments across, but "appeals to logos are the least of what they do."[25] Rather than attempting to plead their case with evidence (logos), argues Minster, the films try to persuade their audiences by the character and authority of their speakers (ethos) and by an appeal to emotion and shared values (pathos). *An Inconvenient Truth*, featuring Al Gore as the ultimate climate hero, is particularly interesting in this regard. In Minster's view, the film's greatest strengths are its successful creation of Al Gore as a strong identification figure and the uplifting narrative about a communal attempt to bring about a more sustainable future with which it ends.

While I agree with most of the points Minster makes, I believe that he does not pay enough attention to the *visual* components of *An Inconvenient Truth* and the way in which they are closely connected to an emotionally engaging narrative about real-world risks. Minster does mention the "cartoons of polar bears looking forlorn" and the "graphs that function as axes of evidence" which frequently appear in the film, but for him these images belong to the film's presentation of evidence and they tend to "operate less for the sake of logos than for the sake of ethos" and thus for the strengthening of Gore's position as an authoritative speaker.[26] When Gore walks up and down in front of the graphs that record CO_2 concentrations and temperatures over the last 650,000 years, Minster claims, these curves are "a literal backdrop for Gore to walk along and participate in" and Gore himself thus becomes "involved in the evidence he presents, both narratively … and corporeally."[27] These are shrewd observations, but I would argue that the graphs as well as a number of other visual elements in the film also operate for the sake of *pathos*, engaging viewers' emotions in a narrative of environmental risk. After all, the film often moves away from Gore and fills the whole screen with these images, thus allowing them to exert their full visual and emotional power on the audience.

As visual media, climate change documentaries must somehow convey climate-related risks—anticipated catastrophes, as Ulrich Beck calls them—*visually*, and this obligation is at the same time their strength and their weakness.[28] It is a strength because impressive images can have strong emotional effects on viewers if they believe that these images are a representation of the real world and therefore consequential; and it is a weakness because these images must visualize something that isn't (yet) there—an *anticipated* catastrophe. So how have filmmakers dealt with this problem? A very common strategy is to provide visual evidence of past changes in natural landscapes and to demonstrate how people are already affected by these changes. We find it in documentaries like Paul Lindsay's *Before the Flood: Tuvalu* (2004), Briar March's *There Once Was an Island* (2010) or Michael Nash's *Climate Refugees* (2010). These films capture climate-related changes in specific ecological and social spaces, warning us that these processes will continue and get worse in the future. We also find this strategy in *The 11th Hour*, which intersperses a long succession of talking heads—all of them designated as "experts" on the topic—with some star appeal and with images of changing landscapes. And so it should perhaps not surprise us to find the same form of visual evidence also in *An Inconvenient Truth*. Naturally, Judy Doyle's critique of the limitations of documentary photography as evidence of truth in the context of climate change campaigning also applies to Guggenheim's film (as well as to the other climate change documentaries I have mentioned). Despite these limitations, however, these images succeed in telling an *emotionally engaging* story about contemporary loss, and, implicitly, about potential future consequences. As Robin Murray and Joseph Heumann have pointed out, "Gore's message gains rhetorical force in the ways that the film uses a comparison and contrast mode to evoke an environmental nostalgia with emotional appeal."[29]

Also, it is important to note that documentary photography is not the only kind of visual evidence used by Guggenheim to cue an emotional response in viewers that will make them more receptive to the narrative of risk that is at heart of the film. He also confronts them with a second set of images that visualize the anticipated catastrophes of an imaginary *future*. Among the most powerful of these is the computer-animated footage of the flooding of various urban centres as a result of projected sea level rise. Even though the potential future disasters are depicted in somewhat abstract and removed terms—especially if we compare them, for instance, with the much more impressive depiction of a similar disaster in Roland Emmerich's *The Day after Tomorrow* (2004)—they are bound to touch viewers in a much more fundamental way if they believe that what they see on the screen is *consequential*. Convincing them that this is the case is the job of Al Gore—and this is why, as Minster demonstrates so convincingly, the film puts so much rhetorical effort into presenting him as an authoritative speaker.

Eitzen has argued that the power of non-fiction film to arouse engaged responses in viewers "is closely tied to an implied entreaty for special attention and concern,"[30] and in his view, our acknowledgement of that entreaty leads to a felt inclination to *intervene*.[31] This inclination, he explains, is the direct result of our cognitive understanding that what we see on the screen is actually *not* fiction but a filmed mediation of the real world. The emotions we feel when watching *An Inconvenient Truth* or another arresting eco-documentary are, in Eitzen's understanding, "quite similar to the responses we would have to seeing the same things first-hand (albeit from a distance that prevents actual intervention, as though through a window)."[32] While this last assertion seems a bit exaggerated, I agree with Eitzen that there is something qualitatively different in our emotional reactions to documentary film. One of the central elements in our enjoyment of fiction film—the fact that we can enjoy *real* emotions while knowing at the same time that there is no way we could possibly influence the occurrences we see on the screen—is missing in our reception of documentaries. The difference between the storm surge in *The Day after Tomorrow* and the flooding of Manhattan in *An Inconvenient Truth* is that we understand that the latter is meant to be a statement about the real world, a visualization of a potential future occurrence we can help to *avert*. The same is true for the relentlessly rising CO_2 graph and the animated polar bear that cannot find a solid piece of ice to float on. The animated bear touches us because it is such a cute and at the same time desperate and doomed animal. What makes things worse, however, is that we are told through the non-fictional mode that it is not *just* a fictional cartoon. Instead, it is *consequential* and thus meant to tell us something about the future fate of real, existing polar bears and our moral duty to *do* something about it.

Guggenheim and Gore have been sharply criticized for their use of computer-animated images of flooded cities and the drowning polar bear. Critics have complained that the film grossly exaggerates the projected increase in global sea levels and abuses the image of the bear for cheap emotional manipulation. Nevertheless, these images are—together with the melting ice caps and the steadily rising CO_2 graph behind Gore's back—among those that are likely to stick in viewers' minds and to influence their future perceptions of climate-related risks. There are certainly multiple reasons for the phenomenal success of the film, among them its ability to position Al Gore as a sympathetic and trustworthy speaker and its emphasis on what Minster calls "collective ascent."[33] But these uplifting aspects of the film are counterbalanced by more painful and negative emotions, such as feelings of loss, regret, and despair, many of which are triggered by powerful visuals and connected to the film's narrative of risk. Only if we consider all of these various appeals to pathos together can we do justice to the film's complex rhetorical strategies. The same is true for *Everything's Cool*, which, as Nicole Seymour shows in her chapter in this volume, strongly relies on irony as its main affective mode, even as Seymour does not always find the film's use of that mode beneficial for its political project.

This reminds us of the fact that not all emotion is good emotion in the sense of supporting an eco-documentary's main rhetorical purpose. Gregg Mitman proposes in the 2009 edition of *Reel Nature* that the "rather abysmal box-office showing" of *The 11th Hour* indicates that "the public was tired of seeing stories of environmental doom and despair."[34] In Mitman's view, *An Inconvenient Truth* did a much better job in this regard, as it balanced its gloomy warnings of large-scale climate change with the emotionally engaging personal story of Al Gore and a good dose of comic relief. However, some viewers may also react with spite or anger to the film's rhetorical strategies, either because they realize that they are being emotionally manipulated or because they simply dislike the sentiment and nostalgia in the presentation of Gore's biography; and so there is hardly ever a guarantee that emotional appeals work with *all* audiences or individual viewers in the intended way. Armstrong's *The Age of Stupid*, to which I will now turn, certainly is closer to *The 11th Hour* in terms of emotional appeal, although there are also brief moments of comic relief. In our context, the film is interesting not only because of its strong reliance on emotional appeals, but also because of its use of an unusual framing device, which all but collapses the boundaries between fiction and non-fiction.

EMOTIONAL APPEALS BETWEEN FACT AND FICTION: *THE AGE OF STUPID*

The first few minutes of *The Age of Stupid* are particularly enticing. After rushing breathlessly through millennia of evolution—the last three seconds of which represent all of human history on Earth—the film confronts us with a matter-of-fact look into our "future" in 2055: a dark, silent, and dying world wrecked by the consequences of unmitigated climate change. A male voice welcomes us to the Global Archive, a vast storage structure that protrudes out of the endless body of water that has now replaced the Arctic icecap. It belongs to an old archivist, who, as one of the last human survivors, is in charge of humanity's cultural artifacts as well as pickled specimens of extinct animals and enormous banks of servers that contain "every film, every book, every scientific report" ever produced by humankind. The Archivist—played by the late Pete Postlethwaite—sits in front of a transparent touch screen and looks back melancholically through "historical" documentary footage of the years 2005–2008, now known as the "the age of stupid." The audience is invited to accompany him on that journey into the past to ponder with him the two questions that torment him: "Why didn't we save ourselves, when we could?" and "What does that say about us as a species?"

These fictitious first scenes of *The Age of Stupid* clearly appeal to *pathos* with their images of pain, decay, and future disaster. What gives the film its particular edge, however, is that it uses contemporary *documentary* footage to criticize the grave stupidities of the film's "past"—and our present—from the perspective of a fictional future. Already in the opening credits *The Age of Stupid* addresses its viewers directly, stating that it will be "starring" all of the fictional and non-fictional characters who appear in the film and "*YOU*"—meaning the viewer—in "the age of stupid." This is what Eitzen calls "an entreaty to viewers" and what he directly relates to the peculiar effect of documentaries on their audiences. A documentary, Eitzen argues, "is an invitation to adopt a particular stance or attitude, a particular mode of response,"[35] and *The Age of Stupid* offers such an invitation as it confronts us with six documentaries that trace the interconnections between the social inequalities and environmental repercussions of our global oil culture, our personal and political inertia, and the current and future risks of unmitigated climate change.

The stories of the six documentary strands are quite diverse and apparently only loosely related in their topics. Armstrong has explained that the original inspiration for her film's structure was Steven Soderbergh's *Traffic* (2000), a fiction film about international drug trafficking that combines in separate storylines the perspectives of different people involved in drug trafficking who never actually meet but whose actions nevertheless affect each other's lives. To

Armstrong this complex interwoven structure seemed ideal for telling a story about fossil fuels and global warming, but when she had finished this first version of the film she found that it was confusing and not at all emotionally engaging. Her solution to the problem was to add a fictional frame narrative to demonstrate *visually* the future consequences of current practices and to give the six documentary strands an overarching meaning through the introduction of an intradiegetic narrator.

As the only fictional character of the film, Pete Postlethwaite's nameless Archivist is crucial for viewers' emotional engagement. As Murray Smith reminds us, character plays a "fundamental role ... in our engagement with fiction,"[36] not least because of viewers' propensity to feel empathy and sympathy for fictional humans played by actors. The fact that actors are trained to portray their characters' emotions in particularly convincing ways facilitates emotional contagion—the processes by which we "catch" others' emotions by looking at their faces or hearing their voices.[37] This process is particularly powerful in the close-up. "The prolonged concentration on the character's face," explains Carl Plantinga, "is not warranted by the simple communication of information about character emotion. Such scenes are also intended to elicit empathic emotions in the spectator."[38] It is hard for us not to be affected by Postlethwaite's rugged facial features and haunted gaze when he looks at us directly through his transparent computer screen. One of the first things he tells us is that "the conditions we experience now were actually caused by *our* behavior in the period leading up to 2015." The Archivist, we are supposed to grasp, is one of *us*, a version of our own future selves in the not-so-distant future; and we are invited to join him on his journey into the past, back into our *present*, and share his feelings of loss and regret. Logos is thus framed and strengthened by pathos as viewers are invited to ponder the potential real-life consequences of their current practices and behaviours.

While most documentary films do not make use of actors (although some do, for example when they re-enact historical events), they still confront us with the faces and voices of human beings. While they might not be as skilful as actors in *performing* thoughts and emotions through body language—an act that Lisa Zunshine has called "*embodied transparency*"[39]—their faces and voices can be particularly powerful precisely because viewers know that they are *not* acting in the professional sense, that they are *not* following the script of a fictional story. Rather, an untrained person is speaking about her experiences, memories, hopes, and fears in the actual world.

The documentary portion of *The Age of Stupid* portrays six individuals living in different corners of the world and invites viewers to engage with their real-life stories from the perspective of a fictional failed future: Alvin DuVernay, an American paleontologist who helped rescue more than a hundred people after Hurricane Katrina, tries to square his traumatic experiences with the fact that he spent his life working for Shell Oil off the coast of New Orleans. Shell also heads the drilling operation in Nigeria that forces Layefa Malini and her community to come to terms with the resulting local poverty and environmental degradation. This instance of transnational environmental injustice is linked to another "oil story," this one about the war in Iraq. Jamila and Adnan Bayyoud, nine and ten years old, have found refuge from the war in Iraq in Amman, where they mend and sell old shoes that are shipped to Jordan from the United States, while at the same time passionately hating American soldiers for killing their father in the war. And there is a fourth "oil story," this one about Jeh Wadia, an Indian entrepreneur in Mumbai who is starting a low-cost airline. Wadia's dream is to get every Indian traveller into an airplane, and he insists that what he does is helping both the Indian economy and the Indian poor. These four stories are contrasted with two others that exemplify the difficulties that environmentalists face in their struggle to reduce the global dependence on fossil fuels and mitigate climate change: Fernand Pareau is an eighty-two-year-old mountaineer in the French Alps who is concerned about the rapid melting of glaciers and joins local protests against the never-ceasing flow of trucks through the Mont Blanc tunnel. Last but not least there is Piers Guy, a wind-farm developer in England whose campaign to build turbines that would produce wind energy in Bedfordshire is vehemently opposed by residents because they believe it will spoil their views and lower their property values.

Cutting back and forth between these six documentary strands, the future Archivist in his lonely Archive, historical news footage, and animated cartoons, Armstrong puts each individual story into the larger context of contemporary interdependence and future devastation. The sequence that introduces Layefa Malini follows one featuring Alvin DuVernay, the American paleontologist who works in oil exploration. The last image we see of DuVernay in that section shows him smiling mischievously at the camera as he states that oil is "greasy and ugly, and smells so much like money it's just beautiful." From here Armstrong cuts to her fictional future Archivist, who, without comment, moves on to a piece of archival BBC news footage that informs viewers that Shell earned "£13,000,000,000 in 2005" and another one stating that "a hefty junk of those profits came from Nigeria, where most of the population lives on less than one dollar a day." The Archivist then touches another icon that starts the documentary strand on Malini, who talks about Shell's activities in the area and the devastating consequences for the local people. Through her editing choices, Armstrong creates from the beginning a cognitive link between Shell's enormous profits and Malini's poor living conditions.

The sequence that follows further strengthens this cognitive link, not least through a number of appeals to viewers' emotions. Armstrong has Malini walk through the unfinished and abandoned construction of the "medical centre" that Shell had promised the community, but has no intention of completing. Malini's sister recently died because of a cholera infection that could not be properly treated. Armstrong includes a brief close-up of the young woman talking about the death of her sister, but she does not dwell on her grief-stricken facial features, which—because of emotional contagion—would be a relatively easy way to provoke an emotional response in viewers. Instead, she includes footage of Malini talking about her project of becoming a medical doctor and about how she is trying to earn the money for it through fishing and the selling of diesel. And it is in this context that viewers are confronted with some of the most powerful scenes in this documentary strand: in a matter-of-fact manner, Malini explains that "sometimes the oil will be all over the fish" she catches and that she has to wash them "with Omo" before eating them. When she opens a small package of the laundry detergent and pours it over the polluted fish, viewers are likely to feel visceral sensations of revulsion and disgust. Armstrong uses a close-up to intensify the effect of these images, an effect that still resonates with viewers when she cuts to a shot of Shell's gas flares burning bright in the Nigerian landscape. The (African) narrator reports that "the local people's health problems are compounded by gas flares burning night and day throughout the Niger Delta. Asthma, bronchitis, skin diseases, and cancer have all been linked."

These pieces of information about water and air pollution in the context of transnational environmental injustice take on additional meaning because they are provided in conjunction with the personal story of Malini, which allows viewers to empathize and sympathize with a specific—and actually existing—human being. Instead of nameless masses somewhere "in Africa," the film offers its audience images of a concrete environment and a protagonist they can identify with (empathy) or feel for (sympathy). However, in her focus on the lives of particular people Armstrong does not lose sight of the larger power structures that determine these individual lives. In the case of Malini's story, her directorial choices not only create a connection between the young Nigerian woman and global processes of resource exploitation and consumption, she also links it to the even larger issue of climate change—and thus to the film's gloomy fictional future—when her narrator reminds viewers that the constant burning of gas flares in the Niger Delta by Shell and other trans-national oil companies produces enormous amounts of CO_2, "more than the annual emissions from 10 million British homes." Later on in the film, Malini's story receives a final twist when she admits on camera that she would like to live exactly like the people in America, with a "good house," "flashy cars," and "drinking good water." Living that kind of life, the young woman says smilingly, "you wouldn't even want to die. You'd just want to stay on Earth forever." While it is easy to sympathize with Malini in this scene, the temporal framing of the film reminds viewers that her wish is part of a much larger problem. Earth, in the fictional future of *The Age of Stupid*, has become a place in which humans can no longer live at all, not only because big corporations, as Malini puts it, "can do whatever they like," but also because individuals like herself have the understandable desire to enjoy the same prosperity and material comforts as people in the industrialized nations—a form of prosperity the planet cannot sustain for seven billion plus people.

In case viewers fail to make such connections, Armstrong has included a few cartoons in her film that explain them in simple and often highly polem-ical terms. Narrated by what sounds like children's voices (actually distorted versions of Armstrong's voice and that of her producer Lizzie Gillett), they inform viewers about the history of war over resources, the ultimate victory of consumerism, the large differences between ecological footprints in differ-ent parts of the world, and many other topics that are addressed in the film. Because of their lighthearted and humorous approach to very serious prob-lems, these cartoons offer comic relief and thus a variation of affective tone for rhetorical effect. Mitman's dismissal of *The 11th Hour* as a dysfunctional story "of environmental doom and despair" suggests that committed eco-docu-mentaries—and specifically climate change documentaries—cannot do with-out some lighter notes because they will otherwise overbear their audience. This is in keeping with much of the scholarly literature on the topic, which, as Rachel Howell points out in her empirical study of the reception of *The Age of Stupid*, tends to display "anxiety that the use of shocking images and disaster narratives reduces efficacy to act because people feel overwhelmed and have a reduced sense of agency."[40] The success of *An Inconvenient Truth*, which deliberately softens the blow of its "inconvenient" message with a good dose of comic relief and a turn towards the hopeful at the end, seems to further support this position.

Howell's study shows that Armstrong's film, too, has been quite effect-ive.[41] Crucial in my context here is that Howell draws a number of conclu-sions regarding the effects of the film's emotionalizing strategies. Specifically, she concludes that the often suspected negative and depoliticizing effect of disaster narratives "largely does not appear to have happened in this case.... Respondents emerged from the film with an increased motivation to take action, and an increased belief that they could do something to prevent climate change getting worse, along with the sense that they are not already doing everything they can."[42] In addition, Howell reports that "one of the most striking results" of her research was that "having seen the film, a large majority of respondents believed that there is a significant possibility of the kind of devastation shown in the film, by 2055."[43] Finally, Howell reports that a significant percentage of respondents felt a "sense of urgency" and that only a very small percentage (about 10 percent) "expressed a sense of depression."[44]

These results seem to suggest that the inclusion of a fictional frame narrative representing a devastated future Earth made a strong impression on viewers. As James Christopher puts it in his review of the film for *The Times*, "the power of this shameless campaigning film is that it gives dates and deadlines" and that its "conclusion is probably spot-on: we are inches away from being the first species on the planet to knowingly kill itself off."[45] Christopher's comment, which is highly emotional and full of conviction, illustrates well the peculiar power that rhetorical eco-documentaries can assert.[46] It also illustrates that viewers clearly understand that despite its mixing of fictional and documentary modes *The Age of Stupid* is not meant to be a fiction film but a *documentary* that makes direct and specific "assertions" about the *actual* world and its uncertain future. In addition, as Howell's study shows, viewers also understood the film as an *entreaty* to rethink their current practices and to do something to stop global warming.

CONCLUSION

Eitzen's differentiation between fiction and non-fiction in terms of its emotional impact thus seems to hold even for a film that, while being *indexed* as documentary, freely mixes "fictional" elements (such as the use of an actor who speaks the monologues provided for him by a film script) and "non-fictional" elements (such as interviews with non-actors and the depiction of their everyday lives in their actual environments). Viewers recognize *The Age of Stupid* as a discourse of consequence and respond to it accordingly, both affectively and cognitively. Before we accept Eitzen's definition of the documentary all too easily, however, we have to remember that fiction films, too, can and have historically been understood as "discourses of consequence" and thus have triggered the corresponding affective and cognitive responses. To name just two examples in the realm of ecocinema: James Bridges' *The China Syndrome*

(1979) is famous for having had considerable effects on the way American audiences felt and thought about nuclear power, aided by the almost contemporaneous nuclear accident on Three Mile Island.[47] Emmerich's *The Day After Tomorrow*, regardless of the fact that it is a rather crude disaster science fiction film, had considerable effects on its audiences' perceptions of climate risk, not least because of the emotionally affecting visuals it offered.[48]

I do not at all think that this makes Eitzen's observations obsolete; on the contrary, as I hope to have shown, his insights can be very helpful in the analysis of the emotional impact of eco-documentaries. My point is rather that we should take this as an incentive and encouragement to look even more closely at the ways in which both fiction and non-fiction films—especially those with environmental themes—are tapping into their viewers' emotions and in what relation these emotions stand to viewers' understanding of real-world risks and problems. The methodological tools of cognitive film theory, I believe, are particularly well-suited for such an analysis, especially when they are supplemented with other modes of analysis, such as empirical audience response studies.

NOTES

1 Dirk Eitzen, "Documentary's Peculiar Appeals," in *Moving Image Theory*, ed. Joseph D. Anderson and Barbara Fisher Anderson (Carbondale: Southern Illinois University Press, 2005), 183–99.

2 Eitzen, "Documentary's Peculiar Appeals," 186.

3 Julie Doyle, "Seeing the Climate? The Problematic Status of Visual Evidence in Climate Change Campaigning," in *Ecosee: Image, Rhetoric, Nature*, ed. Sidney Dobrin and Sean Morey (Albany: State University of New York Press, 2009), 280.

4 Michael Renov, "Introduction: The Truth about Non-Fiction," in *Theorizing Documentary*, ed. Michael Renov (London: Routledge, 1993), 3.

5 Bill Nichols, *Introduction to Documentary* (Bloomington: Indiana University Press, 2001), 1.

6 Nichols, *Introduction*, 1.

7 Nichols, *Introduction*, 1.

8 Nichols, *Introduction*, 2.

9 Noël Carroll, "Nonfiction Film and Postmodernist Skepticism," in *Post-Theory: Reconstructing Film Studies*, ed. David Bordwell and Noël Carroll (Madison: University of Wisconsin Press, 1996), 286.

10 Noël Carroll, "Fiction, Non-fiction, and the Film of Presumptive Assertion: A Conceptual Analysis," in *Philosophy of Film and Motion Pictures: An Anthology*, ed. Noël Carroll and Jinhee Coy (Oxford: Blackwell, 2005), 166.

11 Dirk Eitzen, "When Is a Documentary? Documentary as a Mode of Reception," *Cinema Journal* 35 (1992): 92; Edward Branigan, *Narrative Comprehension and Film* (London and New York: Routledge, 1992), 88.

12 Dai Vaughan, *For Documentary: Twelve Essays* (Berkeley: University of California Press, 1999), 84.

13 Carl Plantinga, "Moving Pictures and the Rhetoric of Nonfiction: Two Approaches," in *Post-Theory: Reconstructing Film Studies*, ed. David Bordwell and Noël Carroll (Madison: University of Wisconsin Press, 1996), 310.

14 Eitzen, "Documentary's Peculiar Appeals," 192.

15 Eitzen, "Documentary's Peculiar Appeals," 193.

16 Greg M. Smith, *Film Structure and the Emotion System* (Cambridge: Cambridge University Press, 2003), 12.

17 Eitzen, "Documentary's Peculiar Appeals," 183.

18 Eitzen, "Documentary's Peculiar Appeals," 183.

19 Eitzen, "Documentary's Peculiar Appeals," 183.

20 Eitzen, "Documentary's Peculiar Appeals," 190.

21 Eitzen, "Documentary's Peculiar Appeals," 184.

22 David Bordwell and Kristin Thompson, *Film Art: An Introduction*, 8th ed. (New York: McGraw-Hill, 2008), 348–49.

23 Paul Slovic, *The Perception of Risk* (London: Earthscan, 2000), xxxi.

24 Slovic, *The Perception*, xxxi.

25 Mark Minster, "The Rhetoric of Ascent in *An Inconvenient Truth* and *Everything's Cool*," in *Framing the World: Explorations in Ecocriticism and Film*, ed. Paula Willoquet-Marcondi (Charlottesville: University of Virginia, 2010), 29.

26 Minster, "The Rhetoric," 30.

27 Minster, "The Rhetoric," 31.

28 Ulrich Beck, *World at Risk* (Cambridge: Polity Press, 2009), 9.

29 Robin Murray and Joseph Heumann, "Al Gore's *An Inconvenient Truth* and Its Skeptics: A Case of Environmental Nostalgia," *Jump Cut* 49 (Spring 2007), http://www.ejumpcut.org/archive/jc49.2007/inconvenTruth.

30 Eitzen, "Documentary's Peculiar Appeals," 184.

31 Eitzen, "Documentary's Peculiar Appeals," 186.

32 Eitzen, "Documentary's Peculiar Appeals," 191.

33 Minster, "The Rhetoric," 37.

34 Gregg Mitman, *Reel Nature: America's Romance with Wildlife on Film* (Seattle: University of Washington Press, 2009), 213.

35 Eitzen, "Documentary's Peculiar Appeals," 184.

36 Murray Smith, *Engaging Characters: Fiction, Emotion, and the Cinema* (New York: Oxford University Press 1995), 17.

37 For a detailed exploration of emotional contagion in the context of film reception, see Carl Plantinga, "The Scene of Empathy and the Human Face on Film," in *Passionate Views: Film, Cognition, and Emotion*, ed. Carl Plantinga and Greg M. Smith (Baltimore: Johns Hopkins University Press, 1999), 239–55.

38 Carl Plantinga, "The Scene of Empathy," 239.

39 Lisa Zunshine, *Getting Inside Your Head: What Cognitive Science Can Tell Us about Popular Culture* (Baltimore: Johns Hopkins University Press, 2013), 23.

40 Rachel Howell, "Lights, Camera ... Action? Altered Attitudes and Behaviour in Response to the Climate Change Film *The Age of Stupid*," *Global Environmental Change* 21, no. 1 (2011): 181.

41 Howell conducted research for her study during twenty-one screenings at the Edinburgh Filmhouse where she randomly selected 244 people willing to participate in her three-part study. Participants had to fill in the first questionnaire before watching the film, a second one after the screening, and—if they had agreed to that—a third one ten to fourteen weeks later. Individual questions were less concerned with the film as film, and more with participants' attitude toward climate change and their willingness to take personal action.

42 Howell, "Lights, Camera," 184.

43 Howell, "Lights, Camera," 181. For a scientific appraisal of the depiction of climate change in *The Age of Stupid*, see Mark Lynas, "The Scientific Basis of 'The Age of Stupid,'" *Spanner*

Films: The Science, 2009, http://www.spannerfilms.net/the_science; and Richard Betts, "The Frightening Vision of the Near Future Depicted in *The Age of Stupid* is Not Science Fiction," *Spanner Films: The Science*, 2009, http://www.spannerfilms.net/the_science.

44 Howell, "Lights, Camera," 181.

45 James Christopher, Review of *The Age of Stupid*. *The Times*, 19 March 2009, http://www .thetimes.co.uk/tto/arts/film/reviews/article1864458.ece.

46 Still, as Howell's reception study also makes clear, climate change documentaries like *The Age of Stupid* face a double problem: their audiences are often atypical of the general public in that they already exhibit high levels of concern about climate change before choosing to see a film on the topic—this was clearly the case for the people in Howell's study ("Lights, Camera," 184). Secondly, the effects these films exert on their already highly aware audiences tend to be short-lived. Howell reports that the follow-up questionnaire sent to participants ten to fourteen weeks after the screening of the film showed that the initial effects, which included "increased concern about climate change, motivation to act, and viewers' sense of agency" had "not persisted," having gone down almost to levels of concern and action before the viewing of the film ("Lights, Camera," 177).

47 For a more detailed discussion of the reception and emotional impact of *The China Syndrome*, see my essay "The Stuff of Fear: Emotion, Ethics, and the Materiality of Nuclear Risk in *Silkwood* and *The China Syndrome*," in *The Anticipation of Catastrophe: Environmental Risk in North American Literature and Culture*, ed. Sylvia Mayer and Alexa Weik von Mossner (Heidelberg: Universitätsverlag Winter, 2014).

48 For a more detailed discussion of the reception and emotional impact of *The Day After Tomorrow*, see my essay "Facing *The Day after Tomorrow*: Filmed Disaster, Emotional Engagement, and Climate Risk Perception," in *American Environments: Climate—Culture—Catastrophe*, ed. Christof Mauch and Sylvia Mayer (Heidelberg: Universitätsverlag Winter, 2012), 97–115.

BIBLIOGRAPHY

The Age of Stupid. Directed by Franny Armstrong. London: Spanner Films, 2009. DVD.

Beck, Ulrich. *World at Risk*. Cambridge: Polity Press, 2009.

Before the Flood: Tuvalu. Directed by Paul Lindsay. London: BBC Four, 2004. DVD.

Betts, Richard. "The Frightening Vision of the Near Future Depicted in *The Age of Stupid* Is Not Science Fiction." *Spanner Films: The Science*. 2009. http://www .spannerfilms.net/the_science.

Bordwell, David, and Kristin Thompson. *Film Art: An Introduction*. 8th ed. New York: McGraw-Hill, 2008.

Boyz n the Hood. Directed by John Singleton. 1991. Culver City, CA: Sony Pictures Home Entertainment, 2004. DVD.

Branigan, Edward. *Narrative Comprehension and Film*. London: Routledge, 1992.

Carroll, Noël. "Fiction, Non-Fiction, and the Film of Presumptive Assertion: A Conceptual Analysis." In *Philosophy of Film and Motion Pictures: An Anthology*, edited by Noël Carroll and Jinhee Coy, 154–71. Oxford: Blackwell, 2005.

———. "Nonfiction Film and Postmodernist Skepticism." In *Post-Theory: Reconstructing Film Studies*, edited by David Bordwell and Noël Carroll, 283–306. Madison: University of Wisconsin Press, 1996.

The China Syndrome. Directed by James Bridges. 1979. Chatsworth, CA: Image Entertainment, 2013. DVD.

Christopher, James. Review of *The Age of Stupid*. *The Times*, 19 March 2009. http://www.thetimes.co.uk/tto/arts/film/reviews/article1864458.ece.

Climate Refugees. Directed by Michael Nash. Los Angeles: LA Think Tank, 2010. DVD.

Damasio, Antonio. *Descartes' Error: Emotion, Reason, and the Human Brain*. London: Vintage, 1994.

The Day after Tomorrow. Directed by Roland Emmerich. Los Angeles: Twentieth Century Fox, 2004. DVD.

Doyle, Julie. "Seeing the Climate? The Problematic Status of Visual Evidence in Climate Change Campaigning." In *Ecosee: Image, Rhetoric, Nature*, edited by Sidney Dobrin and Sean Morey, 279–98. Albany: State University of New York Press, 2009.

Eitzen, Dirk. "Documentary's Peculiar Appeals." In *Moving Image Theory*, edited by Joseph D. Anderson and Barbara Fisher Anderson, 183–99. Carbondale: Southern Illinois University Press, 2005.

———. "When Is a Documentary? Documentary as a Mode of Reception." *Cinema Journal* 35 (1992): 81–102.

The 11th Hour. Directed by Nadia Conners and Leila Conners Petersen. Burbank, CA: Warner Home Video, 2008. DVD.

Everything's Cool. Directed by Judith Helfand and Daniel B. Gold. New York: City Lights Media, 2007. DVD.

Gorillas in the Mist. Directed by Michael Apted. 1988. Burbank, CA: Warner Home Video, 2003. DVD.

Howell, Rachel A. "Lights, Camera … Action? Altered Attitudes and Behaviour in Response to the Climate Change Film *The Age of Stupid*." *Global Environmental Change* 21, no. 1 (2011): 177–87.

An Inconvenient Truth. Directed by Davis Guggenheim. Los Angeles: Paramount Classics, 2006. DVD.

Lynas, Mark. "The Scientific Basis of 'The Age of Stupid.'" *Spanner Films: The Science*. 2009. http://www.spannerfilms.net/the_science.

Minster, Mark. "The Rhetoric of Ascent in *An Inconvenient Truth* and *Everything's Cool*." In *Framing the World: Explorations in Ecocriticism and Film*, edited by Paula Willoquet-Marcondi, 25–42. Charlottesville: University of Virginia, 2010.

Mitman, Gregg. *Reel Nature: America's Romance with Wildlife on Film*. Seattle: University of Washington Press. 2009.

Murray, Robin, and Joseph Heumann. "Al Gore's *An Inconvenient Truth* and Its Skeptics: A Case of Environmental Nostalgia." *Jump Cut* 49 (Spring 2007). http://www.ejumpcut.org/archive/jc49.2007/inconvenTruth.

Nichols, Bill. *Introduction to Documentary*. Bloomington: Indiana University Press, 2001.

Plantinga, Carl. "Moving Pictures and the Rhetoric of Nonfiction: Two Approaches." In *Post-Theory: Reconstructing Film Studies*, edited by David Bordwell and Noël Carroll, 307–24. Madison: University of Wisconsin Press, 1996.

———. "The Scene of Empathy and the Human Face on Film." In *Passionate Views: Film, Cognition, and Emotion*, edited by Carl Plantinga and Greg M. Smith, 239–55. Baltimore: Johns Hopkins University Press, 1999.

Renov, Michael. "Introduction: The Truth about Non-fiction." In *Theorizing Documentary*, edited by Michael Renov, 1–11. London: Routledge. 1993.

Slovic, Paul. *The Perception of Risk*. London: Earthscan, 2000.

Smith, Greg M. *Film Structure and the Emotion System*. Cambridge: Cambridge University Press, 2003.

Smith, Murray. *Engaging Characters: Fiction, Emotion, and the Cinema*. New York: Oxford University Press, 1995.

There Once Was an Island: Te Henua e Noho. Directed by Briar March. On the Level Productions, 2010. DVD.

Vaughan, Dai. *For Documentary: Twelve Essays*. Berkeley: University of California Press, 1999.

Weik von Mossner, Alexa. "Facing *The Day after Tomorrow*: Filmed Disaster, Emotional Engagement, and Climate Risk Perception." *American Environments: Climate—Culture—Catastrophe*, edited by Christof Mauch and Sylvia Mayer, 97–115. Heidelberg: Universitätsverlag Winter, 2012.

———. "The Stuff of Fear: Emotions, Ethics, and the Materiality of Nuclear Risk in *Silkwood* and *The China Syndrome*." In *The Anticipation of Catastrophe: Environmental Risk in North American Literature and Culture*, ed. Sylvia Mayer and Alexa Weik von Mossner, 101–17. Heidelberg: Universitätsverlag Winter, 2014.

Zunshine, Lisa. *Getting Inside Your Head: What Cognitive Science Can Tell Us about Popular Culture*. Baltimore: Johns Hopkins University Press, 2013.

3

Irony and Contemporary Ecocinema:
Theorizing a New Affective Paradigm

Nicole Seymour

enerally speaking, ecocinema is serious business. From low- and mid-budget documentaries (*An Inconvenient Truth* [2006], *The 11th Hour* [2007], *The Cove* [2009], *Queen of the Sun: What Are the Bees Telling Us?* [2010]) to big-budget fiction films (*The Day after Tomorrow* [2004], *The Constant Gardener* [2005], *2012* [2009]), eco-films are markedly sincere, even sanctimonious. In fact, even when leavened by doses of humour (*Erin Brockovich* [2000], *March of the Penguins* [2005], *Happy Feet* [2006]), these films tend to be underwritten by earnest beliefs: Nature is miraculous, Earth is in trouble. In turn, they solicit serious affective responses from viewers, such as reverence, guilt, dread, and conviction.

However, as critics such as Paula Willoquet-Maricondi have noted, serious-ness is not the only affective trajectory possible in ecocinema. Willoquet-Maricondi argues that eco-films can "inspir[e] activism through a rhetoric of opti-mism and humor that does not sacrifice the seriousness of the message."[1] My essay builds on this observation, insisting that serious cinematic messages do not require serious affective modes. I argue, in fact, that the political project of ecocinema *demands* "unserious" affective modes such as irony, self-parody, and playfulness. I focus on irony in particular, taking up the claim of environ-mental sociologist Bronislaw Szerszynski that "the most appropriate philo-sophical foundation for ecological politics is ... a cultural modernism of which a generalised irony is the master trope."[2]

In the first part of this chapter, I present several rationalizations for the use of irony in ecocinema. Surveying a selection of recent fiction and non-fiction films, and viewers' and critics' responses to those films, I consider how irony can address the problems posed by serious affective modes—and foster a self-critical attitude that does not hinder but in fact enables environmentalist work. In the second part of the essay, I offer a close look at the work of contemporary American filmmaker Mike Judge. I propose that Judge's depiction of "average-Joe environmentalism" exemplifies ironic ecocinema. Through these discussions, I hope not just to establish the importance of irony as an affective mode in ecocinema, but to point to an emerging agenda for the medium: to simultaneously look outward and inward, scrutinizing both "the environment" and its mediation.

TOWARD AN IRONIC ECOCINEMA

By most accounts, ecocinema creators want to move their audiences emotionally, and in ways that promote ecologically-minded behaviours. Consider, for instance, that the "Ways to Get Involved" postscript has become *de rigueur* for the contemporary eco-documentary. Many eco-documentaries extend this postscript into the virtual realm. For instance, *Food, Inc.* (2008) has a companion website that offers visitors additional opportunities and tools for action.[3] We can presume that less didactic eco-films—namely, fictional ones—are likewise made with some expectation that audience members will be affected in profound, lasting ways. We might consider, for instance, James Cameron's (often-ridiculed) claim that *Avatar* (2009) has inspired viewers to save the planet. In 2010 he told MTV News that Twentieth Century Fox executives read the initial script and said, "'Can we take some of this tree-hugging, "FernGully" crap out of this movie?'" As Cameron recounts, "I said, 'No, because that's why I'm making the film.'"[4]

But serious affective modes pose several problems in terms of "moving" an audience, be it to tears or protest, or both. For one thing, they run the risk of alienating viewers—perhaps even before they enter the theatre or go online to stream a film. Journalist Catherine Shoard, in an irreverent piece for *The Guardian*, claims that "green films are taking a beating at the box office" due to features such as "dimwit voiceovers and preachy tutting."[5] Similarly, *Telegraph* blogger Lucy Jones told her readers that "there's one thing holding me back [from seeing *Avatar*]: James Cameron has come over all preachy.... He sees it as a 'broader metaphor' of how 'we treat the natural world' and warned that 'we're going to find out the hard way if we don't wise up.' As soon as I read this, I ... zzzzzzzzzzz."[6]

Shoard also implies that market saturation exacerbates audiences' aversion: "the eco-documentary has become as much of a [theatre] staple as the duff geezer flick or the drippy indie romcom."[7] Of course, the romcom is in no apparent danger of demise. But that's precisely the point: Shoard is suggesting that, to increasing numbers of viewers, watching an eco-film seems too much like taking your medicine—or eating your vegetables, as it were. Ecocritic Ursula Heise, drawing on Frederick Buell's notion that we "dwell in crisis,"[8] comes to a similar conclusion: "a steady drumbeat of gloom-and-doom rhetoric is liable to discourage and alienate individuals more than it incites them to action." But, conversely, "too much normalization of crisis might lead to an implicit acquiescence to the environmental status quo."[9]

I propose that irony can allow cultural producers to work between those two positions, neither discouraging viewers nor normalizing crisis. After all, the most basic element of irony is incongruity; incongruity between, say, what is defined as possible or true, and what appears to be possible or true. Thus, for example, irony both emerges from, and can highlight, the gap between scientific evidence of global warming and political pundits' denials that such a phenomenon exists. Al Gore and director Davis Guggenheim exploit this gap in An Inconvenient Truth, mostly to good effect—though, below, I discuss the limitations of their deployment of irony. Indeed, we might say that irony as a mode of affect is alarmist, but in a different sense than, say, dread: as anthropologists James Fernandez and Mary Taylor Huber note, "when things seem misaligned, disproportionate, unexpected, or out of place, philosophers, poets, and everyday people ... often use irony to capture and comment on the pattern of contrasts they discern."[10] The ironist conveys the sense that something is amiss, but not through didactic statement or dramatic handwringing; she presents the audience with two different planes of information, asking it to grapple with the two in order to develop a response.

As a mode defined by incongruity, then, irony is also well-suited to negotiate between the paradoxical desires of ecocinema audiences: the desire for pleasure as well as information, and the desire to be both entertained and validated as thinkers in their own right. As Jones puts it, "I am completely behind stopping the destruction of rainforests and the slaughtering of snow leopards (and the like) but I'm not paying for a Hollywood sermon when I order my popcorn."[11] Simply put, irony can accommodate the hitch that lies at the heart of ecocinema: that most people watch movies because they like to have fun. Ecocinema creators might accept or even embrace that paradox through an ironic stance, rather than proceeding as if the average person enjoys cinematic sermons.

Of course, audience satisfaction and, by extension, profits, are not the only objects in town. As Cameron's statement about his motivations suggests, ethical and philosophical integrity are equally, if not more, important to many ecocinema creators. I propose that irony might be crucial in these regards as well, especially if such creators are willing to embrace the ideological shifts that ecocritics have recently proposed. The past several years have seen a growing belief amongst ecocritics that questioning "nature" is as important as defending nature—and, more importantly, that those two moves are not incompatible. For instance, Noël Sturgeon has argued that a "relentlessly critical examination of claims to the natural is the best way to learn to respect natural beings and processes (including our own natural status as animal-humans ...)."[12] Irony, as a skeptical, humorous mode, encourages such examination. Indeed, to question the category of nature—as construction, as accessible only through mediation—while defending it vigorously is nothing if not ironic.

Bronislaw Szerszynski suggests that irony is in fact a necessary logic of sustainability in our current moment. As he argues, "The persistence of unsustainability is due not simply to the ignorance or duplicity of individuals, or even to the mere logic of the capitalist system, but also to a crisis in political meaning.... The solution to this crisis is not to be found in a simple restoration of political language's reference to a reality outside language, as if language is a flapping sail that can simply be re-secured to its mast."[13] Thus, a serious or sincere environmentalism can prove problematic not just because it is out of step with the postmodern (or post-postmodern) tendency toward irreverence and questioning—and, more specifically, with the ecocritical turn toward skepticism of "nature"—it's also problematic because it assumes that we can solve environmental problems simply by swapping out corporate or capitalist "untruths" for environmentalist "Truth," or that environmental problems arise in the first place because people simply don't know any better.

In an era of multiple, competing truths, and a half-century into the contemporary environmentalist movement, such assumptions seem naïve. Consider, for instance, that while most readers of this essay would agree that evolution is a fact, the declaration "I don't believe in evolution" can keep that fact out of a classroom. Or, to return to ecomedia, consider that a Google search for "*An Inconvenient Truth*" produces the result "*An Inconvenient Truth* lies."[14] A successful campaign against that film's free distribution in public schools in the UK was, in fact, waged by a school governor who complained that the film consisted of "serious *scientific inaccuracies*, political propaganda and *sentimental mush*."[15] The irony was perhaps lost on the school governor, Stewart Dimmock, but should not be lost on us: while recent surveys by researchers such as Peter Doran and Maggie Kendall Zimmerman have found that "the debate on the authenticity of global warming ... is largely nonexistent among those who understand the nuances and scientific basis of long-term climate processes,"[16] Dimmock successfully seized upon small errors in the film to make global-warming deniers look like the mainstream voice of reason. An ironic stance in ecocinema could allow filmmakers to respond to such impasses—to fight for particular environmentalist truths while acknowledging the contingent and contested status of "truth." Indeed, what I've been suggesting, along with Sturgeon, Szerszynski, and others, and as I have argued elsewhere in a different context, is that an ironic, critical position on claims to the natural might in fact be an effective way to defend nature.[17] Among other things, it can account for the multiple ways in which "nature" has been interpreted and deployed—oftentimes, at the expense of the non-human world.

Thus far, I have discussed the relevance of irony to ecocinema as both a cultural product and a form of activism. Those two purposes intersect, of course. But historically, they have done so in rather troubled ways: ecocritics such as Derek Bousé and Gregg Mitman have recognized, as Willoquet-Maricondi puts it, that "an inherent conflict of interests arises between the subject matter—nature—and the conventions of cinema."[18] Consider Mitman's point: "'We are drawn to the spectacle of wildlife untainted by human intervention and will. Yet, we cannot observe this world of nature without such interventions.'"[19] In other words, beyond the paradox of ecocinema as both entertainment product and pedagogical tool, the medium is located at the juncture of two oft-opposed masters: Nature and Technology. Through ironic affect, ecocinema creators might acknowledge, thematize, and/or dramatize the political and philosophical problems that this peculiar location poses, rather than lamenting or ignoring it.

Before surveying the work that a few films have done toward these ends, I will lay out two brief examples of how ecocinematic irony might function in relation to the medium itself. First, it could allow filmmakers to respond to the heterosexism and homophobia that many eco-films, including *March of the Penguins*, have unselfconsciously advanced.[20] Thus, we might imagine an eco-film produced from a campy, queer perspective—ironizing how nature is selectively valued for the ways in which it can advance human agendas, including homophobia. Another specific possibility is that irony would allow filmmakers to respond to the ways in which certain spaces—majestic mountains, say—have been treated more reverentially in ecomedia than others—inner cities, say. While certainly there are fiction and non-fiction eco-films focused on the latter, we have yet to see something like an environmentally degraded neighbourhood rendered in the lush and loving style of a nature documentary. Such a depiction would be jarring, maybe even galvanizing. In short, as ecocriticism increasingly expands its definitions of nature and environment to include less-than-ideal spaces and entities, irony may prove to be a crucial mode of operation.

THE LIMITS OF IRONY

Recently, a few eco-films have explored the use of irony as an affective rhetorical tool. Morgan Spurlock's 2004 documentary *Super Size Me*, though not explicitly environmentalist, takes on relevant issues including food politics and the debate over personal versus public responsibility for human health. The film, as is now well known, depicts the thirty days Spurlock spent eating only fast food from McDonald's, in the process highlighting questionable corporate marketing and consumption practices. Much like its colleagues *An Inconvenient Truth* and *Food, Inc.*—which are, overall, more serious films—*Super Size Me* elicits laughs by juxtaposing overblown corporate rhetoric to on-the-ground experience and evidence. In one infamous DVD extra, for instance, Spurlock shows us that an order of McDonald's fries, kept for ten weeks without refrigeration, looks virtually the same as it did at point of purchase, thanks to "unnatural" ingredients and preservatives.

But while *Super Size Me* was very successful (the twelfth-highest-earning documentary of all time, with a $30 million worldwide gross), Spurlock has since suffered serious backlash from all points on the political spectrum—as have *An Inconvenient Truth*'s Al Gore and kindred documentarians such as Michael Moore. This backlash may have multiple triggers, including dislike of these figures' individual personae; distaste for their gimmicky tactics; the inevitable cycling of popular media into *un*popularity; and the impossible standards of consistency and morality to which the public tends to holds political activists. As regards the first point, Mark Minster observes that "Gore's autobiographical narrative makes the science of global warming digestible, and yet the [adulatory] visual style in which he is often shot renders some of this autobiography unpalatable."[21] As regards the second and fourth points, consider media blogger Gabe Delahaye's comment about Spurlock's less successful 2011 release, *The Greatest Movie Ever Sold*:

> the only thesis statement less in need of proving than "fast food is bad for you" ... is "corporate advertising is everywhere." If Morgan Spurlock's documentaries were a magazine it would put *Duh Aficionado* out of business. Even more importantly, though, he's got his math upside down.... [I]t's still going to cost me $12 to go see this in the theater, so what the FUCK do I care if the movie was paid for by sponsorship agreements? GET [POM Wonderful, the film's sponsor] TO BUY MY MOVIE TICKET AND THEN WE WILL TALK ABOUT WHAT A GREAT TRICK YOU HAVE PULLED OFF, SIR.[22]

Delahaye's commentary—a prime example of a serious message delivered in an "unserious" form[23]—gestures toward another explanation for backlash: the limited character of these filmmakers' senses of irony. As Szerszynski notes, "the irony generally deployed in environmental ... protests is a 'corrective' irony.... Movements reveal situational ironies in order to shame their targets into repentance ...: Schweppes, Shell or British Nuclear Fuels, for example, present themselves as responsible corporate citizens, but are revealed to be otherwise. [These tactics position] the ironist as an outside observer of the irony, on the moral high ground looking down, rather than implicated in it."[24] Thus, we should understand that while irony is an important affective mode for ecocinema, for the many reasons I have outlined above, its impact depends on deployment and context. In the case of media producers such as Spurlock, Guggenheim, and Moore, their ironic/humorous stances lead some viewers to perceive them negatively; as training their smug critical eyes on everyone and everything except themselves and their work. Delahaye, for one, complains that Spurlock has "ma[de] a career out of self-aggrandizing condescension."[25] As Szerszynski concludes, "such a positing of the ethical actor"—on the moral high ground, on the side of the so-called real truth—"seems inadequate for an age in which the logic of politics is that of Baudrillardian simulation."[26]

Besides simply failing to win viewers over, limited irony can contribute to an environmentalist elitism that maligns the working class and the uneducated. Such operations run rife, presumably unintentionally, in Daniel B. Gold and Judith Helfand's "Toxic Comedy Pictures" production *Everything's Cool*, which Netflix categorizes as "Dark" and "Witty." The opening scene of the 2007 documentary follows the filmmakers as they drive to a county fair in a truck bearing the partially completed phrase "Global Warming"; they challenge passersby to complete the phrase *à la* Wheel of Fortune. Whether or not we as viewers actually find this scene funny, it is structured to play for laughs, and self-congratulatory ones at that: since we as viewers know the film's topic to be global warming, we are set up to mock those who don't know this "obvious" answer. *Everything's Cool* thus seizes upon the classic observation that jokes function not to entertain, but to police social boundaries; as Elliott Oring states, "the range of depth of the cultural knowledge that may be required for understanding humor can be considerable."[27] This particular filmic setup, in turn, frames as laughable the responses that Gold and Helfand gather from these white, middle-to-lower-class subjects—including one man's opinion that "I don't think what man does affects [the climate] a lot," and one woman's conclusion that, "One day ... you're gonna be home with [God] and this isn't gonna matter."

Such deployment of ecocinematic humour and irony is troubling not just because of its classist, elitist implications but also, I maintain, because it fails quite hypocritically as an environmentalist strategy. First, such deployment can re-entrench the aversion to environmentalism already felt by many individuals like those featured in *Everything's Cool*—the feeling that environmentalists are educated snobs who sit around and laugh at the little guy. This potential is particularly problematic considering the ways in which big business, especially industries such as coal and oil, successfully frame their interests as coincidental with those of the little guy.[28] The *Everything's Cool* brand of irony leaves *that* troubling irony untouched. Second, this brand of irony works against the film's own structuring premise: that in the early 2000s, "there was an enormous gap between what scientists knew [about climate change] ... and what Americans understood." By poking fun at those who don't understand, the filmmakers threaten to widen that gap rather than close it. Indeed, we might find the humour of *Everything's Cool* to be wildly misplaced: while belief in heaven ("One day ... you're gonna be home with [God] and this isn't gonna matter") may be laughable in the abstract to many environmentalists, it should cease to be laughable if it directly licenses environmental destruction.

As in *An Inconvenient Truth* and Spurlock's films, then, *Everything's Cool* aims its irony at all the structures of truth and authority except its own. For instance, the film features a scientist named Heidi Cullen who was hired as a global warming commentator for The Weather Channel. In one scene, Cullen discusses with her producer the fact that global warming has reduced the number of days that companies can successfully prospect for oil. "The irony of that is not lost on us," she tells him. Cullen then turns to the camera and complains, "I wanted to add the word ironic there [in my newscast]. Why is it ironic? It's basically an education thing. In order for you to know that it's ironic, you have to know that greenhouse gases are a byproduct of fossil-fuel burning. And so then I said, how about if I say, 'a global-warming irony is that oil-exploration's already been impacted'? ... [But] that still wasn't clear enough." The debate continues, as her producer argues, "I just don't know that people will get that." Cullen presses on, "*For me* it just screams out for the word irony" (my emphasis). She thus fails to consider how her position as a scientist affords her a kind of expertise that may alienate the average viewer. Moreover, while her frustration may be rightfully aimed at a dumbed-down news culture, she does not consider how the deployment of *corrective* irony in particular might add fuel to that cultural fire. In other words, it is not necessarily the content of statements such as Cullen's that is so objectionable, but the way in which their articulation frames the receiver.

Werner Herzog's documentary *Grizzly Man* (2005), released two years before *Everything's Cool*, was prompted by a deeply, horribly ironic occurrence: its subject, self-styled wilderness videographer Timothy Treadwell, lived among the wild bears of Alaska and considered them his friends—until one ate him and his girlfriend. Herzog's deadpan narration often matches this central irony, though at times the director seems to take Treadwell's arrogance and self-importance at face value—even going so far as to refer to the bear who attacked him as his "murderer"; a ludicrous designation from an ecological standpoint, as many have observed.[29] Indeed, while *Grizzly Man* seems to understand irony as a useful tool in the critical exploration of human hubris and the use of human technology to mediate encounters with the non-human, its irony is rarely self-directed. While the film, to a large extent, centres on its own making—we watch as Herzog curates and re-presents Treadwell's footage in an attempt to understand his life—the director spends relatively little time theorizing his own role.

Much of Louie Psihoyos's 2009 Academy Award–winning documentary *The Cove* is, likewise, about its own making: we watch as the filmmaking crew figures out how to expose dolphin slaughter in Taiji, Japan. But the crew's investigatory tactics also go largely untheorized. For instance, they never acknowledge the similarities they share with the Japanese men who guard the Taiji cove with video cameras in tow—a failure that has led many critics and viewers to charge the film with cultural insensitivity, if not outright racism.[30] Moreover, the filmmakers' commitment to exposing the truth has been thrown into question by accusations of factual errors and misleading editing, prompting at least one lawsuit.[31] And the filmmakers never fully explain what is so particularly heinous about the fate of the dolphins we see onscreen; what makes their slaughter more worthy of notice than that of other intelligent and sentient animals such as pigs, which many an average viewer consumes regularly. At other times, *The Cove* teeters dangerously close to unintentional self-parody with its sentimental overtures, including activist Ric O'Barry's tale of how Flipper "committed suicide" in his arms—like Herzog's "murder," a rather contentious turn of phrase.

This is not to say that *The Cove* has no light-hearted moments to speak of. In one pivotal sequence, for instance, the filmmakers turn to a cinematic special effects team that gleefully helps them craft imitation rocks to hide the video cameras that will expose the slaughter. (It's debatable whether the light tone of this sequence acknowledges the irony inherent in *faking* nature in order to preserve what the filmmakers perceive as authentic nature.) But the film's overarching mood is an excessively melodramatic one that, coupled with its utter lack of self-consciousness and irony, may actually compromise its very *raison d'être*: moments like O'Barry's tale of Flipper's "suicide" may prompt skeptical viewers to slip out of the film's argumentative hold, or even to laugh, in all the wrong ways.

Surveying this range of contemporary films—from the unserious *Super Size Me* to the super-serious *The Cove*—allows us to see that irony is a useful hermeneutic for ecocinema, but one that must be utilized in a committed and strategic manner if it is to engage, convince, motivate, and/or empower viewers. From a more philosophical standpoint, I have also proposed that thoroughgoing irony, as opposed to limited, corrective irony, can make for an effective environmental ethics in relation to both human viewers and non-human nature; it rejects elitism, superiority, and other values of dominance. All of this is not to say that ecocinematic irony should not, say, aim to counteract ignorance or anti-intellectualism—but, rather, that disdain for the uneducated is unlikely to facilitate the learning that eco-films presume to be crucial in the first place, and, moreover, that an environmentalism articulated in elitist terms cannot serve progressive environmentalist goals like non-dominance. In valorizing thoroughgoing irony, I have also not meant to suggest that ecocinema must be relentlessly flippant—but, rather, that it must train its skeptical eyes on filmic authority as well as on the authority of, say, polluting corporations or ecocidal governments; that it must be able to laugh at itself as well as at others. In the next section, I consider a film that embraces such thoroughgoing irony and self-awareness.

THE IRONIC ECOCINEMA OF MIKE JUDGE

After a controversial limited release by Twentieth Century Fox in 2006, *Idiocracy* failed at the box office but then developed a cult following on DVD and online.[32] We could easily write it off due to its pedigree—*Beavis and Butt-Head* creator Mike Judge co-wrote and directed—and, hence, low-brow appeal. But consider *WebEcoist*'s synopsis of the film: "When two people awake from a 500-year deep freeze, they find that the world has decayed into a glorified garbage dump. Commercialism and anti-intellectualism [have] caused humans to become progressively dumber, eventually leading to the wanton destruction of the planet."[33] While that summary is entirely accurate, it could just as easily describe a serious dystopian thriller, or even some aspects of an eco-documentary—thus proving that serious messages do not require serious modes of affect for their transmission. In other words, *Idiocracy* is affective, and potentially effective, because what's laughable about it—a completely globalized, corporatized human existence at the edge of ecological collapse—is also entirely plausible. Its ironic juxtaposition of the grave with the light-hearted encourages us to both laugh and consider why we're laughing.

While looking out to the external world, *Idiocracy* also allows us to reflect on its status as a film, and its relationship to other eco-films. For one thing, its mining of the dystopian sci-fi plot for comedy prompts us to ask: Why, in other hands, has this same story *not* been funny? More specifically, *Idiocracy* satirizes ecocinema conventions, even as it makes the same points that more serious films do about over-consumption, pollution, and other ecological issues. For instance, the film's voice-over mimics that didactic eco-documentary convention to hilarious effect; in an exaggerated deadpan, the narrator recounts such disasters as "The Great Garbage Avalanche of 2505," and reports on our hero's reception in 2505: "when he spoke in an ordinary voice [those he encountered thought] he sounded pompous and faggy." But perhaps even more amusing is *Idiocracy*'s intertextual status: many of the elements it satirizes have been unselfconsciously taken up by subsequent eco-films. For instance, its opening shot of a whole earth from space, accompanied by dramatic music, anticipates the poster image for *The 11th Hour*, released a year later: a whole earth from space, with footprint imposed on it. The film's visualization of the "Great Garbage Avalanche" is also a spot-on match for the much-lauded opening sequence of *WALL-E*, released two years after *Idiocracy*. Though quirky in execution, the mountains-of-garbage sequence in *WALL-E* is not played for the same level of laughs that Judge's film elicits.

Idiocracy also avoids the elitism associated with the ecocinema creators I've mentioned in particular, and with much environmentalist rhetoric in general. Its protagonist is literally an average Joe, a middle-class white slacker named Joe Bauers (Luke Wilson), chosen because of his very ordinariness to be a subject for the government's top-secret Human Hibernation Program. Scheduled to last just a year, until 2006, the deep-freeze program goes awry and Joe subsequently awakens in the cartoonish dystopia of 2505, where the "intelligent [have] become an endangered species" and the Violence Channel competes for attention with a hit movie called *Ass*. Flummoxed by this futuristic reality, but staunchly good-humoured, Joe revises the lone white hero archetype predominant in dystopian sci-fi and fits instead into the bumbling "comic eco-hero" role described by Robin Murray and Joseph Heumann.[34] But the film subverts that hero archetype even further, giving Joe a mixed-race sex worker named Rita (Maya Rudolph) as his female counterpart in the program and subsequent romantic partner, and a white-trash dim-bulb named Frito Pendejo (Dax Shepard) who proves to be invaluable help.

The potential relatability of these (admittedly ridiculous) characters matters from an environmentalist perspective because, as Minster reminds us, "persuasion is less the goal of rhetoric than identification." As he argues, "it is not so much that films about environmental issues are trying to change audiences' minds, but that they are tapping into latent desires their audiences already have to join the whole, the common."[35] Considering that the "common" in *Idiocracy* is made inseparable from environmental consciousness—and, in turn, that environmental consciousness is framed as common sense, as the province of the common person, we might consider the film an environmentalist document of the most successful order. To wit: *Idiocracy* explicitly conceives of its hero as no smarter than the average film viewer, in contrast to the films I've surveyed—which rely on specialized expert knowledge, and, as I have detailed, potentially alienate viewers with their use of limited and corrective irony. In fact, *Idiocracy* features several scenes wherein Joe's basic, everyday knowledge is treated *as* expert by the ignorant, incurious characters who surround him, including Dwayne Elizondo Mountain Dew Herbert Camacho, the porn-star/professional-wrestler-turned–President of the United States. In one sequence, Joe attempts to convince a government panel that Brawndo "The Thirst Mutilator," an energy drink that has bought out the US Food and Drug Administration and the Federal Communications Commission, should not be used to water crops. (This irrigation system has triggered not just agricultural collapse but natural disasters like dust storms.) When the panel initially rejects his suggestion to use water, chanting the brand's slogan, "Brawndo's Got What Plants Crave. It's Got Electrolytes!" an exasperated Joe replies, "I'm no botanist, but I do know that if you put water on plants, they grow."

The film thus makes the notable point that average citizens/viewers possess a great deal of knowledge about ecological problems and processes; they just need to shake off their passivity and apply that knowledge. In *Idiocracy*, ecology literally becomes the province of the average Joe, not of corporations; presidents; former vice presidents, as in *An Inconvenient Truth*; or scientists, as in *Everything's Cool*. After all, while Joe is determined to be the "smartest man in the world" by the citizens of 2505—and, subsequently, appointed Secretary of the Interior and then voted President after his watering "plan" proves successful—those developments form the film's central joke. Importantly, though, it is a joke that is at once deeply cynical and deeply idealistic. As the narrator concludes, "Okay, so maybe Joe didn't save mankind. But he got the ball rolling, and that's pretty good for an average guy." The film thus insists that the educated, ecologically conscious guy *is* the average guy, the little guy, and not his foil. Embracing this ethos, Joe declares in his presidential victory speech that "there was a time in this country, a long time ago, when reading wasn't just for fags, and neither was writing.... And I believe that time can come again!" The crowd cheers for this sentiment as Joe offers them 2505's version of the thumbs-up: two raised middle fingers.

Sequences like these have become YouTube classics in the past few years. Searches for "Idiocracy" return dozens of clips that have been viewed by millions, including fan-made trailers, mash-ups of different scenes, and, in a stunningly ironic development, commercials for Brawndo that launched a real-life, limited-edition line of the drink aimed at the film's cult audience.[36] I would propose that this broad-based popularity speaks to the effectiveness of Judge's use of ecocinematic irony, if not to the film's success as a whole: he offers the same kind of anti-capitalist ecological critique found in films such as *Super Size Me* and *Food, Inc.*, but with none of the elitism, preaching, or doomsaying. And in fact, *Idiocracy*'s deployment of irony may reveal an important point about its viewers' level of awareness. As Murray and Heumann observe,

> from the 1980s forward, eco-disasters have served as fodder for comedy because audiences know enough about the issue to laugh about it.... By the late 1980s, ... [g]as was unleaded, catalytic converters on cars were mandatory, recycling was on the rise around the country, and new EPA controls were firmly in place. Film audiences, then, didn't need to be warned or taught about environmental problems. And they already had institutions in place that took the issue seriously.[37]

In other words, *Idiocracy* embodies the fact that the purpose of ecocinema is no longer, or no longer *just*, to educate—as many eco-films clearly still believe. Indeed, if audiences are so eco-savvy that they have (potentially) been laughing at eco-comedies for three decades now, there must be another purpose at hand. Of course, eco-comedies remain a small, often obscure lot, compared to the dominant strain of serious, didactic eco-films. And Murray and Heumann may be (optimistically?) overstating their case. But the point is that *Idiocracy* may indicate a shift toward a new task for ecocinema: not just external representation, but self-reflection, and self-reflection *as a form of ecological consciousness*.

CONCLUSION

In this essay, I hope to have dispelled any notion of a serious/unserious binary in ecocinema by arguing that unserious affective modes can do serious work, sometimes even more successfully than serious ones. At the same time, I have qualified this argument by observing that unserious ecocinematic modes are not *inherently* effective, or even necessarily progressive. My discussion of

Everything's Cool, for example, indicates that ecocinematic irony and humour can be just as troubling, if not more so, than the doomsaying or preaching of, say, *Avatar*.

This chapter shares, then, ecocinema's broader concern with film as an environmentalist practice. I have shown that ecologically minded filmmakers face multiple challenges, from attracting and pleasing audiences to responding to contradictory ideological demands. I have argued that an ironic affective stance within ecocinema is a key strategy in meeting these challenges: such a stance can allow films to foment environmentalist agendas, while encouraging us to question both the "eco" and the "cinema" in ecocinema. I have speculated that this is the direction ecocinema is heading, especially as critics begin to address the fact that, as Richard Maxwell and Toby Miller put it, "ecological ethics barely figures into the way media and communication researchers think about media technology."[38] But on a less formal level, an ironic stance might prove helpful to eco-filmmakers themselves, and to ecocritics and environmentalists more generally. It can force us, for one thing, to be more self-aware when it comes to our agendas and how we articulate them.

The last possibility I want to explore here may throw some of my own claims into question—perhaps a not-inappropriate move for an essay that notes irony's self-critical and self-reflexive potential. First, it must be admitted that, for all its potential to enable effective, non-elitist political action, irony can also make for inaction: for smug armchair environmentalism or even slacker apathy. But admitting this creates an opportunity for deeper discussions about the relationship between art and action, and about our hopes and expectations for ecocinema in particular. That is to say, in talking about the work that irony can do when it comes to environment and the representation thereof—its utility, or instrumental value—we must also talk about our definitions of and beliefs around work, utility, and instrumentality. We might scrutinize, for instance, the dearly held assumption that making a movie about environmental crisis will actually help resolve such crisis, or that *writing about* a movie about environmental crisis will actually help resolve such crisis. We might also consider that environmental art can have other ends besides "political action" (however we define that)—such as to diagnose our current moment, or to foster sensibilities suited to that moment. And in fact, in a political climate increasingly hostile to the supposedly useless humanities, we might ask what it means that so many of us on the Left are so similarly insistent that art be clearly "useful" or "impactful."

These are surely conversations for a different essay. So I want to close by musing that, if nothing else, perhaps irony can keep ecocinema creators and ecocritics alike in good humour rather than despair as we undertake work that is difficult, thankless, and—who knows?—maybe even pointless.

NOTES

1 Paula Willoquet-Maricondi, ed., *Framing the World: Explorations in Ecocriticism and Film* (Charlottesville: University of Virginia Press, 2010), 14. Here, Willoquet-Maricondi is referring specifically to Mark Minster's work.

2 Bronislaw Szerszynski, "The Post-Ecologist Condition: Irony as Symptom and Cure," *Environmental Politics* 16, no. 2 (April 2007): 340.

3 See http://www.takepart.com/foodinc.

4 Eric Ditzian, "James Cameron Says 'Avatar' Is Inspiring Environmental Activism," *MTV News*, 17 February 2010, http://www.mtv.com/news/articles/1632038/james-cameron-avatar -inspiring-environmental-activism.jhtml.

5 Catherine Shoard, "The Eco-Documentary: An Endangered Species?" *Guardian*, 15 October 2009, http://www.guardian.co.uk/film/2009/oct/15/eco-documentaries -cove-vanishing-bees.

6 Lucy Jones, "Avatar's Preachy Message about the Environment Is a Turn-off," *Telegraph*, 14 December 2009, http://blogs.telegraph.co.uk/culture/lucyjones/100005572/ avatars-preachy-message-about-the-environment-is-a-turn-off.

7 Shoard, "The Eco-Documentary."

8 As quoted in Ursula Heise, *Sense of Place, Sense of Planet: The Environmental Imagination of the Global* (New York: Oxford University Press, 2008), 142. In *From Apocalypse to Way of Life: Environmental Crisis in the American Century* (New York: Routledge, 2003), Buell declares, "Far from going away, environmental crisis has become a regular part of the uncertainty in which people nowadays dwell" (xiv).

9 Heise, *Sense of Place*, 142.

10 James Fernandez and Mary Taylor Huber, eds., *Irony in Action: Anthropology, Practice, and the Moral Imagination* (Chicago: University of Chicago Press, 2001), 1. Of course, irony can have a normalizing effect as well, but that effect is not inherent to the mode. As Fernandez and Huber observe, "While it may be … common to use irony to criticize someone or something for not meeting expectations or cultural norms … irony is sometimes used to question those expectations or cultural norms themselves" (3).

11 Jones, "Avatar's Preachy Message."

12 Noël Sturgeon, *Environmentalism in Popular Culture: Gender, Race, Sexuality, and the Politics of the Natural* (Tucson: University of Arizona Press, 2009), 23.

13 Szerszynski, "The Post-Ecologist Condition," 338.

14 Sally Peck, "Al Gore's 'Nine Inconvenient Untruths,'" *Telegraph*, 11 October 2007, http://www .telegraph.co.uk/earth/earthnews/3310137/Al-Gores-nine-Inconvenient-Untruths.html.

15 Peck, "Al Gore's 'Nine Inconvenient Untruths'" (my emphases).

16 Peter Doran and Maggie Kendall Zimmerman, "Examining the Scientific Consensus on Climate Change," *EOS* 90, no. 3 (2009): 23, http://tigger.uic.edu/~pdoran/012009_Doran_ final.pdf.

17 In my 2013 book, *Strange Natures: Futurity, Empathy, and the Queer Ecological Imagination* (Urbana: University of Illinois Press), I look at Shelley Jackson's novel *Half Life* as an example of ironic queer-ecological fiction.

18 Willoquet-Maricondi, *Framing the World*, 8.

19 As quoted in Willoquet-Maricondi, *Framing the World*, 9.

20 A few anti-homophobic counterpoints to that film do exist, including Peter Parnell, Justin Richardson, and Henry Cole's 2005 children's book, *And Tango Makes Three* (New York:

Simon and Schuster Children's Publishing), based on the true story of the New York Central Park Zoo's "gay penguins." But the book engages in the same tactics that the film does, depicting animals sentimentally to achieve a particular political purpose.

21 Mark Minster, "Ecocinema as and for Activism: The Rhetoric of Ascent in *An Inconvenient Truth* and *Everything's Cool*," in *Framing the World: Explorations in Ecocriticism and Film*, ed. Paula Willoquet-Maricondi (Charlottesville: University of Virginia Press, 2010), 32.

22 Gabe Delahaye, "*The Greatest Movie Ever Sold* Trailer, You Guys," *Videogum*, 21 March 2011, http://videogum.com/288202/the-greatest-movie-ever-sold-trailer-you-guys/movies/trailer.

23 One might say that this is the *Videogum* ethos: its articles and reader commentaries are utterly irreverent and tongue-in-cheek, yet an intelligent, progressive politics clearly undergirds them. One recent controversy centred around Delahaye's posting of an "upskirt" photo of his celebrity nemesis, Gwyneth Paltrow, whom he sees as a symbol of the out-of-touch elite. Readers took him to task for misogyny, claiming that the move ran counter to the site's spirit.

24 Szerszynski, "The Post-Ecologist Condition," 347.

25 Gabe Delahaye, "*The Greatest Movie Ever Sold* Trailer."

26 Szerszynski, "The Post-Ecologist Condition," 347–48.

27 Elliott Oring, *Jokes and Their Relations* (Lexington: University Press of Kentucky, 1992), 8.

28 "Joe the Plumber," name-checked frequently by the Sarah Palin–John McCain political campaign, is perhaps one of the most prominent examples of the "little guy" articulating big-business concerns. "Joe," also known as Ohio citizen Samuel Joseph Wurzelbacher, most recently made headlines when he spoke at a counter-protest in Wisconsin in the wake of Governor Scott Walker's efforts to abolish the collective bargaining rights of public employees.

29 See Bart Welling's contribution to this volume.

30 See, for instance, Belinda Smaill's contribution to this volume. In his review of the film at http://www.tinymixtapes.com/film/cove (*Tiny Mix Tapes*, n.d.), Alex Preiss remarks, "Unfortunately, the film's depiction of the Japanese borders on being cartoonishly racist, but I'm willing to accept it as a form of heroes-and-villains reductiveness rather than intentional prejudice."

31 See the coverage of the lawsuit from *The Japan Times* (3 December 2010) at http://www.japantimes .co.jp/news/2010/12/03/national/professor-in-cove-sues-film-firms-over-arbitrary-editing.

32 See Chris Garcia's article, "Was 'Idiocracy' Treated Idiotically?" *Austin American-Statesman*, 30 August 2006. According to BoxOfficeMojo.com, the domestic total gross of the film was $444,093, which would be healthy for, say, a mid-budget eco-documentary. See http://www .boxofficemojo.com/movies/?id=idiocracy.htm. (As a point of comparison, *The 11th Hour*, with the star power of narrator Leonard DiCaprio, earned a domestic total gross of $707,343. See http://www.boxofficemojo.com/movies/?id=11thhour.htm.)

33 "12 Films with Dystopian Depictions of Earth's Future," *WebEcoist*, n.d., http://webecoist .com/2009/04/02/12-films-with-dystopian-depictions-of-earths-future.

34 Robin L. Murray and Joseph K. Heumann, *Ecology and Popular Film: Cinema on the Edge* (Albany: State University of New York Press, 2009), 109–226.

35 Minster, "Ecocinema as and for Activism," 36.

36 See "This Joke's for You," *New York Times*, 4 May 2008, for Rob Walker's account of the bizarre Brawndo tie-in at http://www.nytimes.com/2008/05/04/magazine/04wwln-consumed-t .html.

37 Murray and Heumann, *Ecology and Popular Film*, 114.

38 Richard Maxwell and Toby Miller, "Ecological Ethics and Media Technology," *International Journal of Communication* 2 (2008): 331.

BIBLIOGRAPHY

Avatar. Directed by James Cameron. 2009. Los Angeles: Twentieth Century Fox, 2010. DVD.

Buell, Frederick. *From Apocalypse to Way of Life: Environmental Crisis in the American Century.* New York: Routledge, 2003.

The Constant Gardener. Directed by Fernando Meirelles. 2005. Universal City, CA: Universal Studios, 2006. DVD.

The Cove. Directed by Louie Psihoyos. Santa Monica, CA: Lions Gate, 2009. DVD.

The Day after Tomorrow. Directed by Roland Emmerich. Los Angeles: Twentieth Century Fox, 2004. DVD.

Delahaye, Gabe. "*The Greatest Movie Ever Sold* Trailer, You Guys." *Videogum,* 21 March 2011. http://videogum.com/288202/the-greatest-movie-ever-sold-trailer-you-guys/movies/trailer.

Ditzian, Eric. "James Cameron Says 'Avatar' Is Inspiring Environmental Activism." *MTVNews,* 17 February 2010. http://www.mtv.com/news/articles/1632038/james-cameron-avatar-inspiring-environmental-activism.jhtml.

Doran, Peter, and Maggie Kendall Zimmerman. "Examining the Scientific Consensus on Climate Change." *EOS* 90, no. 3 (2009): 22–23. http://tigger.uic.edu/~pdoran/012009_Doran_final.pdf.

The 11th Hour. Directed by Nadia Conners. 2007. Burbank, CA: Warner Home Video, 2008. DVD.

Erin Brokovich. Directed by Steven Soderbergh. Universal City, CA: Universal Studios, 2000. DVD.

Everything's Cool. Directed by Judith Helfand and Daniel B. Gold. New York: City Lights Media, 2007. DVD.

Fernandez, James, and Mary Taylor Huber, eds. *Irony in Action: Anthropology, Practice, and the Moral Imagination.* Chicago: University of Chicago Press, 2001.

Food, Inc. Directed by Robert Kenner. 2008. New York: Magnolia Home Entertainment, 2009. DVD.

Garcia, Chris. "Was 'Idiocracy' Treated Idiotically?" *Austin American-Statesman,* 30 August 2006.

The Greatest Movie Ever Sold. Directed by Morgan Spurlock. New York: Sony Pictures Classics, 2011. DVD.

Grizzly Man. Directed by Werner Herzog. Santa Monica, CA: Lions Gate, 2005. DVD.

Happy Feet. Directed by George Miller. 2006. Burbank, CA: Warner Home Video, 2007. DVD.

Heise, Ursula. *Sense of Place, Sense of Planet: The Environmental Imagination of the Global.* New York: Oxford University Press, 2008.

Idiocracy. Directed by Mike Judge. 2006. Los Angeles: Twentieth Century Fox, 2007. DVD.

An Inconvenient Truth. Directed by Davis Guggenheim. Los Angeles: Paramount, 2006. DVD.

Jones, Lucy. "Avatar's Preachy Message about the Environment Is a Turn-off." *Telegraph*, 14 December 2009. http://blogs.telegraph.co.uk/culture/lucyjones/100005572/avatars-preachy-message-about-the-environment-is-a-turn-off.

March of the Penguins. Directed by Luc Jacquet. Burbank, CA: Warner Home Video, 2005. DVD.

Maxwell, Richard, and Toby Miller. "Ecological Ethics and Media Technology." *International Journal of Communication* 2 (2008): 331–58.

Minster, Mark. "Ecocinema as and for Activism: The Rhetoric of Ascent in *An Inconvenient Truth* and *Everything's Cool.*" In *Framing the World: Explorations in Ecocriticism and Film*, edited by Paula Willoquet-Maricondi, 25–42. Charlottesville: University of Virginia Press, 2010.

Murray, Robin L., and Joseph K. Heumann. *Ecology and Popular Film: Cinema on the Edge*. Albany: State University of New York Press, 2009.

Oring, Elliott. *Jokes and Their Relations*. Lexington: University Press of Kentucky, 1992.

Peck, Sally. "Al Gore's 'Nine Inconvenient Untruths.'" *Telegraph*, 11 October 2007. http://www.telegraph.co.uk/earth/earthnews/3310137/Al-Gores-nine-Inconvenient-Untruths.html.

Queen of the Sun: What Are the Bees Telling Us? Directed by Taggart Siegel. 2010. Chicago: Music Box Films; and Portland, OR: Collective Eye, 2012. DVD.

Shoard, Catherine. "The Eco-Documentary: An Endangered Species?" *Guardian*, 15 October 2009. http://www.guardian.co.uk/film/2009/oct/15/eco-documentaries-cove-vanishing-bees.

Sturgeon, Noël. *Environmentalism in Popular Culture: Gender, Race, Sexuality, and the Politics of the Natural*. Tucson: University of Arizona Press, 2009.

Super Size Me. Directed by Morgan Spurlock. Culver City, CA: Sony Pictures, 2004. DVD.

Szerszynski, Bronislaw. "The Post-Ecologist Condition: Irony as Symptom and Cure." *Environmental Politics* 16, no. 2 (April 2007): 337–55.

"12 Films with Dystopian Depictions of Earth's Future." *WebEcoist*, n.d. http://webecoist.com/2009/04/02/12-films-with-dystopian-depictions-of-earths-future.

2012. Directed by Roland Emmerich. 2009. Culver City, CA: Sony Pictures, 2010. DVD.

Walker, Rob. "This Joke's for You." *New York Times*, 4 May 2008. http://www.nytimes.com/2008/05/04/magazine/04wwln-consumed-t.html.

WALL-E. Directed by Andrew Stanton. Burbank, CA: Walt Disney Video, 2008. DVD.

Willoquet-Maricondi, Paula, ed. *Framing the World: Explorations in Ecocriticism and Film*. Charlottesville: University of Virginia Press, 2010.

PART II

Anthropomorphism and the Non-human in Documentary Film

4

On the "Inexplicable Magic of Cinema"
Critical Anthropomorphism, Emotion, and the Wildness of Wildlife Films

Bart H. Welling

The anthropomorphization of animals, traditionally defined as the one-way projection of uniquely human emotions and characteristics onto non-human beings conceived of as radically "other," was attacked by scientists in the twentieth century as a "dangerous pit" or even a kind of mental disorder.[1] Some scholars in the humanities have also viewed anthropomorphism with deep suspicion, albeit for different reasons. In his seminal 1977 essay "Why Look at Animals?" John Berger treats the massive proliferation of anthropomorphic representations of animals in the modern era not as a *compensation* for the disappearance of wild and domesticated animals from the daily lives of most Westerners, but, paradoxically, as an integral part of this disappearance.[2] However, as important as it is for ecocritics and animal studies scholars to attend to the damage caused by *superficially* anthropomorphic representations,[3] there are good reasons for doubting that a completely "*non*-anthropomorphic relationality" between humans and animals is possible.[4] If Jesús Rivas and Gordon M. Burghardt are right to suggest that anthropomorphism may be the "default condition of the human mind,"[5] then the true challenge is not to purge ourselves of it, but to develop theories from within an inherently anthropomorphic framework that can adequately account for its powerful operations in human minds and cultures, and persuasively analyze the relationship between, on the one hand, anthropomorphic representations and perceptions of non-human beings, and, on the other, the minds and emotions of these beings themselves.

Elsewhere I have placed Burghardt's scientific model of "critical anthropomorphism" in dialogue with W.J.T. Mitchell's theories on "image life," outlining a set of problems relating to anthropomorphism that are best approached from what the film scholar Torben Grodal would identify as a biocultural (as opposed to an "extreme constructivist" or, conversely, a "strong biological") perspective.[6] The following sections comprise a preliminary biocultural and critically anthropomorphic investigation into some of the affective dimensions of anthropomorphism in the production and viewing of wildlife films. Taking a cue from Grodal's study *Embodied Visions: Evolution, Emotion, Culture, and Film* (2009), I examine the emotions evoked by film in evolutionary as well as cultural contexts, treating film's emotional impacts on viewers not as historically unprecedented products of new technologies but, rather, as the results of complex cultural activations and modifications of certain basic, universal "innate dispositions" that have fostered human survival and structured our perceptions of the world for hundreds of thousands of years. Unlike Grodal, however, who focuses mainly on responses to representations of *human* emotions, and who tends to treat animals in film as "transitional objects" for children, with cinematic locations functioning as interchangeable "surface element[s],"[7] I attempt to expand the biocultural frame of reference to encompass the more-than-human emotional landscape in which human emotions originally developed, along with the range of animal feelings to which our emotions are intimately related. What we feel when we watch wildlife films, I argue, does not just depend on techniques employed by filmmakers to promote superficial anthropomorphism or to tap into our innate drive to make sense of the world by comparing animal physiology and behaviour to our own. Rather, I am going to claim that wildlife films can (intentionally in some cases, unintentionally in many others) provide viewers with heavily mediated but potentially transformative modes of access to the emotional lives of our non-human kin. They do this by staging onscreen encounters with sentient creatures—encounters that emerge not from disembodied human scopic regimes but from behind-the-scenes relationships (however close or distant, oppressive or respectful) between filmmakers and the animals with whom they form ephemeral communities while filming.

Before moving any further, though, it should be stressed that I am not arguing, to paraphrase the marketers of Walt Disney Studios' True-Life Adventures, that wildlife documentaries represent "completely authentic, unstaged and unrehearsed" windows on animals' emotional lives.[8] It is true that, in shifting the focus from the "play between the surfaces of bodies" to controversial aspects of "animal interiority,"[9] I am addressing issues that Jonathan Burt,

Cary Wolfe, and other animal studies scholars have largely chosen to sidestep for perfectly understandable reasons. After many years in which "ecopornography" has been the dominant paradigm in wildlife films, it can be difficult to distinguish between superficial anthropomorphism and film techniques that represent animal emotions in more plausible ways, to say nothing of the stigma that is still attached to discussions of animal emotions in various academic circles.[10] Then too, of course, when arguing that film can set in motion a meaningful *relationship* across the picture plane between human viewers and representations of animals who are not literally present and cannot see them, we are flying in the face of any number of postmodern critiques of "the real," of universal human traits, and so on. Some may argue that film is by its very nature a superficially anthropomorphic technology, since it captures selected scenes from the visual and aural commons that all seeing and hearing organisms can perceive, albeit in different ways, and translates them into a medium that only humans and very few other animals can make sense of. I may feel a powerful sense of emotional connectedness to a representation of a northern yellow bat in a wildlife documentary, but if, miraculously, the same exact bat were to chase a flying ant through my open window and encounter me watching images of her on my television set, she would surely not recognize herself on the screen or acknowledge my emotional attachment to her. She would most likely perceive the television set as a blinding and deafening nuisance and consider me a threat to be avoided. Depending on how agitated she became, my earlier feelings of relatedness to, or even affection for, the bat could easily yield to heart-pounding fear.

However, even in the midst of such a potentially alienating encounter between a large earth-bound primate and a small flying mammal, a rapidly growing body of evidence in fields like evolutionary psychology and cognitive ethology suggests that my emotions and the bat's emotions would be influenced by similar drives (e.g., for safety), homologous brain structures (e.g., the hippocampus, which, among other things, helps govern spatial navigation in mammals), and related biochemical processes (e.g., the release of adrenaline as part of the fight-or-flight response). And if our physical meeting were unpleasant, this would not negate the validity of the emotions I had experienced while watching the bat documentary. Grodal argues that "our brains have not entirely adjusted themselves to the new situation" inaugurated by film, in which "what we see and hear is not necessarily real."[11] On a cognitive level we may understand perfectly well that a tiger filmed charging at the camera is not literally present in the theatre, but the "low-level perceptual mechanisms" that trigger emotions would still be activated, to a certain degree, as if we were actually being attacked; our pulses would speed up a bit, our muscles would tense up for a fight or a quick retreat, and we might even break out in a sweat or grab the arm of a loved one sitting next to us.[12] As members of a species that co-evolved with carnivores that were larger, stronger, faster, and equipped with sharper teeth and nails than our ancestors, we would have felt a certain amount of *real fear*, even if the threat triggering it in this case happened to be simulated. If I were to feel terrified on encountering the bat face to face, the ensuing emotional dynamic could not be reduced to a simple conflict of feelings in which the "real" emotion, fear, could be said to drive out the "simulated" emotion, affection. My experience with the live bat might complicate, but would not completely efface, the experience of connectedness that I had lived through while watching her on film. After witnessing and, indeed, sharing the sense of fear and vulnerability that she experienced upon finding herself trapped in my house, I might even be motivated to act both on this shared fear and on my affection for the bat. For example, I might build a bat house in my back yard ... at a safe distance from my window.

Of course, fear is far from the only emotion pertaining to human–non-human interactions either in the theatre or in the woods. A biocultural and critically anthropomorphic approach can go a long way towards explaining what Werner Herzog, in *Grizzly Man* (2005),[13] calls the "inexplicable magic of cinema"—a sense of magic that, I would argue, inspired by Grodal and Mitchell's analyses, is not entirely unique to film, but has evolved from the repertoire of powerful emotions that our ancestors developed both as hunters and prey animals in their own right,[14] and as painters, carvers, sculptors, and users of animal representations that embodied a magical worldview. The next three sections briefly map out a triangular schema that may prove helpful in elucidating how wildlife films capture and structure exchanges of emotion between their producers, their viewers, and the animals whose emotions (not just *behaviours*) they engage with. At their best, wildlife films can facilitate affective exchanges that—as trite as it may sound—can truthfully be described as magical in their ability to shape the emotions of those who watch them.

PRODUCERS AND VIEWERS

Scholars like Gregg Mitman, Derek Bousé, and Cynthia Chris have devoted a good deal of attention to the anthropomorphic techniques that wildlife filmmakers use to elicit emotional responses from viewers. They also offer perceptive and historically nuanced accounts of how these responses have been shaped and channelled so as to foster public support for various human projects, ranging from controversial European and American conservation efforts in Africa[15] to sociobiology's equally controversial attempts to transform scientific and popular views on subjects like human sexuality.[16] Needless to say, the primary ulterior motive guiding filmmakers' anthropomorphic manipulations of viewers' emotions has often been commercial in nature.[17] Viewers of wildlife documentaries seem to find "smiling" chimpanzees and "friendly" dolphins endlessly entertaining, no matter how often they may have been informed that the chimpanzee's "smile" is better described as a "fear grimace"[18] (also used to signal aggression) or that seeing a dolphin "smile" requires similar acts of physiological misrecognition and unwarranted emotional projection.

However, there are various ways in which animals can elude anthropomorphic attempts to exploit their appearances and behaviours in order to elicit certain emotional responses from viewers. Part of the magic of film, as Werner Herzog notes in *Grizzly Man*, can be ascribed to the basic unpredictability of the world, especially where wild animals are involved. Additionally, as Jonathan Burt puts it,

> although the animal on screen can be burdened with multiple metaphorical significances ... the animal is also marked as a site where these symbolic associations collapse into each other. In other words, the animal image is a form of *rupture in the field of representation*.... This rupturing effect of the animal image is mainly exemplified by the manner in which our attention is constantly drawn beyond the image and, in that sense, beyond the aesthetic and semiotic framework of the film."[19]

Burt's analysis of the rupturing effect centres on animal welfare issues, but it would make good sense to extend his claims to the realm of animal emotions. True, the inherent instability of animal images is partly a function of viewers' concerns over how animals are treated by filmmakers, but this instability is also produced, in part, by frequent discrepancies between (a) the emotions that filmmakers want animals to elicit in their audiences and (b) the emotions being experienced—and expressed—by the animals themselves. The rupturing effect is on full display in one scene in the Disney True-Life Adventure *White Wilderness* (1958), in which a young polar bear is shown slipping and rapidly tumbling down a steep, icy mountain slope.[20] The voice-over narration and comical music accompanying the shot encourage viewers to respond to the bear's predicament as a humorous spectacle, but our hard-wired sense of balance and fear of falling—innate dispositions that contribute to our survival, and which evolved in a distant past before humans and bears had even come into being—make it difficult not to share some of the fear and frustration that the polar bear evidently experienced on being pushed down the hill. On a more positive note, the emotional relationship between filmmaker and viewer may approximate the viewer-animal relationship reasonably well. The feelings of parental tenderness and warmth evoked by a dolphin birth scene in another True-Life Adventure, *Mysteries of the Deep* (1959),[21] should not just be written off as superficially anthropomorphic products of 1950s-era heteronormativity and patriarchal control of female sexuality; they are related in evolutionary and neurophysiological terms to the emotions that the dolphin mother was most likely experiencing as she cared for her newborn calf.

Examples like these highlight the importance of not simply focusing on producers' efforts to control what animals mean to viewers, but, rather, of attending to the triangular dynamics at work in human representations of other animals. When examined from this perspective, even the most blatantly ecopornographic documentaries can be seen to harbour the potential to transform how viewers perceive non-human animals. This is not to say that, by connecting emotionally with onscreen animals in a way that holds up to critical anthropomorphic scrutiny, viewers are *guaranteed* a way of resisting filmmakers' efforts to shape their emotions. Documentarians have many tools at their disposal with which to manipulate more legitimate cross-species emotional experiences as well as superficially anthropomorphic ones. In *Winged Migration* (2001), for example, one of the film's hard-working avian subjects is shown grounded with a broken wing on an African beach, desperately trying to escape a horde of hungry crabs.[22] Humans share enough innate dispositions with birds—such as the fear of being eaten—to justify the observation that the terror we may experience on viewing this scene is grounded in biology, and is not simply a by-product of certain cultural anxieties. After following the bird's movements for a few seconds, the film cuts to a shot of the crabs swarming over and devouring … something. The bird? So it would seem, but the filmmakers confess in a DVD interview that the object was a dead fish, and that they had actually rescued the injured bird from the crabs. Obviously, this bit of benign fakery could be defended on the grounds that the bird probably *would* have been eaten if the filmmakers hadn't intervened. Moreover, the scene harnesses real emotions to help dramatize a significant problem for migrating birds: their vulnerability to injury and predation. Of course, this means that the triangular economies of anthropomorphism are still at work; we are still not dealing with a purely human (producer-viewer) emotional exchange. The makers of *Winged Migration* have manipulated their footage to call up a very different emotion than what we would have experienced if we had been informed ahead of time that the film's "dead" avian protagonist was actually a fish, but our feelings of sympathy for the "eaten" bird, if partially misguided, can be productively extrapolated to our everyday interactions with birds, injured animals, and non-human beings in general.

WILDLIFE FILMMAKERS AND ANIMALS

Emotional exchanges between filmmakers and animals have received much less scholarly attention than the producer-viewer leg of the triangle, but, as demonstrated in any number of wildlife documentarians' memoirs, interviews, "how-they-shot-it" features, and other sources, these exchanges have been absolutely central to the making of many wildlife films.[23] Documentaries like *Winged Migration* simply would have been impossible to make if the producers and their non-human subjects had not formed strong affective bonds. Ecopornographic conventions have trained viewers to regard as "natural" such breathtaking shots as *Winged Migration*'s extreme close-ups of wild birds flying in formation (as if we ourselves were birds flying alongside them), but the truth is that untrained birds would never allow an aircraft to get close enough to obtain these kinds of shots—which, by the way, can take months to set up.[24] Even with the most advanced technology at their disposal, it would also have been impossible to track the same groups of migrating wild birds day and night across the vast distances (oceans, deserts, sprawling cities) that the documentary aimed to cover. And the filming of staged sequences that lend the movie much of its pathos—red-breasted geese getting mired in (simulated) industrial pollutants in eastern Europe, a macaw escaping from a wildlife trafficker's cage in South America—would likewise have presented insurmountable ethical and logistical challenges to the producers if they had tried to employ wild birds. Thus, the geese, ducks, and other birds shown in *Winged Migration*'s mesmerizing "formation shots" were hand-raised from birth, imprinting on humans as if they were their actual parents, and trained to follow ultralight airplanes as closely as if the filmmakers were lead birds in their migratory formations.[25] Most of the time, the birds flew as they normally would have done, and presumably experienced emotions quite close to what they would have felt in an all-bird flock.[26]

What do filmmakers feel when working with animals, though? Answers to this question are clearly going to vary depending on any number of factors: the species of animal involved, individual filmmakers'—and animals'—temperaments and shifting moods, location, climate, culturally contingent views of particular animals, and more. For some filmmakers, who might be viewed as the heirs of John James Audubon, aesthetic fascination with a given *species*, ecological process, or plot line can trump concern for the physical and emotional well-being of individual "specimens." The producers responsible for the notorious lemming "mass suicide" scene in Disney's *White Wilderness*, in which lemmings were simply flung off of a river bluff in order to dramatize (erroneous) theories about the rodent's migratory behaviour, obviously fall in this category.[27] At a very different point on the emotional spectrum we find the *Winged Migration* unit responsible for the footage of migrating pelicans. A DVD special feature on the making of the film shows that when their birds refused to eat and became ill, the pelican team worked around the clock to care for them. It would be going too far to claim that the filmmakers' "quasi-maternal" feelings for the pelicans perfectly mirrored the birds' emotional attachment to their adoptive human parents, but the genuine affection that the humans felt for the birds surely involved some of the same biochemical and neurological processes that are activated when people care for their children.[28] Hard-core Cartesians might insist that the birds' attachment to the humans is purely instinctual, while the humans' emotional attachment to the birds is based on a sentimentalized attribution of emotions to the animals that they simply do not possess. However, Mary Midgley's comments on the "basic everyday feelings" that govern the interactions of Asian elephants and their handlers, or mahouts, seem relevant in this context: "Obviously the mahouts may have many beliefs about the elephants which are false because they are 'anthropomorphic'—that is, they misinterpret some outlying aspects of elephant behaviour by relying on a human pattern which is inappropriate. But if they were doing this about the basic everyday feelings—about whether the elephant is pleased, annoyed, frightened, excited, tired, sore, suspicious or angry—they would not only be out of business, they would often simply be dead."[29] It is an anthropocentric fallacy to assume that pleasure, annoyance, fear, anger, and so on are, strictly speaking, *human* emotions at all, and interpreting other sentient creatures' emotions correctly can be a life-or-death matter for wildlife filmmakers and the animals with whom they work as much as it is for elephants and their mahouts.

This fact is illustrated clearly in Leanne Allison and Diana Wilson's 2004 film *Being Caribou* and Karsten Heuer's 2008 book *Being Caribou: Five Months on Foot with an Arctic Herd*.[30] The *Being Caribou* projects document Allison and husband Heuer's thousand-mile trek to follow the massive Porcupine herd of caribou from Canada's Yukon Territory to their calving grounds in Alaska's hotly contested Arctic National Wildlife Refuge (ANWR) and back to the Yukon again. The title gestures towards Allison and Heuer's desire to come as close as humanly possible to experiencing what it means to be a caribou by "sharing the same challenges" as the wild deer.[31] These challenges include starving grizzlies, swarms of biting insects, extreme hunger, exhaustion, blizzards, dangerous river crossings, and the everyday frustrations involved in trying to keep up with a herd of swift quadrupeds which, unlike their bipedal followers, can survive on grass and lichen and run up steep slopes with minimal effort. It goes without saying that the caribou, which have always served as a primary food source for the Gwich'in and other Arctic peoples, do not share a corresponding interest in "being human," and Disney-esque moments of pure interspecies harmony materialize rarely, if ever. Eventually, though, the "huffs and stamping hooves" with which the nervous animals typically signal their awareness of Heuer and Allison's presence give way to a calm acceptance based on mutual trust and creaturely respect.[32] At one point, Heuer writes, he was shocked to discover that the entity walking behind him on an ancient migratory trail was not his wife but a bull caribou. As this caribou and others pull up alongside him, his shock yields to a relaxed attentiveness: "The bulls seemed to sense this: their eyes softened, their breathing quieted, and for a brief, suspended moment we inhaled each other's exhaled breaths. Finally, after so many miles, I was floating with animals instead of chasing them. I was experiencing caribou experiencing themselves."[33] A biologist by training, Heuer is careful to stop short of claiming in passages like this one that he and Allison are "becoming caribou" in a Deleuzian-Guattarian sense,[34] that they have gained unfiltered access to the animals' inner lives. The interesting final sentence in the excerpt constitutes an acknowledgement of another being's full but non-human sentience, not an act of rhetorical "clairvoyance," to paraphrase John Berger.[35] Even though he has good empirical reasons for contending that that the caribou bulls are picking up on and responding to his growing sense of relaxation, Heuer opts for a modest speculative approach ("The bulls *seemed* to sense") to this brief but powerful moment of embodied trans-species dialogue. Heuer and Allison's version of critical anthropomorphism is grounded in a healthy respect for the irreducible physiological, behavioural, and emotional differences as well as the continuities between human beings and caribou beings; their main purpose in factoring in their emotions and intuitions—even their dreams—is to make verifiable or nullifiable predictions about where the caribou will move next, not about how the animals feel. In sharp contrast to *Grizzly Man* Timothy Treadwell's behaviour among his "animal friends," Allison and Heuer resist touching caribou when the opportunity presents itself, but their attempts to make sense of "caribou being" *are* informed by corporeal feedback from the animals. Crucially, they are also guided by forms of indigenous knowledge which modern science has only recently begun taking seriously, but which have allowed the Gwich'in and other groups to flourish in one of the harshest biomes on Earth.

Allison and Heuer's willingness to acknowledge the social subjectivity of individual caribou, and the caribou's reciprocal acceptance of them as "mildly interesting, harmless companion[s],"[36] result in a rare filmmaking opportunity: the partners are able to set up camp among pregnant caribou on ANWR's coastal plain. This is the same part of the refuge, designated Area 1002, that has been in the crosshairs of oil corporations and conservative politicians since before the presidential administration of George H.W. Bush (1989–93). No matter how physically remote Heuer and Allison get from Washington, DC, the contentious politics of US oil exploration are always on their minds; in fact, Heuer travels with a George W. Bush doll in his pack as a humorous reminder of the serious political stakes of the journey.[37] Likewise, the *demands* of relationship with caribou are never far from the *rewards*.[38] Heuer and Allison are apparently never in danger of being attacked by the caribou, but they are keenly attuned to the delicate emotional state of the mothers and infants during the birth process—"They're as fragile as glass right now," Allison whispers into the camera—and they accept the discomforts involved in remaining "hostages in the tent" for five days out of the fear that they might spook the herd, which would result in the separation of cows and calves. But separations occur all too often anyway thanks to grizzly and golden eagle attacks, among other tribulations, and Allison and Heuer's position "migrat[ing] with the herd"[39] opens them up to many unexpected "heart-wrenching" encounters (as Allison puts it in the film) with suffering caribou: lost calves mistaking them for their mothers; an adult female dying in utter misery from a botfly infestation, which they are powerless to cure.

Allison and Heuer's emotional vulnerability comes into sharpest focus at the end of the film and book, when they travel to Washington, DC, to try to share their profoundly transformative experiences with impatient lawmakers in an urban environment that they find newly bewildering after five months in the Arctic. Interspecies politics and petro-politics converge in their attempts to find "the right words to put into the right sentences,"[40] the right images with which to persuade Americans, accustomed to stereotypes of the Arctic as a frozen wasteland, that the lives of caribou and the traditional lifeways of the Gwich'in—along with the well-being of vast numbers of birds and other creatures who migrate to ANWR's coastal plain every summer—are worth more than "sav[ing] a few dollars on our next tank of gas."[41] Appropriately, Heuer's book ends on a note of uncertainty; he writes that he and Allison wondered "whether it was a eulogy we were producing or a successful call to action."[42] Near the end of the film Allison is shown breaking into tears in front of the US Capitol building, worrying that after becoming "hopelessly attached" to the caribou, she and Heuer may have to watch as "their calving grounds [are] drilled, their numbers decline ..." One of the most haunting images in the film is a slow-motion shot of a young caribou racing around the calving grounds in what Heuer has just described in an *in situ* voice-over as "huge, raging fast circles." The shot ends in a freeze-frame and fade-out, with the calf's hooves all bunched together in the air above ground they may, in one sense, never touch again.

CONCLUSION: VIEWERS AND/AS ANIMALS

What do we see when we watch animals in wildlife films, if not simply feathered or furry avatars of human values, ideologies, anxieties, cinematic conventions, and so on? Trying to arrive at a satisfactory answer to this question would take us far beyond the scope of this essay. For now, the best I can do is to follow David Ingram's and Adrian Ivakhiv's examples (see Chapters 1 and 8) in mapping out some of the more promising ways in which ecocritics and animal studies scholars might go about searching for answers. What these approaches have in common, in keeping with Greg Garrard's bold redefinition of ecocriticism as "the study of the relationship of the human and the non-human ... throughout human cultural history and entailing critical analysis of the term 'human' itself,"[43] is that they can shift our focus from first-wave ecocriticism's strangely abstract analysis of *representations* to the study of cinematic anthropomorphism as a dynamic process based on affective, historical, ecological, economic, and other kinds of *relationships* between animals, filmmakers, and viewers.[44] Furthermore, as implied in Garrard's definition, these approaches will require us to engage in modes of interdisciplinary work that will not only entail challenging humanism's assumptions about humanity's position in the biosphere, but will also contribute to the transformation of the humanities into something like what Cary Wolfe means by the "posthumanities,"[45] or (why not?) the "animalities."

The first approach would involve crossing borders between the humanities and the social sciences by conducting the same sorts of "careful, contextual analysis of audience responses" to animals in wildlife films that Ivakhiv advocates doing with respect to other genres of environmental film.[46] Does Leanne Allison's handling of her animal footage in *Being Caribou* add up to a "successful call to action," in Karsten Heuer's apt words, or to a beautiful, but ultimately self-defeating, "eulogy" for the caribou and other animals of the Arctic National Wildlife Refuge?[47] How many of the film's viewers have been inspired to rethink their positions in the world of petro-politics thanks to its progressive approach to trans-species politics? Conversely, in what ways might the film's engagements with animals backfire? Does a scene like an early sequence in which Gwich'in hunter Randall Tetlichi shoots and skins a number of caribou primarily (a) evoke audience members' sympathy for the animals, (b) reinforce a deeply engrained sense of dominion over them, or (c) carry out more complicated types of affective work? One of the clearest signals to emerge from our workshop at the Rachel Carson Center (see Introduction to this volume) is that the days of the "ideal viewer" in the study of environmental film are over; as Ivakhiv notes, we can only hope to resolve debates over the "political impacts" of environmental visual culture by carrying out "detailed ethnographic studies of audience perceptions."[48]

As we do so, the issue of physiological and ethological accuracy in wildlife films—no matter how much derision ecocritical "police work," that is, the censuring of "environmentally incorrect" representations,[49] may have attracted in the past—will undoubtedly take on a new-found significance. For example, if we were equipped with empirical data about how superficially anthropomorphic misrepresentations of animals (e.g., "smiling" chimpanzees) and animal stereotypes[50] can result in ecologically counterproductive attitudes and behaviours on the part of viewers, we would be in a much better position not just to *critique* but to actively *shape* filmmaking and film-viewing trends. Of course, this line of inquiry will not only lead us out of our ecocritical ivory towers by immersing us more deeply in conversations with image-makers and the public. Determining whether a given representation happens to constitute an accurate portrayal or a *mis*representation will necessarily also entail crossing "two cultures" frontiers into territory traditionally controlled by sciences devoted to the study of non-human animal anatomy and behaviour, such as zoology and ethology. There we will find ourselves in the company of other boundary-crossers, such as biosemioticians and cognitive ethologists, whose work on animal communication, thought, and culture will prove invaluable in helping us envision new modes of post-Cartesian engagement with the entanglements of matter and meaning that we find in wildlife films, as in non-human minds, bodies, and communities themselves.[51]

But why should we limit our extramural forays to conversations with fellow academics? Depending on the film we happened to be researching, we might find it more appropriate to consult with members of indigenous communities, ranchers, park rangers, zoo workers, and others (much like the elephant handlers discussed by Mary Midgley) with access to the forms of "craft knowledge"[52] that are instrumental to the co-flourishing of human and non-human animals in everyday life, despite the rejection of this kind of knowledge by most scientists in the past. We may end up crossing the most deeply entrenched border of all as we design intellectually rigorous, but also emotionally resonant and ethically sound, experiments that will integrate lived experiences with non-human beings into our scholarship. One of the most exciting aspects of Garrard's definition of ecocriticism is that it anticipates the development of image-, narrative-, and cultural theory-based methodologies for studying not just animal representations but lives of animals and human–animal relationships in their own right. Among other things, these new forms of scholarship would promote true interdisciplinarity between the sciences and the humanities rather than the colonization of one set of disciplines by the other.

The rich, if often studiously self-concealing, field of human and non-human relationships out of which wildlife films emerge would seem to call for "detailed ethnographic studies"—or, better yet, anthrozoological studies—of its own.[53] One type of anthrozoological work might take "embedded ecocritics," where possible, into the field and the studio to conduct first-hand observational studies of filmmakers and animals at work.[54] This new variety of fieldwork, while difficult to arrange, would afford scholars rare opportunities to assess the amount of "material waste and ecological change,"[55] and perhaps even the emotional and cultural costs for animals, involved in the making of wildlife films. However, it could also help illuminate more complex, and positive, modes of coexistence and trans-species collaboration. (In the future, some students of wildlife film might reinvent the genre itself as a form of scholarship, creating documentaries that would tear down the usual firewalls between main features and behind-the-scenes special features, between seamless, human-free "clairvoyant" shots and messy, human-dominated "how-they-shot-it" accounts).

Another type of fieldwork—safer and cheaper than the first, perhaps, but by no means antithetical to it—would send biocultural scholars down the trail blazed by Mitman, Bousé, Burt, Chris, and others into the vast archive of filmmakers' biographies, letters, interviews, documentary scripts and outtakes, studio and museum records, promotional materials, special Internet features, and other film paratexts. The goal of such work from a critically anthropomorphic perspective would not just be to more fully understand the media ecologies in which moving images of animals circulate,[56] but to recover types of "craft knowledge" that have informed the making of wildlife documentaries, and to reconstruct the anthrozoological contexts that have had a bearing on the behaviour (including the affective responses) of filmed animals. A hybrid version of these approaches, combining archival research with work outside the university, would explore the ways in which filmmaking histories and representations have intersected and clashed with, hidden and revealed, the anthrozoological histories of the eco-cultural borderlands in which—no matter how hard they work to disavow this fact—wildlife films have always, and only, been made. The idea of what counts as a wildlife film will surely be transformed in the process, as scholars work, for example, to uncover how the filmmaking practices that contributed to the image of Africa as an "untouched animal paradise"[57] have, paradoxically, been entangled with the deep co-evolutionary histories of human–non-human relationships on the continent where these relationships first took shape.

So far this chapter has begged the question of what constitutes "the non-human." I have used the term as a synonym for "animal" and its variants, but of course it can also be applied to landforms, ecological processes, weather patterns, and to the digital technologies through which ever-more-convincing simulations of animals can be integrated with footage (computer-edited, and perhaps computer-enhanced) of live animals, further complicating both what we mean by "wildlife films" (does James Cameron's *Avatar* [2009] count?) and how we deal with the play of agencies and subjectivities that characterizes the genre.[58] These areas of inquiry, informed by advances in post-humanist theory and various scientific disciplines, will no doubt prove fruitful for scholars interested in articulating new theories of anthropomorphism. And advanced imaging technologies will certainly prove useful as *tools* as well as *subjects* of biocultural analysis. For instance, functional MRI (magnetic resonance imaging) scans could be employed in tandem with audience surveys to greatly enhance our understanding of why viewers respond to individual animals, species, ecosystems, plots, and other elements of wildlife films in certain ways, and to elucidate some of the continuities and distinctions between watching animals in person and watching them onscreen.[59] Do images of particular types of animals, such as snakes or big cats, trigger type-specific neurological responses in viewers? What about images of different landscapes (boreal forests versus savannahs) and different image formats (photographs versus film clips)? How large a role do differences in age, gender, and culture play in shaping psychological responses to wildlife films? How does the human brain process film representations of animals expressing emotion, as compared to images of humans? What special connections might be drawn between our tendency to anthropomorphize animals and our ancient and apparently "incorrigible" habit, as Mitchell styles it,[60] of anthropomorphizing visual art? To what extent is film itself a wild medium, perceived by the brain as alive, or perhaps even as an animal? Cognitive approaches to wildlife film would not only lead to fascinating insights in the spaces between ecocriticism, animal studies, and the host of interrelated disciplines grouped together by Brian Boyd under the sign of evolutionary psychology,[61] but could result in practical benefits for traditionally stigmatized predators like wolves, or endangered animals that receive less public support than they deserve because they do not conform to human standards of "cuteness." Furthermore, these efforts—cutting-edge technologies notwithstanding—may shed light on the ancient processes through which "the human" and "the non-human" first came into being and continue to co-evolve, and may thus bring valuable empirical evidence to bear on the struggle to transform humanity's ecocidal relationships with other species.

I have just sketched out several ways in which the "inexplicable magic" of wildlife film can be more fully explained—but, I trust, not explained *away*. Just because in the future we may be able to identify the precise neurological, technological, and co-evolutionary processes that are responsible for the powerful sense of awe we might feel while watching animals on film, this does not mean that the sense of awe will inevitably diminish. Nor, for that matter, will biocultural theories of affect in wildlife films necessarily foreclose the possibility of eco-theological or -spiritual explanations of these kinds of responses. If anything, critically anthropomorphic investigations of wildlife films should foster an increased appreciation of the quasi-magical affective powers of wildlife film by bringing our critical labours back within the purview of what the poet Denise Levertov called "animal presence," the charged zone where humans do not merely shape animals but become aware of their own creatureliness and are themselves transformed.[62] Instead of being widely viewed as deceitful emblems of an "irredeemable" modern rupture between humans and their non-human relations, symptoms of scopophilia and other "sick obsession[s]," wildlife films may be resituated within genealogies of animal visualizations going back over thirty thousand years, to the cave paintings of Chauvet in what is now southern France.[63] To adapt Sean Cubitt's wonderful critically anthropomorphic description of David Attenborough's *Blue Planet* series (2001), we may be more prepared to recognize the wildlife documentary as one of the ways in which "the world's unmotivated upsurge" can "well up into us, clasp itself to us, merge with the salt water in our veins."[64] It may become easier to identify the conditions under which wildlife films cease to merely represent the wild and instead become potent performances of wildness, inspiring the kinds of animals who watch them to connect in new ways with the kinds of animals who star in them, rethinking their place in the family of all life.[65]

NOTES

1 See Randall Lockwood, "Anthropomorphism Is Not a Four-Letter Word," in *Perceptions of Animals in American Culture*, ed. R.J. Hoage , National Zoological Park Symposia for the Public Series (Washington, DC: Smithsonian Institution Press, 1989), 42; and Marc Bekoff, *Minding Animals: Awareness, Emotions, and Heart* (New York: Oxford University Press, 2002), 49.

2   See John Berger, "Why Look at Animals?" in *About Looking* (New York: Pantheon, 1980), 24.

3   Lockwood enumerates five categories of anthropomorphism; I am using one of his terms, "superficial anthropomorphism," to gesture broadly toward any variety that is based on mis-understandings of non-human physiology, behaviour, and emotions. Lockwood, "Anthropomorphism Is Not a Four-Letter Word," 45–50.

4   Nicole Merola, "Monkeys, Apes, and Bears, Oh My!: Illuminating the Politics of Human–Animal Relationship in Jill Greenberg's *Monkey Portraits* and *Bear Portraits*," *JAC* 30, nos. 3–4 (Fall 2010): 649 (emphasis added).

5   Jesús Rivas and Gordon M. Burghardt, "Crotalomorphism: A Metaphor for Understanding Anthropomorphism by Omission," in *The Cognitive Animal: Empirical and Theoretical Perspectives on Animal Cognition*, ed. Marc Bekoff, Colin Allen, and Gordon M. Burghardt (Cambridge: Massachusetts Institute of Technology Press, 2002), 10.

6   See Bart H. Welling, "Critical Anthropomorphism in the 'Age of Biocybernetic Reproduction': A Response to Nicole Merola's 'Monkeys, Apes, and Bears, Oh My!'" *JAC* 31, nos. 3–4 (Fall 2011): 660–85.

7   Torben Grodal, *Embodied Visions: Evolution, Emotion, Culture, and Film* (Oxford: Oxford University Press, 2009), 29, 48.

8   Quoted in Gregg Mitman, *Reel Nature: America's Romance with Wildlife on Film* (Cambridge, MA: Harvard University Press, 1999), 110.

9   Jonathan Burt, *Animals in Film*, Locations Series (London: Reaktion Books, 2002), 31.

10 See my essay "Ecoporn: On the Limits of Visualizing the Nonhuman," in *Ecosee: Image, Rhetoric, Nature*, ed. Sidney I. Dobrin and Sean Morey (Albany: State University of New York Press, 2009), 53–77, for an extended definition and numerous examples of ecopornography.

11 Grodal, *Embodied Visions*, 101.

12 The degree to which we would experience fear in this setting would be influenced, of course, by such factors as our age and size, the symbolic and literal place of tigers in the culture to which we belonged, and the extent to which we had been habituated to this kind of scene by earlier films. See Grodal, *Embodied Visions*, 102, 39–41.

13 *Grizzly Man*, directed by Werner Herzog (Santa Monica, CA: Lions Gate Films, 2005).

14 See Grodal, *Embodied Visions*, 107–9.

15 See Mitman, *Reel Nature*, 187–202.

16 See Cynthia Chris, *Watching Wildlife* (Minneapolis: University of Minnesota Press, 2006), 133–66.

17 Jonathan Burt shares an anecdote that, while pertaining to a different branch of the entertainment industry than wildlife documentaries, highlights the considerable appeal that moving images of animals in general hold for people. When one television producer was asked why he had decided to include a dog in his show, he reportedly responded, "A dog is worth two points in prime time. One point is about 850,000 [television] sets. You do the math." Quoted in Burt, *Animals in Film*, 11.

18 See Erica Fudge, *Animal*, Focus on Contemporary Issues Series (London: Reaktion Books, 2002), 26.

19 Burt, *Animals in Film*, 11–12.

20 *White Wilderness*, directed by James Algar, True-Life Adventures Series (Burbank, CA: Walt Disney Productions, 1958).

21 See Mitman, *Reel Nature*, 170–71.

22 *Winged Migration*, directed by Jacques Perrin, Jacques Cluzaud, and Michel Debats (Paris: BAC Films, 2001).

23 In the preface to his *Wildlife Films* (Philadelphia: University of Pennsylvania Press, 2000), xi–xii, Derek Bousé lists many of these sources dating back to the origins of the genre around one hundred years ago.

24 The companion volume to the documentary mentions one extreme case in which a filmmaker waited four months to shoot an albatross display that took up just two and a half minutes of film. All in all, Jacques Perrin and his colleagues only used 0.5 percent of the *three hundred miles* of footage they had shot around the world over the course of several years, compared to an estimated two to four percent for conventional wildlife films and ten to twenty percent for fiction films. Jacques Perrin and Jean-François Mongibeaux, *Winged Migration*, trans. David Wharry (San Francisco: Éditions du Seuil/Chronicle Books, 2001), 228, 247–48.

25 See Perrin and Mongibeaux, *Winged Migration*, 226–54.

26 Jean-Michel Rivaud, one of the pilots involved in the *Winged Migration* project, notes that "in the air, [the birds] really consider you're one of them. And we sometimes took ourselves for birds." Perrin and Mongibeaux, *Winged Migration*, 240. Unfortunately, it would require another entire essay to address some of the thorny ethical issues associated with the making of *Winged Migration*. Derek Bousé, Gregg Mitman, and Cynthia Chris all deal with the use of trained animals in wildlife documentaries, such as Marty Stouffer's popular *Wild America* series on the US Public Broadcasting Service network. On the 1996 controversy surrounding Stouffer's work with animals, see especially Bousé, *Wildlife Films*, 84–87; Mitman, *Reel Nature*, 203–8; and Chris, *Watching Wildlife*, 107–8.

27 *The Fifth Estate*'s two "Cruel Camera" documentaries, aired by the Canadian Broadcasting Corporation in 1982 and 2008, profile this example of fakery, the polar bear scene described above, and many other forms of filmmaking duplicity and cruelty in Hollywood films as well as nature documentaries.

28 This dynamic was complicated, but not contradicted, by the fact that the pelican team was motivated by another strong desire: to contribute to the success of the film by helping their birds recover as soon as possible so that they could adhere to their shooting schedule and stay within their budget. See Perrin and Mongibeaux, *Winged Migration*, 230, 250.

29 Mary Midgley, *Animals and Why They Matter: A Journey Around the Species Barrier* (Harmondsworth, UK: Penguin, 1983), 115. Jean-Michel Rivaud shares a wonderfully matter-of-fact anecdote about how the birds expressed their "basic everyday feelings" in a way that resulted in genuine cross-species dialogue. Once, he notes, "a goose really did speak to me during a flight"; pulling ahead of the other birds, it "squawked at us as if to tell us to slow down, then fell back to its place in the formation again." Had Rivaud dismissed his interpretation of the goose's squawking as nothing more than anthropomorphic projection, he would have failed to come to an important conclusion: "I realized that, in fact, I was going too fast." Perrin and Mongibeaux, *Winged Migration*, 240.

30 *Being Caribou*, directed by Leanne Allison and Diana Wilson (Montreal: National Film Board of Canada, 2004).

31 Karsten Heuer, *Being Caribou: Five Months on Foot with an Arctic Herd* (Minneapolis: Milkweed Editions, 2008), 167.

32 Heuer, *Being Caribou*, 147.

33 Heuer, *Being Caribou*, 196.

34 Pamela Banting kindly shared with me the pre-publication manuscript of her 2010 essay "The Ontology and Epistemology of Walking: Animality in Karsten Heuer's *Being Caribou: Five Months on Foot with an Arctic Herd*"; this observation is based on Banting's argument.

35 Berger's thoughts on "technical clairvoyance" contributed to my original definition of "ecopornography": "Technically the devices used to obtain ever more arresting images—hidden cameras, telescopic lenses, flashlights, remote controls and so on—combine to produce pictures which carry with them numerous indications of their normal *invisibility*. The images exist thanks only to the existence of a technical clairvoyance." "Why Look at Animals?" 14.

36 Barbara Smuts, afterword in J.M. Coetzee, *The Lives of Animals* (Princeton, NJ: Princeton University Press, 1999), 109. In her afterword, psychologist and anthropologist Barbara Smuts

writes that in studying apes and dolphins in the wild, she was "lucky to be accepted by the animals as a mildly interesting, harmless companion, permitted to travel amongst them, eligible to be touched by hands and fins, although I refrained, most of the time, from touching in turn" (109). The animals' acceptance was predicated on her willingness to stop pretending to be a neutral observer and, instead, like Heuer and Allison, to acknowledge her position as a social subject among social subjects.

37 The two Bushes are shown in archival news conference clips at the beginning of the film. In the first clip, George H.W. Bush reacts angrily to news that drilling plans in ANWR had been stymied with the words, "Unfortunately today, the 'extremes' blocked a bipartisan energy bill because they're worrying about the caribou in Alaska when I'm worrying about jobs for the American people! I'll go with the people; let them go with the caribou!" The clip of George W. Bush shows him humorously challenging reporters to travel to ANWR to see it for themselves, implying that if they were to do so, they would realize how undeserving it was of federal protection. By using the clips, Allison frames her trek with Heuer as an ironic way of accepting these two unintentional invitations to "go with the caribou." On their long walk they see what the Bushes have obviously failed to consider: that the Arctic is full of life, including many species besides caribou. (The main caribou narrative in the film is punctuated with many short, non-narrated close-up shots of flowers, insects, birds, ground squirrels, wolverines, and other life forms.)

38 See Smuts's afterword to *The Lives of Animals*, 110.

39 Heuer, *Being Caribou*, 20.

40 Heuer, *Being Caribou*, 231.

41 Heuer, *Being Caribou*, 233.

42 Heuer, *Being Caribou*, 232.

43 Greg Garrard, *Ecocriticism*, rev. ed., New Critical Idiom Series (London: Routledge, 2012), 5.

44 My thinking on wildlife filmmaking as "an extension of other practices of human-animal relations which impact on filmmaking at every level" has been greatly influenced by Jonathan Burt, who argues persuasively that "the variety of animal films, and the variety of roles that animals play in films generally, express the multifaceted nature of human–animal relations, which in themselves are not necessarily systematic." Burt, *Animals in Film*, 88–90.

45 Cary Wolfe edits the Posthumanities book series published by University of Minnesota Press. For a whirlwind tour of the brief but vibrant history of animal studies in the humanities, along with a useful overview of some of the problems confronting scholars interested in promoting the post-humanities, see Wolfe's essay "Human, All Too Human: 'Animal Studies' and the Humanities," *PMLA* 124, no. 2 (March 2009): 564–75.

46 Adrian Ivakhiv, "Green Film Criticism and Its Futures," *Interdisciplinary Studies in Literature and Environment* 15, no. 2 (Summer 2008): 18.

47 Heuer, *Being Caribou*, 232.

48 Ivakhiv, "Green Film Criticism," 13.

49 Robert Kern, "Ecocriticism: What Is It Good For?" in *The ISLE Reader: Ecocriticism, 1993–2003*, ed. Michael P. Branch and Scott Slovic (Athens: University of Georgia Press, 2003), 260.

50 On animal stereotypes, see Jonathan Balcombe, *Pleasurable Kingdom: Animals and the Nature of Feeling Good* (London: Macmillan, 2006), 38–39.

51 Here I have in mind Karen Barad's book *Meeting the Universe Halfway: Quantum Physics and the Entanglement of Matter and Meaning* (Durham, NC: Duke University Press, 2007).

52 Mitman, *Reel Nature*, 60. In thinking about the cross-fertilization possible between scientific and other forms of knowledge, I have been inspired by the example set by Donna Haraway in

books like *When Species Meet*, Posthumanities Series (Minneapolis: University of Minnesota Press, 2008).

53 Ivakhiv, "Green Film Criticism," 13. For a highly readable introduction to the field of anthrozoology, see Hal Herzog, *Some We Love, Some We Hate, Some We Eat: Why It's So Hard to Think Straight about Animals* (New York: HarperCollins, 2010).

54 Sarita Siegel provides a thoughtful early example of what these kinds of studies might look like in her account of "the role anthropomorphism plays in the filmmaker's craft" from an insider's perspective, as the director of a documentary about orangutans on Borneo. See Siegel, "Reflections on Anthropomorphism in *The Disenchanted Forest*," in *Thinking with Animals: New Perspectives on Anthropomorphism*, ed. Lorraine Daston and Gregg Mitman (New York: Columbia University Press, 2005), 196–222.

55 Ivakhiv, "Green Film Criticism," 19.

56 See Ivakhiv, "Green Film Criticism," 18–23.

57 Mitman, *Reel Nature*, 197.

58 This point was informed by Donna Haraway's chapter "Crittercam: Compounding Eyes in Naturecultures," in *When Species Meet*, 249–63.

59 I owe the idea of using fMRI scans in this way to Alexa Weik von Mossner, who has started carrying out path-breaking interdisciplinary work on environmental perception with psychologists and other scientists using this new technology, and who provided me with something of a crash course on cognitive approaches to literature and film in the months leading up to the workshop that she and Arielle Helmick organized at the Rachel Carson Center.

60 W.J.T. Mitchell, *What Do Pictures Want? The Lives and Loves of Images* (Chicago: University of Chicago Press, 2005), 54.

61 See Brian Boyd, *On the Origin of Stories: Evolution, Cognition, and Fiction* (Cambridge, MA: Belknap Press of Harvard University Press, 2009), 39.

62 Levertov, "Come into Animal Presence," *Poetry*, April 1960, http://www.poetryfoundation .org/poetrymagazine/poem/17534#poem. I will have to defer the task of clarifying the connections and disparities between *live* animal presence and *filmed* animal presence to future essays. See Anat Pick's recent study *Creaturely Poetics: Animality and Vulnerability in Literature and Film* (New York: Columbia University Press, 2011) on film as a "zoomorphic stage that transforms all living beings—including humans—into creatures" through its inherent "immediacy and materiality," qualities that contribute to the "absorption of the human figure within the leveled plain of the photographed world." The book also features a perceptive discussion of John Berger's "thesis of disappearance and loss" and Jonathan Burt's response to it, among many other things. Pick, *Creaturely Poetics*, 105–6.

63 On Polly Toynbee's argument that the modern fascination with wildlife films constitutes a "sick obsession," see Burt, *Animals in Film*, 25. This sentence encapsulates the progression in my own thinking about wildlife films that occurred between writing "Ecoporn" and publishing "Critical Anthropomorphism in the 'Age of Biocybernetic Reproduction'" a few years later.

64 Sean Cubitt, *EcoMedia*, Contemporary Cinema Series (Amsterdam: Rodopi, 2005), 59.

65 I would like to express my gratitude to the Rachel Carson Center for Environment and Society for sponsoring the workshop where the first version of this essay was delivered, and to the German government for funding such an amazing institution! The Center's Arielle Helmick was instrumental in getting me to Munich and arranging for a truly wonderful experience there, and Alexa Weik von Mossner went out of her way both to help me feel at home and to provide all of the workshop participants with a friendly, challenging, invigorating, and incredibly instructive opportunity to collaborate on the essays gathered in this volume.

BIBLIOGRAPHY

Balcombe, Jonathan. *Pleasurable Kingdom: Animals and the Nature of Feeling Good.* London: Macmillan, 2006.

Banting, Pamela. "The Ontology and Epistemology of Walking: Animality in Karsten Heuer's *Being Caribou: Five Months on Foot with an Arctic Herd.*" Unpublished manuscript, 2010.

Barad, Karen. *Meeting the Universe Halfway: Quantum Physics and the Entanglement of Matter and Meaning.* Durham, NC: Duke University Press, 2007.

Being Caribou. Directed by Leanne Allison and Diana Wilson. Montreal: National Film Board of Canada, 2004. DVD.

Bekoff, Marc. *Minding Animals: Awareness, Emotions, and Heart.* New York: Oxford University Press, 2002.

Berger, John. "Why Look at Animals?" In *About Looking,* 3–28. New York: Pantheon, 1980.

Bousé, Derek. *Wildlife Films.* Philadelphia: University of Pennsylvania Press, 2000.

Boyd, Brian. *On the Origin of Stories: Evolution, Cognition, and Fiction.* Cambridge, MA: Belknap Press of Harvard University Press, 2009.

Burt, Jonathan. *Animals in Film.* Locations Series. London: Reaktion Books, 2002.

Chris, Cynthia. *Watching Wildlife.* Minneapolis: University of Minnesota Press, 2006.

"Cruel Camera." *The Fifth Estate,* Canadian Broadcasting Corporation, May 1982 and January 2008.

Cubitt, Sean. *EcoMedia.* Contemporary Cinema Series. Amsterdam: Rodopi, 2005.

Fudge, Erica. *Animal.* Focus on Contemporary Issues Series. London: Reaktion Books, 2002.

Garrard, Greg. *Ecocriticism.* Rev. ed. New Critical Idiom Series. London: Routledge, 2012.

Grizzly Man. Directed by Werner Herzog. Santa Monica, CA: Lions Gate Films, 2005.

Grodal, Torben. *Embodied Visions: Evolution, Emotion, Culture, and Film.* Oxford: Oxford University Press, 2009.

Haraway, Donna. *When Species Meet.* Posthumanities Series. Minneapolis: University of Minnesota Press, 2008.

Herzog, Hal. *Some We Love, Some We Hate, Some We Eat: Why It's So Hard to Think Straight about Animals.* New York: HarperCollins, 2010.

Heuer, Karsten. *Being Caribou: Five Months on Foot with an Arctic Herd.* Minneapolis: Milkweed Editions, 2008.

Ivakhiv, Adrian. "Green Film Criticism and Its Futures." *Interdisciplinary Studies in Literature and Environment* 15, no. 2 (Summer 2008): 1–28.

Kern, Robert. "Ecocriticism: What Is It Good For?" In *The ISLE Reader: Ecocriticism, 1993–2003,* edited by Michael P. Branch and Scott Slovic, 258–81. Athens: University of Georgia Press, 2003.

Levertov, Denise. "Come into Animal Presence." *Poetry,* April 1960. http://www.poetry foundation.org/poetrymagazine/poem/17534#poem.

Lockwood, Randall. "Anthropomorphism Is Not a Four-Letter Word." In *Perceptions of Animals in American Culture,* edited by R.J. Hoage, 41–56. National Zoological

Park Symposia for the Public Series. Washington, DC: Smithsonian Institution Press, 1989.

Merola, Nicole. "Monkeys, Apes, and Bears, Oh My!: Illuminating the Politics of Human–Animal Relationship in Jill Greenberg's *Monkey Portraits* and *Bear Portraits*." *JAC* 30, nos. 3–4 (Fall 2010): 645–81.

Midgley, Mary. *Animals and Why They Matter: A Journey Around the Species Barrier*. Harmondsworth, UK: Penguin, 1983.

Mitchell, W.J.T. *What Do Pictures Want? The Lives and Loves of Images*. Chicago: University of Chicago Press, 2005.

Mitman, Gregg. *Reel Nature: America's Romance with Wildlife on Film*. Cambridge, MA: Harvard University Press, 1999.

Perrin, Jacques, and Jean-François Mongibeaux. *Winged Migration*. Translated by David Wharry. San Francisco: Éditions du Seuil/Chronicle Books, 2001.

Pick, Anat. *Creaturely Poetics: Animality and Vulnerability in Literature and Film*. New York: Columbia University Press, 2011.

Rivas, Jesús, and Gordon M. Burghardt. "Crotalomorphism: A Metaphor for Understanding Anthropomorphism by Omission." In *The Cognitive Animal: Empirical and Theoretical Perspectives on Animal Cognition*, edited by Marc Bekoff, Colin Allen, and Gordon M. Burghardt, 9–18. Cambridge: Massachusetts Institute of Technology Press, 2002.

Siegel, Sarita. "Reflections on Anthropomorphism in *The Disenchanted Forest*." In *Thinking with Animals: New Perspectives on Anthropomorphism*, edited by Lorraine Daston and Gregg Mitman, 196–222. New York: Columbia University Press, 2005.

Smuts, Barbara. Afterword in *The Lives of Animals*, by J.M. Coetzee, 107–20. University Center for Human Values Series. Princeton, NJ: Princeton University Press, 1999.

Welling, Bart H. "Critical Anthropomorphism in the 'Age of Biocybernetic Reproduction': A Response to Nicole Merola's 'Monkeys, Apes, and Bears, Oh My!'" *JAC* 31, nos. 3–4 (Fall 2011): 660–85.

———. "Ecoporn: On the Limits of Visualizing the Nonhuman." In *Ecosee: Image, Rhetoric, Nature*, edited by Sidney I. Dobrin and Sean Morey, 53–77. Albany: State University of New York Press, 2009.

White Wilderness. Directed by James Algar. True-Life Adventures Series. Burbank, CA: Walt Disney Productions, 1958.

Winged Migration. Directed by Jacques Perrin, Jacques Cluzaud, and Michel Debats. Paris: BAC Films, 2001.

Wolfe, Cary. "Human, All Too Human: 'Animal Studies' and the Humanities." *PMLA* 124, no. 2 (March 2009): 564–75.

5

Emotion, Argumentation, and Documentary Traditions
Darwin's Nightmare *and* The Cove

Belinda Smaill

Media attention to the acceleration and consequences of environmental degradation has been increasing over the past two decades. However, the influence of environmentally focused documentary was cemented with the success of *An Inconvenient Truth* in 2006.[1] The cluster of films concerned with environmental advocacy has grown exponentially since this time. Often referred to as "eco-documentaries" in the popular press, this category includes examples exploring a broad range of issues such as food industries, climate change and habitat endangerment, water supply and allocation, sea level rise, diminishing fish stocks, and the oil industry.[2] These films consistently investigate and publicize the corporate control of natural resources and the impact of industry practices on the environment and/or wildlife and, at times, on the consumer. This cluster of documentaries has emerged in tandem with the resurgent popularity of feature-length documentary and the growing mainstream interest in environmental issues.[3]

At first glance, this cluster, with its strong focus on critiquing commercial interests and government inaction, shares much with films that are couched in traditions of radical leftist documentary filmmaking. For Jane Gaines, mimetic technologies, such as documentary, "have the power to explosively reproduce, to reproduce the world before us as well as to reproduce its intensities onscreen, and to reproduce them most strategically in the bodies and hearts and minds of viewers."[4] It is this aim to politicize, in an "explosive" manner, that motivates a history of political filmmaking. Documentary is unique within this history due to its capacity to provoke a felt sense of continuity between the world of the viewer and the world of the film, or a "same world sensation."[5] In this film historical tradition, filmmakers frequently take up a position within a social movement, explicitly locating themselves on one side of the political divide, eschewing the notion of the distanced observer. In her description of those reporting on the labour strikes in the 1930s in the USA, Paula Rabinowitz argues that those who take up the tools of representation necessarily also must forge an allegiance to either side of the battlelines. She aptly describes this as a "sentimental contract": "an either-or situation demands that both reporter and reader must choose sides within a dichotomous class structure. In repor-tage, documenters serve not only to witness but to intervene."[6] This mode of filmmaking, one that seeks to participate in social and political transformation, is also one that endeavours to rally and construct a public—a constituency that, however contingently, recognises a need for change. For Helen Hughes, an important aim of the eco-doc is "to visualize the environment as a shared physical and imaginary space ... in ways that promote the popularity of activ-ism and environmental justice."[7] The eco-doc can be contextualised within a history of documentary filmmaking while also offering its own specific mode of address to the viewer.

This chapter focuses on two documentaries, *Darwin's Nightmare* (2004) directed by Austrian filmmaker Hupert Sauper, and *The Cove* (2009), an American production directed by Louis Psihoyos.[8] *Darwin's Nightmare* and *The Cove* offer two distinctly different ways of taking up Rabinowitz's pos-itionality. Each functions in different ways to advocate for environmental or ecological politics. Yet they also have much in common. Both concentrate on a specific geographical location and explore the socio-cultural, industrial, and environmental issues emerging from the harvesting of a particular marine spe-cies. Both engage the viewer in an unfolding narrative that centres the spectacle of non-human life (the fish and the dolphin) within a delineated geo-cultural location. My interest in these two very visible examples[9] within this grouping of documentary revolves around how they work at the intersection of para-digms of radical filmmaking and environmental advocacy.

Significantly, both Gaines and Rabinowitz frame their analysis with a nod to the importance of emotion in the work of political documentary. Emotion is inevitably bound up with the motion of political change and underpins the way documentary appeals to and engages with audiences, whether the emotions are hope, pleasure, outrage, or dismay.[10] For this reason, I explore how non-human life, the fish in *Darwin's Nightmare* and the dolphin in *The Cove*, is posed within this emotional address, or sentimental contract. I analyze how it is produced within the rhetorical argument, formally and narratively. In both cases the image of the non-human is central to the formulation of an emotional political address to viewer. The second feature of these films that I discuss is the issue of looking across cultures in the context of production and reception. In both *Darwin's Nightmare* and *The Cove*, non-Western modernity is perceived as the location of a particular ecological and social problem. I investigate how the desire for knowledge, for a mastery of the world, that documentary so powerfully facilitates might be enabled in the documentaries in terms of this problem. I question how the desire to attribute a rationale for the problem lends itself to narratives that unfold in familiar, and at times ethnocentric, ways.

THE COVE AND DARWIN'S NIGHTMARE: THE NON-HUMAN, EMOTION, AND DOCUMENTARY RHETORIC

Since John Berger's observations in "Why Look at Animals?" (1980), much work has been done on understanding the importance of the image of animals in visual culture.[11] In this section I look at how aspects of the two documentaries weave together histories of signification and already familiar ideological formations, including discourses pertaining to food, fish, and humanness. The representation of animals in documentary is bound to other elements that constitute the rhetorical and generic framework of the text, such as voice-over, interviews, and editing. Through the mechanics of argument and aesthetics, the films work to institute particular modes of identification with social actors and with the non-human animals. The notion of identification I draw on here is one specifically facilitated by documentary. As Elizabeth Cowie describes, "documentary informs us of the world, offering us identities in the images and stories of other lives that it presents that become fixed as known and knowable through its account and explanation of the world it shows."[12] Identification in this respect is both rational, requiring knowledge, and emotional, requiring an engagement involving a degree of emotion on the part of the viewer.

The Cove focuses on Taiji, a small fishing town in southern Japan where, between September and March, dolphins are rounded up and harvested for sale as live specimens and for processing as meat. This practice had not been widely publicized and the documentary narrative is posed from the perspective of a handful of activists whose aim it is to reveal the extent of this killing. The most vocal and committed activist is Ric O'Barry and the film tells the story of O'Barry's transformation from the dolphin trainer for the television series *Flipper* in the 1960s to marine advocate in the present day. The film explicitly seeks to alert viewers to not only the killing of large numbers of dolphins in Taiji, but also the negative effects of keeping dolphins in captivity and the Japanese government's role in facilitating the destruction of the animal. Central to the film is the expedition, undertaken by the small group of activists, including the director, Louis Psihoyos, to covertly gather evidence of the practices of Taiji fishermen.

The film opens with images of slaughtered dolphins being processed at night. These activities are shot with a military-grade thermal imaging camera the activists succeeded in smuggling into the country. The scenes are black and white, much like a photographic negative. This imagery is repeated in two scenes when the group, described at one point in the film as an *Ocean's Eleven*–style ensemble, undertakes to clandestinely film in the cove one night. Their aim is to not only capture the slaughter on film but as Psihoyos states to the camera, "to do something that will make people change." The mission is presented with the immediacy and exhilaration of a Hollywood thriller narrative as the group works to evade the fishermen who have previously responded with hostility to their endeavour.

Alongside this mission to uncover and reveal the activities in Taiji, *The Cove* makes a strong case for the exceptionalism of dolphins. At points in the film they are grouped with other cetaceans, such as whales, but the focus overall is on the special status of dolphins. The discussion of the abilities of dolphins is conveyed through a collage of images and interviews with activists. This collage presents anecdotes of dolphins swimming playfully with divers and surfers and the capacities of dolphin sonar and consciousness. After one nighttime excursion to the cove, one of the divers participating in the covert mission states: "The most horrifying thing about the whole dive that night was that you could hear them communicating and you knew that the next morning that would be the end of it. There would be silence forever." Soon after this O'Barry states in voice-over: "It's not about intelligence. It's about consciousness. They are self-aware like humans are self-aware. That means we look in the mirror and we know exactly what we're looking at. I don't believe that the fishermen here are aware of that." The images in this sequence are taken from stock footage and show dolphins underwater, playfully responding to the camera or to their own image in an underwater mirror. These visuals sit alongside many other montages of stock footage drawn from nature documentaries, aquatic theme parks, and the *Flipper* series. The argument for dolphin exceptionalism is then juxtaposed with the routine destruction of the dolphins in the cove, which comes to be framed as almost homicidal, approaching the horror of human murders.

The visual and auditory evidence of the activities in the cove is central to the documentary. The revelation of these images offers a climax for the group's clandestine activities. In the footage shown near the end of the film the water of the cove is stained red from the blood of the dolphins as they are killed with spears and hauled into boats. This imagery seems to be some of the little primary footage shot by the filmmakers (as opposed to sourced from elsewhere) that depicts dolphins in the film.

If a central aim of the documentary is to pose the dolphin as a subjective being and establish a form of dolphin consciousness, the argument verbalized by the activists is the primary platform for this. The slaughter of the dolphins is a spectacle, and alone, would do more to discourage identification with the dolphin. Yet it works in tandem with the anecdotal evidence in the voice-overs, as I have said, to present as a massacre of exceptional creatures. In an earlier scene activists watch from the beach as a young dolphin trailing blood, makes its way to the beach before disappearing under the water. A review in *Time Magazine* seems to be describing this moment when stating: "This is like seeing baby seals clubbed to death, except that as adorable as baby seals are, no one has yet made a case for their being potentially smarter than humans, which is exactly what *The Cove* does for dolphins. To watch bleeding dolphins struggle for their last breath, to actually hear their agony, is devastating."[13] The documentary seeks a recognition in the viewer of the consciousness of the dolphin who is herded into the cove—that they understand the horror they are about to confront.[14]

Significantly, *The Cove* encourages an emotional response to not only the dolphin slaughter, but also the practice of consuming dolphin meat. As the documentary acknowledges, very few Japanese people actually eat dolphin meat. Yet sequences show dolphin meat packaged and on supermarket shelves labelled as whale meat and children eating from lunch boxes (with the inference that they are some of those who were required to consume dolphin as part of the Taiji school lunch program). As Emma Roe notes, food comes to be considered edible through a particular and normalizing set of "intimate biomaterial connections between bodies that eat and bodies that are eaten."[15] Another effect of emphasizing dolphin exceptionalism is that the cetacean appears as "too sentient" to be food; the requisite normalizing process is disrupted. The intimate material relation between humans and dolphins in the documentary is not one that facilitates consumption—it is one that fosters an affective or bodily recognition that dolphins are inedible just as humans are inedible. The dolphin meat becomes even less viable as food when it is reported that there are high levels of mercury in the Taiji area that have contaminated the marine life. *The Cove* seeks identification with a world in which dolphins are first and foremost sentient beings, aware of their relations with each other and with humans. It is a subjective being that is too close to human to be food and is, similarly, too human (and extraordinary) to be killed or harvested in the way that other animals or fish regularly are.

However, *The Cove* does not simply present the dolphin as an object of emotional identification. The recognition of the dolphin's exceptionalism sits alongside the intense identification that the film seeks with the activists and with O'Barry in particular. These are the speaking subjects of the documentary, asking the viewer to see as they see and feel as they feel. Alignment with and immersion in the momentum of the activist movement is a key strategy of *The Cove* and of documentary that seeks social change more broadly. The persuasiveness of the documentary owes much to the onscreen presence of the filmmaker activist and his compatriots. Writing almost thirty years ago, Thomas Waugh described an influential paradigm for radical, "committed" documentary that draws not on the social impact of documentaries (or the change in consciousness in the audience), but rather on the trace of desire that motivates the production of the film. Filmmakers produce radicalizing documentaries when they "work *within* actively ongoing political struggles; by making films not only about people engaged in these struggles but also *with* and *by* them as well."[16] Committed documentary makes explicit its production within or alongside organized social movements. Working towards a more proximate relationship between the filmed and the filmmaker, these works emphasize solidarity. This exemplifies Rabinowitz's notion of the sentimental contract. *The Cove*, asks the viewer to join in solidarity with the interviewees/activists onscreen, to share in the empathy and passion they exude. These individuals provide another avenue through which to "read" the dolphins. In this case it is via the emotional momentum of human endeavour, as the object of activism.

Darwin's Nightmare again positions a marine species at the centre of the narrative. Although the fish, the Nile perch, is ostensibly the focus of the film, it soon becomes clear that the fish is made to objectify a complex network of human interaction and exploitation. This documentary, like *The Cove*, presents a delineated geo-cultural location (the community of Mwanza on the shores of Lake Victoria in Tanzania) and explores the social and environmental situation that has emerged in the wake of the introduction of the Nile perch into the lake. An industry has developed around exporting large numbers of this now plentiful fish to Europe and the film gradually exposes the negative consequences of this industrialization. *Darwin's Nightmare* formulates a more layered emotional address to the audience than *The Cove*. The fish takes on a malevolent quality in this documentary, negating any possibility of empathy. The spectacle of the Nile perch poses a materiality that deems it, again, inedible but in this case the fish is an object of disgust. Moreover, the unfolding horror of the situation in this community is transposed onto the image of the corpse of the fish in its many manifestations. In this sense, the fish is an emotional object that is consistently framed as abject, thus again disturbing the viewer's expectations of the representation of fish and food.

The film is made up of observational footage and numerous interviews with various personalities in the communities and industries around the lake such as factory workers and fishermen, homeless children, sex workers, and the Russian pilots who fly the fish to Europe. The picture presented is one of emerging catastrophe. The situation is exposed to the viewer through a gradual unfolding of information offered by these different informants, often at the off-screen prompting of the filmmaker. Interviews consistently feature questions about the cargo the Russian planes bring into Tanzania. Eventually it becomes apparent that that the planes are full of illegal arms and munitions that fuel the wars in Africa. The sex workers who are employed by the Russian pilots flying these planes are interviewed and in the course of filming one of them, Eliza, is murdered by a client. AIDS is widespread in the itinerant communities of fishermen on the shores of the lake. The homeless children of families, either impoverished or destroyed by AIDS, battle over scraps of food and get high from the fumes of melting plastic containers used to package the fish. While the fish is at the heart of this decline, the industry it has produced is also a source of survival for many. The fish is variously cast in a number of roles—it is a predator that has destroyed the ancient ecosystem, a catalyst for industrial growth *and* social decline while, of course, providing food for locals as well as for export.

Significantly, while *Darwin's Nightmare* does not offer images of the causalities in the Congo or Angola,[17] the violence inflicted on the street kids, or the physical effects of the AIDS epidemic, the film does offer sublime imagery of the body (the corpse) of the fish. Early in the documentary we are shown the factory in which the fish is processed. Rather than depicting the fillets neatly prepared for packaging as we see in *The Cove*, the camera concentrates on the leftover waste of bones, heads, and innards as they are swept into bins from a conveyor belt. At a later point in the film we are informed that displaced farmers in surrounding communities buy this waste at low cost. Images show fish parts offloaded by trucks and eventually hung and dried on open-air racks infested with maggots and scavenging birds. Later fish heads will be fried and sold by vendors to the locals. The omnipresent spectacle of the huge fish carcass dominates the second half of film and comes to provide a visual metaphor for the violence and decay verbalized in the interviews.[18]

The power of this visual metaphor can be found in the way that the Nile perch is framed as an object of disgust. Sara Ahmed writes, "while disgust *over takes* the body, it also *takes over* the object that apparently gives rise to it."[19] When it generates disgust in the viewer, an object becomes wholly disgusting. As a foodstuff, the fish meat is meant to be eaten. There is an intercorporeal dimension to this as the fish becomes integrated into the human body after it is eaten. However, when it generates disgust, the recognition of this potential intercorporeality then leads to rejection of the object. As Deborah Lupton observes, "meat is linked to violence, aggression, the spilling of blood, pain; it constantly trembles on the border between self/other and purity/contamination. Because it is the product of the death of animals, meat is also more strongly linked than any other food to rottenness and pollution."[20] *Darwin's Nightmare* exploits these associations between pollution and flesh to accentuate a contaminating quality in the images of the fish meat and to reject (along with a rejection of the disgust object) the slim benefits of the introduction of the fish. The decline in the film, as the title suggests, registers for the audience a backward social and non-human evolution in which decay is foregrounded. Here it is Tanzanians, rather than dolphins, who are the victims (and speaking subjects) and who must not only subsist in the shadow of the fish industry but also consume the fish "waste."[21] The perpetrators are less clearly rendered when compared to *The Cove* and are symbolically posed, as I discuss in the next section, through the terms of capitalism and globalization.

Unlike *The Cove*, *Darwin's Nightmare* does not pose the filmmaker, or even the stories represented, as part of an explicit movement for social change. Yet it clearly invites the viewer to recognize a social problem that is the outcome of political and commercial forces. If it is not a "committed documentary" in Waugh's sense, *Darwin's Nightmare* is certainly not a "public education" film in the Greirsonian sense. Instead, it emphasizes techniques of direct or observational cinema within its mosaic of styles. Barry Keith Grant describes observational filmmaker Frederick Wiseman's approach in his first film, *Titicut Follies* (1967), as "that of detached observer. Yet the film is also carefully structured to advance its maker's personal sense of moral outrage."[22] As Grant observes, Wiseman avoids didacticism while constructing argument through the careful use of editing that serves to produce irony, inversion, evidence, and summation. While not usually considered part of the canon of political filmmaking, Wiseman's work nevertheless appeals to the viewer to engage with the logic of a defined political perspective. Similarly, *Darwin's Nightmare*, rather than explicitly offering argumentative instruction, is *aligned* with an implicit argumentative, subjective position. The filmmaker may not be as unequivocally driving onscreen events as in *The Cove*, but nor is he a distanced, disinterested observer. The rhetorical impetus of the documentary unfolds in ways that structure a compelling argument. The implications of the introduction of the Nile perch are made known through the many interviews in the film, and through the use of irony and juxtaposition, but it is also *felt* through the imagery of the fish and its polluting malevolence. This spectacle addresses the audience and infers a negative presence and teleology. The "same world sensation"[23] the film invites is centred on this intersection of visual visceral knowledge and knowledge of the social impact and repercussions of the introduction of the fish.

As I have noted, these films contribute to a recent cluster of documentary filmmaking. They present themes related to questions of food, humanness, and the relation between the social and the non-human. Aiming to rally a constituency of viewers, these documentary arguments channel familiar traditions in the documentary endeavour in order to address new questions in relation to environmentalism and ecology. The turn to subjectivity in documentary by the 1990s that Michael Renov describes as "a kind of experiential compass guiding the work toward its goal as embodied knowledge"[24] is evident in the highly authored observational slant of *Darwin's Nightmare* and in *The Cove's* emphasis on the actions and passion of the activists. Both films, albeit in different ways, engage the sentimental contract invoked by Rabinowitz. Further, the non-human animal is the object of struggle and persuasion that is also made available to the audience in recognizable ways, primarily through identification with the perspective of the filmmaker-subject.

DOCUMENTARY DESIRE

Just as they share a subjective argumentative structure, the two documentaries in question also concentrate their cameras on non-Western cultures, producing images from an authorial perspective that looks across cultural borders and largely addresses audiences in the Euro-American world. This is not unusual for eco-documentaries, which frequently take up globalizing concerns—they traverse continents to follow environmental issues and questions of food production. However, in both *Darwin's Nightmare* and *The Cove*, non-Western modernity is perceived as the location of a particular problem, whether it is the cultural and nationalistic traditions that perpetuate the slaughter of dolphins or the social impact of the Nile perch that is devastating the community around the lake.

The Cove is an American production directed by Louis Psihoyos and produced by the Oceanic Preservation Society based in Colorado. *Darwin's*

Nightmare is directed by an Austrian, Hupert Sauper, and is a French/Belgian/Austrian co-production. Both films are the work of North American or European filmmakers and have been marketed and distributed largely with European and anglophone audiences in mind. *Darwin's Nightmare* achieved two-thirds of its box office takings in Europe (predominantly in France) and in the former French colonies in North Africa, while *The Cove* found its primary audience in the USA. There are longstanding ethnographic traditions that haunt interpretations of images of Western filmmakers travelling to locations such as Japan and Africa. These representations frequently codify subjects so that, as Bill Nichols points out: "they occupy a time and a space which 'we' must recreate, stage, or represent."[25] The two documentaries under consideration depart from this tradition while nevertheless inviting spectatorial desire for particular images and narratives about these sites of "otherness."

Over the decades that cinema studies have been borrowing from the methods of psychoanalysis, discussions of desire and pleasure have been almost taken for granted in the discipline's study of fiction film and securely tied to the unconscious in spectatorship theory. I wish to denaturalize these associations and build on approaches that incorporate desire into an analysis of emotion and documentary. The notion of documentary "epistephilia," a desire for and pleasure in knowledge, is well established in Nichols's work. This is a distinctive form of social engagement that is engendered by documentary, a genre that is associated with a privileged access to the texture and complexity of the social world. Cowie extends this by understanding the way viewers bring different expectations to texts conventionally deemed "factual" or "fictional": "the demand for the distinction these terms imply itself constitutes a *desire* for a certainty of the knowable, of the world as testable, producing a split between the two domains: one of proper, true knowledge and a second domain of improper, untrue fabrications."[26] I investigate how the desire for knowledge, for a mastery of the world that documentary so powerfully facilitates, might be enabled in these documentaries.

Important in this respect is the way epistephilia can be coupled with the notion that knowledge is ordered in particular ways that make it recognizable to a constituency of viewers—documentaries make sense of and represent the world through reference to established textual patterns. These recognizable formations frequently do the work of satisfying the desire for knowledge acquisition. In the case of *The Cove*, epistephilia revolves around the visual evidence of a problem (the dolphin slaughter) and the clear presentation of "why and how" this occurs. It seeks a rationalization of the perpetrators' motivations. In the first instance, rhetorical strategies in the film build towards a desire for what is, as I have noted, eventually captured—footage of the whole cove running red with the blood of the dolphins as they are killed. In the second instance, it is knowledge about which aspect of Japanese society, its people or its culture, is responsible for maintaining what is presented as a barbaric practice.

In her discussion of tolerance, Wendy Brown describes the manner in which no legal Western practice is ever marked as barbaric within Western (dominant) codes of representation. She notes that the effect of this "is to tar the non-West with the brush of the intolerable for harboring certain practices that are not only named barbaric, that is, uncivilized in contrast to our practices, but coerced, that is, unfree compared to our practices. The limits of tolerance are thus equated with the limits of civilization or the threat to civilization."[27] Non-Western practices Brown refers to as examples include female genital cutting, widow suttee, or polygamy. The activity of killing dolphins aligns, in many respects, with these practices. Yet, does this "unjust" practice become equated with non-Western (Japanese) society in *The Cove*, which is in turn deemed uncivilized?

Midway through the film O'Barry's voice-over notes that knowledge of the dolphin slaughter and the harvesting of dolphin meat is limited to a relatively small group of people. This is despite the claim by fishermen that consuming dolphin is a traditional practice. Showing interviews with people on Tokyo streets who claim they know nothing about the treatment of dolphins or consumption of dolphin meat, the film is at pains not to present all Japanese as involved in the dolphin harvest. The authorities in Taiji and those on the International Whaling Commission (IWC) representing Japan perpetuate and protect the Japanese right to harvest dolphins. Following a suggestion in the film that this is due to an economic concern with protecting livelihoods, a member of the IWC representing one of the small Caribbean nations bribed by Japan to support their interests offers what is posed as the singular rationale or the "why" of the narrative arc. He states that this activity continues to be supported due to the "remnants of traditional notion of empire" and a nationally felt resistance to succumbing to international will to desist eating cetaceans. Thus, the authorities' ongoing protection of the dolphin and whale meat industries and the dolphin harvest are *not* posed as the barbaric tradition of a non-Western culture, but rather the Japanese are positioned as passively standing by while those in power perpetuate this practice. O'Barry's voice-over states that Japanese culture abides by the ethos that "the nail that sticks out must be pounded down." This suggests that in Japan dissent and individual autonomy is discouraged. The projection of "uncivilized" behaviour is displaced as the film locates blame in relation to other cultural factors—mass compliance and traces of a history of imperialism. In sum, while the population is not broadly "barbaric" in Brown's sense, they are nevertheless posed as stereotypical and intolerable because Japanese culture is somehow at fault.

There are other features of *The Cove's* rhetorical arc that further support a binarization between the West and the non-West. Japanese individuals are, for the most part, represented by physically and verbally aggressive fishermen, evasive and wary officials, or self-interested representatives on the IWC. While the film is about specifically Japanese activities, it offers only a small number of Japanese individuals the status of speaking subjects. An exception is the two city councillors in Taiji who protest the use of dolphin meat in the school lunch program (on the grounds that it has high levels of mercury). The councillors speak for less than a minute, with their concerns largely stated in O'Barry's voice-over. Similarly, the documentary does not seek out interviews with or acknowledge the work of any Japanese environmental activists in Japan or elsewhere. Adding to this, the town of Taiji is cast as a place of conspiratorial malevolence. This allows for a fluid dualism in which the team of North American activists are impassioned, active, resourceful, and aligned with the best (civilized) interests of the dolphins. They are worthy, renegade outsiders in the town, encouraging a strong identification with their position as outsiders and non-Japanese. *The Cove* weaves a narrative that presents American audiences with a decisive and convincing source of advocacy. It does this through appealing to viewer desire for recognizable stories about the non-Western other. While the film attributes the slaughter and its cover up to a select group, their actions are described with reference to culture and tradition.

In the case of *Darwin's Nightmare* the desire for knowledge is again focused on exploring a problem in a non-Western culture. However, this documentary does not focus on questioning and gathering evidence about the other's actions and motivations. Instead, *Darwin's Nightmare* works to steadily build an intricate picture of what is happening in Mwanza and compels the audience to engage in a process of recognizing the relationships of cause and effect that constitute an expanded portrait of the impact of the fish. It is not clear until some way into the film what the detail of this impact is. The growing recognition encouraged by the film positions the viewing subject as, cumulatively, the subject of knowledge. For Cowie, this positioning encourages an identification with the social actors and this contributes to the pleasurable experience documentary affords.[28] In one scene a factory worker, with factory work continuing behind him and while holding a fillet of Nile perch, describes how the fish fillets are too expensive for the ordinary Tanzanian due to the costs of processing. From off-screen the filmmaker asks him about the newspaper reports concerned with the growing famine in Tanzania. The worker seems to agree that he has seen the reports but looks confused about the jump from one line of questioning to another. This is an observational moment—by the time this scene appears late in the film the viewer is easily able to make the leap that the worker, it seems, cannot.

This exploratory narrative does not pose a hierarchized dichotomy between West and non-West as in *The Cove*. Instead it presents a much broader delineation between the exploited and the exploiter and this is posed loosely as Tanzania (Africa) and Europe. The network of relations that comes to light in the film highlights the ways different groups in Mwanza participate in this system of exploitation. This network includes factory owners and workers, fishermen, the night watchman at the Fisheries Institute, the sex workers, and the Russian pilots. The pilots are, to some degree, placed outside the teleology of decline that the documentary depicts. They are upwardly mobile and seem to be obfuscating the full nature of their cargo. Yet late in the film one pilot admits, with much dismay, that he transports guns into Africa and leaves with export goods for Europe. He observes that the children of Angola receive guns for Christmas, and the children of Europe receive grapes. The pilot laments: "This is business." Many of those interviewed in the film do not present as clear victims, in part because they are also negotiating the environment in which they find themselves in order to survive and, at times, prosper.

The fact that *Darwin's Nightmare* is not simply a story of ecological catastrophe is evidenced by the scant attention given to the scene of the introduction of the fish. Primarily, the fish is a visual metaphor for decay and an object that facilitates global trade. The social relationships of cause and effect that are the focus of the film are illustrated across the body of the fish but also across the black bodies and faces of the Tanzanians who are both visual objects of difference and beauty (and at times social decline), and as interview subjects, the source of much of the information conveyed in the film.

While there is no unambiguous perpetrator in *Darwin's Nightmare* who can be clearly represented onscreen, the film circles around and infers that the source of the problem should be located in global trade and global capitalism. This documentary, with its wide array of interviews with Mwanzan locals, casts the African other as informant, contributing to the tapestry of evidence the film produces. One man, possibly a fisherman, explicitly articulates the hegemonic order at the heart of the documentary when he states that "God unfortunately created the world and he provided limited natural resources. Therefore people scramble for natural resources.... Who is to get and who is to miss.... Maybe we start viewing the Europeans as stronger than the rest. Because they are the people who own the IMF. They are the people who own the World Bank. They are the people who own the world trade." Tanzania, in this sense, is depicted as caught up in the Western hegemony of global trade. At the heart of this trade is the fish. Significantly, despite the many interrelated issues represented in *Darwin's Nightmare*, the scope of the film is relatively narrow in its focus on the Mwanza community. AIDS, environmental degradation, poverty, and homelessness are all problems facing sub-Saharan Africa more broadly and while the film does not deny that this is the case, it offers a microcosm that localizes all of these issues around the Nile perch.

The Cove's success has been achieved, in part, by elaborating a chain of cause and effect that opposes the activists' agency, integrity, and resourcefulness to the unjust (cultural) actions or passive inaction of the Japanese. In the case of *Darwin's Nightmare*, however, the problems in Mwanza that emanate from the introduction of the fish are attributed to the complex fabric of European capitalism. In this respect, while the Tanzanians participate in and perpetuate the industry that has built up around the fish, the source of this exploitation is located off-screen, a continent away. It is the piecing together of the patchwork of the multifaceted impact of the European-driven industry that addresses audience desire for mastery and knowledge.

CONCLUSION

In his discussion of documentary "politicality," John Corner offers an outline that defines the "character of documentary as a form of political discourse" and its capacity to formulate an "explicit address to questions of institutional power (both as structure and process)."[29] While *Darwin's Nightmare* and *The Cove* share many features (such as the focus on a marine life form, the setting of a delineated social geographical area) the style of their politicality and the questions they pose are markedly different. One is concerned with animal rights and the plight of the dolphin. It advocates for this animal on the grounds that it is exceptional in the non-human world. The other explores a twinned environmental/social catastrophe, offering a dystopian vision of the Mwanzan predicament, and is more concerned with the ecosystem and human rights than animal rights. However, continuing a long tradition of documentary practice, both films invite the viewer to enter into the emotional contract proposed by the argument—through the passion of and empathy for the activists and the dolphin or through the recognition of the web of social crises that accompanies the disgust and horror evoked by the fish carcass.

The Cove has been successful in its aim to publicize and change the treat-ment of dolphins in Japan.[30] In comparison, while *Darwin's Nightmare* was fol-lowed by calls for consumer boycotts,[31] it also met a storm of controversy that revolved around the truth claims of the film. Ruby B. Rich writes that Sauper

> has been both praised and reviled, the attacks carried out by proxy writers aligned with foreign-trade interests. The viciousness of the attacks was reminiscent of those on the young Michael Moore's *Roger and Me*, except that Sauper had not re-edited any footage or chronology. He had all his facts courtesy of African-based NGO sources. Most recently, the Tanza-nian government has gone after both Sauper and his subjects in Tanzania, who have been punished with firing, arrest, and threatened deportation.[32]

Published criticisms of the film were the subject of libel cases in 2008 and 2009.[33] *Darwin's Nightmare* melds observational techniques with an allegorical thematization and it is perhaps this creative treatment of actuality, to borrow Grierson's well-known phrase, that also drew accusations that the film was sensationalist and misleading. Darin Kinsey associates the film with "a new genre of sensationalist and proactive documentary films."[34] This claim lacks an appreciation of the histories of documentary referred to above by Gaines and Rabinowitz that pose a long-standing relationship between emotion (and the quest to mobilize viewer sensation) and the documentary project.

In Chapter 6 of this volume Robin Murray and Joseph Heumann suggest that the difference in advocacy outcomes between these two documentaries is due to the ontological status of the arguments presented—*The Cove* is con-cerned with animal rights while *Darwin's Nightmare* references arguments of organismic ecology. I argue that in evaluating the way these films circulate, con-sideration should also be given to the *means* by which identification is encour-aged or discouraged and the way knowledge is organized. In both instances the films have strong ties to well-established documentary codes and traditions. While they seek recognition of the immediacy of problems facing the environ-ment or the non-human world, and thus are concerned with new objects of debate and education, there is much to be gained by understanding how this emerging cluster of documentary operates within a lineage of documentary practice and critique.

NOTES

1 *An Inconvenient Truth*, directed by Davis Guggenheim (Los Angeles: Paramount Classics, 2006), DVD.

2 Titles, just to name a few, include: *Food Inc.* (2009), *Crude* (2009), *The 11th Hour* (2007), *Flow: For Love of Water* (2008), *The End of the Line* (2009), *King Corn* (2007), *Life and Debt*

(2001), *A Crude Awakening* (2006), *Frack Nation* (2013), *The Last Ocean* (2012), *Gasland* (2010), *Green* (2009), *Shark Water* (2006), *Trashed* (2012), *The Hungry Tide* (2011), *The Island President* (2011), and *Climate Refugees* (2010).

3 Helen Hughes offers some reasons for the rise of eco-docs in "Humans, Sharks and the Shared Environment in the Contemporary Eco-Doc," *Environmental Education Research* 17, no. 6 (2011): 735–49.

4 Jane Gaines, "The Production of Outrage: The Iraq War and the Radical Documentary Tradition," *Framework* 48, no. 2 (2007): 40.

5 Gaines, "The Production of Outrage," 44.

6 Paula Rabinowitz, "Sentimental Contracts: Dreams and Documents of American Labour," in *Feminism and Documentary*, ed. Janet Walker and Diane Waldman (Minneapolis: University of Minnesota Press, 1999), 43.

7 Hughes, "Humans, Sharks and the Shared Environment," 737.

8 *Darwin's Nightmare*, directed by Hubert Sauper (New York: Homevision, 2004), DVD; *The Cove*, directed by Louis Psihoyos (Santa Monica, CA: Lions Gate, 2009), DVD.

9 Notably, both of these films have enjoyed wide distribution. In terms of box office takings alone (without accounting for DVD distribution), *The Cove* has so far earned over US$1 million internationally and *Darwin's Nightmare* almost US$3 million according to Box Office Mojo (http://www.boxofficemojo.com). These are significant figures for documentary. Both have also received numerous awards, with *Darwin's Nightmare* nominated for an Oscar for Best Documentary Feature in 2006 and *The Cove* winning this award in 2010.

10 This is an argument I establish more fully elsewhere: Belinda Smaill, *The Documentary: Politics, Emotion, Culture* (Basingstoke, UK: Palgrave Macmillan, 2010).

11 John Berger's "Why Look at Animals?" is the opening chapter of his *About Looking* (New York: Pantheon, 1980). For examples of more recent scholarly work that has explored the importance of the image of animals in visual culture, see Jennifer Fay, "Seeing/Loving Animals: André Bazin's Posthumanism," *Journal of Visual Culture* 7, no. 1 (2008): 41–64; Jonathan Burt, *Animals in Film* (London: Reaktion Books, 2002); and Lorraine Daston and Gregg Mitman, eds. *Thinking with Animals* (New York: Colombia University Press, 2005).

12 Elizabeth Cowie, *Recording Reality, Desiring the Real* (Minneapolis: University of Minnesota Press, 2011), 88.

13 Mary Pols, "Rescue at Sea," *Time Magazine*, 10 August 2009, http://www.time.com/time/magazine/article/0,9171,1913757,00.html.

14 Akira Lippit observes "language brings consciousness and with it, the consciousness of consciousness and its absence, or death." He goes onto observe, "according to a logic peculiar to Western thought from Epicurus to Heidegger, animals are incapable of a proper death. That is, because animals are said to have no knowledge of death as such, they simply perish without death as death." Akira Mizuta Lippit, "The Death of an Animal," *Film Quarterly* 56, no. 1 (2002): 11. Other scholars have made a case for dolphin communication and thus consciousness (Bateson 1972) and animal consciousness (Bergson 1920). *The Cove* errs from Lippit's characterization, especially the final visual climax.

15 Emma Roe, "Things Becoming Food and the Embodied, Material Practices of an Organic Food Consumer," *Sociologia Ruralis* 46, no. 2 (2006): 118.

16 Thomas Waugh, ed., *Show Us Life: Toward a History and Aesthetics of the Committed Documentary* (Metuchen, NJ: Scarecrow, 1984), xiv.

17 One aspect of the social fabric *Darwin's Nightmare* represents includes Russian pilots who fly fish fillets as exports to Europe and fly back into Africa importing arms that fuel the conflicts in Angola and the Congo.

18 This is akin to Lippit's analysis of Eisenstein's use of animal slaughter as a metaphor for the brutality of labour relations. However, while for Lippit "Eisenstein's animals intervene at the

limits of representation, here the death of human beings" (Lippit, "The Death," 14), the fish carcass signifies the limits of documentary representation—historical excess. As Bill Nichols notes in *Representing Reality* (Bloomington: Indiana University Press, 1991), historical complexity always escapes full representation in documentary. In this sense the decaying fish alludes to what is impossible to portray fully—the detail of the social scene and human experience in Mwanza following the fateful introduction of the fish.

19 Sara Ahmed, *The Cultural Politics of Emotion* (New York: Routledge, 2004), 85.

20 Deborah Lupton, *Food, the Body and the Self* (London: Sage, 1996), 117.

21 John Corner offers an insightful reading when noting that the visual design of *Darwin's Nightmare* serves to convey aspects of "politicality." He refers to the way the "recurrent image of giant Russian transport aircraft coming in to land, or taking off, over the lake makes symbolic connection with the 'predatory' in relation to the fish, to Africa-Europe relations and to globalized capitalism." John Corner, "Documenting the Political," *Studies in Documentary Film* 3, no. 2 (2009): 115.

22 Barry Keith Grant, "Ethnography in the First Person: Fredrick Wiseman's *Titicut Follies*," in *Documenting the Documentary: Close Readings of Documentary Film and Video*, ed. Barry Keith Grant and Jeanette Sloniowski (Detroit: Wayne State University Press, 1998), 239.

23 Gaines, "The Production of Outrage," 44.

24 Michael Renov, *The Subject of Documentary* (Minneapolis: University of Minnesota Press, 2004), 178.

25 Nichols, *Representing Reality*, 67.

26 Elizabeth Cowie, *Recording Reality*, 86.

27 Wendy Brown, *Regulating Aversion: Tolerance in the Age of Identity and Empire* (Princeton: Princeton University Press, 2006), 191.

28 Cowie, *Recording Reality*, 30–32.

29 Corner, "Documenting the Political," 113–14.

30 For one example of this impact, see Coco Masters, "Japan Gets Its First Chance to See *The Cove*," *Time Magazine*, 16 September 2009, http://www.time.com/time/world/article/0,8599,1923252,00.html.

31 As Hughes notes, French audiences in particular perceived a need for consumer action in response to the situation in Mwanza. Helen Hughes, "Scrutiny and Documentary: Hubert Sauper's *Darwin's Nightmare*," *Screen* 53, no. 3 (2012): 246–65.

32 Ruby B. Rich. "Documentary Disciplines: An Introduction," *Cinema Journal* 46, no. 1 (2006): 112.

33 For an outline of these cases, see Hughes, "Scrutiny and Documentary," 252.

34 Darin Kinsey, "Nightmare or Delusion," *Environmental History* 12 (2007): 322.

BIBLIOGRAPHY

Ahmed, Sara. *The Cultural Politics of Emotion*. New York: Routledge, 2004.

Bateson, Gregory. *Steps to an Ecology of Mind*. New York: Ballantine Books, 1972.

Berger, John. *About Looking*. New York: Pantheon, 1980.

Bergson, Henri. *Mind-Energy: Lectures and Essays*. New York: Henry Holt, 1920.

Brown, Wendy. *Regulating Aversion: Tolerance in the Age of Identity and Empire*. Princeton: Princeton University Press, 2006.

Burt, Jonathan. *Animals in Film*. London: Reaktion Books, 2002.

Corner, John. "Documenting the Political." *Studies in Documentary Film* 3, no. 2 (2009): 113–29.

The Cove. Directed by Louie Psihoyos. Santa Monica, CA: Lions Gate, 2009. DVD.

Cowie, Elizabeth. *Recording Reality, Desiring the Real*. Minneapolis: University of Minnesota Press, 2011.

Darwin's Nightmare. Directed by Hubert Sauper. New York: Homevision, 2004. DVD.

Daston, Lorraine, and Gregg Mitman, eds. *Thinking with Animals*. New York: Colombia University Press, 2005.

Fay, Jennifer. "Seeing/Loving Animals: André Bazin's Posthumanism." *Journal of Visual Culture* 7, no. 1 (2008): 41–64.

Gaines, Jane. "The Production of Outrage: The Iraq War and the Radical Documentary Tradition." *Framework* 48, no. 2 (2007): 36–55.

Grant, Barry Keith. "Ethnography in the First Person: Fredrick Wiseman's *Titicut Follies*." In *Documenting the Documentary: Close Readings of Documentary Film and Video*, edited by Barry Keith Grant and Jeanette Sloniowski, 238–53. Detroit: Wayne State University Press, 1998.

Hughes, Helen. "Humans, Sharks and the Shared Environment in the Contemporary Eco-Doc." *Environmental Education Research* 17, no. 6 (2011): 735–49.

———. "Scrutiny and Documentary: Hubert Sauper's *Darwin's Nightmare*." *Screen* 53, no. 3 (2012): 246–65.

An Inconvenient Truth. Directed by Davis Guggenheim. Los Angeles: Paramount Classics, 2006. DVD.

Kinsey, Darin. "Nightmare or Delusion." *Environmental History* 12 (2007): 322–24.

Lippit, Akira Mizuta. "The Death of an Animal." *Film Quarterly* 56, no. 1 (2002): 9–22.

Lupton, Deborah. *Food, the Body and the Self*. London: Sage, 1996.

Masters, Coco. "Japan Gets Its First Chance to See *The Cove*." *Time Magazine*, 16 September 2009. http://www.time.com/time/world/article/0,8599,1923252,00.html.

Nichols, Bill. *Blurred Boundaries: Questions of Meaning in Contemporary Culture*. Bloomington: Indiana University Press, 1994.

———. *Representing Reality*. Bloomington: Indiana University Press, 1991.

Pols, Mary. "Rescue at Sea." *Time Magazine*, 10 August 2009. http://www.time.com/time/magazine/article/0,9171;1913757,00.html.

Rabinowitz, Paula. "Sentimental Contracts: Dreams and Documents of American Labour." In *Feminism and Documentary*, edited by Janet Walker and Diane Waldman, 43–63. Minneapolis: University of Minnesota Press, 1999.

Renov, Michael. *The Subject of Documentary*. Minneapolis: University of Minnesota Press, 2004.

Rich, Ruby B. "Documentary Disciplines: An Introduction." *Cinema Journal* 46, no. 1 (2006): 108–15.

Roe, Emma. "Things Becoming Food and the Embodied, Material Practices of an Organic Food Consumer." *Sociologia Ruralis* 46, no. 2 (2006): 104–21.

Smaill, Belinda. *The Documentary: Politics, Emotion, Culture*. Basingstoke, UK: Palgrave Macmillan, 2010.

Waugh, Thomas, ed. *Show Us Life: Toward a History and Aesthetics of the Committed Documentary*. Metuchen, NJ: Scarecrow, 1984.

6

Documenting Animal Rights and Environmental Ethics at Sea

Robin L. Murray and Joseph K. Heumann

The Academy Award–winning documentary *The Cove* (2009) captures viewers' attention immediately with its opening shots in Taiji, Japan, where its unlikely hero Ric O'Barry discusses the origin of his mission: "Here it is … the town of Taiji, the little town with a really big secret," he exclaims as he points to a seemingly idyllic village beside the sea. Dolphins are memorialized in the Taiji Whale Museum and exalted by both locals and tourists in pleasure boats shaped like smiling dolphins.[1] But, as O'Barry reveals, "hundreds of thousands of dolphins have died there," and it is his mission to fight for the dolphins' rights and reveal the senseless slaughter to the world.

The Cove and two other documentaries regarding the fishing industry— *Darwin's Nightmare* (2007) and *The End of the Line* (2010)—grapple with issues surrounding fishing for what *New York Times* seafood writer Paul Greenberg calls our "last wild food" in his *Four Fish*.[2] All three documentaries seek to address what their filmmakers see are environmental catastrophes: dolphin slaughter, biosphere destruction, and massive over-fishing. But only *The Cove* effects the changes it proposes. Whereas *Darwin's Nightmare* and *The End of the Line* reveal little known eco-disasters, *The Cove* goes further. It not only unmasks the slaughter of dolphins that leaders in Taiji work hard to hide, it also provides a call to action that is both heard and followed to successfully slow the carnage in the cove.

We assert that *The Cove* successfully slows the slaughter of dolphins because it draws on the emotional appeal of animal rights arguments in its strong advocacy for the dolphins of Taiji. *Darwin's Nightmare* and *The End of the Line* less successfully motivate changes in fishing practices because they immerse themselves in wise-use environmental arguments similar to Aldo Leopold's land ethic rather than animal rights rhetoric. *Darwin's Nightmare* provides a passionate critique of the human consequences of destroying Lake Victoria's ecosystem. And both *Darwin's Nightmare* and *The End of the Line* more logic-ally connect with long-term environmental solutions. Since it meets its goal to significantly slow and even end dolphin slaughter, however, *The Cove* employs the most effective rhetorical approach—an emotionally appealing strategy grounded in the animal liberation movement's claim that sentient animals are equal to humans because they too feel pain.

Highlighting its environmental bent from its opening, *Darwin's Nightmare* introduces its perspective differently than does *The Cove*. Instead of empha-sizing an animal liberation approach, the film illustrates the consequences of a disrupted biotic community by contrasting the struggles of impoverished local Africans with their prosperous Eastern European economic colonizers. While European pilots appropriate the only fish remaining in Lake Victoria, the town and its people collapse in poverty and neglect. In the streets, boys run on crutches and cry in the face of bullies. Girls sing to the sound of a synthe-sizer and sleep on the sidewalk. "They take the fish to the factory," police officer Marcus explains, and the European pilots fly the prepared perch back to their homeland. With these opening shots, the film's focus has been established—an interrogation of the dire economic and environmental consequences of intro-ducing Nile perch into the Lake Victoria ecosystem.

With a blatantly environmental message, *The End of the Line* contrasts a seemingly pristine ocean with its disastrous future. Close-ups of sea life and sky show the damage that has occurred over years of exploitation by humans. Those images are contrasted with shots of untouched coral, neon-coloured fish, and crabs. Violin music amplifies the ocean's unspoiled beauty in what Ted Danson reveals is a "Marine Protected Area" in the Bahamas. Here sea life is protected from humanity, "the most efficient predator." The music becomes ominous now as a shark swims by, but the crescendo rises when the hand of a fisherman brings up a line and nets of fish, trawling that the narrator explains is "like plowing a field seven times per year." We are the predators, the image tells us, and the title, *The End of the Line* rolls on the screen.

The End of the Line and *Darwin's Nightmare* draw on the biotic arguments of organismic ecology to substantiate their respective arguments against human-ity's exploitation of marine life. *The End of the Line* asserts and supports a straightforward argument against overfishing in our oceans around the world. *Darwin's Nightmare* effectively demonstrates the negative consequences of introducing the non-native (and carnivorous) Nile perch species into a freshwater lake (Lake Victoria). Both films highlight the need for a biotic community undisrupted by human intervention—either by industrializing the fishing industry or experimenting with a marine biosphere in Africa. But both also lack the emotional force found in the animal rights approach taken in *The Cove*. Combining an organismic ecology approach with animal rights arguments may provide the punch missing from these films' rhetoric.

ALDO LEOPOLD'S LAND ETHIC AND ORGANISMIC APPROACHES TO ECOLOGY: *THE END OF THE LINE* AND *DARWIN'S NIGHTMARE* IN CONTEXT

The organismic approach to ecology underpinning both *The End of the Line* and *Darwin's Nightmare* is based on Aldo Leopold's land ethic and Frederic Clements's approach to ecology. Leopold and Clements view a plant community as a living organism that evolves through succession. According to Clements, the living organism of a plant community changes over time: "The unit of vegetation, the climax formation is an organic entity. As an organism, the formation arises, grows, matures, and dies…. The climax formation is the adult organism, the fully developed community."[3] The organismic school of ecology emphasizes the need for such biotic communities and "rejected Social Darwinist assumptions of a nature characterized by Thomas Henry Huxley as 'red in tooth and claw,' for a nature of cooperation among individuals in animal and human communities."[4] Warder C. Allee and Alfred E. Emerson—organismic ecologists at the University of Chicago after World War I—saw the workings of the natural world as a model for healing societal problems. Aldo Leopold applied human ethics to the natural world, constructing a manifesto, "The Land Ethic," which encouraged an ecologically centred view of the land as a biotic pyramid in which humans were a part. In Leopold's view, humans had "the scientific and ethical tools to follow nature and heal it."[5]

An organismic approach to ecology views the natural world as a set of communities where living creatures cooperate in interconnected relationships. Ideally, humans, too, interact with the natural world cooperatively rather than seeking to exploit and ultimately destroy it. For Leopold and other organismic ecologists, humanity should see both nature and society as an organism in which each natural element, both human and non-human, contributes a part. From this perspective, humans thrive only when they seek to sustain rather than exploit the natural world around them because they too are part of this whole organism in which the whole is greater than the sum of its parts. Our societies prove most effective when each member is seen as equally important because he or she contributes to the success of the whole. Biotic communities work in similar ways. To sustain natural resources, we must maintain these cooperative communities.

Both *The End of the Line* and *Darwin's Nightmare* emphasize the need to work toward such sustainable development, nurturing the natural world rather than exploiting it as only a source of food. *The End of the Line* warns us against the corporate fishing that is depleting our seafood supply so astronomically that our oceans will be virtually empty of fish in a few decades. Instead, the film asserts, we should implement sustainable fishing practices that maintain aquatic life and nurture the oceans' biotic communities. *Darwin's Nightmare*, on the other hand, demonstrates how our greed for a particular type of fish— perch—has irrevocably disrupted the biosphere of Lake Victoria. Because of the changes in the fishing industry caused by the overabundance of perch and Westerners' taste for this fish as food, human life has also been irrevocably disrupted, demonstrating how interconnected human and non-human nature remain.

UNIVERSALIZING THE BIOTIC COMMUNITY IN *THE END OF THE LINE*

The End of the Line argues for an ethical approach to the ocean environment that embraces sustainability. The film exclaims, "Imagine a world without fish!" and asserts that based on the current rate of fishing, the world will see the end of most ocean life by 2048. By juxtaposing what should be emotionally appealing images of protected pristine seas with spectacles of predation, *The End of the Line* successfully argues for organismic approaches to ecology. The survival of human nature is indelibly intertwined with that of the non-human nature of the seas. To sustain fish for future human consumption we must preserve its aquatic biotic community. Because it fails to integrate an animal rights perspective, however, the film's call to action is weakened.

Reviews laud the film's exposé of what Andrew Schenker calls "a new threat to the planet's sustainability."[6] Nathan Lee of *The New York Times* declares that *The End of the Line*, an Official Selection at the Sundance Film Festival, "expos[es] the damages wrought to the sea by the usual suspects: industrialized food production, unchecked capitalism, and soaring consumer demand," for example, and highlights the film's focus on "an over fishing so severe that the world's piscatorial stock may be completely depleted by 2048."[7] Roger Ebert also notes the film's documentation of "what threatens to become an irreversible decline in aquatic populations within 40 years."[8]

Measures of how effectively the film conveys this horrific message vary, however. Although Roger Ebert asserts that the film "is constructed from interviews with many experts, a good deal of historical footage, and much incredible footage from under the sea, including breathtaking vistas of sea preserves, where the diversity of species can be seen to grow annually,"[9] Nathan Lee states that the film's propositions "are slathered in laughable scare music."[10] Andrew Schenker goes further and condemns the film's effectiveness arguing, "the picture fails to build a rigorous enough argument to sustain [its] indignant tone."[11] According to Schenker, "if over fishing is to take its place among that growing catalogue of woes already assaulting the American conscience … it will certainly take a far more cogent polemicist than [director] Rupert Murray to make it stick."[12]

For us, however, *The End of the Line* effectively appeals to this American conscience, illustrating the consequences of industrialized fishing and consumerism. The film demonstrates the catastrophic consequences of over-using marine resources by contrasting areas of the ocean with and without "fair use" fishing strategies. Our exploitation is killing the sea, making what was a renewable resource into a death pool. Fair use strategies exploit the sea's resources without regard for the future of sea life. Wise use strategies will help sustain them. The film documents evidence that validates this key argument.

To begin with, the Newfoundland, Canada, cod shortage is held up as evidence. In 1992, what had once been the most abundant cod-fishing area in the world became "fished out." Forty thousand people lost their jobs. Cod became an endangered species in Canada, so much so that its population has not regenerated despite a moratorium. The levels of cod became so low that the fish were unable to recover.

Near extinction of the blue fin tuna serves as a second compelling case supporting the film's horrific assertion. Once caught in the thousands, catches of blue fin tuna have declined by 80 percent in the last twenty-two years. Although *The End of the Line* does focus on specific species of tuna, it explains that these examples merely particularize a more general trend: species after species of fish have collapsed in the world's oceans because developed nations crave seafood. Even fish in developing nations such as Senegal are sold to Europeans, forcing West Africans into poverty and starvation. The collapse of marine species also disrupts the oceans' biotic community, destroying a balance of predator and prey found in the ocean food chain. Reasons for these major declines are explored—all related to a move toward large-scale industrial fishing in the 1950s. But the film primarily demonstrates that the number of fish available in the world's oceans will hit zero by 2048 at the current rate of fishing. Marine life is fragile; it is a finite resource that will disappear if we do not change the way we harvest fish.

The film offers a variety of solutions to this catastrophic future of our seas, all of which are based in organismic approaches of ecology that embrace sustainable development and biotic community. Alaska's conservation methods are held up as one example of a better way. Alaska strictly enforces a 200-mile fishing limit. The state also controls the number of fishing boats and enforces quotas on fishing levels. Exploitation of marine resources there is only 10 percent, compared to 50 percent in the North Sea. In Alaska, fishermen are willing to take a cut in the harvest so they can continue to catch fish.

The film also suggests that consumers should demand to know where their fish comes from and how it is caught in order to support a sustainable fishing industry such as that described by the Marine Stewardship Council. According to *The End of the Line*, some corporations are leading this drive toward sustainability. In 2011, Wal-Mart began selling only Marine Stewardship Council–sustainable fish, for example. Two-thirds of the fish Birdseye sells come from sustainable sources, and 99 percent of McDonalds's fish come from sustainable sources, the film explains. These examples reinforce Charles Clover's facts from the book version of *The End of the Line* that served as the source for the film.[13]

The End of the Line also argues against industrialized fish farming and argues instead for the opening of more marine preserves where commercial fishing is off limits. Sea life will begin to recover if we increase the percentage of protected marine preserves from less than one percent to a global network of 20–30 percent of the world's oceans. These massive marine preserves would help the seas regenerate themselves. By implementing and enforcing fishing limits, changing our eating habits, abiding by rules, and decreasing capacity, we can manage the sea for its recovery. As the narrator explains, we can act now. With this generalized focus on the biotic community of Earth's oceans, *The End of the Line* moves beyond individualized animal rights arguments and embraces a sophisticated theory of organismic ecology.

Whether or not the film's rhetoric will result in activist responses from viewers, however, is yet to be seen because the film is available primarily by accessing a website rather than through wide release. Despite multiple positive reviews and awards, including one from Sundance, the film has not found a mainstream distributor in the United States. Dogwoof Pictures—a UK company—is distributing the DVD through the film's website: endoftheline.com. The website provides multiple resources for reclaiming the oceans and offers educational screenings of the film. But one screening at a Salt Lake City high school that was documented in a YouTube video resulted in laughter rather than outrage. These unwanted emotional responses undercut the attempts made in the film to evoke compassion or "sustain [an] indignant tone," as

Andrew Schenker put it. These responses also conflict with appeals to pathos that might sway opinions or promote changes in fishing or consumption behaviours. Both *Darwin's Nightmare* and *The End of the Line* demonstrate that arguments against overfishing that are based in organismic ecology may not change behaviours.

DARWIN'S NIGHTMARE AND ANIMAL WELFARE: ECOLOGY MEETS HUMAN RIGHTS

Despite its engagement with organismic approaches to ecology, *Darwin's Nightmare*'s human rights argument provides a way to connect the "land ethic" with animal rights. *Darwin's Nightmare* attempts to connect human rights with ecology and demonstrate that—as J. Baird Callicott asserts—"animal welfare ethicists and environmental ethicists have overlapping concerns."[14] In this case, the disruption of an aquatic community has had devastating effects on both aquatic and human life.

Darwin's Nightmare limits its argument to one species, as does *The Cove*, and highlights the need for "rights." But this connection between organismic ecology and human rights falls flat for two reasons: it focuses on a non-native species that has become an unwanted predator rather than a sentient species with which we can sympathize. And it fails to adequately connect the perch with human rights violations on shore. It does not extend its human rights argument to animal rights. *Darwin's Nightmare* also offers no solutions to the problem it exposes: humanity's intervention in the biosphere of Lake Victoria disrupted the evolutionary trajectory and destroyed what was once a thriving aquatic biotic community. In *Darwin's Nightmare*, the ecological message is clear, but because there is no call to action, the film's ability to connect human and non-human nature is weakened. The ecological message needs the force of an animal rights argument to succeed.

Drawing on Mary Midgley's altruistic vision of animal welfare, Callicott explains how an animal welfare ethic aligns well with organismic ecology. According to Callicott, "since we and the animals who belong to our mixed human-animal community are coevolved social beings participating in a single society, we and they share certain feelings that attend upon and enable sociability—sympathy, compassion, trust, love, and so on."[15] He further asserts,

> Mary Midgley's suggested animal welfare ethic and Aldo Leopold's seminal environmental ethic thus share a common ... understanding of ethics as grounded in altruistic feelings. And they share a common ethical bridge between the human and nonhuman domains in the concept of

community—Midgley's "mixed community" and Leopold's "biotic community." [By] [c]ombining these two conceptions of a metahuman moral
community we have the basis of a unified animal-environmental ethical
theory.[16]

A unified animal ethics-environmental ethical theory acknowledges preferences for specific examples of human or non-human nature but places more
value on community. This holistic perspective rests on the notion that both
Midgley's mixed and Leopold's biotic communities matter. Films that illustrate an animal welfare ethic like Midgley's provide a way to connect animal
liberation and environmentalism. These films work toward interdependence
between human and non-human nature instead of the valorization of the individual no matter how it disturbs both the mixed and biotic communities.

Darwin's Nightmare highlights the need for such interdependent connections by showcasing the consequences of disrupting them. Deemed a "fully
realized poetic vision" by David Denby of *The New Yorker*,[17] *Darwin's Nightmare* emphasizes the importance of interdependence not only between human
and non-human nature, but also among human and non-human species. The
film chronicles the consequences of a little evolutionary experiment: introducing Nile perch into Lake Victoria. Fifty years after their introduction, the
perch have destroyed 210 species of African cichlids that once thrived in the
lake and controlled the lake's oxygen levels. Now, according to the International
Union for Conservation of Nature's International Climate Congress in Kenya,
falling oxygen levels coupled with the perch's cannibalism may destroy the
fishing industry, turning the lake into a "barren sinkhole."

The perch have destroyed the biotic community of the lake, becoming a species overwhelming all others and—as Belinda Smaill asserts—have taken on
"a malevolent quality."[18] But the perch have also negatively affected the human
community. According to David Rooney, director Hubert Sauper "focuses on
the ripple effect of a globalized economy in a specific microcosm to weigh the
casualties of the New World Order."[19] The destructive behaviours of these
perch may ultimately destroy the fishing industry, but their introduction into
the lake has already changed the industry and the market that sustains it. With
huge perch available for export, countries bordering on the lake—especially
Tanzania—can no longer rely on the lake for their own sustenance. Instead
they catch perch for a factory where they are prepared for shipment to Europe
where—according to the film—two million white people eat Lake Victoria
fish each day.

The film's emotional appeals are centred on the human consequences of the
dominance of perch in the lake. Tanzanians are starving because their lake has

become a Darwinian nightmare marketplace for Eastern European business-
men. These economic colonizers provide nothing for the people living near
the lake. Rather, they contribute even further to their impoverished state and
to the destabilization of their neighbours, since they fly weapons to warring
African countries—including Liberia, the Democratic Republic of Congo,
and Sudan—and fuel conflicts that have left more than a million dead. On
their return, pilots from Ukraine fly perch back to Europe, while hungry and
orphaned Tanzanian children sleep on the streets. The human biotic community has thus disintegrated. Tanzanians who once lived interdependently with
the lake's fish can no longer feed themselves. Their lake has been decimated,
first by the Nile perch, and then by the European colonizers who further disrupt their community.

To document the effects of such an evolutionary disaster, *Darwin's Nightmare* attempts to evoke emotional responses to the plight of Tanzanians near
the lake. The film opens and closes on views of the European cargo planes
landing in and leaving Tanzania, all piloted by white European men who look
well fed in contrast to Tanzanians pulling an out-of-control cart full of perch
in the impoverished town or fishing on Lake Victoria, the source of the Nile
and birthplace of civilization. Both the fishermen and the boys pulling the
cart take them to the factory, explains Marcus, a police officer. The film also
shows us how both fishermen and boys suffer because their source of food has
become a commodity. Fishermen and their families starve. Some fishermen die
on the lake, leaving wives and children to mourn them. Many children end up
orphaned and living on the street where they fight over scraps of food and fall
into a drug-induced sleep on sidewalks and in doorways.

These images arouse empathy for suffering fishermen and their sons, but
the women in this colonized community are left with even fewer choices.
After their husbands die of AIDS, fishing accidents, or war, they care for their
children until they starve to death, die from fumes exuded by smoking perch
corpses, or sell themselves to the European cargo pilots. Some of the women
work in brothels and bars constructed for their colonizers and some also die
at the hands of their so-called benefactors—as does Eliza, a beautiful young
woman highlighted in the film. The lone fish factory employs only four thousand people and pays as little as possible—a dollar a day for a night guard, for
example.

The film personalizes each of these struggles, appealing effectively to the
audience's emotional responses: It foregrounds Eliza's attempts to figure out
her life and showcases her glowing smile and her powerful voice singing her
country's anthem, "Tanzania." It also focuses on Raphael, a night guard fearing

for his life (since the previous guard had been murdered); Jonathan, a painter who documents the life on the streets he left behind; a group of boys fighting to survive on the street; and the cargo pilots themselves. Some of the pilots even regret their part in the arms sales that contribute to so many deaths.

Although the film highlights personalized emotional appeals, director Hubert Sauper takes the argument further, asserting that *Darwin's Nightmare* stands as evidence that "the old question, which social and political structure is the best for the world, seems to have been answered. Capitalism has won."[20] For Sauper, the changes in the communities around Lake Victoria are evolutionary and demonstrate that "the ultimate forms for future societies are 'consumer democracies,' which are seen as 'civilized' and 'good.' In a Darwinian sense, the 'good system' won. It won by either convincing its enemies or eliminating them."[21]

Despite the European Union's claim that Nile perch from Lake Victoria have not been allowed in EU market countries since 1999, the exporting continues, leaving a Syrian factory owner free to play with a dancing fish wall hanging while the UN discusses a food shortage in Tanzania and starving children fight for food. As Noel Murray suggests, "only a movie could catch the irony and horror of an office manager proudly showing off his Billy Bass while local children beat each other senseless over handfuls of rancid rice."[22] Tanzanians rally and pray for food while watching a film about Jesus as a fisherman. Factory workers pack fish in boxes and onto cargo planes, leaving only bones and fish heads for the locals. Eliza is killed, leaving her friends to mourn, and a one legged-boy walks down empty railroad tracks. A man reads a *BBC Focus on Africa* magazine claiming there are no supplies for Tanzania and explains that it would be a good idea for his son to be a pilot, so he can bring back supplies from Europe. Boys in the street smoke glue from empty soda bottles and sleep, and another plane takes off in a storm with thunder in the background. A Tanzanian woman watches from the ground.

Sauper used a minimalist unit to shoot *Darwin's Nightmare*, relying only on himself, his camera, and his companion, Sandor, to document the figures he followed throughout the film. But, according to Sauper, "when you look out for contrasts and contradictions, reality can become 'bigger than life.' So in a way it was easy to find striking images because I was filming a striking reality." This poignant reality demonstrates the need for an interdependent biotic community.

Even though Sauper argues that Tanzania's dilemma is a product of evolution, we assert that *Darwin's Nightmare* shows us what happens when the biotic communities of and between non-human and human nature are disturbed.

Here, unlike *The Cove*, the film demonstrates that a single species—either the Nile perch or the European colonizer—can destroy its environment and even itself. Instead of arguing for animal liberation, the film upholds the need for interdependent community. The consequences of its destruction are monumental and ultimately end in both lake and land turning into barren sinkholes.

But ultimately the film stands only as a warning against disrupting other biospheres, for it falls short of explicitly connecting the introduction of the perch with the cultural degradation surrounding the lake. Despite the powerful emotionally charged images of desperate Tanzanian men, women, and children, the film suggests it is too late for Lake Victoria and, perhaps, for Tanzania. *Darwin's Nightmare* connects the need for a biotic community with human rights, but it excludes the "call to action" that might address Lake Victoria's disastrous condition. *The End of the Line* demonstrates that arguments against overfishing that are based in organismic ecology may or may not change behaviours. Documentaries with animal rights–driven arguments, however, may produce real change.

ANIMAL RIGHTS VERSUS ENVIRONMENTALISM: THE VALUE OF "SENTIENCE"

Animal rights and environmentalism are sometimes seen as resting on similar values and grounded in similar calls to action: if we save the animal world, we save the environment might be the call. According to Peter Singer, for example, "Animal Liberation is Human Liberation too,"[23] and "human equality … requires us to extend equal consideration to animals"[24] and preserve their rights as we might other human rights, as in the civil rights or women's rights movements. Yet the organismic environmental movement of pioneers like Aldo Leopold advocates for the good of all life as part of an ecosystem, a position counter to the animal rights movement's focus on individual "sentient" animals, as Singer, for example, would have it.

The animal rights movement, however, typically bases its arguments on principles of the human rights movement and nineteenth century utilitarianism, which defined *good* as pleasure, and *bad as* pain. Creatures capable of feeling pleasure and pain, in Singer's view, have the same rights as humans because their "sentience" gives them inherent value. Other elements of non-human nature without such "sentience" do not share the same rights and are defined as "vegetables," which are living creatures somewhere between the oyster and shrimp. According to Rebecca Raglon and Marian Scholtmeijer, "advocates for nonhuman animals note the similarities between human and other animal species and argue for rights for animals based on that closeness."[25] From Peter Singer's groundbreaking 1975 work, *Animal Liberation*, to Norm Phelps's 2007 overview, *The Longest Struggle: Animal Advocacy from Pythagoras to PETA*, animal advocates base their arguments on the close connection between humans and non-human animals.[26]

The principles of organismic environmentalism, on the other hand, valorize biodiversity and interdependence and draw on Aldo Leopold's land ethic, which "enlarges the boundaries of … community to include soils, waters, plants, and animals, or collectively: the land."[27] So, as Raglon and Scholtmeijer note, animal advocacy is not necessarily associated with the environmental movement because the two movements "essentially developed along separate lines."[28] However, connecting animal rights and environmentalism, through what Mary Midgely calls "animal welfare,"[29] can provide a space for interdependence between human and non-human nature. While animal rights principles focus on individuals, such a focus may disrupt Aldo Leopold's concept of the "biotic community,"[30] a principle that rests on the belief that humans are simply members of a community of living things that interact cooperatively and with equal ethical value. One species—humans or other "sentient" beings—is not constructed as a conqueror but as a group of "biotic citizens."[31]

Robert H. Schmidt differentiates between animal rights and animal welfare as a step toward aligning animal treatment with the environmental movement. As Schmidt explains, "the animal rights movement has as its underlying foundation the perception that animals have rights equal or similar to those of humans (the principle of equal consideration of interests; Singer 1980).… In their view, biomedical, agricultural, and other uses of animals have no place in society unless the same treatment could ethically be given to humans."[32] The animal welfare movement, on the other hand, "is particularly concerned with reducing pain and suffering in animals."[33] Schmidt sees focusing the discussion on animal welfare rather than animal rights as a way to "follow … the direction of the rapidly increasing numbers of people concerned about environmental issues in general and animal utilization in particular."[34] Mary Midgley agrees and grounds the animal welfare ethic in a biosocial perspective that connects well with the ideas Aldo Leopold outlines in *A Sand County Almanac*.[35] Documentaries focusing on animal treatment, however, sometimes foreground animal rights rather than animal welfare, potentially discouraging alignment with environmentalism. *The Cove* most effectively draws on this rhetoric.

THE COVE, SENTIENCE, AND EMOTIONAL APPEALS

The Cove has received nearly universal acclaim, earning the 2009 Academy Award for Best Documentary Feature, perhaps because it is, according to Andrew O'Hehir, "a grim tale of murdered dolphins and poisoned school kids" that spins into "an amazing, real-life spy story video."[36] O'Hehir claims that the film "raises troubling questions about how badly we have befouled the 70 percent of our planet that's covered with water, and about why we have treated the species closest to us in intelligence with such cruelty and contempt."[37] Justin Chang declares, "Eco-activist documentaries don't get much more compelling than The Cove, an impassioned piece of advocacy filmmaking that follows Flipper trainer-turned-marine crusader Richard O'Barry in his efforts to end dolphin slaughter in Taiji, Japan."[38] According to Chang, "it's hard not to feel that there's something uniquely barbaric about the destruction of this exceptionally intelligent, human-friendly species."[39] Even Noel Murray, who calls the film "muddled," suggests that "The Cove offers a lot to think about in terms of the future of fishing, and Psihoyos' gift for fiction-feature conventions does make a seemingly unpalatable subject entertaining."[40]

Murray's critique of the film, however, like other reviewers' accolades, rests on its reliance on the point of view of dolphin advocate Ric O'Barry, who, as Murray suggests, sides with "anyone who wants to protect dolphins, whether they want to shutter Sea World or not."[41] The Cove, then, is both praised and condemned because it valorizes an animal rights ethic. Animal rights ethicists like Peter Singer argue that dolphins as a species deserve the same liberation movements as do human groups. As Singer contends, the film suggests that speciesism should be eradicated, just as racism and sexism should be abolished, primarily because animals are so much like humans.

To support his claim, Singer asserts that humans are considered morally superior only because they belong to the species Homo sapiens. He also suggests that using this membership to define superiority is completely arbitrary. Instead, we should consider sentience—the capacity of a being to experience pleasure and pain—as a plausible criterion of moral importance. If we use sentience as a criterion, we extend to other sentient creatures the same basic moral consideration, the principle of equality. In other words, we ought to extend to animals the same equality of consideration that we extend to human beings. Singer, like O'Barry, also connects certain animals more closely with humans, defining them as persons, a category that includes both sentience and self-awareness over time. In The Cove, O'Barry defines dolphins as both sentient and self-aware, offering these characteristics of persons as reasons for ensuring their safety and freedom.

The Cove demonstrates dolphins' connections with humans through Ric O'Barry's recollections of interactions with the dolphins he captured and trained for the television series Flipper (1964–68). According to O'Barry, he captured and trained the five female dolphins that played Flipper in the television series, translating the script into dolphin action each day. The dolphins' skills and intellect surprised and impressed even O'Barry. They even recognized themselves in the show when they saw themselves on O'Barry's television. O'Barry lived in the house at the end of the dock featured in the series, so he came in contact with the dolphins almost every waking hour. When the show ended, however, the dolphins were sold to an aquarium where they entertained crowds, seemingly smiling throughout the show—"nature's greatest deception," according to O'Barry. This connection with humans unfortunately leads to their harm or even death. The aquarium life is so stressful for dolphins, says O'Barry, that they must take Maalox and Tagamet every day. They travel forty miles a day in the wild. Captivity not only confines them, but also interferes with their sonar. O'Barry explains, "When they are captured and put in a concrete tank surrounded by screaming people, the noise causes stress." Even the sound of the filtration system was found to kill dolphins and had to be modified.

O'Barry's commentary demonstrates both their sentience (ability both to feel pleasure and pain) and their self-awareness (ability to recognize themselves on television), arguing effectively that dolphins should be preserved because destroying them means destroying living things of equal value to humans. Dr. John Potter reinforces their value by aligning it with dolphins' ability to respond to American Sign Language and connect with humans on an emotional level. According to Mandy-Rae Cruikshank, one of the divers in the film, a dolphin swam with her and invited her to rub its belly. Surfers recount stories of dolphins saving them from shark attacks. According to the film, then, dolphins have worth, so they deserve to live. They also deserve the freedom all persons of equal worth deserve.

While *The Cove* establishes the worth of dolphins, it also assumes, because they have historically been viewed as sentient creatures, that viewers will immediately call for action, once the slaughter at Taiji Cove is revealed. Ric O'Barry's attempts to film the slaughter are continually hampered by local authorities until he partners with the film's director Louie Psihoyos. O'Barry became a dolphin advocate after one of the dolphins he had trained killed herself in his arms by cutting off her own oxygen supply. Freeing as many dolphins as possible and preventing their slaughter is his life's work.

Dolphins are such great performers they have become a huge commodity, worth $150,000 apiece for *Sea World* shows. Because thousands of dolphins migrate to Taiji each year, dolphin trainers purchase dolphins there, bringing $2.3 million a year to the area. The remaining dolphins herded into the cove are slaughtered for food. O'Barry needed filmic proof to present to the world, so he could stop the catastrophe.

Filmmaker Louie Psihoyos and Netscape CEO Jim Clark joined forces with O'Barry to accomplish this mission, helping him build a team of experts to plant cameras and microphones, even utilizing George Lucas's Industrial Light and Magic to construct artificial rocks in which to hide cameras in the cove. They bring in world-class divers, a military expert, and a rock concert organizer to facilitate the mission, and the film documents the process these experts follow to plan and execute their goal to film the slaughter in two stages: they first plant audio equipment, and then, in Mission 2: The Full Orchestra, the team hides cameras around the cove.

The film asserts both logical and emotional reasons why the dolphins should be saved. For example, it provides practical reasons why humans should avoid dolphin meat, if they value their health, explaining that the meat has toxic levels of mercury; yet it is donated to area schools for lunch programs and disguised as whale meat in Tokyo markets. A history of problems with mercury poisoning is shown to support this claim, especially those recounting mercury poisoning in Minamata, Japan, in 1956, when the government covered up toxicity levels caused by industrial dumping. Fetuses were most affected, so children were born deformed, losing sight and hearing.

The slaughter that the crew of *The Cove* captures on film goes on for days and becomes the climax of this powerful documentary. It also serves as the strongest animal rights argument in the film. Before all recording devices have been planted in the hidden cove, the team films a dolphin trying to get away, leaving a trail of blood in the water in its wake. After the team plants the audio equipment, they listen to the dolphins scream in the cove. The sounds demonstrate that each dolphin is aware of its coming death. They anticipate their own slaughter, O'Barry explains.

But it is after all cameras are planted that the most shocking evidence against such slaughter is revealed. O'Barry and the team watch monitors showing fishermen on shore around a fire telling stories about whaling missions around the globe. Other shots show fishermen standing in boats and placing barriers across the cove. The fishermen herd the dolphins in, disorienting them with constant tapping noises. Once inside the cove, the fishermen begin the slaughter, stabbing dolphins repeatedly with harpoons. The water turns red with blood. Dolphin screams fill the soundtrack. The harpooning continues until all the dolphins are dead. The water is ruby red, but dolphins caught in nets are pierced again and again. They try to escape but are caught in this cove fortress.

Carcasses are ripped on board the boats, but fishermen smoke nonchalantly, even diving into the bloody water in search of more bodies. The dolphins are dragged like harpooned whales. These images contrast with majestic shots of dolphins swimming freely in the sea.

The footage of the slaughter becomes O'Barry's proof of dolphin sentience. Their suffering is clear on the video screen he shows a town spokesman and the members of the International Whaling Commission. And these shocking images get results because they appeal both to audiences' emotions and their rational understanding of the issue of dolphin slaughter. Small countries paid off by the Japanese leave the IWC, and dolphin meat is no longer allowed in school lunches, for example. By building an argument that demonstrates dolphins' equality with humans, based on sentience and self-awareness, *The Cove* draws on animal rights arguments. It also effectively takes those arguments one step further: because dolphins are sentient and self-aware, their slaughter must end.

CONCLUSION

The focused rhetoric of *The Cove* succeeds where the environmental ethics perspective of *Darwin's Nightmare* and *The End of the Line* fails to convey the same emotional power. Ultimately, even though animal liberation arguments may privilege some elements of the natural world over others, such an individualized approach has been shown to have more effective results. According to Ric O'Barry, the Taiji dolphin slaughter was suspended in September 2009 because of the publicity surrounding *The Cove*,[42] and as of March 2, 2011, Taiji fishermen were returning to traditional fishing practices rather than dolphin slaughter.[43] Even though dolphin killing continues, it has "drastically decreased compared to previous seasons," O'Barry explains.[44]

Today O'Barry continues to garner support from Japanese journalists and local students and community members in Wakayama City, Tokyo, and other cities throughout the country and around the world. He sees this response to *The Cove* as a major victory: "Our Save Japan Dolphins Team and I have been meeting with media for years about the dolphin slaughter in Japan, but now the Japanese media is coming to us!" According to O'Barry, they opened *The Cove* in Japan despite intense opposition and a press conference after the film's release "was attended by over 100 media representatives, including every major broadcast outlet."[45] As of October 2011, Ric O'Barry's "Save Japan Dolphins" project continues its fight to end the slaughter of dolphins and stop the capture and live trade of dolphins to zoos and aquariums around the world. The organization and its Earth Island Institute core have sparked an Animal Planet series called *Blood Dolphin$* as well as a large team of volunteers who continue to create worldwide pressure against dolphin slaughter. Because of the continuing success of *The Cove*, dolphin slaughter is on the wane. In October 2011, for example, volunteer observers noted that "while Taiji dolphin hunters have tried several times over the past few days to herd dolphins into the notorious Cove in Taiji, they have failed, and the dolphin pods escaped them."[46] Although hunters did herd a pod of 28–30 striped dolphins into the cove on October 4, 2011, the number of dolphin deaths continues to diminish.

Perhaps, then, films taking an organismic approach to eco-resistance might learn from the strategies invoked in a powerful animal liberation film like *The Cove*. As Holmes Bolston III explains, "development in the West has been based on the Enlightenment myth of endless growth.... [Yet] none of the developed nations have yet settled into sustainable culture on their landscapes."[47] By moving from an animal rights perspective to an animal welfare approach, environmentalists may find a way to individualize environmental issues without diluting the need for a biotic community.

An animal welfare approach may provide an emotional centre missing from both *Darwin's Nightmare* and *The End of the Line* and, perhaps, facilitate an eco-activist response that culminates in the powerful resistance that is central to *The Cove*. *The End of the Line* could, for example, "humanize" selected species of aquatic life, demonstrating that they, like humans, have rights or it could provide further emotional connections between humans and the ocean biosphere. For its part, *Darwin's Nightmare* could reinforce the connection between the human rights issues broached in the film and the species destruction caused by the introduction of Nile perch into Lake Victoria, emphasizing how species destruction leads to cultural disruption because we are all part of the "land." Such a focus on both individual species and their biotic communities could have the same result as the animal rights focus of *The Cove*: more than two million signatures from 151 countries on a petition that will, it is hoped, end dolphin slaughter for good.

NOTES

1 *The Cove*, directed by Louie Psihoyos (Santa Monica, CA: Lionsgate, 2009), DVD.

2 *Darwin's Nightmare*, directed by Hubert Sauper (New York: International Film Circuit, 2004), DVD; *The End of the Line*, directed by Rupert Murray (London: Dogwoof Pictures, 2009), DVD. Paul Greenberg, *Four Fish: The Future of the Last Wild Food* (New York: Penguin, 2010).

3 Frederic Clements quoted in Carolyn Merchant, *American Environmental History: An Introduction* (New York: Columbia University Press, 2007), 182.

4 Merchant, *American Environmental History*, 184.

5 Merchant, *American Environmental History*, 185.

6   Andrew Schenker, review of *The End of the Line*, Dogwoof Pictures, *Slant Magazine*, 14 June 2009, http://www.slantmagazine.com/film/review/the-end-of-the-line/4267.

7   Nathan Lee, "Consumption and Extinction," *New York Times*, 19 June 2009, http://movies.nytimes.com/2009/06/19/movies/19end.html.

8   Roger Ebert, "*The End of the Line*: Fish Not Bitin' Today," *Chicago Sun Times*, 15 July 2009, http://rogerebert.suntimes.com/apps/pbcs.dll/article?AID=/20090715/REVIEWS/907159995.

9   Ebert, "*The End of the Line*."

10 Lee, "Consumption and Extinction."

11 Schenker, review of *The End of the Line*.

12 Schenker, review of *The End of the Line*.

13 Charles Clover, *The End of the Line: How Overfishing Is Changing the World and What We Eat* (New York: New Press, 2006).

14 J. Baird Callicott, "Animal Liberation and Environmental Ethics: Back Together Again," in *The Animal Rights/Environmental Ethics Debate: The Environmental Perspective*, ed. Eugene C. Hargrove (Albany: State University of New York Press, 1992), 249.

15 Midgley cited in Callicott, "Animal Liberation," 252.

16 Callicot, "Animal Liberation," 254.

17 David Denby, "Candid Cameras: Three New Documentaries," *New Yorker*, 6 March 2006, http://www.newyorker.com/archive/2006/03/06/060306crci_cinema?currentPage=all.

18 See Belinda Smaill, Chapter 5 of this volume, 108.

19 David Rooney, review of *Darwin's Nightmare*, *Variety*, 21 September 2004, http://www.variety.com/review/VE1117924973.

20 David Sauper, "Filming in the Heart of Darkness," *Darwin's Nightmare*, n.d., http://darwinsnightmare.com/darwin/html/startset.htm.

21 Sauper, "Filming in the Heart of Darkness."

22 Noel Murray, review of *Darwin's Nightmare*, *A.V. Club*, 9 November 2005, http://www.avclub.com/articles/darwins-nightmare,4217.

23 Peter Singer, *Animal Liberation* (New York: Avon Books, 1975), vii.

24 Singer, *Animal Liberation*, 1.

25 Rebecca Raglon and Marion Scholtmeijer, "'Animals Are Not Believers in Ecology': Mapping Critical Differences between Environmental and Animal Advocacy Literatures," *ISLE: Interdisciplinary Studies in Literature and Environment* 14, no. 2 (2007): 121.

26 Singer, *Animal Liberation*; Norm Phelps, *The Longest Struggle: Animal Advocacy from Pythagoras to PETA* (New York: Lantern, 2007).

27 Aldo Leopold, *Sand County Almanac* (New York, Oxford UP, 1949), 204.

28 Raglon and Scholtmeijer, "Animals Are Not Believers in Ecology," 121.

29 Midgely cited in Callicott, "Animal Liberation," 252.

30 Leopold cited in Callicott, "Animal Liberation," 252.

31 Leopold, *Sand County Almanac*, 223.

32 Robert H. Schmidt, "Why Do We Debate Animal Rights?" *Wildlife Society Bulletin* 18, no. 4 (1990): 459.

33 Schmidt, "Why Do We Debate Animal Rights?" 459.

34 Schmidt, "Why Do We Debate Animal Rights?" 460.

35 Midgley cited in Callicott, "Animal Liberation," 254.

36 Andrew O'Hehir, "Beyond the Multiplex," *Salon.com*, 2 March 2006, http://www.salon.com/topic/beyond_the_multiplex.

37 O'Hehir, "Beyond the Multiplex."

38 Justin Chang, review of *The Cove*, *Variety*, 19 January 2009, http://www.variety.com/review/VE1117939389?refcatid=31.

39 Chang, review of *The Cove.*

40 Noel Murray, review of *The Cove, A.V. Club,* 30 July 2009, http://www.avclub.com/review/the-cove-31085.

41 Murray, review of *The Cove.*

42 Ric O'Barry, "Goodbye (for now) to Taiji," *Save Japan Dolphins,* 29 September 2009, http://savejapandolphins.blogspot.ca/2009/09/goodbye-for-now-to-taiji.html.

43 Ric O'Barry, "Taiji Fishermen Catching Fish, Not Dolphins," *Save Japan Dolphins.* 2 March 2011, http://savejapandolphins.org/blog/post/taiji-fishermen-catching-fish-not-dolphins.

44 Ric O'Barry, "A Big Year in Review," *Save Japan Dolphins,* 2 December 2010, http://savejapandolphins.org/blog/post/a-big-year-in-review.

45 O'Barry. "A Big Year in Review."

46 Ric O'Barry, "Dolphins Elude Dolphin Killers in Taiji," *Save Japan Dolphins,* 3 October 2011, http://savejapandolphins.org/blog/post/dolphins-elude-dolphin-killers-in-taiji.

47 Homes Bolston III, "Environmental Ethics," in *The Blackwell Companion to Philosophy,* 2nd ed. (Oxford: Blackwell, 2003), 528.

BIBLIOGRAPHY

Bolston, Homes, III. "Environmental Ethics." In *The Blackwell Companion to Philosophy,* 2nd ed., 517–29. Oxford: Blackwell, 2003.

Callicott, J. Baird. "Animal Liberation and Environmental Ethics: Back Together Again." In *The Animal Rights/Environmental Ethics Debate: The Environmental Perspective,* edited by Eugene C. Hargrove, 249–61. Albany: State University of New York Press, 1992.

Chang, Justin. Review of *The Cove. Variety,* 19 January 2009. http://www.variety.com/review/VE1117939389?refcatid=31.

Clover, Charles. *The End of the Line: How Overfishing Is Changing the World and What We Eat.* New York: New Press, 2006.

The Cove. Directed by Louie Psihoyos. Santa Monica, CA: Lionsgate, 2009. DVD.

Darwin's Nightmare. Directed by Hubert Sauper. New York: International Film Circuit, 2004. DVD.

Denby, David. "Candid Cameras: Three New Documentaries." *New Yorker,* 6 March 2006. http://www.newyorker.com/archive/2006/03/06/060306crci_cinema?currentPage=all.

Ebert, Roger. "*The End of the Line*: Fish Not Bitin' Today." *Chicago Sun Times,* 15 July 2009. http://rogerebert.suntimes.com/apps/pbcs.dll/article?AID=/20090715/REVIEWS/907159995.

The End of the Line. Directed by Rupert Murray. London: Dogwoof Pictures, 2009. DVD.

Greenberg, Paul. *Four Fish: The Future of the Last Wild Food.* New York: Penguin, 2010.

Lee, Nathan. "Consumption and Extinction." *New York Times,* 19 June 2009. http://movies.nytimes.com/2009/06/19/movies/19end.html.

Leopold, Aldo. *Sand County Almanac.* New York: Oxford University Press, 1949.

Merchant, Carolyn. *American Environmental History: An Introduction.* New York: Columbia University Press, 2007.

Midgley, Mary. "The Mixed Community." In *The Animal Rights/Environmental Ethics Debate: The Environmental Perspective,* edited by Eugene C. Hargrove, 211–25. Albany: State University of New York Press, 1992.

Murray, Noel. Review of *The Cove*. *A.V. Club*, 30 July 2009. http://www.avclub.com/review/the-cove-31085.

———. Review of *Darwin's Nightmare*. *A.V. Club*, 9 November 2005. http://www.avclub.com/articles/darwins-nightmare,4217.

O'Barry, Ric. "A Big Year in Review." *Save Japan Dolphins*, 2 December 2010. http://savejapandolphins.org/blog/post/a-big-year-in-review.

———. "Dolphins Elude Dolphin Killers in Taiji." *Save Japan Dolphins*, 3 October 2011. http://savejapandolphins.org/blog/post/dolphins-elude-dolphin-killers-in-taiji.

———. "Goodbye (for now) to Taiji." *Save Japan Dolphins*, 29 September 2009. http://savejapandolphins.blogspot.ca/2009/09/goodbye-for-now-to-taiji.html.

———. "Taiji Fishermen Catching Fish, Not Dolphins." *Save Japan Dolphins*, 2 March 2011. http://savejapandolphins.org/blog/post/taiji-fishermen-catching-fish-not-dolphins.

O'Hehir, Andrew. "Beyond the Multiplex." *Salon.com*, 2 March 2006. http://www.salon.com/topic/beyond_the_multiplex.

Phelps, Norm. *The Longest Struggle: Animal Advocacy from Pythagoras to PETA*. New York: Lantern, 2007.

Raglon, Rebecca, and Marion Scholtmeijer. "'Animals Are Not Believers in Ecology': Mapping Critical Differences between Environmental and Animal Advocacy Literatures." *ISLE: Interdisciplinary Studies in Literature and Environment* 14, no. 2 (2007): 121–40.

Rooney, David. Review of *Darwin's Nightmare*. *Variety*, 21 September 2004. http://www.variety.com/review/VE1117924973.

Sauper, David. "Filming in the Heart of Darkness." *Darwin's Nightmare*, n.d. http://darwinsnightmare.com/darwin/html/startset.htm.

Schenker, Andrew. Review of *The End of the Line*. *Slant Magazine*, 14 June 2009. http://www.slantmagazine.com/film/review/the-end-of-the-line/4267.

Schmidt, Robert H. "Why Do We Debate Animal Rights?" *Wildlife Society Bulletin* 18, no. 4 (1990): 459–61.

Singer, Peter. *Animal Liberation*. New York: Avon Books, 1975.

PART III

The Effects and Affects of Animation

7

Animation, Realism, and the Genre of Nature

David Whitley

The ground that this paper sets out to explore really takes us back to first principles. I want to consider, from a fresh angle, cinema's uniquely affective power in enabling reflection on the environment within which we live. Anat Pick has described this power as inherent within "cinema's immediacy and materiality—its corporeal, zoomorphic quality or creatureliness."[1] Pick's argument seeks to reposition André Bazin's theories of cinematic realism, so that these will serve as a basis for developing what she calls a "creaturely poetics": a way of reading the significance of animality within film that moves beyond an anthropocentric perspective. It is significant that Pick deems it necessary to ground her argument on theories of realism for this purpose, since cinema's capacity to engage viewers' perception of the world with full sensory detail would seem to be one of its founding characteristics. As Noël Carroll puts it, "Movies became a worldwide phenomenon—and a lucrative industry—precisely because in their exploitation of pictorial recognition—as opposed to symbol systems that require mastery of processes such as reading, decoding or deciphering in order to be understood—they rely on a biological capability that is nurtured in humans as they learn to identify the objects and events in their environment."[2] Carroll suggests that a substantial reason for cinema's affective power over audiences, its ability to provide intensity as well as emotional satisfaction, resides in its harnessing the force of this primary mechanism for recognizing things that exist in the world. As a consequence of this alignment with the biologically endowed powers of human perception, popular film narratives are imbued with extraordinary clarity and accessibility.

143

Since the reality of nature is precisely what we cut ourselves off from in modern societies, this would seem to provide a particularly useful starting point for an ecologically orientated analysis of film.

An alternative—though perhaps ultimately complementary—starting point for analysis may be derived from the idea that film, rather than simply clarifying a particular view of reality on behalf of viewers, may enable reflection on the contradictions inherent in any culturally mediated perception. Sean Cubitt expresses this notion lucidly when he argues:

> Though many films are predictably bound up to the common ideologies of the day, including ideologies of nature, many are far richer in contradictions and more ethically, emotionally and intellectually satisfying than much of what passes for eco-politics today. Fine art and popular media alike can, at their best, be far more than symptoms of their age. They can voice its contradictions in ways few more self-conscious activities do, because both want to appeal to the senses, the emotions and the tastes of the hour, because both will sacrifice linear reason for rhetoric or affect, and because both have the option of abandoning the given world in favour of the image of something other than what, otherwise, we might feel we had no choice but to inhabit.[3]

Cubitt positions the power of cinema's appeal to the senses here in a context that suggests that the exploration of contradictions may be just as important in determining the quality of audiences' emotional engagement as the clarity and coherence of a storyline. In doing so, he also suggests that non-realist perspectives—"the option of abandoning the given world in favour of something other"—may be equally significant. But what is the relationship between the affective power of cinema that is generated by its capacity for realism and film's capacity to explore contradictions, which may involve embracing non-realist alternatives? This paper probes some of the underlying issues involved here by focusing on an exemplary case study, a comparison between the acclaimed documentary *March of the Penguins* (2005) and a Hollywood children's animation, *Happy Feet* (2006), that was partly inspired by it. In developing a close analysis of the way realist and non-realist aesthetics are linked to each other in these two related films, I hope to open up some of the more subtle and complex dimensions involved in these issues.[4]

Leo Braudy's 1998 essay "The Genre of Nature" provides a very useful theoretical underpinning for this discussion. Braudy argued, in this seminal essay, that a case could be made for a genre of nature having emerged in the 1980s within film. The significance of this genre, for Braudy, lay in its providing an arena within popular culture that could act as a "sounding board or

lightning rod for deep rooted audience concerns."[5] These "deep rooted concerns" arose out of contradictions within public attitudes that were not easily
resolved—such as the perceived need for continuing economic growth and
technical progress, set off against feelings of loss and detachment as environments became degraded and nature appeared to "shrink." Narratives of popular
"films of nature" had come to embody these concerns in more satisfying ways
than political discourses and public life more generally, since the films had more
affective power, touched unresolved issues in their audiences obliquely, and did
not have to present a coherent outcome that could be perceived as unpersua-
sive, unpalatable, or simply false. Indeed, although the films Braudy ascribed to
this genre did generally resolve key elements in their plots with some form of
definitive closure, the cultural work they performed lay not in this closure, but
precisely in the films' articulation of irresolvable contradictions, now opened
up to audiences' thought and feeling in distinctive and compelling ways.

Braudy is careful not to give his proposed "genre of nature" too much cat-
egorizing force. He sees the films that emerge in this mode as having a distinctive orientation in terms of the transformative work they do on older genres as
these are pressed into service in new ways to engage with different dimensions
of contemporary identity and what is perceived to be "natural." In this respect,
"films of nature appear to constitute something between a genre and a cultural
code, neither an explicitly codified or codifiable form nor a bundle of thematic
coincidences, but a product of the inadequacy of established narrative modes
and systems of production to deal effectively with the new world the audience
inhabits."[6] Nevertheless he suggests that key elements of this protean genre
of nature may be specified. Among them, Braudy identifies: a prevalence of
protagonists who might be termed "primitives"—children, animals, Neander-
thals; a nostalgia for a lost past in which it was possible to live more simply
and authentically, or for residual elements in the present that emblematize
that past; and a hunger for what are described as "ceremonies of innocence."
Ceremonies of innocence are needed to "restore the natural core of belief, in the
world, in the country, and in the self."[7] They embody the desire, experienced
particularly acutely in a period of cultural crisis, for a restored innocence, "an
untouched and perhaps impossible freshness,"[8] that is perceived, in its most
radical forms, as "a standard by which to judge and a hammer to smash the
unnatural impositions on the individual by social and political power."[9]

The value of Braudy's theory, in the context I wish to explore now, seems to
me twofold. First, it avoids the trap of viewing popular cinema reductively, in
the way that some strands of environmentally orientated criticism have done:
judging films according to rather inflexible criteria of the degree to which they

represent the reality of the natural world, or assessing the ideological assumptions on which film narratives appear to be based according to the degree of fit with an environmentally sensitive ideal. For all the inherent difficulties in applying Braudy's more protean concept of genre to a very broadly conceived category of "nature film," and despite the problems of academic rigour involved in identifying cultural anxieties with enough specificity, this approach does attempt to treat audiences and popular films seriously in their own terms. The second advantage, though, is that the theory enables one to examine closely what happens when a narrative genre is transformed in response to the kinds of cultural pressures and anxieties that Braudy identifies. This, as we shall see, is particularly relevant to the context I wish to examine now. There is a curious, and potentially illuminating, paradox involved in the transformation that takes place between the poetic realism of the documentary *March of the Penguins* and the ersatz exuberance of the children's animation *Happy Feet*. For, oddly, it is the latter film that bears the weight of cultural anxieties concerned with lost or degraded environments much more explicitly. The lightweight fantasy appears to be carrying a heavier load.

THE POETICS OF DOCUMENTARY REALISM: *MARCH OF THE PENGUINS*

Let us begin by looking in more detail at *March of the Penguins*. This is a documentary film, co-scripted by the director, Luc Jacquet, and first released in a French language version. The film follows the life cycle of a single species, the emperor penguin, photographed—often exquisitely—in its natural environment of Antarctica. There is nothing very distinctive about this as a brief for a nature documentary. A narrative charting the life cycle of a single species over the period of a year is one of the commonest plot structures for this genre and *March of the Penguins* might well be taken as characteristic of this tradition. If there is anything remarkable about the content—as opposed to the treatment—that is the focus of the film, then, it perhaps resides in the singular focus on one species, seen for long periods as completely isolated from all other animals, and indeed even from plant life forms. The emperor penguins' long winter vigil, during which they incubate and hatch their eggs, takes place in conditions so extreme in an inner part of the Antarctic landscape, that no other bird, mammal, insect, or hint of even the most primitive form of vegetation seems to accompany them for substantial sections of the film. Such isolation is rare—even for limited periods of the year—within the earth's ecosystems and, although it receives no explicit comment in the film, one might argue that it helps establish a keynote of strange purity, akin to the quality of innocence that Braudy sees as such a fundamental component of the emergent genre of nature. Looked at in this way, at least, the life cycle format that is so standard to the nature documentary form could be viewed as being imbued with a special quality that makes it available, implicitly, to perform work as a kind of ceremony of innocence.

If the relative isolation of the birds in their breeding ground represents a potentially transformative element in *March of the Penguins* development of the nature documentary genre, this is undoubtedly rendered more powerful by the symbolic role that the Arctic and Antarctic landscapes take up within contemporary cultural consciousness. For the polar ice caps have come to embody—at a literal level—the widespread perception of a natural world that is shrinking.[10] They feature regularly as news items, as one of the prime indicators of the pace and extent of climate change. The polar regions appear to focus anxiety in a particularly vivid, almost axiomatic form about this issue. But on a less acknowledged level, the shrinking ice caps also provide a symbolic focus for the intensification of feelings of imminent loss that characterizes contemporary experience. *March of the Penguins* thus engages audiences within a cultural nexus that connects to a whole substructure of feelings about a natural world at a point of profound, probably irreversible change. The ceremonies of innocence that the creatures depicted in the film enact on our behalf may be related—legitimately I think—to this larger substructure of cultural anxiety, even though the film itself never makes this link explicit.

The line of argument I have been pursuing here may also help account for the aspect of the film which nearly all audiences and critics of the English language version do notice explicitly (though not always appreciatively)—the way it treats its subject with a distinctive kind of poetic lyricism.[11] The subtext of cultural anxieties about environmental loss and change helps license the poetic treatment of the subject, in other words. This poetic treatment is justified in other ways too, by the extremity of the conditions endured by the penguins and by the purity of light and form that the ice bound environment embodies. The poeticization of the narrative in *March of the Penguins* is orchestrated in the English language version through a voice-over narration performed by Morgan Freeman that interprets key events in the animals' lives in metaphorical forms. Interestingly, the French version of the film develops this poetic license through personification more than metaphor, narrating the events from the penguins' lives by using several actors who "speak" the penguin's thoughts *in situ*, rather than omnisciently from outside. In the English version however, which will be the subject of my analysis henceforth, the narration begins with an evocation of the long view through geological time, reminding us that the continent of Antarctica was once tropical, rich in vegetation and animal life forms, and that the emperor penguins are vestiges or survivors from this time. This evocative framing of the narrative serves to connect the extraordinary and extreme conditions of the Antarctic with more widespread contexts of life on earth with which audiences are more familiar. But it is also a pretext for the metaphorical gloss that is offered on the penguins' capacity to adapt to extreme change and survive. The positioning of the penguin's story as a survival narrative—"a tale of life over death"—is almost immediately reprised to yield a more emotional and perhaps surprising underlay. "But more than that, this is a tale about love," Morgan Freeman intones, giving the words the full weight of his distinctive, tough, gravelly voiced humanity.

There is, of course, a long history of extending the use of the word "love"—perhaps the most fundamental of the spiritual and emotional capacities that distinguish human beings—to animals. Although Descartes famously characterized animals as machines, within the sentimental traditions engaged with nature that developed from the eighteenth century onwards the ascription of love, at least to certain kinds of animals, became commonplace. Meanwhile, in a parallel but related development, the range of earlier literary and artistic traditions in which animal behaviour symbolized aspects of human emotion and attitudes became extended, with the analogical links often being expressed with greater sentimental license. By the late nineteenth century, even that most cautious of hypothesizers, Charles Darwin,[12] had no qualms about ascribing love in an unqualified manner as the emotion signified by certain kinds of animal behaviour.[13] So the move to foreground love as a primary motivating force for animal behaviour in *March of the Penguins* is by no means unique, though it remains striking. What is distinctive though is the way this opening move connects with a chain of other, powerfully emotive metaphors that encourage viewers to deepen their understanding of the penguins' behaviour in human terms. The most important of these are the metaphors of the "dance"—which is used to interpret the difficult process whereby the single egg is transferred from its incubatory hollow under the female's body to an equivalent space beneath the male—and the unique "song," uttered by the chick, that enables the returning parent to find it. I want to look briefly now at the way these metaphorical extensions of the role of love are developed in *March of the Penguins*, both because of what this strategy reveals about the power of the film itself to connect audiences with environmental perspectives, but also because the animation *Happy Feet* picks up and develops these metaphors in much more extended and fantastical forms that we will analyze later.

We need to recognize first that, within the realist aesthetic of the documentary form, these metaphors inevitably set up the potential for a double reading. The discrepancy between what is seen and what is narrated, in other words, may make the viewer as aware of mismatch as of metaphorical aptness, in terms of the degree to which the animals' behaviour fits human terms of reference. This potential gap is engendered by the realism of image and diegetic sound, both of which serve to resist appropriation in human terms, at the same time as the poetic metaphor enables connection and alignment with human identity and feeling. Thus the penguin chicks' unique signature "songs," faithfully reproduced on the film's soundtrack, sound nothing like songs to the human ear but are rather a series of chirrupings, each bird's noise indistinguishable to the audience from any others. The metaphor of "song" encourages the audience to appreciate the art and affective power of the penguin chicks' utterance however, the way each apparently atonal sequence of sounds is able to draw the intended penguin parent listener in closer to being reunited with its chick along a secret cord (or chord) of love. Without this metaphorical alignment, the sound itself has little affective power for the audience, lacking beauty, grace, or distinction of any kind in human terms. The metaphor works ideally to induce a sense of wonder, encouraging viewers to apprehend the otherwise unassimilable birdness of the animals' communication as equivalent to the lyrical power of song. Sean Cubitt recognizes the extraordinary effect bird songs may have on listeners, when he suggests how these "complex communications ... alien though they are and open to all sorts of non-linguistic interpretations, overcome us."[14] Underlying this sequence then is an attribution of a kind of Orphic power, that must be reconciled with the realistic particulars of the penguins' animal otherness.

A similar kind of doubleness is enacted in the sequences depicting the penguins' "dance." There is very little that is "dance-like" in human terms about the exchange of the egg between parent birds we see being enacted. Unlike a human dance, the egg exchange is conducted through a series of awkward shuffling movements, the scaly feet beneath the birds' apparently portly bodies revealed by the camera as big, tough, and ungainly. The animals' slow tentativeness appears to betoken apprehension, rather than the grace and harmony of dance, an apprehension that the audience is encouraged to internalize in dramatic form, since the near immediate freezing and destruction of any egg that slips out of the penguins' grasp is offered visually as a graphic alternative to the successful transfer that should consummate the "dance" sequence. Here too then the audience is invited to wonder at the difference of the penguins' ritual from human modes of interaction through dance, as much as to identify with the animals through the proffered metaphorical alignment. The disjunction here (which exemplifies what Ivone Margulies has defined as the "registered clash of different material orders")[15] perhaps functions partly as comic charm. But the deeper emotions activated are of pathos inherent in the potential loss of an offspring. The dance sequence is also set off by its proximity to the courtship scenes, where the penguins are shown earlier on as expressing the intimacy of their bond as procreating parents. In these scenes the camera dwells in extreme close-up mode on the birds' beaks, nape and head, as they conduct an extraordinarily beautiful series of bowing and entwining movements around each other's bodies. This slow sequence is accompanied by a musical soundtrack that is indeed the equivalent of an intimate and lyrical slow dance. There is no doubt that the emotive power of the exchange of eggs is substantially enhanced by its alignment with the poetic form in which the courtship is represented both visually and aurally for the audience; the distance between the birds' movements and human forms of art is here perceived to be at its most minimal.

The analysis above, then, is intended to explore an aspect of one of the most vexed and complex issues within ecocriticism: the degree to which representations of nature that have the power to strike chords of affinity within humans tend to do so by occluding the real otherness of non-human life forms. The poetics of any art form that seeks to engage imaginative empathy, as well as understanding, at a profound level will almost inevitably have to cross and recross this boundary. And it is often a difficult critical judgment to assess which side of the line any particular work of art ultimately falls on. In the case of *March of the Penguins*, it may be worth noting that the environment, as well as the animals, supplies much of the emotive force, however. In a sense, the Antarctic landscape has an irreducible otherness—indeed otherworldliness—which it would be difficult for the most androcentrically inclined filmmaker to completely cancel out. *March of the Penguins* is filmed in a way that encourages perception of this otherworldliness to play to the qualities of "purity" and "innocence" seen by Braudy as central to the genre of nature, however. There are no signs of human activity of any kind in the film itself; the shots selected are particularly beautiful in terms of light quality and the long winter vigil is edited down to a short sequence, over which the aurora lights in the sky cast their strange, scintillating brilliance continually. Moreover, although this is no doubt accidental rather than intended, the shape of the land over which the penguins travel is oddly reminiscent of the landscape in Hollywood Westerns, redressed in resplendent white. The Western genre, as Braudy notes, has repeatedly invoked nostalgia for an originatory innocence and it may be that the penguins' journey has some undertones of the primitive frontier ethos of the Western. Whether or not this is persuasive, it is undoubtedly true that the shape of the Antarctic landscape (or the environmental modelling as the animators put it) is altered significantly in *Happy Feet* and it is to this, as well as other significant changes, that I now want to turn attention.

HAPPY FEET: HYPERREAL ANIMATION AND MUSICAL FANTASY

Although critics were divided over whether the voice-over narration in *March of the Penguins* was offputtingly schmaltzy or movingly poetic, there is no doubt that audiences found the film as a whole deeply engaging. Indeed it is reputed to be the second-most commercially successful documentary ever made. The project of transforming this material into a successful children's animation clearly involved aesthetic risks, perhaps more so as the source material was itself in the film medium. At least one critic summed up the whole film as "weird" and took the conceit of transforming the birds into a troupe of—literally—all singing and dancing performers to be bizarrely ill-judged. Paul Arendt opined that *Happy Feet* was a "bewildering combination of anthropomorphic perversity and environmental polemic, all scored to cheesy pop hits.... It's as if the filmmakers watched *March of the Penguins* together and said to each other: 'You know what this really needs? Disco.'"[16] This critical standpoint has some parallels with the opprobrium directed towards Francis Ford Coppola when he viewed the Vietnam War through the medium of the 1960s popular music in *Apocalypse Now* (1979). Coppola had transformed Conrad's *Heart of Darkness* (1899), it was suggested, into a kind of luridly visceral "jungle disco."[17] Neither critique is particularly fair, but both highlight perceived dangers in mixing pop culture with serious subjects. In the case of *Happy Feet*, the danger is obviously one of tasteless commodification, the empathetic reverence towards nature displayed in *March of the Penguins* repackaged as pop in the Antarctic, with the additional celebrity allure of film star voice-overs. However, the cue for this musical reinterpretation of the penguins' lives is the original documentary's use of "dance" and "song" as metaphorical interpretations of central aspects of the birds' behaviour. And it is by no means clear that *Happy Feet* simply abandons all claims to develop viewers' sympathetic understanding of the plight of wild creatures in taking these metaphors literally as a pretext for anthropomorphized disco routines. Quite the reverse in fact, since the ending of the film clearly requires it to be interpreted as a moral fable that attempts to inculcate sympathy in the audience, from the animals' point of view, in an ecological crisis. How can these apparently incompatible projects possibly square up?

Two aspects seem particularly relevant to the argument I am developing here. The first of these is that *Happy Feet* is distinctive in terms of the degree to which it operates within a hyperrealist visual aesthetic. Both the penguins and the landscape are rendered with as realistic a texture as the animated medium will allow. While it is true that Disney's virtual colonization of the children's animated feature mode pushed mainstream animated filmmakers towards a much more realist aesthetic generally, and that each technological innovation within the medium has been exploited to heighten the realist effect, few films have taken this quite as far as *Happy Feet*. Even Pixar's *Finding Nemo* (2003), which set a new benchmark for the realistic depiction of the environment in the animation industry, deliberately held back from using the full power of CGI to mimic the effects of light and form with total fidelity. Andrew Stanton has related how at one point the team managed to create a texture for the underwater reef scenes that was virtually indistinguishable from that produced in popular nature documentaries, such as David Attenborough's *Blue Planet* series.[18] But they then reduced the realistic texture slightly, preferring a look that had slightly more of the feel of art. They felt that the freedom available in the animation medium would have been compromised if the world they were depicting edged too close to reality. Yet *Happy Feet* looks in many ways more hyperreal than its Pixar predecessor, despite the fact that the song and dance routines required by the script are considerably less plausible than any of the fishes' movements in *Finding Nemo*. One wonders why this should be? Could the commitment to an extraordinary degree of realism in the film be designed—perhaps unconsciously—to sustain its environmental ethics in a context where the fantastical play of its musical conceits might otherwise undermine these? Would penguin figures whose features were enhanced to look more like humans—in the mode pioneered by *Bambi*, for instance—have fallen so far into the cuteness trap that it would not have been possible to retrieve any environmental concerns from the narrative with even a vestige of authenticity? This is certainly debatable.

Although a number of critics have seen the film's earnest attempt to drama-tize environmental issues from the animals' viewpoint at the end as artistically flawed, this aspect of the film would arguably have been less effective without a base in palpable reality. Oddly, the scene that seems to me to be most effective in this respect is where the film's penguin hero, Mumble, awakes to find himself in the penguin enclosure of a zoo. Trapped behind glass viewing panels, the artificial penguin environment seen here is itself a simulacrum of the Antarc-tic, conceived with hyperrealistic detail so that even the ground has precisely the texture of snow encrusted ice. "Try the water," urges one of the long-term, brain-dead penguin inmates Mumble encounters there, "it's really real." The film captures the multiple ironies of the human need to stage nature as spec-tacle here with some deft satire, imbued with touches of bizarre surrealism.

While it is true the effectiveness of the satire is undermined by the clumsiness with which the plot is engineered towards a feel-good ending (Mumble's dance routine is supposed to communicate to the human spectators the penguins' need to have their dangerously depleted fish stock restored) it could be argued that child audiences need an optimistic balance of some kind. Indeed the perception that emphasizing environmental degradation too exclusively may have a psychologically demotivating effect has become a significant issue for environmental education recently. Certainly the imagery of industrial scale fishing in *Happy Feet* is as dark as anything in *Finding Nemo* and more politically pointed. If the plot lacks the intelligent direction and artistry of a fully realized moral fable, such as Stanton's *WALL-E* (2008), then it is at least well intentioned and in many ways ambitiously original in the elements it attempts to combine.

The second aspect of the film I want to examine is the interplay and transformation of genres that give significance to this hyperrealist detail. Braudy's theory suggests that it may be through the subtle transformations enacted on older genres, rather than through overt self-conscious didacticism, that recent films of nature enact their most fundamental cultural work. The source materials that *Happy Feet* uses—the details of emperor penguins' egg exchange, the significance of a uniquely encoded "song" for species survival, predators such as leopard seals and skuas, and the evocative nature of the Antarctic setting—all derive from the documentary mode, as we have seen. But the genre through which this material is reinterpreted is clearly not documentary at all, and is best seen in relation to the history of children's animation. Indeed, original though *Happy Feet* is in many respects, its main genre affiliation is really to the classic Disney model—romantic comedy, combined with adventure quest, and staged with conventions of the Hollywood musical. In this respect the affiliation to the genre of the musical is perhaps most interesting and definitive. In the wake of Richard Dyer's 1977 essay "Entertainment and Utopia,"[19] a number of film scholars have explored the notion that the musical has a distinctively utopian dimension. As Barry Langford summarizes: "the musical shows us what utopia would *feel* like: the reconciliation not simply of individual characters … or even of communities … but of space, style and expressive form. It is quite literally harmonious experience, charged in Dyer's account with the energies of intensity, transparency, abundance and community."[20] Of course, this utopian project still takes place within a set of social ideologies and, despite staging a transformative fantasy, may well be ultimately conservative in its effects. Langford goes on to note how Dyer's later work emphasizes the degree to which the "privilege of joyous self-expression in the classic musical is policed along racial lines—it is a privilege enjoyed only by whites, never by performers of colour."[21]

However, it is striking how many of the key terms invoked in this analysis—particularly the *feel* of a strangely intensified "space, style and expressive form" seem directly relevant to *Happy Feet*. Moreover, the plot of this film works precisely on a bifurcation, or rupture, in the way the "privilege of joyous self-expression" is perceived within the penguin community. The main protagonist Mumble is isolated and ridiculed—in a classic ugly duckling mode—because of his inability to express himself through song, like all other penguins, but instead through a special aptitude for dance and movement. This could be interpreted as an instance of what Michael Dunne has described as a standard trope of the American film musical where characters can often "discover their true feelings by dancing."[22] Perhaps more pertinently for my line of inquiry here, though, Mumble's "difference" could also be seen as marking him out for a role embodying restorative energies. Rick Altman suggests that, in the genre he describes as "folk musical," a common typology is where "one of the lovers represents the stability of the earth, the other energy and movement."[23] The penguin community requires Mumble's movement and interaction with humans to provide any chance of shoring up the region's damaged ecology.

The utopian ending of the film brings together both these expressive modes in a closing, Busby Berkeley style, ensemble number. Mumble persuades the rest of the penguin community to join with him in a dance that links humans and animals together again in harmonious understanding. This certainly stretches credulity in terms of realism (but then the musical is distinctive as the only major Hollywood genre that is non-realist in its aesthetic). However, one might understand the expressive rupture that the film seeks to heal within the penguin community as also being metonymic in terms of its association with the wider rupture that has taken place in the environment. Mumble's deviant expressive mode is not causatively linked to the way human activity is perceived as impacting on the pristine ecology of the Antarctic. But it is associated with this, in that Mumble's status as an outsider pushes him outwards in a heroic quest to communicate with humans and restore ecological harmony. One could perhaps see this as the mode through which the traditional genre of the musical is adapted so that it can perform cultural work in the new genre of nature. The social rupture within the penguin community is twinned with the rupture of environmental crisis.

Support for this viewpoint can be found in the imagery of the film, particularly the landscape. Although relatively little is done to enhance the appearance of the animals to make them look more like humans, the Antarctic environment is modelled in more distinctive forms. The shape of the land in *March of the Penguins*—long flat plains, rugged enclosed canyons, steep faced hills and cliffs in the middle distance—looks like an icebound version of the classic Western, as suggested earlier. In *Happy Feet* everything in the landscape is literally heightened, however, so that it acquires a much more dramatic force of its own. Indeed it is very close, at times, to iconic images of the Romantic sublime, with huge sweeps of vertiginous mountain imparting an upward surge and energy to the viewpoint, particularly at key moments of crisis in the story. Since the concept of the Romantic sublime is in itself expressive of rupture, projected spiritually onto nature, the film may well be reaching out for an imagery that resonates with the split it seeks to heal.[24]

CONCLUSION

What, then, are the implications of this case study? Primarily, the study raises questions about the role of realism in films that dramatize environmental themes. Part of the purpose of this paper has been to explore the emotional, as well as cognitive, significance of cinema's capacity to bring realistic images of the world—including parts of earth few of us are ever likely to see first-hand—within audiences' purview. But what is the significance of extending the reach of areas that we feel we "know" in some way like this? And to what extent is "knowing"—even when construed in terms of images recording real life—ultimately an imaginative act, grounded on a poetics as much as upon empirically grounded detail? In focusing on the poetics of even the most real-istically grounded representations of nature in the way I have done here, I am suggesting that the affective dimension should be central to our understand-ing of how films work. As Graham Walters (producer of *Finding Nemo*) puts it, "ultimately, what you have to do in animation—any kind of filmmaking, really—is direct the audience's eyes to where you want them to go, to not just soak in the environment, but feel it."[25]

This study suggests that it is impossible to assess the impact of films that appear to have potential for connecting viewers with nature without engaging with the poetics of the film form within which such narratives are produced. Jonathan Burt has suggested that, rather than seeing nature films as a kind of "replacement for reality, they seem more like the point of entry for our engage-ment with the natural world: an active moral gaze made possible, even struc-tured, by the technology of modernity."[26] My case study of the relationship between two related films has also focused on the way genres shape narratives to do distinctive kinds of work for us and raises questions about the value of film genres with a non-realist aesthetic—particularly for the young—in developing ecocritical perspectives. Do we need to develop a different critical vocabulary and set of theories to appreciate the kinds of work that films in a non-realistic idiom may perform? And how do we make judgments about film narratives where realistic and fantasy elements are mixed? Is ecocriticism in general too enthralled to realism anyway? Or is the only really viable antidote to a culture that commodifies and packages every aspect of nature to feed consumers' desires an art that insists on representing realistic detail with scrupulous care and integrity? Finally is it the function of cinema—perhaps especially popular cinema—to provide an arena within which the unresolved anxieties of a culture can be rehearsed and exercised in forms that remain pleasurable, rather than to serve as a tool for didactic intentions, however worthy? These are all large—perhaps ultimately unanswerable—questions. But I hope the small scale analysis presented here may at least take us some way further in bringing what is crucial within these questions into clearer focus.

NOTES

1 Anat Pick, *Creaturely Poetics: Animality and Vulnerability in Literature and Film* (New York: Columbia University Press, 2011), 5.

2 Noël Carroll, *Theorizing the Moving Image* (Cambridge: Cambridge University Press, 1996), 81.

3 Sean Cubitt, *EcoMedia* (Amsterdam: Rodopi, 2005), 1–2.

4 *March of the Penguins*, directed by Luc Jacquet (Burbank, CA: Warner Bros, 2005), DVD; *Happy Feet*, directed by George miller, Warren Coleman, and Judy Morris (Burbank, CA: Warner Bros, 2006), DVD.

5 Leo Braudy, "The Genre of Nature: Ceremonies of Innocence," in *Refiguring American Film Genres: Theory and History*, ed. Nick Browne (Berkeley: University of California Press, 1998), 279.

6 Braudy, "The Genre of Nature," 281.

7 Braudy, "The Genre of Nature," 296.

8 Braudy, "The Genre of Nature," 292.

9 Braudy, "The Genre of Nature," 296.

10 Interestingly, some recent theorists have seen the figure of the animal as itself in a state of "perpetual vanishing" within contemporary culture. See, for instance, Anat Pick: "Animals dwell in the spectral state of an active disappearance." Pick, *Creaturely Poetics*, 5.

11 See, for instance, Paul Arendt's 2005 review: "The effect is somewhat spoiled by Morgan Freeman's soothing, sentimental narration, which coats the action like treacle over ice cream." Paul Arendt, review of *March of the Penguins*, British Broadcasting Corporation, 1 December 2005, http://www.bbc.co.uk/films/2005/12/01/march_of_the_penguins_2005_review.shtml.

12 Charles Darwin, *The Expression of the Emotions in Man and Animals* (London: John Murray, 1872).

13 For what remains one of the richest accounts of shifts in intellectual and emotional attitudes towards animals from the sixteenth to the early nineteenth century, see Keith Thomas, *Man and the Natural World: Changing Attitudes in England 1500–1800* (Harmondsworth, UK: Penguin, 1984).

14 Cubitt, *EcoMedia*, 26.

15 Ivone Margulies, *Rites of Realism: Essays on Corporeal Cinema* (Durham, NC: Duke University Press, 2003), 3.

16 Paul Arendt, review of *Happy Feet*, British Broadcasting Corporation, 4 December 2006, http://www.bbc.co.uk/films/2006/12/04/happy_feet_2006_review.shtml.

17 The evocative and darkly atmospheric journey that Marlowe makes upriver in Conrad's novella is transposed onto the setting of the Vietnam War in Coppola's film, with a diegetic soundtrack of late iconic 1960s popular music, including songs by Jimi Hendrix and the Rolling Stones.

18 Stanton stated that the coral reef environment was "already so fantastical that you can't exaggerate it. But we realized we could simplify things, putting a sense of order to it. That's when we cracked it and got that slightly fantastical view of reality." Quoted in Mark Cotta Vaz, *The Art of Finding Nemo* (San Francisco: Chronicle Books, 2003), 22. Stanton offers a fuller reflection on the team's pulling back, in the final version of the film, from the most realistically sensuous version of the reef they had produced, in the interviews provided as additional material for the DVD version of the film. *Finding Nemo*, directed by Andrew Stanton (Emeryville, CA: Disney-Pixar, 2004), DVD.

19 Richard Dyer, "Entertainment and Utopia," in *Genre: the Musical*, ed. Rick Altman (London: Routledge and Kegan Paul, 1981).

20 Barry Langford, *Film Genre: Hollywood and Beyond* (Edinburgh: Edinburgh University Press, 2005), 91.

21 Langford, *Film Genre*, 91.

22 Michael Dunne, *American Film Musical: Themes and Forms* (Jefferson, NC: McFarland, 2004), 67.

23 Rick Altman, *The American Film Musical* (Bloomington: Indiana University Press, 1989), 307.

24 For a parallel argument on the role of the Romantic sublime as a space generating ecological awareness in popular film, see Pat Brereton, *Hollywood Utopia: Ecology in Contemporary American Cinema* (Bristol: Intellect Books, 2005).

25 Graham Walters, quoted in Cotta Vaz, *The Art of Finding Nemo*, 23.

26 Jonathan Burt, *Animals in Film* (London: Reaktion, 2002), 47.

BIBLIOGRAPHY

Altman, Rick. *The American Film Musical*. Bloomington: Indiana University Press, 1989.

Arendt, Paul. Review of *March of the Penguins*. British Broadcasting Corporation, 1 December 2005. http://www.bbc.co.uk/films/2005/12/01/march_of_the_penguins_2005_review.shtml.

———. Review of *Happy Feet*. British Broadcasting Corporation, 4 December 2006. http://www.bbc.co.uk/films/2006/12/04/happy_feet_2006_review.shtml.

Braudy, Leo. "The Genre of Nature: Ceremonies of Innocence." In *Refiguring American Film Genres: Theory and History*, edited by Nick Browne, 278–310. Berkeley: University of California Press, 1998.

Brereton, Pat. *Hollywood Utopia: Ecology in Contemporary American Cinema*. Bristol: Intellect Books, 2005.

Burt, Jonathan. *Animals in Film*. London: Reaktion, 2002.

Carroll, Noël. *Theorizing the Moving Image*. Cambridge: Cambridge University Press, 1996.

Cotta Vaz, Mark. *The Art of Finding Nemo*. San Francisco: Chronicle Books, 2003.

Cubitt, Sean. *EcoMedia*. Amsterdam: Rodopi, 2005.

Darwin, Charles. *The Expression of the Emotions in Man and Animals*. London: John Murray, 1872.

Dunne, Michael. *American Film Musical: Themes and Forms*. Jefferson, NC: McFarland, 2004.

Dyer, Richard. "Entertainment and Utopia." In *Genre: the Musical*, edited by Rick Altman, 175–89. London: Routledge and Kegan Paul, 1981.

Happy Feet. Directed by George Miller, Warren Coleman and Judy Morris. Burbank, CA: Warner Bros, 2006. DVD.

Langford, Barry. *Film Genre: Hollywood and Beyond*. Edinburgh: Edinburgh University Press, 2005.

March of the Penguins. Directed by Luc Jacquet. Burbank, CA: Warner Bros, 2005. DVD.

Margulies, Ivone. *Rites of Realism: Essays on Corporeal Cinema*. Durham and London: Duke University Press, 2003.

Pick, Anat. *Creaturely Poetics: Animality and Vulnerability in Literature and Film*. New York: Columbia University Press, 2011.

Thomas, Keith. *Man and the Natural World: Changing Attitudes in England 1500–1800*. Harmondsworth, UK: Penguin, 1984.

8

What Can a Film *Do?*
Assessing Avatar's Global Affects

Adrian Ivakhiv

What better study of cinematic affect than a blockbuster that broke all box-office records to become the most widely seen movie of all time, a film that explicitly portrays an eco-social utopia being viciously attacked by— and successfully fighting off—a colonial-capitalist army bent on domination and exploitation of nature for commercial profit?

Studies of cinema affect, to be convincing, must address audience responses, but these are highly variable and difficult to evaluate. *Avatar's* many spin-offs—from books and other commercial products to fan websites and activist appropriations in diverse global contexts—provide a broad base for analysis of the film's cognitive and affective impacts. This chapter will analyze *Avatar's* "global affects" with the aid of a process-relational model of cinema that understands the film experience as an affective-cognitive journey into a film-world that comes to interact, in variable ways, with the cognitive-affective potencies of the real, extra-filmic world.

Films, in this model, unfold in a series of material, perceptual, and social ecologies. They provide audio-visual material that viewers encounter as spectacle, or, in terms of C.S. Peirce's logical-phenomenological categories, as "firstness"; as narrativity, or "secondness"; and as exo-referentiality, or "thirdness." And they enact "worlds" that consist of geomorphic object-worlds, anthropomorphic subject-worlds, and biomorphic interperceptual dynamic-worlds. Seen in this framework, *Avatar's* divergent responses—from the seething critiques of many on both the political Right and Left to the enthusiastic forms of identification it elicited among many younger viewers, including some claiming to suffer from "post-Pandoran depression"—can be made sense of according to the ways these different viewers responded to the film. Critics, for instance, viewed the film primarily exo-referentially, by comparing it with other films and reading it through ideological and other theoretical frameworks. Fans primarily responded to the combination of spectacular effects and the straightforwardly heroic-melodramatic narrative, but also through a very specific exo-referential lens that followed the film's own eco-social resistance narrative. Communities of environmental activists in developing countries have especially found that narrative useful in communicating their own struggles in the global media environment.

The result is a film that not only affords a diversity of readings, but that makes available a range of affects for worldly projects that far exceed a single two-hour experience at the cinema. In what follows, I briefly expand upon the process-relational model of cinema that I have mentioned, and then apply this model to *Avatar*. I examine audience responses, including critiques from the political Right and Left, observations from anthropologists, environmentalists, and indigenous observers, and the responses of *Avatar*'s online fan communities. In the end I argue that *Avatar* successfully elicited strong "eco-affects" among many fans, and that it generated a variety of widespread conversations on socio-ecological topics, but that its potentials for bringing about a changed ecological sensibility was hampered by its tight and unoriginal narrative structure. If films are to be judged—as I argue they should—both by the *extent* of "eco-affects" that they generate and the *depth, resonance, and cognitive complexity* of those affects, then *Avatar* did very well on the first criterion and less well on the second. For a Hollywood blockbuster, that nevertheless makes it, if not unique, at least somewhat remarkable.

A PROCESS-RELATIONAL ACCOUNT OF CINEMA

The process-relational model on which I draw in this chapter has been developed in detail elsewhere.[1] Given space constraints, I will introduce that model here only to the extent that is necessary for understanding *Avatar*. This model of cinema draws on the philosophies of Alfred North Whitehead, Charles Sanders Peirce, Gilles Deleuze, and others, to argue that what is most *real* in the universe is relational process. All real entities, in this view, ultimately consist of such process, that is, the process of realizing subjective responses to factors that are given in experience. This process of mutual "subjectivation" and "objectivation"—the becoming-subject that entails a becoming-object of other things—occurs for any real entity, from humans and other complex animals "on down" to smaller organisms, cells, molecules, and beyond, and potentially "up" to larger and more complex systems. In tracing the various interactions of experiential process and the emergent, systemic relations that arise from them, such an understanding can account for the makings of the universe. A process-relational ontology differs from traditional ways of understanding the world in that instead of focusing on material or ideal causes alone (as would materialist or idealist ontologies), or on the interplay of the two (as would dualist forms of reasoning), process-relational thinking assumes that the material and the ideal are two sides of the same event, which is the processual event or encounter that is at the heart of all and any experience. Experience is, in this sense, defined in very basic terms: it is relational responsiveness and encounter. And the universe is, in this model, experiential "all the way down." Everything that appears to be non-experiential is an artifact of perception, an object created in and through its relationship with a subject, each of which arises in time out of the manifold causes leading up to it together with the creativity (however small or large) that constitutes subjectivation.[2]

A process-relational account of cinema focuses on how films and other moving-image media *enact film-worlds*; how viewers enter into and navigate those film-worlds, which constitutes the *film-experience*; and how the two processes interact with the material, social, and perceptual ecologies within which they arise and unfold. According to this understanding, a film *is* what a film *does*—materially, socially, and perceptually. And what it does for its viewers, primarily, is generate worlds that they enter and engage with, cognitively and affectively. Cinema is, in this sense, cosmomorphic: it provides for the morphogenesis, the coming into form, of worlds. At least three dimensions of these worlds are relevant to our analysis: (1) the object-world, which expresses cinema's "geomorphism," its taking on the form of a stable, material-like world that is there, given for agents like us to act within; (2) the subject-world, which, for human viewers, is its "anthropomorphism," the world of those recognized as active, human-like subjects and agents within it; and (3) the interperceptive life-world, the world of things that are lively and dynamic, a world constituted by an interactive to-and-fro between subject- and object-making, which is the film-world's "biomorphism." Just as experience consists of subjectivation and objectivation, both of which emerge out of an interactive to-and-fro between elements that arise spontaneously or causally from moments of experience, so the cosmomorphism of a filmic world also consists of a becoming-subject-world, a becoming-object-world, and a dynamic, interperceptive relational process from which these two emerge and congeal at either end. Ultimately, there is only relational process, but out of this process, in all its permutations, arise subjectively experienced worlds.

Viewers' experiences of film-worlds unfold according to another trio of relations. There is, first, the thick immediacy of cinematic spectacle, the shimmering texture of image and sound as it strikes us and resounds in us affectively; this is the moving image that *moves* us most immediately and directly. Second, there is the sequential unfolding of film's narrative "eventness," the one-thing-after-anotherness which we follow in order to find out what happens next and where it will lead. And third, there is the proliferation of meanings that arise once our already-existing worlds are set into motion by what we see, hear, witness, and follow in watching a film or video. I call these three layers or dimensions cinema's *spectacle*, its *narrativity*, and its *signness* or *exo-referentiality*; and the results of each of these as they impact us are, respectively, the affective, the narrative, and the referential or semiotic. Analyzing these three triads—the film-world created by a film in its geomorphism, biomorphism, and anthropomorphism; the film-experience generated as a viewer negotiates that world, in its spectacular, narrative, and exo-referential dimensions; and the relations between the film-world/experi-ence and the extra-filmic world, in their materiality, sociality, and interpercep-tuality—provides for an ecocritically comprehensive understanding of films in their similarities and differences.

AVATAR'S ECO-APOCALYPTIC FILM-WORLD

On the surface, *Avatar* presents a world in which a military-industrial-colonial network is pitted against an eco-pagan tribal world that the former is attempt-ing to subdue for its own gain. For the film's viewers, this conflict sets up the possibility of cognitively and emotionally navigating the differences between these two counterposed systems. Following its main characters, especially the ex-marine Jake Sully, who defects from the first system to the second one, viewers can also think and feel what it means to vacate the first one and "try on" the second. In the development of its storyline, the film presents a clash which is resolved through military and political means: specifically, through the cobbling together of a multi-species alliance of indigenous Pandorans, people and other creatures, along with a few key human defectors, so as to fight off the colonial oppressors represented by Colonel Quaritch and his SecFor human-machine army.

The making of *Avatar* mobilized massive resources of what might be called the industrial-entertainment complex, or even the military-industrial-enter-tainment complex. Among other things, it required the creation of new techno-logical capabilities, including advanced 3-D and motion-capture technology, which contributed to the excitement generated around the making and staging of the film. Its effects included not only the reactions and responses of viewers, but the generation of many products and profits. *Avatar* set the bar for immersive cinema higher than it had been set before. I will leave aside the material and social impacts of the film's making, distribution, and consumption in what follows, and focus instead on the perceptual, intellectual, discursive, and emotional/affective impacts of the film. The latter constitute the "perceptual ecologies," as I am calling them, in and around the film.

By many measures the most successful film ever made, seen by more viewers around the world than any other film in history, *Avatar* offers perhaps the best case study of the collective traversing of an eco-apocalyptic film-world by cinema audiences.[3] At once an eco-social utopia and a dystopia, the film brings together a combination of geomorphic and anthropomorphic effects. It depicts the contact between a society much like ours—a mining company exploiting the resources of a foreign land, which in this case is the planet Pandora, a lush, vegetated moon in the Alpha Centauri star system—and a tradition-bound indigenous society called the Na'vi. The latter is presented as radically other: they are blue-skinned and ten-foot-tall, for starters, and they live in a state of harmony with Pandoran "nature" that clearly eludes the planet's human invaders. While the human colony is engaged in scientific efforts to communicate and learn about the Na'vi and their world, these biological and anthropological efforts are trumped by the imperative to mine the ore of the mineral unsubtly named "unobtanium," which happens to be found in greatest abundance beneath the sacred trees of the Na'vi. Former marine Jake Sully is brought in to replace his deceased brother in a genetic engineering program that produces human-Na'vi hybrids to communicate and interact with the indigenous inhabitants, and when Sully is rescued by the Na'vi princess, Neytiri, and is granted the opportunity to learn Na'vi ways directly, he gradually "goes native." When the mining colony, with its private security army SecFor, initiates war in order to take control of the resources protected by the Na'vi, Sully and a few other compatriots are forced to take sides. They join the Na'vi and help corral a sweeping coalition of species to fight back and force the human army off the planet.

Two aspects of the film make it especially interesting from a process-relational perspective: the film's success as sheer spectacle, especially in its biomorphic generation of a captivating alien world; and the film's seeming capacity to generate different interpretations, readings, and meanings. Let us examine each of these in turn.

THE SPECTACLE OF *AVATAR*

The spectacle of *Avatar* is what elicited the greatest interest in the early stages of the film's reception.[4] The film is spectacular on multiple fronts: there are its immersive 3-D effects, CGI, and advanced motion-capture technology; there are the thrills-and-chills of its lengthy, high-tech and rapid-fire battle scenes; and, of greatest interest for an ecocritical reading, there is the film's scintillating portrayal of the biotic life of Pandora, perhaps the most seductive and alluring vision of another planet ever presented in cinema. *Avatar* was Cameron's long-time dream film, one he had first thought of making in the 1970s, but only began to write in the early 1990s, and one that was to push the technology of computer graphics, motion-capture, and 3-D cinema to levels heretofore unseen. Both *Avatar* and Cameron's previous blockbuster, *Titanic*, reflect their director's love of deep sea diving: the earlier one in the many submersible scenes of the *Titanic* wreck, the later one in the way the world of Pandora comes alive in bioluminescent splendour. As one online commenter and scuba diver put it, there is "no other ecological encounter which is so alien to our physiology, and so decentering. When one dives there is a kind of avatarship experience of suspension." The diving features, he argued, can be easily recognized,

> when Sully first playfully and childishly smacks luminescence to stimu-
> late it. A junior diver is the one that touches everything (often killing it
> to some degree). But it is not the portrayal of diving that Cameron was
> after […]. It was the kinesthetic transferral, the displacement, the suspen-
> sion, the alien drift, the wobbly wonder that bombards a diver, no matter
> how experienced. When every single living thing in an environment is
> physiologically superior to you. When every single living thing is aestheti-
> cally more beautiful. When your own suspension is technological and pre-
> carious before what can only be called a *witnessing*. The effect is ecological.[5]

The novelty of the 3-D experience is underlined by the film's repeated empha-
sis on seeing, from the recurrent shots of Sully's eyes and the first-person shots of his avatar's view of the Na'vi and their world, to the frequently repeated Na'vi greeting "I see you," intended as an acknowledgment of empathetic understanding of another. Sully is a fairly typical Hollywood action hero. He is disadvantaged to start with, being a disabled survivor of warfare, marginalized and ridiculed in multiple contexts: among the mercenaries sent to Pandora to defend the human colony, the scientists of the avatar program, and the Na'vi themselves. But he triumphs over adversity to become the sixth in a succession of Na'vi spiritual leaders known as Toruk Macto, with the ability to tame the birdlike creature known by that name and to unite the Na'vi clans. Following

Sully's trajectory can be a particularly immersive experience for viewers. In a study of the film's capacity for eliciting viewer empathies, Lisa Sideris notes that studies with virtual body transfers show a strong sense of ownership and identification with one's avatar body well after one has "returned" to one's own body.[6] Sully's transformation and "empathic education," Sideris demonstrates, remains "imperfect and incomplete," inasmuch as it shows him cutting corners and reverting, on numerous occasions, to the "jarhead" mentality that supposedly characterized his identity as a marine.[7] This leaves the film open to critiques that it exhibits the very colonial assertiveness it is attempting to curtail. It is, in this sense, a flawed and compromised version of the sorts of empathic tracts that have characterized the environmental movement, from Aldo Leopold's poignant account of the "fierce green fire" in a dying wolf's eyes to Rachel Carson's efforts to "think myself into the role of an animal that lives in the sea."[8] How viewers *follow* Sully in their identifications thus becomes one of the points at which viewer responses begin to diverge.

In its luxurious depiction of the Pandoran world, which takes up much of the film's first half, viewers have the option of enjoying this world, finding it beautiful, compelling, and attractive; of failing to enjoy it, finding it fearful or unattractive (it is, after all, full of horrific creatures); or of moving between these two extremes, for instance, being won over by its beauty in the same way that Sully is apparently won over. With its 3-D graphics and the immersive camera work and character movement (real and animated/simulated), the film elicits a strong sensation of movement into a biomorphically rich and strange world. But the filmic spectacle of the Pandoran biosphere is upstaged in the film's second half by the spectacle of war between the Na'vi, with their coalition of animal allies, and the high-tech military machine. Here the film recalls Cameron's work on the *Terminator* series. Viewers have the option of enjoying the spectacle and the bodily sensations of warfare—hunting and being hunted, shooting and being shot at, flying mounted on strange birds, and the jarring sensation of sudden attack, all in extremely rapidly edited jolts—and of enjoying their identification with one side or the other. Or they can enjoy the implicit message that "war is hell" (identifying with the underdogs, and perhaps appreciating the point that there may be times when we must take up arms in self-defense). Or, finally, they can reject all of these forms of enjoyment—which accounts for the critical response of those who disliked the film.

NARRATIVE STRUCTURES AND THE MANY READINGS OF THE FILM

To understand how viewers come to align with one of these responses, we need to examine more closely how the narrative structures these options for us. In its narrativity, the film is not very original. It is a traditional linear narrative of an encounter and conflict between two cultures, which seemingly takes the side of the underdogs but insists on casting the hero as a renegade member of the overdog (white, human) group. This hero is a traditional masculine point of identification: it is his struggles that we follow, and in the end he triumphs, "gets the girl," and even becomes a messiah. Geomorphically, there is a "here" and a "there": the mining colony represents the industrial-capitalist Earth we all know, while the alien world of the Pandoran Na'vi is the Zone we ourselves enter, explore, take pleasure in and, arguably, come to dominate. In this metaphorical meeting between West and non-West, the first is expanded by taking on something of its Other through a transmission that ultimately depends on the technology of the transfer—the avatarship of Jake Sully. Robert Hyland is not alone in reading all of this as a "colonial control narrative," where the white, male ex-marine masters and subordinates a series of others: starting with his own alien avatar body and extending to the Pandoran terrain, Na'vi language and culture, various beasts, which he literally penetrates to force them to do his bidding, the Na'vi princess, and finally the entire Na'vi people.[9]

At the same time, there is no denying that the conflict is between two radically different cultures and ways of life, and that the Na'vi, with or without Jake Sully, present an imagined alternative to the society that is dominant on *our* planet. What makes the film interesting in this respect is the way it lays its structuring oppositions onto one another, opening itself up to a range of exo-referential analogies and allegorical interpretations. It is these that were the focus of the second stage of the public debate over the film once the attention to the 3-D and CGI subsided. Allegory is a classic instance of exo-referentiality: a case of something in the film standing in for something else in the real world. A list of common allegorical interpretations of *Avatar* would include at least the following: the human takeover of the planet as an allegory of rampant resource extraction, neo-colonialism, rainforest destruction, US militarism, the global military-industrial complex, the Iraq War, the "War on Terror," and the genocide of indigenous peoples; the relationship between the humans and the Na'vi as a form of anthropological encounter, of "cultural understanding through immersion," of cultural imperialism and of the "white messiah complex"; the destruction of Hometree as a metaphor for the September 11 attack on the World Trade Center; and Pandora as an allegorical representation of the Gaia hypothesis, of the internet, or of cinema itself.[10] Let us look at a few of these more closely.

One of the ways in which American audiences grappled with the film was through the lens of the decades-long "culture wars" between the liberal left and the conservative right. Read as a liberal-environmentalist credo, the film became a lightning rod for right-wing critics, who typically lambasted both its superficiality and its thinly disguised attack on corporate militarism, which the critics found "anti-American."[11] Its depiction of Na'vi religion triggered right-wing critiques of its animism, pantheism, paganism, eco-religion, and New Age "hippie spiritualism."[12] Critics on the left, meanwhile, divided themselves between those celebrating the film's anti-corporate, anti-militarist, anti-imperialist, and pro-indigenous and ecological sentiments, and those critiquing its contradictions and ironies. Political theorist and media critic James Der Derian called it "the best anti-war film since *Dr. Strangelove*"; it "spectacularly ... repudiates the utility of war" and that "manages to entertain and to critique, to revel in the pleasures and to expose the pathologies of the military-industrial complex within a wholly new media-entertainment matrix."[13] Others derided the film's racism. Slavoj Žižek, for instance, lambasted its suggestion that "a paraplegic outcast from earth is good enough to get the hand of a beautiful local princess, and to help the natives win the decisive battle" and that "the only choice the aborigines have is to be saved by the human beings or to be destroyed by them," that is, that "they can choose to be the victim of imperialist reality, or to play their allotted role in the white man's fantasy."[14] In other words, the Na'vi can either be real and lose (to "imperialist reality"), or be fake (a "white man's fantasy") and win. Yet one could counter-argue that such critics are stacking the deck: couldn't losing (getting crushed by the imperialist machine) be just as fake, since it is only a movie, and, as we know, the real people at the other end of the imperialist wars of our time—Afghanistan in particular comes to mind—have not so clearly lost? And couldn't winning—with the help of a few white humans, but against the vast majority of them—be equally real if one's victory inspires people around the planet to rise up against their resource-robbing oppressors? A film is not only what happens between the dimming and the turning back up of the lights. It is also what happens in our discussions, dreams, and lives as we work with the images, sounds, and symbols it makes available to us. In this sense, the judgments of Žižek and other critics may be premature.

In an analysis that takes in Cameron's entire *oeuvre*, Lacanian theorist Todd McGowan argued that the film pits a Spielbergian "paternal" ideology, which convinces us that the social order is solidly founded in the patriarchal authority represented by Colonel Quaritch, against the eco-maternalism of Eywa, the mother-goddess of the Na'vi. The latter represents an ideology of wholeness, plenitude, and the "sense of belonging to a transcendent network of significance."[15] Cameron is not alone among contemporary filmmakers in questioning patriarchy in favour of an ecological or maternalist holism. In McGowan's reading, however, there is a productive tension between the maternal as plenitude, visible in the Na'vi belief that Eywa "does not take sides" but "protects the balance of life," and the maternal as itself divided: Eywa does, in the end, take sides and get drawn into the political. Yet the final struggle between Sully and Quaritch, McGowan writes, "has all the trappings of Hollywood's ideological denouement" in which "the psychology of the villain takes center stage": Quaritch's "individual homicidal psychosis trumps the villainy of the structural evil and allows the spectator to personalize evil."[16]

In contrast to McGowan's neo-Lacanian argument, is the prevailing tenor of pro-ecological views expressed about the film (widespread and easily found among online responses), which could be called eco-maternalist. Eywa, in this view, is triumphant and this ought to be celebrated.[17] From another perspective, however, all of these messages are undercut by the implicit message that it is technology and Hollywood magic—the Image Industry—that enchants, seduces, and delivers us from evil. The tension between the film's ostensibly critical message and its technological wizardry recalls a similar debate that arose over the film *Jurassic Park*. As ecopsychologist Renee Lertzman put it, "While the film purports to be proenvironmental—'Enter the world,' the tagline says—the psychic message delivered by the story is about leaving the world. [...] Don the glasses and leave our world of plastic cups and sticky soda, and drift among the trees and exotic species likely to be endangered on our own planet."[18] And more than in most fantasies, what that psychic message is about is new life, maybe eternal life, through the New Age sciences of neuro-energetics, gene splicing, and virtual reality. Jake Sully the Na'vi avatar (not the marine) is, after all, a zombie and a drone: his body is a remote-controlled, genetically engineered robot that comes to life, echoing the fantasy of a hypercapitalist American dream of remaking oneself as someone else entirely.

This fantasy underlying the avatar theme is the crux of social ecologist Max Cafard's lengthy and searing indictment of the film.[19] Cafard calls *Avatar* "the most important film in history," unsurpassed "in showing the ways in which ideology turns things into their precise opposite."[20] Its explicit message "that civilization is oppressive and destructive and that we should break with it, smash its power, and go to live in egalitarian, ecological communities instead" and its delivery of this message using the most sophisticated affective technologies in history conspire to blind viewers to the fact that the film's "ability to inspire any active opposition to war and imperialism is nil."[21] Instead it offers "pseudo-subversive images," commodified forms of dissent providing only imaginary substitutes for action.[22] The minimal actions it inspires—such as the "Home Tree Initiative," which Twentieth Century Fox developed in partnership with The Earth Day Network to plant a million trees in 2010 by signing up adopt-a-tree "warriors of the earth"—have borne little fruit. Cafard caustically notes that the initiative only managed to enlist 290,000 "adoptive tree parents" by the end of the year,[23] but one could argue that this is not bad, for what it's worth.[24] The film's "most powerful ideological message" and "final truth," in Cafard's reading, is the message that only "the Drone," the "latest product of the drive for technological domination [...] from a distance," "can save us."[25] The Drone, he writes, "reveals the *telos* of superpower military-industrial technology." While "the dominated can be more intensely terrorized," the dominators are rendered less and less vulnerable (though fantasies of vulnerability paradoxically increase as tolerance of risk declines).[26] Along related lines, Caleb Crain attacks the movie's "moral corruptness," arguing that its anti-imperialism and anti-corporatism are red herrings planted to distract us from "the movie's more serious ideological work: convincing you to love your simulation—convincing you to surrender your queasiness." On Pandora, he writes, the Na'vi are "digital natives" and "all the creatures have been equipped by a benevolent nature with USB ports in their ponytails."[27] At the very least, it is reasonable to agree that the film navigates a tension between technophilia and technophobia, and that this tension plays itself out between its overt "symbolic" message (in a Lacanian sense) and its implicit "imaginary" or "real" function.

TRACING THE FILM'S EFFECTS

The theme of encounter between colonialists and indigenous people made the film particularly interesting to cultural anthropologists and to non-westerners. One anthropologist, writing on the environmental anthropology listserv E-ANTH, characterized the film as being "like a giant anthropological piñata," while others noted the resemblance between the film's "avatars" and the real-world "human terrain avatars" of the US military's occupation of Iraq.[28] Anthropology's deep historical implication within militarism and colonialism gets its own reflection in the film's depiction of scientist Grace Augustine and her human-Na'vi avatar project. Yet many on the same listserv reported audiences as far apart as Brazil and Malaysia leaving theatres energized and mobilized for discussing issues of imperialism, globalization, capitalism, and struggles over control of resources. The film's pro-mining humans, one anthropologist suggested, are recognized as the same faces as those of private security companies at extractive mines around the world, at a time when human rights abuses at such mines are up to an all-time high.[29]

Avatar's popularity gave it currency among media-savvy environmental and indigenous activists as widely dispersed as South America, Palestine, and South and East Asia. It encouraged activists in the occupied Palestinian village of Bil'in to paint themselves blue in a protest march that resulted in the Israeli army tear-gassing and sound bombing the activists.[30] Footage of the incident juxtaposed with clips from *Avatar* circulated on YouTube. Bolivia's indigenous president, Evo Morales, praised the film as an "inspiration in the fight against capitalism."[31] In Ecuador, members of various indigenous groups were impressed with the parallels between the Na'vi and their own struggles against mining corporations and corporate or governmental military proxies. A little digging reveals that this meeting of indigenous people and movie screens, as reported in media and disseminated widely on websites, was arranged by Lynne Twist of the Pachamama Alliance after reading a blog post suggesting that very thing.[32] Proceeds from the film have gone to fund reforestation projects in South America, and in India a tribal group appealed to James Cameron to help them stop the open-cast mining of a mountain by the (somewhat perversely named) Vedanta Resources mining company.[33] In China, meanwhile, as the film broke box office records and the government moved to restrict the film to a small number of 3-D screens, presumably because of its (counter-) revolutionary potential, tourist operators promoted the Huangshan and Zhiangjiajie mountains as models for the "hanging mountains" of Pandora.[34]

Environmentalist responses echoed this mixture of activist and pragmatic sentiments and motivations. Writing on the Mother Nature Network blog, Harold Linde called it "without a doubt the most epic piece of environmental advocacy ever captured on celluloid," which hits "all the important environmental talking-points—virgin rain forests threatened by wanton exploitation, indigenous peoples who have much to teach the developed world, a planet which functions as a collective, interconnected Gaia-istic organism, and evil corporate interests that are trying to destroy it all."[35] James Cameron encouraged these readings, calling Pandora "an evocation of the world we used to have," "before we started to pave it and build malls, and shopping centers."[36] Others, taking advantage of the attention to the film, explored its themes by looking for real-world analogues among indigenous peoples fighting off corporate exploitation in the Peruvian Andes, Malaysian Borneo, the Ecuadoran rainforest, the Indian Himalayas, and elsewhere.[37]

Indigenous responses were not so much positive as they were pragmatic, and many were prefaced by low expectations that Hollywood could possibly reflect their perspective. In a nuanced account, Cherokee professor Daniel Heath Justice acknowledged the film's value for drawing attention to indigenous issues, but took it to task for its simplistic narrative and its distancing of the audience "from any complicity with these evils on our world" and thereby making "real and lasting change" all the less likely. Audiences can identify with cartoon heroes but "are exempted from the hard work that actually accompanies the struggles for decolonization, social and environmental justice, and peace."[38] On the other hand, an extensive mixed-methods study of responses to the film among Native and non-Native Hawaiians showed that the "vast majority" of those surveyed "were able to identify moral messages from the film months after viewing it," retaining "pro-'environment' messages," including "of the importance of humans connecting to the land," and "readily identif[ying] the connection between Hawaii's history and Avatar's plotline." Indigenous Hawaiians, in particular, "identified and related to messages" concerning the film's animist spiritual sensibilities and "the need to respect culture."[39]

Beyond these responses among organized discursive communities—of environmentalists, anthropologists, politically motivated intellectuals, and indigenous people—it is the film's uptake by its most active fans, particularly those who constituted new online communities on the basis of the film itself, that indicates to us its most telling *affective* impacts. Media reports in early January began to note a phenomenon that came to be called "post-Pandoran depression," a malady apparently suffered by those for whom the real world of Earth seemed lackluster in comparison with the alluring world of the Na'vi.[40] Discussions of this "depression" first emerged on the website Avatar-Forums.com under threads with titles like "Ways to cope with the depression of the dream of Pandora being intangible," with the number of posts on the topic eventually reaching over three thousand.[41] Examining the discussion, one finds a combination of eco-despair—the response, according to ecopsychologists, that many people feel when they come to recognize the extent of the ecological crisis—and something more like virtual reality withdrawal. Because *Avatar* is a movie and not the kind of VR environment that is repeatedly visited by gamers, and yet it comes close, in its 3-D version, to being as immersive as a VR game, the withdrawal symptoms are hidden or subsumed into the seemingly more real ecological reality check. The film's version of the "wilderness sublime" is made real, if not hyperreal, in the intensity of its cinematic portrayal. And the equally intense depiction of the viciousness of the colonizers' land grab, the assault on people and nature, and the accompanying Trail of Tears–like dispersal of the Na'vi, is hardly mitigated by the reprieve they seem to gain at the film's end—a reprieve that anyone who knows history understands can only be temporary at best, or wishful thinking at worst. What awaits our inevitable return to Earth, then, can be doubly disappointing.

Help was well on its way, however, for those suffering from the malady: in the form of video games, soundtracks, growing online communities, and even dictionaries and biological and social history field guides to Pandora.[42] The web forums Avatar-Forums.com and Naviblue.com grew to several thousand members each, and within a year of the film's release close to a million posts had been published on some thirty thousand separate topics.[43] Many "depression" sufferers typically sought to reimmerse themselves in the fictional Avatar world, for instance, by listening to the film's soundtrack, painting Pandoran landscapes, writing Avatar sequels, spending time on the Avatar web forum, and viewing the film repeatedly. Others, however, showed strong spiritual or political leanings, with some producing conversion narratives accounting forms of new-found activism on behalf of real-world communities whose plight resembled that of the fictional Na'vi.[44] Spiritual themes among fans, according to at least one study, showed a strong selectivity in favour of a focus on the film's ecological, pantheistic, and animistic themes and away from a concern with the film's violence and seeming technophilia.[45]

CONCLUSION

Gauging the level of activism triggered by Avatar in light of critiques like Cafard's, for whom its capacity for contributing to activism is nil, is not an easy task. The film is a hybrid of pop culture and radical critique that has set in motion a series of material, social, and perceptual-affective currents around the world. It presents various forms of cinematic excess—spectacle beyond what the narrative seems to warrant—including its luxurious depiction of the Pandoran world, but also its rather conventional cinematic glorification of war. Its exo-referentialities offer audiences many openings for interpretation, and viewers tend to follow the ones they are most responsive to. If there is a single coherent message, it is arguably something to do with the seemingly insatiable human craving for possessible objects, represented in the film by the quest for unobtanium, but which even children could substitute for the things most desired on Earth: oil, diamonds, toys, eternal life. But the film's response to this craving is contradictory. The text suggests the answer is through developing a culture that satisfies itself with what is in its midst (on the Na'vi life-world of Pandora), not elsewhere (on the distant planet Pandora). But this Buddhist-like message about the suffering induced by craving for objects that are really ungraspable processes, is, as Cafard writes, "contradicted by the film itself as a technologically utopian project, and by its plot elements that involve either explicit or mystified technological liberation." In the end, he writes, "the film ironically affirms precisely the same project that it negates."[46] As Lertzman notes, "It is not only the minerals on Pandora that are 'UnObtainium' but the idealized image of nature before the Fall itself: the fantasy of returning to the Garden that continues to plague most of us with any form of environmental consciousness."[47] If the Pandoran world becomes an elsewhere that is more attractive than our own lives in *this* world, as appears to be the case for at least some of those afflicted by "post-Pandoran depression," then we have simply replaced one set of fantasies with another.

But this, in the end, is the basis of *all* cinematic power: moving images draw us into them, their worlds lure and captivate us, drawing their beholders into their gravitational fields for the period of a couple of hours or so, but in some cases for much longer. In the case of *Avatar*, its film-world is a shimmering, vibrant, three-dimensional place, a world of movement in which sensory delight and wonder seem rediscoverable in the context of a rich floral and faunal paradise. In its creation of a dazzling alternative ecology, the film represents cinematic biomorphism at its best. Through the eyes of its main character, it presents a world that comes alive as ecologically and spiritually *different* and somehow *more alive* than the world of today's industrial capitalism. In this, it may elicit in environmentalists memories of experiences they may have had in the natural world, or perhaps of experiences they may have had while watching other films *about* the natural world (and its indigenous protectors). These memories contribute to viewers' ability to sympathize with the lead characters in the movie, both human (at least on the side of the "good guys") and Na'vi, whose struggles seem to reflect the struggles of people in *this* world that these viewers may sympathize or find a resonance with.

But this same film-world is also a place of technical wizardry and messianic violence, where the complexities of the real world's political ecologies have been rendered into a black-and-white caricature. *Avatar* has presented opportunities for activists to stake their own cases in a new set of image-frames, but its potential to deepen audiences' engagement with the elusive materialities of the world's real ecologies may be more limited than its fans would like. That, at least, would be the claim of many of the film's critics. At the same time, fandom, once triggered, sets off on its own trajectories, which in this case may include those that turn viewers into radical activists. Few blockbuster films do this, so the ones that might are worth paying attention to. Extensive, longitudinal studies of *Avatar* fan communities do not yet exist, as of this writing. If and when such studies are carried out, we will be able to say more about whether, and to what extent, *Avatar* has succeeded in generating long-term socio-ecological change in its fans.

What the film has done, however, aside from generating revenue and new products (along with the waste that almost inevitably accompanies them), is to generate certain affective sensibilities among its fans—sensibilities that these fans associate with ecology or eco-spirituality—and to raise certain socio-ecological issues into popular discussion. For environmentalists, this is more than most Hollywood blockbusters do. The film's contradictions have thus become a way for those who agree with the "message" to debate whether and to what extent that message is undercut by the "medium"—namely, by an ultra-expensive, technologically dependent, and rather violent form of escapist entertainment. It is, in this sense, a product of the military-industrial-*entertainment* complex turned against some of the manifest goals of the military-industrial complex. It is an internal critique of western, technological society, or rather of some of its aspects, presented by and within one of the most powerful vehicles of that same society. Among certain of the communities that have expended energy in debating it, the film will no doubt remain controversial precisely because of this paradoxical character.

NOTES

1 See Adrian Ivakhiv, *Ecologies of the Moving Image: Cinema, Affect, and Nature* (Waterloo, ON: Wilfrid Laurier University Press, 2013).

2 Process-relational thought has emerged in many times and places, including ancient Greece (Heraclitus and the Stoics), India (Nagarjuna and the Madhyamika philosophers), China (Zhuang Zhu, the T'ian-t'ai and Hua-Yen Buddhists), and in the early and late modern West in such philosophers as Bruno, Spinoza, Leibniz, Schelling, Bergson, Peirce, James, Dewey, Whitehead, Hartshorne, Simondon, Deleuze, Guattari, and Rescher. For a few recent articulations, see Nicholas Rescher, *Process Metaphysics: An Introduction to Process Philosophy* (Albany: State University of New York Press, 1996); David Ray Griffin, *Founders of Constructive Postmodern Philosophy: Peirce, James, Bergson, Whitehead, and Hartshorne* (Albany: State University of New York Press, 1993); and Isabelle Stengers, *Thinking with Whitehead: A Free and Wild Creation of Concepts* (Cambridge, MA: Harvard University Press, 2011).

3 With its gross receipts of nearly three billion dollars exceeding the gross national product of seventy-seven countries, it is, as Max Cafard observes, "the highest-grossing film of all time—in the U.S., in at least thirty-one other countries worldwide, and as far as we know, in the entire universe." Max Cafard, "Intergalactic Blues: Fantasy and Ideology in Avatar," *Psychic Swamp: The Surre(gion)al Review* 1 (2010): 9.

4 Viewer polls conducted during the opening weekend showed that the 3-D effects were the largest draw, and that all demographics gave the film a positive ("A" average) grade. See Neil Miller, "*Avatar* Opens to Big Returns, but Staying Power Is the Key," *Film School Rejects*, 21 December 2009, http://www.filmschoolrejects.com/news/avatar-opens-to-big-returns-but-staying-power-is-the-key.php.

5 Kvond, comment on "Avatar: Panthea v. the Capitalist War Machine," *Immanence* blog, 21 December 2009, http://blog.uvm.edu/aivakhiv/2009/12/21/avatar-panthea-v-the-capitalist-war-machine; Kvond, "Avatarship and the New Man: Reading Ideology, Technology and Hope," *Frames/sing*, 21 December 2009, http://kvond.wordpress.com/2009/12/21/

avatarship-and-the-new-man-reading-ideology-and-hope. On the other hand, Joshua Clover complains that most of the movie "looks like a series of Roger Dean album covers from 1970s prog-rock albums, set in motion. The technology is improving, but the achievement does not yet feel like a profound change in our experience of cinematic volume equivalent to Greg Toland's deep focus, the introduction of CinemaScope, or the onset of the Steadicam." Joshua Clover, "The Struggle for Space," *Film Quarterly* 63, no. 3 (2010): 6.

6 Lisa Sideris, "I See You: Interspecies Empathy and *Avatar*," *Journal for the Study of Religion, Nature and Culture* 4, no. 4 (2010): 465.

7 Sideris, "I See You," 471.

8 See Sideris, "I See You," 472ff.

9 Robert Hyland, "Going Na'vi: Mastery in *Avatar*," *CineAction* 82/83 (2011):12.

10 Catherine Grant perspicuously sifts through the many allegorical readings to be found online and in the press in "Seeing through *Avatar*: Film Allegory 101," *Film Studies for Free*, 27 January 2010, http://filmstudiesforfree.blogspot.com/2010/01/i-see-you-on-avatar-and-allegory .html. The Wikipedia article "Themes in Avatar" provides a thorough distillation of the film's many themes and interpretations. See http://en.wikipedia.org/wiki/Themes_in_Avatar. The cinema analogy is my own addition, which I have not seen elsewhere, but which is consistent with the argument made in my *Ecologies of the Moving Image*.

11 Many of these responses, by such commentators as Glenn Beck, John Podhoretz, and others, are documented on the Wikipedia "Themes in Avatar" article (see "Anti-Americanism").

12 See, for instance, Ross Douthat's op-ed "Heaven and Nature" in *The New York Times*, 20 December 2009, http://www.nytimes.com/2009/12/21/opinion/21douthat1.html?_ r=3&th&emc=th; Kathryn Reklis, "'New' Pantheism Enters the Oscar Race," *Immanent Frame*, 1 February 2010, http://blogs.ssrc.org/tif/2010/02/01/new-pantheism-enters-the -oscar-race; and Nathan Schneider, "The Religion of *Avatar*," *Immanent Frame*, 30 December 2009, http://blogs.ssrc.org/tif/2009/12/30/the-religion-of-avatar.

13 James Der Derian, "'Now We Are All Avatars,'" *Millennium: Journal of International Studies* 39, no. 1 (2010): 182–83.

14 Slavoj Žižek, "Return of the Natives," *New Statesman*, 4 March 2010, http://www.newstates man.com/film/2010/03/avatar-reality-love-couple-sex.

15 Todd McGowan, "Maternity Divided: *Avatar* and the Enjoyment of Nature," *Jump Cut* 52 (2010), http://www.ejumpcut.org/archive/jc52.2010/mcGowanAvatar.

16 McGowan, "Maternity Divided."

17 See, for instance, Vincent M. Gaine's "The Emergence of Feminine Humanity from a Tech-nologised Masculinity in the Films of James Cameron," *Journal of Technology, Theology and Religion* 2, no. 4 (2011): 1–41.

18 Renee Lertzman, "Desire, Longing and the Return to the Garden: Reflections on *Avatar*," *Ecopsychology* 2, no. 1 (2010): 42.

19 Cafard, "Intergalactic Blues."

20 Cafard, "Intergalactic Blues," 10.

21 Cafard, "Intergalactic Blues," 29.

22 Cafard, "Intergalactic Blues," 25.

23 Cafard, "Intergalactic Blues," 26.

24 Cafard argues that planting trees is a mere ruse for product promotion and marketing, which helps explain why the film had partnered with McDonald's and Coca-Cola for promotion. He quotes the film's website that "by filling out and submitting this registration form [to adopt a tree] I understand and agree that Twentieth Century Fox Home Entertainment may send me information about upcoming products, promotions and services and may use information about my activities on Fox web sites to determine what products, promotions and services are likely to be of interest to me." "Until," he interprets, "they can plant something directly in

your brain that determines what your interests are, they need a little bit of cooperation on your part to effectively track and check up on you." Cafard, "Intergalactic Blues," 27.

25 Cafard, "Intergalactic Blues," 31.

26 Cafard, "Intergalactic Blues," 38.

27 Caleb Crain, "Don't Play with That, or You'll Go Blind: On James Cameron's *Avatar*," *n+1*, 1 January 2010, http://www.nplusonemag.com/dont-play-or-youll-go-blind.

28 Kerin Friedman, "*Avatar*," *Savage Minds*, 24 December 2009, http://savageminds.org; David Price, "Hollywood's Human Terrain Avatars," *CounterPunch*, 23 December 2009, http://www .counterpunch.org/price12232009.html.

29 E-ANTH listserv communication, 29 January 2010, http://www.aaanet.org/sections/ae/ index.php/listserv.

30 "Palestinians Dressed as Na'vi from the Film Avatar Stage a Protest against Israel's Separation Barrier," *Telegraph*, http://www.telegraph.co.uk/news/picturegalleries/worldnews/7222508/ Palestinians-dressed-as-the-Navi-from-the-film-Avatar-stage-a-protest-against-Israels -separation-barrier.html. Media theorists Henry Jenkins and Stephen Duscombe refer to such activist appropriations of popular media imagery as "participatory" and "spectacular" forms of cultural activism. See Henry Jenkins, "Avatar Activism," *Le monde diplomatique*, 15 September 2010, http://mondediplo.com/2010/09/15avatar.

31 "Evo Morales Praises 'Avatar,'" *Huffington Post*, 12 January 2010, http://www.huffingtonpost .com/2010/01/12/evo-morales-praises-avata_n_420663.html.

32 See, "Avatar and the Amazon," reported by Melaina Spitzer, *PRI's The World*, 29 January 2010, http://www.pri.org/search/node/avatar%20and%20the%20amazon; "Avatar Is Stimulating Some Very Juicy Conversation," *Tom-Atlee's posterous*, 27 January 2010, http://tom-atlee .posterous.com; "Avatar and Making All the Difference in the World," *Tom-Atlee's posterous*, 12 February 2010, http://tom-atlee.posterous.com.

33 Kathryn Hopkins, "Indian Tribe Appeals for *Avatar* Director's Help to Stop Vedanta," *Guardian*, 8 February 2010, http://www.guardian.co.uk/business/2010/feb/08/ dongria-kondh-help-stop-vedanta.

34 Pete Stanton, "China Pulls *Avatar* from Their Cinemas Fearing Civil Unrest," *Moviefone*, 19 January 2010, http://blog.moviefone.com/2010/01/19/china-bans-avatar-from-their-cinemas -fearing-civil-unrest; Moon, "Avatar Lands on a Wrong Mountain?" *China Decoded*, 4 January 2010, http://www.chinadecoded.com/2010/01/04/avatar-lands-on-a-wrong-mountain.

35 Harold Linde, "Is *Avatar* Radical Environmental Propaganda?" *Mother Nature Network*, Karl Burkart's blog, 4 January 2010, http://www.mnn.com/green-tech/research-innovations/blogs/ is-avatar-radical-environmental-propaganda.

36 "SRK Means India for Cameron," *Times of India*, 20 March 2010, http://timesofindia .indiatimes.com/entertainment/bollywood/news-interviews/SRK-means-India-for -Cameron/articleshow/5702067.cms?referral=PM.

37 See Jeremy Hance, "The Real Avatar Story: Indigenous People Fight to Save Their Forest Homes from Corporate Exploitation," *mongabay.com*, 22 December 2009, http://news.mongabay .com/2009/1222-hance_avatar.html; Rohini Hensman, "Of *Avatar* and Adivasis: How James Cameron's *Avatar* Relates to the Exploitation of Indigenous People of the World and India," *Over the Top: Raising a Regional Ruckus* (*Himal SouthAsian*), 28 January 2010, http:// himalmag.com/blogs/blog/2010/01/28/of-avatar-and-adivasis. See also Žižek, "Return of the Natives."

38 Daniel Heath Justice, "James Cameron's *Avatar*: Missed Opportunities," *First Peoples: New Directions in Indigenous Studies*, 20 January 2010, http://www.firstpeoplesnewdirections.org/ blog/?p=169.

39 Rachelle K. Gould, Nicole M. Ardoin, and Jennifer Kamakanipakolonaheʻokekai Hashimoto, 'Mālama the ʻĀina, Mālama the People on the ʻĀina': The Reaction to *Avatar* in Hawaiʻi," *Journal for the Study of Religion, Nature and Culture* 4, no. 4 (2010): 450, 452.

40 Jo Piazza, "Audience Experience 'Avatar' Blues," *CNN Entertainment*, 11 January 2010, http://www.cnn.com/2010/SHOWBIZ/Movies/01/11/avatar.movie.blues/index.html.

41 Matthew Holtmeier, "Post-Pandoran Depression or Na'vi Sympathy: *Avatar*, Affect, and Audience Reception," *Journal for the Study of Religion, Nature and Culture* 4, no. 4 (2010): 415.

42 Dictionaries include Marki and Tirea Aean's *Definitive Na'vi Dictionary* and NeotrekkerZ's *Na'vi in a Nutshell*, both available at www.learnnavi.org. Field guides include Maria Wilhelm and Dirk Matheson's *James Cameron's Avatar: An Activist Field Guide—A Confidential Report on the Biological and Social History of Pandora* (New York: It Books, 2009). See also Henry Jenkins, "Avatar Activism and Beyond," *Confessions of an Aca-Fan*, 22 September 2010, http://henryjenkins.org/2010/09/avatar_activism_and_beyond.html; and Jenkins, "Avatar Activism," (*Le monde diplomatique*).

43 Britt Istoft documents that the web forums Avatar-Forums.com and Naviblue.com had some 8,000 and 5,500 members each, respectively (it's not clear how many of these members overlapped), and that over 850,000 posts had been logged on some 27,000 subjects within nine months of the film's release. Britt Istoft, "*Avatar* Fandom as Nature-Religious Expression?" *Journal for the Study of Religion, Nature and Culture* 4, no. 4 (2010): 401.

44 Holtmeier, "Post-Pandoran Depression," 416–18. See also Jenkins, "Avatar Activism."

45 Istoft argued that the technological violence "evoked little response" among the fan groups he studied. Istoft, "*Avatar* Fandom," 411.

46 The quote here is from Cafard, "Intergalactic Blues," 33. I explored the connection between the Lacanian and Buddhist understandings of desires in a series of blog posts reviewing and responding to an article by John Clark. ("Max Cafard" is Clark's radical pen name.) See Adrian Ivakhiv, "Nagarjuna, Ecophilosophy, and the Practice of Liberation," *Immanence*, 14 November 2009, http://blog.uvm.edu/aivakhiv/2009/11/14/nagarjuna-ecophilosophy-the-practice-of-liberation; and Ivakhiv, "Nagarjuna and Ecophilosophy, pt. 2," *Immanence*, 14 November 2009, http://blog.uvm.edu/aivakhiv/2009/11/14/nagarjuna-ecophilosophy-pt-2.

47 Lertzman, "Desire," 42.

BIBLIOGRAPHY

Avatar. Directed by James Cameron. Los Angeles: Twentieth Century Fox, 2009. DVD.

Cafard, Max. "Intergalactic Blues: Fantasy and Ideology in *Avatar*." *Psychic Swamp: The Surre(gion)al Review* 1 (2010): 9–41.

Clover, Joshua. "The Struggle for Space." *Film Quarterly* 63, no. 3 (2010): 6–7.

Crain, Caleb. "Don't Play with That, or You'll Go Blind: On James Cameron's *Avatar*." *n+1*, 1 January 2010. http://www.nplusonemag.com/dont-play-or-youll-go-blind.

Der Derian, James. "'Now We Are All Avatars.'" *Millennium: Journal of International Studies* 39, no. 1 (2010): 181–86.

Douthat, Ross. "Heaven and Nature." *New York Times*, 20 December 2009. http://www.nytimes.com/2009/12/21/opinion/21douthat1.html?_r=3&th&emc=th.

Friedman, Kerin. "*Avatar*." *Savage Minds*, 24 December 2009. http://savageminds.org.

Gaine, Vincent M. "The Emergence of Feminine Humanity from a Technologised Masculinity in the Films of James Cameron." *Journal of Technology, Theology and Religion* 2, no. 4 (2011): 1–41.

Gould, Rachelle K., Nicole M. Ardoin, and Jennifer Kamakanipakolonahe'okekai Hashimoto. "'*Mālama* the *'Āina*, *Mālama* the People on the *'Āina*': The Reaction to *Avatar* in Hawai'i." *Journal for the Study of Religion, Nature, and Culture* 4, no. 4 (2010): 450–52.

Grant, Catherine. "Seeing through *Avatar*: Film Allegory 101." *Film Studies for Free*, 27 January 2010. http://filmstudiesforfree.blogspot.com/2010/01/i-see-you-on -avatar-and-allegory.html.

Griffin, David Ray. *Founders of Constructive Postmodern Philosophy: Peirce, James, Bergson, Whitehead, and Hartshorne*. Albany: State University of New York Press, 1993.

Hance, Jeremy. "The Real Avatar Story: Indigenous People Fight to Save Their Forest Homes from Corporate Exploitation." *Mongabay.com*, 22 December 2009. http:// news.mongabay.com/2009/1222-hance_avatar.html.

Hensman, Rohini. "Of *Avatar* and Adivasis: How James Cameron's *Avatar* Relates to the Exploitation of Indigenous People of the World and India." *Over the Top: Raising a Regional Ruckus (Himal SouthAsian)*, 28 January 2010. http://himalmag .com/blogs/blog/2010/01/28/of-avatar-and-adivasis.

Holtmeier, Matthew. "Post-Pandoran Depression or Na'vi Sympathy: *Avatar*, Affect, and Audience Reception." *Journal for the Study of Religion, Nature, and Culture* 4, no. 4 (2010): 414–24.

Hopkins, Kathryn. "Indian Tribe Appeals for *Avatar* Director's Help to Stop Vedanta." *Guardian*, 8 February 2010. http://www.guardian.co.uk/business/2010/feb/08/ dongria-kondh-help-stop-vedanta.

Huffington Post. "Evo Morales Praises'Avatar.'" 12 January 2010. http://www.huffington post.com/2010/01/12/evo-morales-praises-avata_n_420663.html.

Hyland, Robert. "Going Na'vi: Mastery in *Avatar*." *CineAction* 82/83 (2011): 10–16.

Istoft, Britt. "*Avatar* Fandom as Nature-Religious Expression?" *Journal for the Study of Religion, Nautre and Culture* 4, no. 4 (2010): 394–413.

Ivakhiv, Adrian. *Ecologies of the Moving Image: Cinema, Affect, and Nature*. Waterloo, ON: Wilfrid Laurier University Press, 2013.

———. "Nagarjuna, Ecophilosophy, and the Practice of Liberation." *Imma-nence*, 14 November 2009. http://blog.uvm.edu/aivakhiv/2009/11/14/ nagarjuna-ecophilosophy-the-practice-of-liberation.

———. "Nagarjuna and Ecophilosophy, pt. 2." *Immanence*, 14 November 2009. http:// blog.uvm.edu/aivakhiv/2009/11/14/nagarjuna-ecophilosophy-pt-2.

Jenkins, Henry. "Avatar Activism and Beyond." *Confessions of an Aca-Fan*, 22 September 2010. http://henryjenkins.org/2010/09/avatar_activism_and_beyond.html; and "Avatar Activism." *Le monde diplomatique*. 15 September 2010. http://mondediplo .com/2010/09/15avatar.

Justice, Daniel Heath. "James Cameron's *Avatar*: Missed Opportunities." *First Peoples: New Directions in Indigenous Studies*, 20 January 2010. http://www.firstpeoples newdirections.org/blog/?p=169.

Kvond. "Avatarship and the New Man: Reading Ideology, Technology and Hope." *Frames/sing*, 21 December 2009. http://kvond.wordpress.com/2009/12/21/ avatarship-and-the-new-man-reading-ideology-and-hope.

———. Comment on "Avatar: Panthea v. the Capitalist War Machine." *Imma-nence* blog, 21 December 2009. http://blog.uvm.edu/aivakhiv/2009/12/21/ avatar-panthea-v-the-capitalist-war-machine.

Lertzman, Renee. "Desire, Longing and the Return to the Garden: Reflections on *Avatar*." *Ecopsychology* 2, no. 1 (2010): 41–43.

Linde, Harold. "Is *Avatar* Radical Environmental Propaganda?" *Mother Nature Network. Karl Burkart's Blog*, 4 January 2010. http://www.mnn.com/green-tech/research-innovations/blogs/is-avatar-radical-environmental-propaganda.

McGowan, Todd. "Maternity Divided: *Avatar* and the Enjoyment of Nature." *Jump Cut* 52 (2010). http://www.ejumpcut.org/archive/jc52.2010/mcGowanAvatar.

Miller, Neil. "*Avatar* Opens to Big Returns, but Staying Power is the Key." *Film School Rejects*, 21 December 2009. http://www.filmschoolrejects.com/news/avatar-opens-to-big-returns-but-staying-power-is-the-key.php.

Moon. "Avatar Lands on a Wrong Mountain?" *China Decoded*, 4 January 2010. http://www.chinadecoded.com/2010/01/04/avatar-lands-on-a-wrong-mountain.

Piazza, Jo. "Audience Experience 'Avatar' Blues." *CNN Entertainment*, 11 January 2010. http://www.cnn.com/2010/SHOWBIZ/Movies/01/11/avatar.movie.blues/index.html.

Price, David. "Hollywood's Human Terrain Avatars." *CounterPunch*, 23 December 2009. http://www.counterpunch.org/price12232009.html.

Reklis, Kathryn. "'New' Pantheism Enters the Oscar Race." *Immanent Frame*, 1 February 2010. http://blogs.ssrc.org/tif/2010/02/01/new-pantheism-enters-the-oscar-race.

Rescher, Nicholas. *Process Metaphysics: An Introduction to Process Philosophy*. Albany: State University of New York Press, 1996.

Schneider, Nathan. "The Religion of *Avatar*." *Immanent Frame*, 30 December 2009. http://blogs.ssrc.org/tif/2009/12/30/the-religion-of-avatar.

Sideris, Lisa. "I See You: Interspecies Empathy and *Avatar*." *Journal for the Study of Religion, Nature and Culture* 4, no. 4 (2010): 457–77.

Stanton, Pete. "China Pulls *Avatar* From Their Cinemas Fearing Civil Unrest." *Moviefone*, 19 January 2010. http://blog.moviefone.com/2010/01/19/china-bans-avatar-from-their-cinemas-fearing-civil-unrest.

Stengers, Isabelle. *Thinking with Whitehead: A Free and Wild Creation of Concepts*. Cambridge, MA: Harvard University Press, 2011.

Telegraph. "Palestinians Dressed as Na'vi from the Film *Avatar* Stage a Protest against Israel's Separation Barrier." http://www.telegraph.co.uk/news/picturegalleries/worldnews/7222508/Palestinians-dressed-as-the-Navi-from-the-film-Avatar-stage-a-protest-against-Israels-separation-barrier.html.

Times of India. "SRK Means India for Cameron." 20 March 2010. http://timesofindia.indiatimes.com/entertainment/bollywood/news-interviews/SRK-means-India-for-Cameron/articleshow/5702067.cms?referral=PM.

Wilhelm, Maria, and Dirk Matheson. *James Cameron's* Avatar: *An Activist Field Guide—A Confidential Report on the Biological and Social History of Pandora*. New York: It Books, 2009.

Žižek, Slavoj. "Return of the Natives." *New Statesman*, 4 March 2010. http://www.newstatesman.com/film/2010/03/avatar-reality-love-couple-sex.

9

Animated Ecocinema and Affect
A Case Study of Pixar's UP

Pat Brereton

This chapter will focus on a case study of Pixar's *UP* which ostensibly appears to subvert the branded studio model of Disney, while promoting a new generational engagement with ecological and other issues. Pixar's success is due, not only to their superior skills and craftsmanship across scripting and animation, but also to their careful and effective eco-branding and marketing. From Disney to Pixar: both ends of the production/distribution spectrum feed into the general public consciousness, framing important ecological debates that urgently need to be appreciated and addressed. While much theoretical analysis concentrates on the semiosis of the text, little work is done with regard to suggesting or at least inferring how actual audiences' emotions and pleasures are addressed. This paper attempts to capture some of the extra-textual features of audience engagement by focusing on DVD bonus-features as a bridge between the text and the creative makers of *UP*, who in turn speak directly to their audiences and affirm the film's affective eco-credentials.

The uses and benefits of DVD bonus features to frame creative intentionality and speak more directly to audience affect is part of a book on contemporary smart cinema recently completed for Palgrave.[1] Underpinning part of this investigation is the desire to question how fictional film might be read as more ecologically provocative and support long-term emotional/affective engagement with mass audiences. Building upon *Hollywood Utopia* (2005), I continue to explore how "feel good" narratives remain significant in keeping the environment at the centre of human consciousness. Much of this ecological research remains focused on the mediating and staging of global risk and how such texts help to create eco-imaginaries. To further promote this long-term project, this chapter will also draw on the tools of textual reception studies to help demonstrate how these resultant affects and emotional connections can be illustrated through a close reading of UP.

FROM INDUSTRIAL TO SMART ARTISANAL ANIMATION

A related question that interests me with regards to this study of Pixar—which has been recently subsumed into the Disney family—centres around what specifically animation, as an aesthetic form, can add to an ecological address that conventional fictional film might be less capable of constructing and engaging with.[2] "Disney's films are a revolt against partitioning and legislation, against spiritual stagnation and grayness. But the revolt is lyrical. The revolt is a daydream." This surprisingly positive projection is attributed to none other than the great Russian filmmaker Sergei Eisenstein.[3] More recently David Whitley has suggested that Disney is above anything else preoccupied within the realms of feelings.[4] Whitley, alongside numerous other scholars, convincingly argues that the Disney oeuvre, especially early works like Bambi (1942) and The Jungle Book (1967) have played an important role in educating the public about the environment.[5]

Conventional left cultural critics continuously seek to break "the Disney spell," much less "the Pixar magic," by interrogating the "magic" inside. It is suggested at one extreme that Disney's trademark innocence operates on a "systematic sanitization of violence, sexuality, and political struggles concomitant with an erasure or repression of difference."[6] Jack Zipes contextualizes this surprisingly uniform, almost Althusserian, critique by affirming that Walt Disney "capitalised on American innocence and utopianism to reinforce the social and political status quo. The great 'magic' of the Disney spell is that he animated the fairy tale only to transfix audiences and divert their potential utopian dreams and hopes through the false promises of the images he had cast on the screen."[7]

Meanwhile, Patrick Murphy's provocative essay subtitled "The Androcentric Animation of Denatured Disney" (1995) strikes at the heart of such left criticism, which remains more appropriate and relevant for my reading of the Pixar-Disney connection. According to Murphy, escapism in Disney is "based on denying wild nature as an integral part of the biosphere at the world level and as part of individual character at the personal level. The denial of wild nature serves the fabrication of a timeless, universal, and unchanging order, articulated in part by means of cultural values and generalization."[8] Furthermore, critics suggest that the androcentrism of Disney animation is both ideologically consistent and, at the same time, incoherent. The consistency resides in the objectification and subordination of life forms, while the incoherence resides in the philosophical justifications and ideological formations that naturalize them. As Murphy points out, "Disney consistently attempts to reflect a sense of 'virginal' innocence, promoting the 'magic' of childhood often through characters' friendship or ability to communicate with animals, while at the same time reflecting the cultural drive towards the conquest of nature, through promoting a capitalist work ethic among dwarfs, princes, mice, servants and heavily anthropomorphized animals."[9]

The Disney aesthetic ostensibly only favours those who have already adapted "ethically correct attitudes," according to Ariel Dorfman, a radical critic of American culture.[10] Not surprisingly, he perceives Disney as the ultimate exponent of cultural imperialism and pronounces that such utopic cinematic and real spaces appeal to but also abuse "the child in all of us." They "immobilise us into a state of 'pre-Adam and Eve' goodness." The same thing, Dorfman continues, happens to nature in Disney films, with everything "anthropomorphized and reduced to narrative elements which provide simplistic causal effects structures."[11] Dorfman's quip that Disney does to nature what *Playboy* does to sex—believing Disney promotes an infantile view of life and nature, without allowing "nature" to have its own identity outside of man's control—remains conceptually shocking and certainly attention grabbing. Such control however, is not the violent, aggrandizing sort, which subverts nature to serve man's greed. No, the Disney agenda is essentially benevolent and "oozes goodness." But this goodness is defined as a rejection of any political, social, or economic change. "In Disney films," writes Dorfman, "criticising establishment values can't be understood as a form of knowledge but merely as senseless destruction."[12] Like Murphy cited earlier, Dorfman believes such stifling protectionism also serves to misconstrue and dangerously misrepresent what he regards as the liberating power of nature.[13]

General academic criticism has of late become less vitriolic, yet continues to be framed within conventional ideological terms.[14] Crudely rehearsed, such analysis calls upon ideological false-consciousness arguments, whether consciously or not, that seek to dismiss mass audiences as being almost hypnotized by the commercially potent, yet synthetic and sentimental, nature of the Disney—and by extension the Pixar—project. I would counter this crude assessment however, using the lens of deep ecological criticism, to suggest that while this so-called "Disneyfication of nature" might continue to display a reductive, anthropomorphic simplification of nature, it becomes at least potentially progressive by generating smart ecological metaphors for audiences to engage with. This is most particularly evident within the Pixar canon. Such narratives also signal a wide range of ecological risks and call upon core eco-philosophical debates within and beyond the surface representational simulacrum. Essentially, if I were to be overtly provocative and adopt a utopic cultural studies position, I would go so far as to suggest that just because the Disney/Pixar aesthetic encapsulates a commercial facade, this does not necessarily predetermine that prototypical massified audiences cannot at the same time detect and even project deep ecological models and interpretations from within such seductive narratives and representational formats. But of course such a hypothesis would need extensive and robust audience testing to rise above mere conjecture or wishful thinking.

The utopic tension and fault line in celebratory pronouncements on Disney are best expressed by Adrian Ivakhiv, in a comprehensive overview of ecocinema entitled "Green Film Criticism and Its Futures" (2008). Ivakhiv is initially delighted with scholarship that seeks to expose an ecological agenda in popular film, including my own *Hollywood Utopia* (2005), and its willingness to go out on an "interpretive limb." According to Ivakhiv, one can "hardly quibble with the assertion about the pliability rather than the fixity of spectacular images of nature—as in the first encounter with simulated dinosaurs in *Jurassic Park*."[15] He takes issue however, with my suggestion that "audiences often find ways to subvert their controlling ideologies,"[16] because, in his view, there is "no documentary or audience-ethnographic evidence provided to support it."[17] As already suggested, I would unreservedly agree with this caveat and, together with critics like Martin Barker and others, I have frequently called for extensive empirical research to help understand and appreciate audience pleasures. Textual analysis inferences about the role of Pixar in seeding a (smart) ecological agenda are certainly only conjecture, nothing more, and require extensive empirical analysis to evaluate such a hypothesis. Furthermore, this lack of robust audience research to help underpin and critique film studies' preoccupation with grand theoretical analysis has become a major concern in the academy and needs to be addressed with some urgency.

A few successful Hollywood filmmakers, especially Steven Spielberg and Peter Weir, ostensibly address ecological issues, yet, as Ivakhiv points out, they by no means have "contributed to revolutionary change," much less other filmmakers including the subject of this chapter, namely the creators of Pixar.[18] I would continue to reiterate however that this is certainly not the modus operandi of commercial Hollywood cinema. While Weir possibly qualifies as a more reflective eco-filmmaker, his work is most successful at "winging it" and having it both ways, in many ways like James Cameron's recent eco-blockbuster *Avatar* (2009). Both directors explicitly call upon a cautionary ecological agenda, while at the same time appeasing mass audiences with conventional generic tropes. Such directors, including those at Pixar, draw upon the growing popular preoccupation with ecological idealism, while also succumbing to the embrace of visual spectacle and special effects. Commercial filmmakers are nonetheless extending their repertoire, as audiences appear to become more ecologically literate and aware, with studios like Pixar being particularly adept at positing an ecological agenda through broadening and deepening their narrative address and enticing mass audiences to extend their engagement with a more radical form of ecological engagement.

Again drawing upon Ivakhiv's criticism and perceptive analysis and following the Walt Disney theme park and highly criticized model of consumption, *Jurassic Park*—which loosely doubles for the Disney project—can also be decoded and "structured as a ride."[19] According to Sarah Franklin it "offers a movie of a theme park which in turn becomes the main attraction of [real-life] theme parks" in a process that "doubles in on itself to generate revenues upon revenues premised on the magic of Hollywood spectacle in making possible anything imaginable."[20] But surely this well-rehearsed criticism must simply be acknowledged as a pre-given truth, with the commercial imperative of blockbuster cinema remaining at the forefront of any discussion of mainstream cinema. I will argue, however, that Pixar, now in the shadow of the Disney brand, strives to embrace more innovative aesthetics and themes that speak to new generational audiences, while at the same time overlaying a finely tuned, commercially driven agenda. To help tease out this thesis, I will draw on the DVD bonus features attached to *UP*—which is by all accounts less overtly ecological than *WALL-E* (2008) for example. But first of all I will explore the changing dynamics of engaging with the audiences of animation, from simply treating them as children to encouraging more reflexive and active engagement.

PEDOCRATIZING THE (DISNEY) AUDIENCE

"To maximise profitability and ensure its survival the industry has to *paedocratize* its audience—in effect, to address it as children, with child-like preoccupations and qualities."[21] This approach has a long history in the critical literature around Disney. For example Kipling's unforgettably vivid "Mowgli" in *Jungle Book* (1996) and James Matthew Barrie's cocky hero, the boy who wouldn't grow up, *Peter Pan* (1953) both reveal the depth of adult investment in a utopian childhood state. Childhood is placed at a tangent to adulthood, perceived as special and magical, precious and dangerous. As Marina Warner points out, "the injured child has become today's icon of humanity."[22] David Buckingham's ongoing educational research clearly highlights and reinforces a dominant reading of the subject: "The ways which media texts ... articulate ... anxieties—and attempt to assuage them—are clearly 'ideological.' Media texts may offer fantasies that compensate for children's own lack of power, but they often do so on adult terms.... Yet, the ways in which the media 'speak to' children's concerns and thereby help to construct them—are in need of much more systemic analysis."[23] As suggested by such scholars, emotions cannot be separated from cognitions and from the social context in which they are displayed. Furthermore, it is extremely important to try to uncover how texts activate children's, and by extension adults', emotional engagement. Meanwhile, Robin Wood remains unconvinced that such texts can address such a project and dismisses such sentiments "as masquerading as idealized nostalgia for (a) lost radicalism."[24] Wood further argues that films like those from Disney in particular cater to "the desire for regression to infantilism."[25] In his overly elitist dismissal of popular texts, Wood speaks of how "young children require not-quite-endless repetition" and how the 1980s variant "is the curious and disturbing phenomenon of children's films conceived and marketed largely for adults—films that construct the adult spectator as a child."[26] At least, he continues, the old 1930s series from which many of the most successful recent movies have been adapted, were "not taken seriously, on *any* level," suggesting that new audiences are encouraged not to worry since "Uncle George [Lucas] (or Uncle Stephen) [Spielberg (or Uncle Walt Disney)] will take you by the hand and lead you through Wonderland. Some dangers will appear on the way, but never fear, he'll also see you safely home; home being essentially those 'good old values.'"[27]

Sharon Zukin remains less strident in her analysis, while pinpointing Disney's overall cultural ambiguity, which at the same time hints at its primary importance: the Disney World "is built for visual consumption" and "offers both a panorama and a collage of postmodernity,"[28] to which one could most certainly add the huge development in the animation industry—all of which serves to blur the boundaries between high and low culture. Pixar's contemporary digital aesthetic most especially helps to frame these tensions and tropes from a fresh angle. I would suggest in response that just because there appears to be little physical depth behind eco-narratives like *Bambi* or the cardboard cut-outs making up its visual aesthetic, this does not in itself mean that they cannot serve at the same time a very useful cognitive and emotional purpose. Like all signs and icons, particularly provocative ones, which involve "childhood innocence" and "nature," it is what they stand for that is important above all else. At times crude ideological criticism can often get in the way of understanding and appreciating the layering of eco-utopic significance and emotional affect encrusted in such potent cultural signifiers.[29]

Brian Butler is most provocative in affirming that the "unapologetic quality of the Hollywood narrative can serve as a therapeutic tool because of the reluctance on the part of academics to promote any positive ideals."[30] Or, as I have suggested elsewhere, "while academic theory has enormous difficulty articulating, much less legitimising, various foundational beliefs, Hollywood has no qualms whatsoever in promoting them."[31] In other words, Hollywood movies remain valuable as artifacts for "seeing ecology," especially its emotional affect, and for framing large-scale ethical debate.

ANIMATION: THE GENESIS OF A NEW MODEL OF CREATIVITY

As a uniquely successful studio, Pixar effectively blends industrial big-production branding, using the advantages of new innovative techniques for animation, alongside more artisanal "indie" methods of creative development. At the outset, this may appear somewhat contradictory, nevertheless Pixar's general business/creative formula works extremely well and this chapter suggests such a production formula can also be read as evidence of a new brand of smart eco-animation. As many in the industry affirm, "doing animation is like watching grass growing" and, according to a founding director, John Lasseter, "where you spend time in this medium is during the last 10% of the project." In computer animation, Lasseter explains, "it's easy to make things move, but it's the minute detail work at the end that makes it look so real."[32] Lasseter recalls how in 1983 a job offer came from Lucasfilm, where there was some brilliant computer-based research being carried out under Ed Catmull. After just three years, however, Lucas decided to divest this computer division to focus instead on filmmaking. For $10 million, the late Steve Jobs got a core group of about forty-five talented Lucasfilm people together and, under Catmull as president, the fledgling company began producing and marketing the Pixar Image Computer, a 3-D graphics system.

Pixar Studios remains best known for its CGI-animated feature films, which use PhotoRealistic RenderMan to generate high-quality images. Over its short lifespan the studio has produced about a dozen very successful and labour-of-love, quality feature films, most notably *Toy Story* (1995) and two sequels, *A Bug's Life* (1998), *Monsters Inc.* (2001), *Finding Nemo* (2003), *The Incredibles* (2004), *Cars* (2006), *Ratatouille* (2007), *WALL-E* (2008), and *UP* (2009), together with other short projects—and there are sequels in the pipeline. In a very useful essay for film studies in the *Harvard Business Review* (2008), Catmull teases out the core creative ethics of Pixar, which involves adapting the mantra of empowering your creative people and giving them control over every stage of ideas development.[33] Pixar, Catmull affirms, with no hint of modesty, is a community in the true sense of the word: "We think that lasting relationships matter, and we share some basic beliefs. Talent is rare. Management's job is not to prevent risk but to build the capacity to recover when failure occurs. It must be safe to tell the truth."[34] The founding executive goes on to hypothesize that "if you give a good idea to a mediocre team, they'll screw it up. But if you give a mediocre idea to a good team, they'll make it work."[35] This eulogy for creative teamwork continues in a similar vein with the assertion that "quality is the only bar all Pixar films have to reach." According to Catmull, this strategy goes beyond the movie to "the DVD production and extras, and to the toys and other consumer products associated with other characters."[36]

One would have liked to test the veracity of this self-gratifying communal business ethic and quality blueprint, as well as its application for the creative process of filmmaking, by examining the add-ons that might record "real-life" production meetings, for instance. However, such useful discussions, which might help film students learn about the creative process, are seldom included with add-ons. This probably helps to maintain the illusion of authenticity and the one-off nature of the creative process. Only in hindsight, apparently, can such business strategies be rationalized and evaluated. It is hard to imagine a commercial news company or other creative media organization taking the risk of allowing open access or, more critically, relinquishing total editorial control to a live "fly on the wall" outside television documentary crew. "Discussion meetings are usually a work-in-progress; there is no ego," explains Catmull. He continues to sell his utopic vision of creative management by suggesting that "nobody pulls any punches to be polite. This works because all the participants have come to trust and respect one another ... the problem solving powers of this group are immense and inspirational to watch."[37] This sounds like an idealized working environment that could only exist on paper, but it nevertheless helps to illustrate Pixar's creative dynamic and most especially the emotional intentionality of the final text.

SMART DIGITAL CINEMA: FINDING ITS ANIMATED VOICE

"The question is not whether cinema will die," claims David Norman Rodowick, "but rather just how long ago it ceased to be."[38] In *The Virtual Life of Film* (2007), Rodowick argues that the most productive response to the gradual erasure of cinema's photomechanical basis is a combination of mournful nostalgia and forward-looking optimism. In Martin Fradley's view, Rodowick's book makes "an impassioned call to arms regarding the continued importance of cinema studies in the wake of the so-called digital divide."[39] This so-called digital divide is, I suggest, most keenly manifested in new animation cinema. Rodowick goes on to admit that he too may be out of time:[40]"those of us who subjectively were formed in a cinematic culture ... may not be capable either perceptually, psychologically, or philosophically of evaluating the new onto-logical era: a contemporary regime of multiple digital screens, from the cam-corder to the laptop to the iPod to the videogame."[41] This is our new ontology, affirms Rodowick, as "we seek a new generation of philosophers."[42] Pixar, with its successful franchise and creative innovative work practices, has helped to promote a renewed preoccupation with such major ontological debates, which have implications for framing a smart ecological aesthetic and its emotional affect for new audiences. The notion of smart cinema has been popularized following Jeffrey Sconce's seminal essay in *Screen* (2002), where he argued that such films reflect the presence of a growing culture of irony and parody.[43] These aspects are certainly evident in much of Pixar's output and certainly in *UP*, directed by Peter Doctor, which I argue helps to forge a more reflexive emotionally driven semiosis.

UP: AN ECO-READING

In certain ways the storyline of *UP* is reminiscent of David Lynch's *Straight Story* (1999), dealing in a non-sentimental way with the journey of old age.[44] This is by all accounts a very unusual and risky project for a big budget, osten-sibly children's film, which actively seeks to appeal to the child in all of us and certainly to question the ideological criticism of Dorfman, Murphy, and others cited above. Nonetheless, like *WALL-E*, *UP* has enough elements to keep the kids happy, without necessarily "pedocratizing" them with its magical, trans-formative engagement with landscape and people. The vignette at the start of the movie, showing a couple's life, is one of the most evocative and poignant in film history. While the storyline at times veers toward the surreal, it also includes escapist elements, which echo pure Disney. One could argue that the mixture and play on varying ideas takes the story into more unusual places than even *WALL-E* strived to explore, through its more explicit eco-cautionary tale.

But how can one read *UP* as a smart eco-narrative that effectively uses emotional affect? The story dramatizes conventional developers trying to get their hands on an old man's (Karl) picturesque house, after his wife (Ellie) has died. In a related subplot set up like the black and white newsreel at the start of *Citizen Kane* (1941), the idealized hero Muntz, who inspires the young Karl and his girlfriend with the catch phrase "adventure is out there," ends up trying to capture a very rare and exotic bird to reclaim his good name. Human beings often know the price of everything but the value of nothing. The little boy (Russell) who is a stowaway with the old man in his journey of discovery is a very unconventional loner who needs a surrogate dad. We have to have faith in ourselves as human beings, remains an ever-present theme and driving force in Disney, a trope that pervades Hollywood's DNA. Nonetheless, at least this relatively conventional story is given a smart twist.

Both creative directors (Bob Peterson and Pete Docter) who speak on the audio commentary were apparently struck by how old people are "so cool" and of course play with the idea of getting away from everything, as the geeky kid and old man need to escape their predetermined existence. The writers were also inspired by the old *King Kong* movie and other black and white adventure flicks.[45] The title *UP* remains enigmatic; with Karl wanting to literally go "up," but needs to come down eventually to (re-)connect with people.[46] The image of an idealized, even exotic, place in *UP* helps to project an internal dream fantasy, which turns out in reality to appear like an unstable, volcanic-type topography. Only by digging deeper, through the add-ons or other inter-textual investigation, does one discover that this actually presents a real earthly landscape, which has rarely been seen by the general (Western) public.

The bonus features provide the necessary ecological key to connecting with this exotic landscape, in a mini-documentary entitled *Adventure Is Out There*.[47] It narrates a real-life documentary on the backstory of discovering Paradise Falls and the famous Tepui cliff outcrops in Venezuela. The cliffs rise over a thousand metres and are very inaccessible; only a few humans have ever set foot on top of them. The documentary follows the Pixar creative team's long trip to this inaccessible geographical location. They start climbing up the cliff with some difficulty, while their indigenous guides, some apparently wearing flip-flops, are incredibly agile and sure-footed. The creative outsiders speak of how the landscape looks like the moon or even Mars, and understand their journey to Venezuela as a journey back in time to an older landscape. "It was so old," one of them says, "it seemed to have wrinkles like the old man." Following the animators' journey/touristic exploration, a history and geography lesson is afforded. They try to capture the "colour," emotional affect, and authenticity of this exotic place with their cameras, paint brushes, and even poetry, stimulated by physically seeing the place first-hand and capturing this pristine habitation's authenticity for their animation work.

The animators certainly used every medium available to capture the look and feel of the place for their virtual computer work, while drawing on their journey to the actual place. As a result, they felt they earned the right to use the Papui: "We were on a journey of faith," they emote in the documentary, and we also are informed that it was "a wild adventure for the makers of the film." Apparently, the creative team needed the actual visceral sensation of the landscape to help them engage with the resultant simulated, digital process. Such an emotional journey is set up to appear most professional and cutting edge, in contrast to witnessing a more conventional Disney team investing in such authenticating pre-production research exercises to help them to accurately reflect the flora and fauna of a utopic animated space.[48] A recent coffee-table study of the look and feel of UP, Tim Hauser's The Art of UP (2009), has a chapter entitled "Seeking Simplexity," which captures the engaging ecological aims of the Pixar creative team.[49]

Beginning to imagine how their film might look, the team used various techniques, including drawing what they saw and experienced to "[make] it more visible." This certainly feeds off Catmull's earlier pronouncements on how to maximize the creative process and support the unique look and feel of the movie. The team had great fun for example with the dog's voice, using speeded-up audio and digital manipulation to record their squeaky human voices—an ironic sense of playfulness the more sentimentalized and anthromorphized Disney-focused aesthetic would not normally embrace.

The use of music in particular by Michael Giacchino remains most effective in relaying a very smart and reflexive emotional register, inspired by earlier historical diegetic strategies—one even recognizes most recently the renewed power of such counterpointing in the Oscar-winning French silent feature The Artist (2012). From the very simple but haunting violin and piano riff, which becomes Ellie's signature tune as we are first introduced to her; to the quick succession of emotions from happiness, to adventure, to the excitement of marriage and the disappointment of not having children and growing old together—all done through a super-quick montage vignette, yet emotionally anchored and glued together—Giacchino's score is very simple but effective. The audience is quickly initiated onto a rollercoaster ride of emotions and probably the most difficult emotional turn is to handle the transition as Karl has to face life on his own without his beloved Ellie. This transition could have become mawkish and depressing so easily, but because of the great sensitivity in developing his character and playing with the aches and pains of old age, the audience quickly grows to accept his new state of affairs and remains empathetic with him—rather than just for him—as he faces a new struggle to "find himself" in this late stage of life. This is a theme shunned by most mainstream Hollywood cinema, which of course focuses on the more lucrative teen market. Wrapping such a "passages of life" storyline within a children's animation produces a most effective emotional transition. Furthermore, the powerfully enigmatic music in particular, which was inspired by classics from the 1950s and 1960s, never simply just "winks at the audience," but always connects with a deeply appreciated surfeit of affective emotion, as clearly evidenced by the care the creative team speak about in their various bonus features.

The false goal and narrative resolution of planting his iconic house on the cliff, as captured in the drawing from their childhood imagination, finally does not satisfy the old man. Karl learns from his antagonist Muntz, who continues looking backward, to finally look forward and have faith in the future. Eventually finding the empty pages in his wife's scrapbook, he discovers the "real meaning of adventure." "Being in a relationship is an adventure," is the clear message left by his beloved Ellie. Of course it's strange that only now does he closely examine the scrapbook—but then film often obfuscates basic logic. Nonetheless the audience clearly gets the powerful emotional connection and motivational rationalization for this story thread, which is all that matters, as the creative team informs us with total confidence on the add-ons.

"It's a very emotional movie," explains Peterson and Docter in their voice-over commentary, "we did not hold back." Lots of people can connect with the truth and authenticity of the protagonists. The movie becomes very personal, drawing on the directors' family memorabilia, which makes it particularly authentic. The creative team members within the add-ons take us through the cognitive and affective heuristics as they explain: "We see grandpa's stuff and grandma's stuff: the two chairs still side by side on the exotic island. Now at last he can clean the home by getting rid of what is no longer needed, alongside the baggage of life. External actions of the character help to express his interior transformation, which was weighing him down and can now finally be exorcised. A house is just a house." Nonetheless, the creative team is careful to note, Karl is not finally abandoning his great love for Ellie, as this would have been too much for audiences to take emotionally. As film scholars, we are of course reticent to take creative team at face value, and fully appreciate the PR function of bonus features. Nonetheless, we can learn a lot about how audiences' cognitive/emotional affects are cued, framed, and constituted by such insightful insider analysis.

The creative team goes on to suggest how if this were a Capra film, this would be the conclusion after the antagonist has been defeated, but Karl brings the elixir of life back home and places the "Grape Soda" badge, which was Ellie's identifiable signifier, onto his new protege Russell, thereby passing on the romantic action-adventure baton to a new generation. "What more can an older generation hope to do in their lives"—becomes the ultimate expression of human (entopic) rejuvenation. Ellie's life, passion, and inspiration can now live on through a new generation. The underpinning point of the movie is that ordinary things like sitting on the curb and counting cars (with a huge air-blimp surrealistically floating overhead) is all that matters. What a smart and simple ending, which at one level cross-connects and refers back to the sentimental Disney canon—yet at the same time maintains a level of quirkiness, most notably with the blimp, which enables the text to also speak to a "new generation of children."

Little things are what matters; travelling is great, but coming home is best. Such homespun philosophy, embodied in many classics, most notably *The Wizard of Oz* (1939), speaks to a long tradition within Hollywood and most particularly Disney narratives. Karl replays a "true" paternal role as he counts red/black cars on the stoop outside the ice-cream shop with his surrogate grandson. This is also what the young boy imagined "good relations" between father and son would be. Together with the young boy, the old man has learned the lesson of passing on his wisdom and passion for life, as he presents the sacred talisman, which was given to him by his geeky tomboy girlfriend. Ellie has finally taught him how to have fun; what greater skill could one generation pass on to the next?

FINAL COMMENTS

Such emotional engagement and closure, I suggest, pushes the erstwhile sentimentalism of the Disney project into more reflexive and smart trajectories. This high resolution, hyperrealistic animation aesthetic certainly helps to foreground the raw emotions on display in an engaging roller-coaster experience. Nevertheless, the digital aesthetic would not have been as emotionally affective if the script and final storyboard was not as well-honed and "simplex." Furthermore, rather than "denying wild nature," as Disney critics often alleged, especially with regards to identifiable forms of androcentrism, this style of animation and storytelling remains capable of both embracing various contradictions and at the same time drawing on deep ecological and ontological analyses of human and animal behaviour—all the while, ensuring emotions are not separated from cognitions, especially as demonstrated through a reflexive array of musical registers that speak to "childhood innocence" in a way that is certainly not patronizing its smart audiences. As the analysis of various bonus features reveal, the creative team strives to remain true to the heart/emotions of the characters, building on the Disney/sentimental identification approach, while at the same time injecting layers of reflexive play and engagement that speak to contemporary mass audiences everywhere.

All of Pixar's film projects including *UP* can be read as presenting a very slick aesthetic and in varying measures evoke a deep ecological sensibility. The Pixar brand of production has pushed the creative envelope developed by Disney to address new smart agendas, while also teasing out important global issues, be they somewhat newer issues of ecological degradation (*WALL-E*) or perennial issues of old age and rejuvenation explored in *UP*, which are often ignored in youth-fixated animated culture. The Pixar brand also calls upon all forms of nostalgia attached to memories of childhood that serve to produce effective ecological "teacherly texts" dramatizing various ontological dilemmas, which will remain with us forever. Pixar's engagement with these issues certainly refuses to succumb to conventional safe forms of passive emotional sentimentality.

NOTES

1 Note my reading of *UP* in this study is also part of a chapter on Pixar from my book *Smart Cinema: DVD Add-ons and New Audience Pleasures* (New York: Palgrave Macmillan, 2012) but has been reframed for this chapter.

2 Paul Wells argues animated films are especially protean and more difficult to define in relation to the way they use generic codes than their live action equivalents. Cited in David S. Whitley, *The Idea of Nature in Disney Animation* (Aldershot, UK: Ashgate, 2008), 7.

3 See Jay Leyda, ed., *Eisenstein on Disney* (London: Methuen, 1986).

4 Whitley, *The Idea of Nature*.

5 Douglas Brode goes so far as to claim that Disney output (television, film, theme parks, etc.) "played a major role in transforming mid-1950s white-bread toddlers into rebellious teenage youth of the late sixties." *Multiculturalism and the Mouse: Race and Sex in Disney* (Austin: University of Texas Press, 2005), 2. New Age films about the earth and valuing an environmental orientation can certainly be recognized within early Disney animations. Of course I am fully aware of such a risky—some might even say foolhardy—validation of the power of Disney, which pulls against the much more strongly held opinion around Disney's affirmation of a regressive establishment dogma and values.

6 Elizabeth Bell, Lynda Haas, and Laura Sells, eds., *From Mouse to Mermaid: The Politics of Film, Gender and Culture* (Bloomington: Indiana University Press, 1995), 7.

7 Jack Zipes, "Breaking the Disney Spell," in *From Mouse to Mermaid: The Politics of Film, Gender and Culture*, ed. Elizabeth Bell, Lynda Haas, and Laura Sells (Bloomington: Indiana University Press, 1995), 22.

8 Patrick Murphy, "'The Whole Wide World Was Scrubbed Clean': The Androcentric Animation of Denatured Disney," in *From Mouse to Mermaid: The Politics of Film, Gender and Culture*, ed. Elizabeth Bell, Lynda Haas, and Laura Sells (Bloomington: Indiana University Press, 1995), 125. Murphy continues that in ecology we speak of "wild systems" and places as part of a process, "with its active manifestations contingent, indeterminate, and contextually particularistic, and thus continuous demonstrations of the principle of difference." The Disney ethos on the other hand, Murphy claims, promotes escapism from the indeterminacy of these "wild systems" through denial of process and difference. This is helped by the relative primitiveness of the mimetic animation aesthetic. Up till recently, Murphy concludes, Disney animation consistently displayed "static" depictions of both nature and women in particular, rather than just one or the other: "Both are based on androcentric hierarchies and dichotomies

with women and nature objectified for the benefit of the male subject." Murphy, "The Whole Wide World," 126.

9 Murphy, "The Whole Wide World," 126.

10 Ariel Dorfman, *The Empire's Old Clothes: What the Lone Ranger, Babar and Other Innocent Heroes Do to Our Minds* (New York: Pantheon Books, 1983), 137.

11 Dorfman, *The Empire's Old Clothes*, 159. It is frequently affirmed that Disney's animators do not empower characters and therefore by extension the audience. I would certainly take issue with such a generalization in my reading of Pixar's movies and suggest how these contemporary tales have extended and developed the Disney aesthetic and mindset to address smart new audiences, which in turn appear to subvert classic themes and restrictive, conventional ideological preoccupations in the process.

12 Dorfman, *The Empire's Old Clothes*, 166.

13 Similarly Schickel argues that the drive in Disney's success story is toward a sort of "multiple reductionism; wild things and wild behavior were often made comprehensible by converting them to cuteness, mystery was explained with a joke, and terror was resolved by a musical cue ... (or a discreet averting of the camera's eye from the natural process)." Richard Schickel, *The Disney Version* (London: Weidenfeld and Nicolson, 1968), 51.

14 In *Deconstructing Disney*, Eleanor Byrne and Martin McQuillan continue to simply reaffirm how conventional cultural imperialist and ideological messages are encoded in films like *The Little Mermaid* and *Beauty and the Beast*. See Eleanor Byrne and Martin McQuillan, eds., *Deconstructing Disney* (London: Pluto, 1999).

15 Adrian Ivakhiv, "Green Film Criticism and Its Futures," *Interdisciplinary Studies in Literature and Environment* 15, no. 2 (Summer 2008): 11.

16 Pat Brereton, *Hollywood Utopia: Ecology in Contemporary American Cinema* (Bristol: Intellect, 2005), 72.

17 Ivakhiv, "Green Film Criticism," 11.

18 Ivakhiv, "Green Film Criticism," 11.

19 Sarah Franklin, "Life Itself: Global Nature and the Genetic Imaginary," in *Global Nature, Global Culture*, ed. Sarah Franklin, Celia Lury, and Jackie Stacey (London: Sage, 2000), 202–3.

20 Franklin, "Life Itself," 203.

21 John Hartley, cited in David Buckingham, *Moving Images: Understanding Children's Emotional Responses to Television* (Manchester: Manchester University Press, 1996), 277.

22 Marina Warner, *Six Myths of Our Time: Managing Monsters—The Reith Lectures* (London: Vintage, 1994), 35.

23 Buckingham, *Moving Images*, 311.

24 Robin Wood, "Papering the Cracks: Fantasy and Ideology in the Reagan Era," in *Movies and Mass Culture*, ed. John Belton (New Brunswick, NJ: Rutgers University Press, 1995), 203.

25 Wood, "Papering the Cracks," 216.

26 Wood, "Papering the Cracks," 205.

27 Wood, "Papering the Cracks," 207.

28 Sharon Zukin, "Postmodern Urban Landscapes: Mapping Culture and Power," in *Modernity and Identity*, ed. Scott Lash and Jonathan Friedman (London: Wiley-Blackwell, 1992), 232.

29 In this paper I'm self-consciously setting up Disney's apparent "one-dimensional morality tales" as a straw man to tease out how Hollywood animation might have become transformed and complicated by the more reflexive, smart agendas of Pixar creators, who in turn strive to address in new ways many of the concerns explored through the canonical Disney output. Exploring how the creative people at Pixar hold audiences "by the hand," yet appear less directive and therefore insinuate a new relationship with new generational audiences, remains the core transformation; they construct a more robust small-scale and sophisticated animated aesthetic, which nonetheless remains anchored within a predetermined Disney storytelling tradition.

30 Brian E. Butler, "Seeing Ecology and Seeing as Ecology: On Brereton's *Hollywood Utopia* and the Andersons' *Moving Image Theory*," *Film Philosophy* 11, no. 1 (June 2007), http://www.film-philosophy.com/2007v11n1/butler.pdf.

31 Brereton, *Hollywood Utopia*, 35.

32 John Lasseter, cited in Burr Snider, "The *Toy Story* Story: How John Lasseter Came to Make the First 100-Percent Computer-Generated Theatrical Motion Picture," *Wired* 3, no. 2 (December 1995), 1.

33 Ed Catmull, "How Pixar Fosters Collective Creativity," *Harvard Business Review* (September 2008): 3, http://cogsci.uwaterloo.ca/courses/Phil447.2009/pixar.pdf.

34 Catmull, "How Pixar," 3.

35 Catmull, "How Pixar," 3.

36 Catmull, "How Pixar," 6. The growing dominance of DVDs for home consumption has joined with economics to play a powerful role in repositioning a new global brand like Pixar animation. DVD is now part of a home-based digital universe, connected to a "high-tech" aesthetic that presumes the superiority of digital over analog and forever marvels over the advances of computer-age wizardry.

37 Catmull, "How Pixar," 7.

38 David Norman Rodowick, *The Virtual Life of Film* (Cambridge, MA: Harvard University Press, 2007), 26.

39 Martin Fradley, review of David Rodowick's *The Virtual Life of Film*, *Quarterly Review of Film* 60, no. 1 (Fall 2010): 71.

40 In pursuit of the continuities between celluloid and digital, Rodowick shrewdly notes that mimesis remains the Holy Grail of a commercial cinema seemingly in thrall to the imaginative wonderland of CGI animation. Above all other formats this has been taken to extremes, as it became more and more photo-realist. In industrial terms, of course, nothing has changed: the business has simply adopted new technology. And despite purists' objections, the difference between 35 mm and digital projection is often overstated (and more often unnoticed). "If the digital is such a revolutionary process of image making," asks Rodowick, why then must its "technological and aesthetic goal" become "conceptually indiscernible from an earlier mode of image production?" Rodowick, *The Virtual Life*, 11.

41 Rodowick, *The Virtual Life*, 180.

42 Rodowick, *The Virtual Life*, 180.

43 Jeffrey Sconce, "Irony, Nihilism and the New American 'Smart' Film," *Screen* 43, no. 4 (Winter 2002): 349–69.

44 For a detailed discussion of *Straight Story*, see Brereton, *Hollywood Utopia*, 124–30.

45 DVD bonus features and contemporary smart films are particularly influenced by, and seek to actively reference, such old films as part of the cinematic pleasure—both emotional and cognitive—for new generational audiences.

46 One wonders however if audiences fully appreciate such smart word play, without the assistance of the commentary.

47 The bonus features on the DVD of *UP* include: "Partly Cloudy" (a theatrical trailer); "Doug's Special Mission"; "The Many Endings of Muntz"; "Adventure Is Out There"; "Exclusive Animated Short Films: Dug's Special Mission"; and, as is common, "Director's Commentary."

48 At the July 2011 symposium on Ecocinema and Affect in Munich, which served to kick-start this volume, another delegate, David Whitly, suggested that this was not necessarily true and that at least for several successful Disney features, like *Bambi* and *The Lion King*, great effort was taken to capture the likeness of animals and their environment.

49 Tim Hauser, *The Art of UP* (San Francisco: Chronicle Books, 2009).

BIBLIOGRAPHY

Bell, Elizabeth, Lynda Haas, and Laura Sells, eds. *From Mouse to Mermaid: The Politics of Film, Gender and Culture*. Bloomington: Indiana University Press, 1995.

Belton, John, ed. *Movies and Mass Culture*. London: Athlone, 1996.

Brereton, Pat. *Hollywood Utopia: Ecology in Contemporary American Cinema*. Bristol: Intellect, 2005.

———. *Smart Cinema: DVD Add-ons and New Audience Pleasures*. New York: Palgrave Macmillan, 2012.

Brode, Douglas. *Multiculturalism and the Mouse: Race and Sex in Disney*. Austin: University of Texas Press, 2005.

Buckingham, David. *Moving Images: Understanding Children's Emotional Responses to Television*. Manchester: Manchester University Press, 1996.

Butler, Brian E. "Seeing Ecology and Seeing as Ecology: On Brereton's *Hollywood Utopia* and the Andersons' *Moving Image Theory*." *Film Philosophy* 11, no. 1 (June 2007). http://www.film-philosophy.com/2007v11n1/butler.pdf.

Byrne, Eleanor, and Martin McQuillan. *Deconstructing Disney*. London: Pluto, 1999.

Catmull, Ed. "How Pixar Fosters Collective Creativity." *Harvard Business Review* (September 2008). http://cogsci.uwaterloo.ca/courses/Phil447.2009/pixar.pdf.

Dorfman, Ariel. *The Empire's Old Clothes: What the Lone Ranger, Babar and Other Innocent Heroes Do to Our Minds*. New York: Pantheon Books, 1983.

Fradley, Martin. Review of David Rodowick's *The Virtual Life of Film*. *Quarterly Review of Film* 60, no. 1 (Fall 2010): 70–74.

Franklin, Sarah. "Life Itself: Global Nature and the Genetic Imaginary." In *Global Nature, Global Culture*, edited by Sarah Franklin, Celia Lury, and Jackie Stacey, 188–98. London: Sage, 2000.

Hauser, Tim. *The Art of UP*. San Francisco: Chronicle Books, 2009.

Ivakhiv, Adrian. "Green Film Criticism and Its Futures." *Interdisciplinary Studies in Literature and Environment* 15, no. 2 (Summer 2008): 1–28.

Leyda, Jay, ed. *Eisenstein on Disney*. London: Methuen, 1986.

Murphy, Patrick. "'The Whole Wide World Was Scrubbed Clean': The Androcentric Animation of Denatured Disney." In *From Mouse to Mermaid: The Politics of Film, Gender and Culture*. Edited by Elizabeth Bell, Lynda Haas, and Laura Sells, 125–36. Bloomington: Indiana University Press, 1995.

Rodowick, David Norman. *The Virtual Life of Film*. Cambridge, MA: Harvard University Press, 2007.

Schickel, Richard. *The Disney Version*. London: Weidenfeld and Nicolson, 1968.

Sconce, Jeffrey. "Irony, Nihilism and the New American 'Smart' Film." *Screen* 43, no. 4 (Winter 2002): 349–69.

Snider, Burr. "The *Toy Story* Story: How John Lasseter Came to Make the First 100-Percent Computer-Generated Theatrical Motion Picture." *Wired* 3, no. 2 (December 1995):1–6.

UP. Directed by Pete Docter. Emeryville, CA: Pixar, 2009. DVD.

Warner, Marina. *Six Myths of Our Time: Managing Monsters—The Reith Lectures*. London: Vintage, 1994.

Whitley, David S. *The Idea of Nature in Disney Animation*. Aldershot, UK: Ashgate, 2008.

Wood, Robin. "Papering the Cracks: Fantasy and Ideology in the Reagan Era." In *Movies and Mass Culture*, edited by John Belton, 203–29. New Brunswick, NJ: Rutgers University Press, 1995.

Zipes, Jack. "Breaking the Disney Spell." In *From Mouse to Mermaid: The Politics of Film, Gender and Culture*, edited by Elizabeth Bell, Lynda Haas, and Laura Sells, 21–42. Bloomington: Indiana University Press, 1995.

Zukin, Sharon. "Postmodern Urban Landscapes: Mapping Culture and Power." In *Modernity and Identity*, edited by Scott Lash and Jonathan Friedman, 221–47. London: Wiley-Blackwell, 1992.

PART IV
The Affect of Place and Time

10

Moving Home
Documentary Film and Other Remediations of Post-Katrina New Orleans

Janet Walker

A recent talk by the pioneering human geographer Yi-Fu Tuan was advertised under the provocative title "Home as Elsewhere."[1] These might be construed as fighting words for New Orleanians who departed precipitously under a mandatory evacuation order as Hurricane Katrina bore down, or self-evacuated later through the sludge, or were—finally—bused or flown to random locations around the country.[2] "Don't call us refugees!" the displaced rebutted with vigour, protesting against the washing away of their citizenship with the material trappings of their lives.[3]

In the weeks and months following the storms (Hurricane Rita on the heels of Katrina), many of these evacuees tried in vain to return to apartments in the low-income housing projects spared from ruinous flooding but shuttered by the Housing Authority of New Orleans and later demolished after strongly contested New Orleans City Council decision-making.[4] For others, the struggle continues to rebuild dwellings and neighbourhoods destroyed by the hurricanes and high water.

It is entirely apposite, therefore, that a major emotional and structural tension in "post-Katrina documentaries" holds anger over dispossession together with heartfelt longing to return. As I have discussed elsewhere, Spike Lee's widely-acclaimed *When the Levees Broke: A Requiem in Four Acts* (2006) alternates rhythmically between interviews conducted "out of place" (with people posed against lighted, patterned scrims) and "situated testimonies" from the maw of the destroyed city. The narrative arc of Carl Deal and Tia Lessin's

Trouble the Water (2008) (re)traces the self-evacuation and return of its charismatic protagonist-inhabitants.[5]

These and other post-Katrina documentaries, including *Still Waiting: Life After Katrina* (Ginny Martin, 2007), *A Village Called Versailles* (S. Leo Chiang, 2009), and the aptly titled *Right to Return: New Home Movies from the Lower 9th Ward* (Jonathan Demme, 2007),[6] deploy thoughtful survivor interviews toward a critique of the "natural disaster" as a neutralist discourse. "There is no such thing as a natural disaster"[7] "separable from the consequences of human actions,"[8] assert activists, activist films, and a range of scholars writing at the intersection of social ecology and critical race studies. The area's flood control engineering was not only woefully inadequate prior to the 2005 storm season but also profoundly inequitable. Socially disadvantaged segments of the population—already more likely to be living in low-lying, less well-maintained, and environmentally compromised sectors of the city—were, as a result, disproportionately affected when disaster struck.[9] Sufficient money must be federally allocated and the flood control system re-engineered and rebuilt to withstand major weather events and protect the city's inhabitants equally, without regard to race or class.

There is much to appreciate about this combination of social ecological critique and grassroots advocacy germane to the post-Katrina documentary oeuvre. Indeed, part of the work of this chapter is to contemplate the deep significance of people's former homes and communities—"the power of place-as-remembered," in Edward S. Casey's words[10]—in the context of the struggle for a racially and economically equitable plan for the return of all who wish to return. *And yet*, as Tuan evocatively remarked, the family table that is a source of pride can become sharp-edged in the dark. And it is ecological night in New Orleans. The canals cut into wetlands that used to buffer the city have become along with the Mississippi River–Gulf Outlet Canal (a portion of which is referred to colloquially as the "hypodermic needle") instruments of destruction against which the body may not be able to defend itself. "What happened to New Orleans," explain William Freudenburg and co-authors, "is a story of the way humans can rearrange the contours of the land they settle on, doing so in ways that make it, and hence themselves, more vulnerable and exposed—inadvertent authors of their own distress."[11]

I accept the understanding of this hurricane disaster as inseparable from geopolitical formations of the human-built environment; and I accept as well that entrenched prejudices and discriminatory policies are barring the return of the 9th Ward as a close-knit community and seedbed of New Orleans culture. At the same time, I believe it behooves us all—including humanities scholars normally focused on the discursive realm—to take seriously the tangible geographical constraints to rebuilding communities exactly as they were and where they were; to use our humanities training, precisely, to comprehend the epistemological aspect of the material environment and help enact the just remediation of New Orleans and the Gulf Coast. By "remediation" I mean to suggest and bring into relation both the amelioration of environmental quality and the creation of new media works, for the benefit of people and places.

As a chapter in *Moving Environments: Emotion, Affect, Ecology and Film*, this essay will draw on concepts of affect to develop our understanding of how post-Katrina films may function as "bodies of affective intensity"[12] through which New Orleans may be experienced, imagined, and remediated, now and in years to come.

AFFECT/MEDIA/GEOGRAPHY

The literature of affect emerging from sociology and geography is most relevant here for its focus on the production of place. Citing the work of political philosopher and social theorist Brian Massumi, who draws in turn from philosopher precursors Bergson and Spinoza, a number of human geographers and social scientists have come to understand affect as a kind of "vector of the intensity of the encounter between bodies (non-human and human) of whatever scale and consistency," or "between a multiplicity of processes, corporeal and incorporeal."[13]

Affect, they assert, is not synonymous with emotion. Some define it as a broader category,[14] whereas others,[15] more closely following Massumi, distinguish the two by characterizing *emotion* as "a subjective content, the sociolinguistic fixing of a quality of an experience which is from that point onward defined as personal"[16] and *affect* as a "point of emergence" between multiple levels including "mind and body," "volition and cognition," "body depth and epidermis, past and future, action and reaction."[17] A major problem Massumi seeks to address in setting out his titular "Autonomy of Affect" is the absence of "an asignifying philosophy of affect" capable of getting at additional matters of the expression of image and event. The "expression-event" as a "system of the inexplicable" is not adequately explained, he argues, by the semiotic approaches (linguistic, logical, narratological, structural, ideological, "or all of these in combination as a Symbolic")[18] that have defined contemporary cultural theory.

Without being willing (or conceiving it possible) to throw out either the baby of representation or the bathwater of subjectivity, I am keenly interested in this literature of affect for its usefulness in placing into relationship bodies, the human-built environment, and the natural environment, all under the foundational premise of human geography, as articulated by Henri Lefebvre, that "*(social) space is a (social) product.*"[19] Cameron Duff, in the journal *Environment and Planning D: Society and Space*, sets out his understanding of affect "as a specific manifestation of a body's ... lived force or action potential" with a practical and place-making dimension.[20] Likewise, Nigel Thrift characterizes affect not only as a "form of thinking," but more precisely as a "different kind of intelligence about the world" that is a "vital element of cities" and that shades "almost every urban activity with different hues we all recognize."[21] The thrust of this complex literature on the geopolitics of affect, therefore, is away from analytics of signification, representation, and ideology and toward an analytics of the affective co-constitution of body and place.

In developing the question of how the cinematic medium—long understood as a representational mode *par excellence*—fits into this terrain of affect studies, I wish to signal a difference between my angle of approach and that of David Ingram (in this volume). Whereas Ingram, differentiating between and drawing from two theories of film and affect, explores with acuity how phenomenological and cognitivist theories—and especially the combination thereof—may illuminate a spectator's visceral, bodily response to a film,[22] I am not primarily interested in spectatorial affect. Rather, with Sean Carter and Derek P. McCormack, my focus is on "how the matter of affect is implicated in the emergence and popular enactment of geopolitical cultures."[23] This "emergence" and "enactment" of affect may certainly involve a film spectator's visceral response, but of no less importance are the cities themselves as "roiling maelstroms of affect";[24] the faces, bodies, and perambulations of actual urban inhabitants that both affect the city and are affected by it;[25] and, finally, cinematic technologies and images as "bodies of affective intensity."[26]

This is the perspective from which I seek to study the various affective modalities of the post-Katrina documentary. Beginning with sequences from Jonathan Demme's *Right to Return* where affect intensifies from the painful "accidenting" of home, the chapter will point to alternate modalities that exert, in Tuan's words, "the tug of an envisaged elsewhere."[27] Not as a defensive measure or berm against the rising tide, but rather as an act of courage, the documentary *Land of Opportunity* (Louisa Dantas, 2010), I submit, figures mobility and mapping as possibility, and home as the sedimentation of memory and community within a geographically shifted present. Although he was of course referring to those who move by choice—and Katrina is complicated in that regard—Tuan's words might nevertheless be heard in a key of hope and solace: "to be alive," he teaches, "is to be separate; to break out of home's cocoon for the chillier, more invigorating air outside."[28]

HOME IN NEW ORLEANS

On the evening of 9 April 2008 at the fifth annual New Orleans International Human Rights Film Festival, the award-winning feature and documentary film director Jonathan Demme presented his documentary study of devastation and courage to an audience of receptive visitors and vociferous locals. Present were Pastor Melvin Jones, Jr. and long-time activist and co-founder of the Common Ground Collective Malik Rahim, both of whom appear in the film. Comprised of footage shot over the course of a year between January 2006 and January 2007 and concentrated on people and places in and uprooted from the area, *Right to Return: New Home Movies from the Lower 9th Ward* represents the director's ongoing commitment to use his talent and reputation to support New Orleans residents in their quest to return and rebuild.[29]

The documentary includes observational footage but is primarily testimonial in nature, organized as a series of portraits of selected individuals or small groups of people who recount their Katrina experiences, describe the current state of their surroundings, and register their views and pleas, often in direct-address to Demme (who shot much of the film himself). Melvin Jones remembers out loud how he and other church brothers worked together in dire conditions to rescue about seventy stranded residents. The film then facilitates Jones's powerful case for the return of residents to New Orleans East and the Lower 9th Ward. Displaced New Orleanians must stake their property claims, he asserts, against plans by officials to delay the return of services to African American residents—some of whom are poor—and ultimately appropriate the land: "What the federal government wants to do is build some high rise condominiums along the river down to Holy Cross ... wait it out so that the people in those areas don't come back, and then shore up the levees to what they need to be, and then bring in condominiums, golf courses.... [T]hey want to make it a 'boutique city.'" In its structure as an unfolding series of vignettes in which we "meet" an individual or small group, witness his, her, or their story, and then move on down the road to the next person or group, Demme's film differs from that of Spike Lee, who has interspersed interviews with evacuees conducted while they were away with interviews of returnees, and presented individual interviews cut up and distributed across the whole film according to subtopic. Also, *When the Levees Broke* includes substantial archival footage from professional news media and private sources, and harkens back to the period before the storm. *Right to Return* concentrates on the here, the now, and the experiential, thus leveraging affective analysis by foregrounding the profilmic level of mediation—people "playing" themselves in the city they inhabit.

The import of *Right to Return*'s format resides, therefore, in the immediacy of subjects' mind-body experiences and physical trajectories rather than in the development of their verbal accounts mainly as evidence for a broader rhetorical argument. The distinction is one of emphasis, especially when viewed from the perspective of the ultimate indivisibility of the affective and the semiotic. In both films, the testimonials are emotionally charged and deeply affecting; and they contribute to the advancement of the social ecological critique. But Demme's and other locally produced documentaries are even more centrally and palpably concerned with affective intensities accruing from the material existence of local and localized residents—the individuals and clusters of people making their way back—in relation to broader affective communities including gathered and home audiences.[30]

The passage featuring Carolyn Parker is exemplary in this regard, and indeed, Demme has gone on to direct a feature-length documentary about this charismatic woman (*I'm Carolyn Parker* [2011]).[31] Parker and her daughter, Kyrah Julian, arrest Demme's attention and ours, with the film(ing) conferring on them importance as witnesses to history and the status of urban "pioneers." Of crucial importance in the establishment of both is these women's self-emplacement on—and the stand they are making from—the front porch of their home in the process of being remodelled. Julian describes how, from the distance of Syracuse, New York (where she was just beginning her university studies when the hurricane hit), she didn't know for some time what had become of her mother. Her mother takes up the story of Julian's experience, looking into Demme's eyes. The shot is a close-up from a hand-held camera that hovers as if hypnotized. Behind Parker, on the green siding of the house, are visible the spray-painted markings of the responders who came after the storm to check for survivors and the bodies of the deceased. "1 dog," we make out in the bottom triangle of the X. She concludes (in a different shot), "But as far as us leaving, as far as us abandoning our homes, abandoning our neighbourhoods? No, *I'm a pioneer for the Lower 9th Ward* for New Orleans, Louisiana. I've been staying here all my life and it takes more than Katrina to make me leave" (fade to black). Parker also gives us a tour of the inside of her home where, arrayed on a bare surface, are the remnants of her glassware collection from the 1960s.[32]

The interior of a home that has been gutted for rebuilding, the mouldy drywall stripped away, is another iconic location from which people speak in the post-Katrina documentary. After a shot of the blue exterior of a house, we are inside with Herreast Harrison, wife of the late Donald Harrison, Sr., Big Chief of several different Mardi Gras tribes. "The house has been remediated," she reports. "All that's left is for the beams to either be removed or for them to put Kilz [mould abatement product] on it." In several shots from between the bare studs of the home, the camera hovers around Harrison who, remembering the family history, addresses Demme: "… and all of my children grew up here. My husband found this house in 1965 and I hated it, just hated it. Hated it! I don't think I ever fell in love with it until after he was gone…. Because we were supposed to get another house. I always thought it was too small or wasn't constructed correctly."

Several things about these sequences are paramount, especially in relation to affect studies. First, the forceful delivery of the monologues. The riveting looks of the interlocutors bore right past the camera presumably into Demme's face, betraying a superhuman physical restraint that I read, perhaps paradoxically, as amplifying our own visceral engagement. Second, the situational aspect of the testimonies. On the foundations of homes in New Orleans we behold the concrete footing of person and structure, teetering after Katrina and re-established before our eyes, in part through the cinematic support of the filming. The passage beautifully exemplifies Edward S. Casey's insight, following Merleau-Ponty, that "the appropriation of familiar places is accomplished by the lived body, which has 'a knowledge bred of familiarity.'"[33] Quoting phenomenologist Erwin Straus, Casey elaborates: "The kind of space that figures here is an 'attuned space,' a space with which one feels sympathetic at some very basic level…. In the ambiance of attuned space, it is correspondingly difficult *not* to feel at home; for this is the very space that inheres in the place one has made one's own through establishing such dimensional features as level, distance, and directionality."[34] Writing about another group of people under threat of being washed out from the landscape—the indigenous protestors of major river damming projects in India that have already displaced hundreds of thousands of formerly proximate residents—Bishnupriya Ghosh evokes an "ecologics," or "logic of *oikos* (or the household) … in an interconnected system (*oikonomia* or economy) of human and nonhuman relations."[35] "Together testimony and framing text transmit knowledge in an enmeshed form so that we may engage in a sensuous struggle with those who refuse to move."[36] The presentation of these "ecologically lodged" subjects, she argues, ultimately moves (and moves *us*) to an aspirational collectivity. Likewise, these post-Katrina segments not only represent, but actually enact an in-habitation or "ecologics" that lodges Katrina survivors and film spectators under the same roof.

Third, these sequences are notable for "the exceedingly close tie" they establish "between body memory and memory of place."[37] Parker's and Harrison's physical movements within the homes they thereby remember and reanimate are veritable illustrations of Casey's phenomenology of remembering, or the way in which "moving in and through a given place, the body imports its own implaced past into its present experience: its 'local history' is literally a history of locales."[38] With their words and bodies, Parker and Harrison describe not only "attuned spaces" but also a kind of contingency of memory, body, place, and objects. After talking about the different paint colours she had tried on its exterior, and the flowers planted in the front of the house she hadn't ever liked, Harrison—with her voice and bodily presence—explicitly connects the man, the memories, and the house's current tangibility: "But I really love this house now. I really love it. 'Cause all my memories are here, of a life lived with the Big Chief Donald Harrison, Sr. What a man. Quite a man. And I miss him so. And I want to put it back together in his memory." Be they deliberate or dreamy, forceful or tentative, the words, gestures, and postures of Demme's filmic interlocutors re-make the neighbourhoods of New Orleans.

WALKING IN NEW ORLEANS

The movement of people through the neighbourhoods is also significant. Casey's words resonate once again: "The lived body is coterminous with place because it is by bodily movement that I find my way in place and take up habitation there."[39] In the second part of *Right to Return*, the sequential vignette structure gives way to neighbourhood touring and the production of gathering. We join Pastor Melvin Jones and his fellow minister James Gibson driving and also travelling on foot through the Lower 9th Ward, taking in the changed surroundings and interacting with people in the neighbourhood. Clusters of people are encountered (and presumably drawn out by the presence of Jones, Gibson, and Demme with his camera). They tell stories of survival, of what is no more, of what shouldn't be and what might be. David Reed, remembering people who died and how his brother and three others clung to the top of a tree for eighteen hours before being rescued (the camera pans to the very tree), speaks from within a group of people, including an older neighbour who plans to rebuild and Al "Carnival Time" Johnson, whose 1959 composition "Lower 9th Ward Blues" opens the film. Malik Rahim, at the headquarters of Common Ground, meets a group of Common Ground volunteers, college students from out-of-state on their way back from cleaning out storm drains. Demme introduces them to Rahim who thanks them for their sacrifice.

Here exemplified are the "pedestrian speech acts" fundamental to our understanding of the constructedness of cities.[40] "Walking in the city," Michel de Certeau teaches, "is a process of *appropriation* of the topographical system on the part of the pedestrian (just as the speaker appropriates and takes on the language)," "a spatial acting-out of the place (just as the speech act is an acoustic acting-out of language)," that "implies *relations* among differentiated positions."[41]

Out in the neighbourhood, first James Gibson and later Malik Rahim remembers New Orleans's 9th Ward. Gibson interrupts the personal history he's recounting to Demme to identify through the car window the ruins of Joseph Hardin Elementary where he was a student in the 1960s. He reminisces about running track and how he "had some great teachers." Moving along, he points out the downed house of a family whose name he mentions, and the empty lot where another family's house one stood. Now out of the car, standing on the street, he re-enacts through gestures a previous visit to the altered surroundings: "After the storm, I came back. Things were so ... turned over that ... I actually got disoriented in the neighbourhood that I grew up in. I drove down here in my car and I went on the other street, Tupelo, just to see some other houses on Tupelo." The camerawork here describes a joint choreography, dancing on the dilapidated street: hand-held, moving in to a close-up on Gibson as he speaks, and panning left to the street itself in the direction Gibson indicates. "And I made my way, going that way, toward Galvez, and when I came on Galvez I turned, make the left turn, and I came back up on St. Maurice to pass in front of my house again, and I got disoriented." At this point the camera swings 180 degrees around the back of Gibson, and then pans right, toward where Gibson is now pointing. Amazed at the weird turn of events, he continues as the camera moves back onto him after pausing for a moment on Jones listening from a few paces back: "I mean it just doesn't look the same ..." This is all one shot. There follows a cut from Gibson's face to the houses on the street.

Three temporalities coexist (the childhood time in the neighbourhood; the prior, spatially confused visit; the return with Demme and camera) as do several spaces (the physical street as it was and had evolved over time; the street in the mind's eye; the street as it is). "Right now, actually right now just standing right here now I can actually go back and just hear, just hear the people sitting on their porches just talking and the kids playing in the neighbourhood. I can actually hear that right now ... in my mind I'm picturing something different, but with my physical eyes I see something else." It is not the loss of just any city or any neighbourhood that matters here, but rather the loss of *New Orleans*—particularly 9th Ward residents, landmarks, and culture—that is being mourned and is at stake. "NOLA," an often affectionate nickname for New Orleans, Louisiana, is a "thick" place, in Casey's term, a place "contrived in the imbrications of affect, habit, and meaning."[42] The fear expressed by Jones of an imminent "boutique city" where culture is performed for tourists while former inhabitants, especially those who are poor and/or African American, are elbowed out of the city, is affective and founded.

What I have been describing is the socially responsible and locally grounded, *iconic* post-Katrina documentary: a mode of expression in which persons define themselves and are defined in relation to a specific place where the traumatization of subjects is expressed both by their own words and emotion and by the distressed landscape in which we find them. Bodies, places, and things become articulate relationally, and moreover, as Nigel Thrift explains in his brilliant essay on "affect in cities" and "affective cities," "cities and affect interact to produce a politics."[43] Through its pedestrian speech acts, *Right to Return* rearticulates the severed connections among persons, homes, and neighbourhoods, and in so doing contributes to the first stage of re-inhabitation.

THE PROJECTS

It just so happened that the festival screening of *Right to Return* took place the night before the razing of the Lafitte housing projects was scheduled to begin. After some delay, which had served to raise hopes that these better-built projects in the 6th Ward would be spared in contrast to three other Roosevelt-era Works Progress Administration complexes already in the process of being torn down, Mayor Ray Nagin had signed the demolition order a couple of weeks prior.[44] It therefore came to pass that the sense of outrage and activism the film captures in the voices, faces, walks, and histories of its subjects spilled over the edges of the screen and into the community venue. Jones had lived in the Lafitte projects as a child prior to his family's move to the first African American subdivision, Pontchartrain Park, he says in the film. At the screening, person after person spoke for saving the Lafitte.[45]

One of the main threads of Luisa Dantas's *Land of Opportunity*, shot over the course of more than four years and finished in 2010, is the story of the razing of the St. Bernard public housing development in the 7th Ward.[46] This film too contains affecting passages like the one in which Gibson resuscitates the memory of a populated Lower 9th Ward. A major example is the lyrical sequence in which the shuttered St. Bernard housing project is brought back to life by the on-site presence and articulated memories of resident/activist Kawana Jasper. We see Jasper coming toward us down the sidewalk pushing a little girl in a stroller, and then entering the development through the gate of a cyclone fence topped with razor wire. "At one point before the hurricane I used to say I can't wait to get out of here ... so my kids could be in a better environment. But they say you never miss it 'til it's gone.... But we not welcome." She too criticizes city planners whom she describes as trying to make it "like Las Vegas," with poverty-stricken people relegated to the outskirts of a city for the rich and for tourists. Reciting her former address—as do so many displaced residents with the certainty of habit mixed with amazement that it is no more—Jasper motions upward to "3841 Duplessis." The camera follows, for a shot washed in light, evoking the home movie footage we see next: two small boys and an older one tossing a football in the open space between housing blocks.

While both films elegiacally evoke the past, I deem *Land of Opportunity* much more involved than *Right to Return* in the imagination and active materialization of a new city plan for New Orleans's future. Of course this temporal shift may be ascribed in part to necessity, since the time of the filming extended beyond the life of these buildings. But *Land of Opportunity* is profoundly expressive of what I take to be a greater range of affective modalities for rememoration and remediation, encompassing as it does: migration out of state; multiple working-class groups in the city, including people from elsewhere;[47] community-activism and participation in the urban planning process; and the graphic as well as the conceptual qualities of the map, the blueprint, and the architectural rendering. I will examine the latter two.

The multiple segments with New Orleans to Los Angeles transplant Tr'Vel Lyons are a case in point of positive out-migration: thoughtful about the past *and* geographically expansive. The teenager almost cries when on a visit to his former home in East New Orleans he salvages a domino out of the set his father gave him. He reflects on the meaning of the find with reference to a TV commercial about firmer attachment to old toys over new. But in a passage shot several years later, after we've seen the domino Scotch-taped to the wall of his LA apartment and heard him comment, "I'm a little piece of New Orleans in LA," we learn that Tr'Vel has been accepted to UCLA and will be attending on a scholarship. Even initially, on the occasion of his graduation from middle school, the emphatic but ambiguous comment, "Katrina, you *did* something!" was accompanied by his statement, "I'm happy I graduated in California."

I understand the presentation of Tr'Vel's mobility as film work that resists a nostalgic view of home, or the sort of "regime of feeling" that Thrift critiques as "likely to lead to a new kind of velvet dictatorship." Favouring instead a "productive, forward sense of life which strives to engage positively with the world," the film contributes to the forging of a new "politics of affect."[48] Quoting Félix Guattari, Thrift makes it clear that this desirable politics of affect is fundamentally spatial: an "ethics and politics of the virtual that decorporealizes and deterritorializes contingency, linear causality and the pressure of circumstances and significance that besiege us."[49] Dantas's film describes an expansive cartography of labour, mobility, and affect in which a domino may be reattached and a young man (and his viewers) made exuberant, elsewhere.

THE CITY, AS IT HAPPENS

Striving to rectify a perceived "neglect of affect in the current urban literature," Thrift argues its conceptual productivity for a critique of the political form he terms "engineering of affect."[50] The latter is a "rather worrying" tendency, Thrift believes, since it implies a top-down choreography of human possibilities through the built environment.

Post-Katrina New Orleans represents an unfortunate case in point.[51] Insurance compensation, tax incentives, mortgage assistance, and other grants awarded through the state's "Road Home" housing recovery program overwhelmingly favoured homeowners and higher-income households over renters and those living in poverty, a large proportion of whom are black. And the Lower 9th Ward, although approximately 50 percent owner-occupied, was 96 percent black[52] and predominantly low-income.[53] Sociologists and others have therefore corroborated Melvin Jones's and Kawana Jasper's horrified vision of an "engineered" New Orleans by projecting, measuring, and in many cases also decrying a "smaller, more White and Hispanic, more affluent, and more tourism/entertainment-oriented" post-Katrina city.[54]

To respond to the problem of the "engineering of affect," Thrift calls for "new forms of political practice that value democracy as functional disunity."[55] Yoosun Park and Joshua Miller, along with the editors of and contributors to *There Is No Such Thing as a Natural Disaster*, recognize not only that "ongoing environmental risks for poor people and people of color are consistently higher than for white people and those who are economically privileged,"[56] but also the importance of asking, in the aftermath of Katrina, "What will be rebuilt, and for whom, and how?"[57] "It is ... clear," they state unequivocally, "that *New Orleans should not be restored to its former racially divided, poverty-stricken, flood-prone design*."[58] On the basis of lessons learned, this particularly valuable article calls for pre-disaster planning and post-disaster relief work and macro-planning to be carried out by health and human services workers *with the participation of grassroots groups*.

Grassroots interventions in the city planning process are certainly taking place in New Orleans, and it is the involvement in this process that lends the nuanced *Land of Opportunity* its activist dimension (although the title may also be read as sadly ironic). In the tradition of the great committed documentaries[59] such as *Harlan County, USA* (Barbara Kopple, 1975), the film's presentation and performance of reconfigured geographies of home go a long way, I believe, toward realizing Thrift's call for a democratic geopolitics of affect and urban space. Vanessa Gueringer's signature gathering near the beginning of the film constitutes a pedestrian speech act with a purpose. Garbed in a red ACORN (Association of Community Organizations for Reform Now) T-shirt, going house to house or FEMA (Federal Emergency Management Agency) trailer to FEMA trailer gathering signatures to secure a local community voice in the official planning process, she is not only encountering neighbours but also canvassing the neighbourhood: "I'm determined to make them understand, you are not going to side-step us," she asserts to a man and woman as they sign the petition. The reoccupation of the St. Bernard public housing development is also documented by the film. On the anniversary of Martin Luther King, Jr.'s birthday in 2007, former residents came from near and far to reinhabit the complex that had been shuttered and the premises locked by order of the New Orleans Housing Authority in concert with federal government policy. We see Civil Rights attorney Bill Quigley announce that whereas the complex had housed 1,500 families, the redevelopment plans accommodate 500, with only 160 slated for people who are income-eligible for public housing. In front of the news media, on foot and in wheelchairs, people push open the gate and march in. Banners reading "Survivors Village" and "HANO Displaced Us Not Katrina" are unfurled or hung from the balconies, foodstuffs cleaned out of refrigerators and pantries, and walls scrubbed. Children are running around, and there's chicken on the barbeque. On this day, the former residents knowingly risk arrest. "Our people could be living in here.... We were a big family," says Kawana's mother Sharon Jasper.

The film provides historically important documentation of demonstrations and meetings at every level and involving multiple constituencies that Dantas attended with her subjects, filmed, and, in this way, joined. Ranging from a handful to a roomful people, from familiar to public personages (residents among themselves or with Mayor Nagin, Make It Right founder Brad Pitt with Angelina Jolie and Bill Clinton, and Barack Obama campaigning in New Orleans in November of 2007), and from congenial to irate attitudes, these encounters are the growing pains of the city against the hard reality that many. New Orleanians were and are still unable to return for lack of financial means.

One meeting for residents—or would-be residents—consists of the presentation of a plan for mixed housing designed to replace the St. Bernard development after its subsequent demolition during the extended period of filming. Kawana Jasper speaks up from the audience to ask how many of the units and what type will be available for displaced low-income families. The developer answers that the plan allows for one-third public housing, one-third tax credit eligible and forty percent market rate. Jasper follows up with a pointed question: "How do you all feel, knowing what kind of land you all took over and that was public housing? ... It's depressing; it's tearing families apart; it's splitting them here and there." Indeed, the population of the St. Bernard area had been 6,427 in the 2000 census and was recorded as 974 in 2010, after the demolition of the public housing complex.[60] Columbia Parc at the Bayou, built on the footprint of St. Bernard, has far fewer units, and only a portion of these are allocated for people receiving public-housing assistance.[61]

Demme's film does include a passage in which Carolyn Parker's statement, from a public hearing in January 2006, that she's "heard *nothing* really for the 9th Ward" is audible on the soundtrack while the camera tracks down the streets of the Lower 9th Ward.[62] But of the two films, *Land of Opportunity* is much more focused on documenting the ongoing planning process, with all its limits and potentialities, as a *collective enterprise* (albeit one in which dedicated individual leaders arise) rather than documenting individual "pioneers" in their single-family dwellings. Alfred Aubry is shown living with his family in a FEMA trailer while waiting—and waiting—for his ruined house to be legally demolished so he can rebuild. But he is also shown, in one of the particularly hopeful sequences of the film, talking with renowned architect and urban planner Andres Duany in front of a posted map of the Gentilly neighbourhood. "Is there any idea you have that will make people say this is much better than before ...?" asks Duany. "I used to always have dreams of growing stuff over there," Aubry responds, pointing to a spot on the map as Duany really listens. Aubry continues, "I found out that's what I'm made to do on this earth." "Grow!" says Duany. "Grow things," affirms Aubry. "So, could we make community gardens for you ...?" The reaction shot of Aubry is stunning, his face intent with possibility.

The film's (carto)graphic *mise-en-scène* also makes a contribution as futurity practice. The walls of the public forums are hung with photographic maps, blueprints, and architectural elevations. Open floor space is taken up with foam-core placards on easels. Tables are strewn with planning documents and tools. These elements are not just iconographic—part of what we see in the film's diegesis—but become fully graphic as maps fill the screen. The signature gathering sequence with Vanessa Gueringer ends with a wall-mounted map of the Gentilly neighbourhood filling the shot, graphically completed by the presence of a gesturing hand.

This motif comes to fruition later in the film during a Lower 9th Ward Planning Meeting. The sequence opens with two sets of hands moving coloured markers on a photographic map. "We said we're working on the schools right now. OK, so MLK and we said we want another one. Two elementary schools."[63] The film cuts to six people around the table, engaged with the process, joking and laughing about whether the area right by Gueringer's house will be zoned for commercial use. "All right, where's our hospital, ya'll? Hospital? Yeah. I'd like a hospital. Let's dream big." Soundtrack music starts up and a montage of shots of people planning. Black and white, men and women together remaking the city as an eminently livable space.

This is my favourite sequence. Overflowing with affective intensity. Residents dreaming big. The embodiment and graphic rendering of "democracy as functional disunity." As Gueringer exhorts her neighbours: "If we don't take hold of the process these people put in place, they're just gonna step on you. It's true that we've been stepped on in the past, but you got the opportunity for your voice to be heard." I acknowledge that the next sequence shows Gueringer depressed about the havoc Katrina wreaked and the incredible arduousness of the process ("a lot to be dealing with aside from trying to get your house together ... fighting the insurance company ... fighting everybody just to survive"), but this too is part of the film's remarkable documentation of a city in the making.

These films and others like them contribute to the verbal, performative, and semiotic insistence, not just on equal *right* of return for disadvantaged residents but on *quality and place* of return as well. When will water and power be connected? What kind of city might be envisioned and how richly diverse and environmentally safe can it be? Dantas's film seems to me particularly significant in that the voices of its subjects are raised and bodies of its subjects mobilized not only in memory of prior inequities of environment and evacuation but also in the projection of future possibilities. From this perspective, recent reports that African Americans are returning, perhaps more slowly than white residents but yet more steadily,[64] are heartening.

THE SAFE DEVELOPMENT PARADOX: MOVING HOME, RECONSIDERED

And yet, what if the geography of the city—taking into account elevation, wetlands erosion, and extreme weather conditions exacerbated by global warming—makes it more or less safe or even unsafe to return, depending on the specific location of the neighbourhood? As I suggested at the start, it is one thing to advance a polemic against the neutralist discourse of the "natural disaster" and quite another to ignore tangible, if mutable, features of the physical environment. To comprehend and participate in thinking through this quandary, interdisciplinary research is necessary: back and forth reading of epistemologies of knowledge in humanities-based film and critical race studies and in social- and natural science-based studies of the environment.

When the city of New Orleans expanded in the twentieth century, building proceeded, as hazard and reconstruction researchers explain, "off the natural levee [of the riverbanks], across the Metaire Ridge toward the vulnerable wetlands near Lake Pontchartrain."[65] Protected by a system of levees, floodwalls, pumps, and floodways overhauled and overseen in the late twentieth century by the US Army Corps of Engineers, the city's pre-Katrina population resided in a bowl, half of which was below sea level.

As such, New Orleans history and geography exemplify "a long-term pattern of societal response to hazard events" known as the "safe development paradox."[66] That is to say that as humans strive to reduce the consequences to people and society of relatively frequent events, they end up *increasing* vulnerability to major, rare events. Just as the prevention or suppression of small forest fires "leads to the buildup of combustible material that increases the catastrophic potential of fires that escape rapid suppression," in New Orleans "the construction of levees induces additional development leading to much larger losses when the levee is eventually overtopped."[67] The very construction projects undertaken to ensure the safety of residents are actually increasing their vulnerability though a false sense of security and neighbourhood tenability. This is the so-called "levee effect."[68]

As R.W. Kates et al. indicate, the goal of rapid recovery of the familiar may conflict with aspirations "to reconstruct in a safer, better," albeit slower, manner.[69] And passionate demands for resources to rebuild in certain African American neighbourhoods—as Carolyn Parker puts it, "*something* for the 9th Ward"—may clash with feasibility, betterment, and environmental sustainability. While "adaptive actions" have been taken in the rebuilding of the levees, in the reconstruction of houses to elevate them and make them more resistant to wind and flooding, and in the preparation of a new evacuation plan, Kates et al. (writing in 2006) deplore the fact that "no actions have been taken to change land use or even to restore wetlands."[70] Thus, in the absence of this major intervention, the other measures are grossly inadequate or even dangerous in encouraging a false sense of security. While I accept the critique of the city planning process as being racially and economically inequitable[71] and admire the courage of residents like Carolyn Parker who are remodelling their own homes, it is nevertheless the case that some of the homes, even those that have been expertly as well as lovingly rebuilt in the Lower 9th Ward, remain vulnerable to destruction by future hurricanes and floods. As Parker's daughter Kyrah Julian herself states in *Right to Return*: "It doesn't matter how many times we rebuild, no matter how high the houses are off the ground. None of that matters. It doesn't matter how many hurricane-proof shutters we put on our houses. We're always going to have floods if we don't do something about the wetlands. We lost about ten years' worth of wetlands in one year."

CONCLUSION

I have been for many years a scholar of testimonial documentary, deeply invested in acts and audio-visualizations of witnessing the emotional and affective as well as the discursive content of survivor testimony. Certainly, if we humans are to live in peace on this planet, we must listen and attend to one another. Here I have advanced the related arguments that in the life and documented life of testimony, location and setting matter enormously, and that a certain literature of affect sheds light on the co-constitution of persons and places through connected points of affective intensity.

In addition, I have made the perhaps more painful argument that forms of testimony vary in their ability to signal the best or most feasible relationship to place and way forward. This study of the various spatial modalities of the post-Katrina documentary concludes that testimonies grounded not only in heartfelt memory and desire and not only in the concrete foundations of individual homes, but also by collective embodiments of the planning process are most capable of restoring "the affective fecundity of place."[72] Dantas, Gueringer, and their interlocutors inspire us to dream big, and, further, to dream and plan in a socially and ecologically sustainable manner.

I write with eyes cast west toward the Fukushima Daiichi Nuclear Power Plant; the situation is dire. In the words of Freudenburg et al., "we are all from New Orleans, and the Katrinas that lurk on the other side of the horizon threaten us all."[73] Sometimes, it is necessary to move out of harm's way. Interdisciplinary studies and creative works that help us assess when it is possible to move back home and when home itself must move are of particular value.

NOTES

I would like to express my warm thanks to Alexa Weik von Mossner and Arielle Helmick for their inspiring concept and for convening the contributors to this volume at the Rachel Carson Center for Environment and Society in Munich, Germany; and to the Center itself for generous hospitality. I am also grateful to the other workshop participants for their brilliant thoughts, lively conversation, and astute feedback on my initial draft. A big thank you to Luisa Dantas for sharing her film with me prior to its official release. Finally, this essay is dedicated to my late colleague, Dehlsen Professor of Environmental Studies William Freudenburg, in recognition of his tremendous legacy as a scholar, teacher, and humanizing presence in our midst.

1   Yi-Fu Tuan, "Home as Elsewhere" (talk delivered as part of the Geographies of Place Series of the Interdisciplinary Humanities Center at the University of California, Santa Barbara, 9 March 2011).

2 According to CNN, on 6 September 2005 Mayor Ray Nagin ordered law enforcement agencies to remove by force if necessary everyone remaining in New Orleans not involved in clean-up efforts. "New Orleans Will Force Evictions," CNN, 7 September 2005, http://www.cnn.com/2005/US/09/06/katrina.impact/index.html?_s=PM:US.

3 The expression "blew away our citizenship" or "washed away our citizenship" has entered common parlance. For strenuous objections to the media calling displaced New Orleanians "refugees," see Act II, Chapter III of *When the Levees Broke: A Requiem in Four Acts*, directed by Spike Lee (New York: HBO, 2006).

4 Bryan Harris, "City Prepares to Demolish Projects," WDSU News, 21 December 2007, http://www.wdsu.com/City-Prepares-To-Demolish-Projects/-/9854144/11011320/-/oi7he2z/-/index.html.

5 Janet Walker, "Rights and Return: Perils and Fantasies of Situated Testimony after Katrina," in *Documentary Testimonies: Global Archives of Suffering*, ed. Bhaskar Sarkar and Janet Walker (New York: Routledge, 2010), 83–113.

6 See also *The Drive: Lower 9th Ward*, directed by Tim Ryan and Matt Wisdom (2006); and *Witness: Katrina*, produced by Rebecca Snedeker, Sarah Pagura, Stacy Wolff, and Dustin Park for Siskel/Jacobs Productions (Washington, DC: National Geographic Channel, 2010).

7 See, as representative and exemplary, Chester Hartman and Gregory D. Squires, eds., *There Is No Such Thing as a Natural Disaster: Race, Class, and Hurricane Katrina* (New York: Routledge, 2006).

8 Yoosun Park and Joshua Miller, "The Social Ecology of Hurricane Katrina: Re-Writing the Discourse of 'Natural' Disasters," *Smith College Studies in Social Work* 76, no. 3 (2006): 10.

9 Park and Miller, "The Social Ecology," 12–18.

10 Edward S. Casey, *Remembering: A Phenomenological Study* (Bloomington: Indiana University Press, 2000), 197.

11 William R. Freudenburg et al., *Catastrophe in the Making: The Engineering of Katrina and the Disasters of Tomorrow* (Washington, DC: Island Press, 2009), 7–8.

12 Sean Carter and Derek P. McCormack, "Film, Geopolitics and the Affective Logics of Intervention," *Political Geography* 25 (2006): 235.

13 Carter and McCormack, "Film, Geopolitics," 234. See also Brian Massumi, "The Autonomy of Affect," *Cultural Critique* 31 (Autumn 1995): 83–109; and Massumi, "The Automony of Affect," chap. 1 in *Parables for the Virtual: Movement, Affect, Sensation* (Durham, NC: Duke University Press, 2002).

14 Cameron Duff, "On the Role of Affect and Practice in the Production of Place," *Environment and Planning D: Society and Space* 28 (2010): 881–95.

15 Carter and McCormack, "Film, Geopolitics," 234.

16 Massumi, "The Autonomy," 88.

17 Massumi, "The Autonomy," 94.

18 Massumi, "The Autonomy," 87.

19 Henri Lefebvre, *The Production of Space*, trans. Donald Nicholson-Smith (Malden, MA: Blackwell, 1991; original French edition, 1974), 6.

20 In "On the Role of Affect," Duff cites Gilles Deleuze, *Spinoza: Practical Philosophy*, trans. R. Hurley (San Francisco, CA: City Lights, 1988), 882.

21 Nigel Thrift, "Intensities of Feeling: Towards a Spatial Politics of Affect," in "The Political Challenge of Relational Space," special issue, *Human Geography* 86, no. 1 (2004), 57. Thrift explicates four major definitions or "translations" of affect: phenomenological with "traces of social interactionism and hermeneutic" (60); psychoanalytic, especially Freudian; Spinozan-Deleuzian; and Darwinian.

22 Ingram (this volume) references Anne Rutherford, "Cinema and Embodied Affect," *Senses of Cinema* 25 (2003), http://sensesofcinema.com/2003/feature-articles/embodied_affect.

23 Carter and McCormack, "Film, Geopolitics," 230.

24 Thrift, "Intensities of Feeling," 57.

25 Duff, "On the Role of Affect," 884.

26 Carter and McCormack, "Film, Geopolitics," 235.

27 Tuan, "Home as Elsewhere."

28 Tuan, "Home as Elsewhere."

29 Extracts from the film and an interview with Demme are available for online viewing through the *Tavis Smiley* show, "Right to Return" (Arlington, VA: Public Broadcasting Service, 2007), The Smiley Group, http://www.pbs.org/wnet/tavissmiley/features/right-to-return.

30 Spike Lee's follow-up, *If God Is Willing and Da Creek Don't Rise* (2010), is more like Demme's work in its demonstration of Lee's continued concern with issues of racial justice in post-Katrina New Orleans and attention to individuals whose lives are now interwoven with his. The last section of the film concentrates on people he had interviewed previously whose traumatic response is ongoing.

31 This documentary had its world premiere at the Venice Film Festival in September 2011 and its US premiere, as *I'm Carolyn Parker: The Good, the Mad, and the Beautiful*, the same month at the Woodstock Film Festival.

32 A clip of Parker's segment, in a slightly different cut than the festival version of the film, has been posted by Demme's production company, Clinica Estetico, to Vimeo: http://vimeo.com/27164138.

33 Casey, *Remembering*, 192; quoting Maurice Merleau-Ponty, *The Phenomenology of Perception*, trans. C. Smith (New York: Humanities Press, 1962), 144.

34 Casey, *Remembering*, 192; quoting Erwin Straus, *The Primary World of Senses*, trans. J. Needleman (Glencoe, IL: Free Press, 1963), 388–90.

35 Bishnupriya Ghosh, "'We Shall Drown, But We Shall Not Move': The Ecologics of Testimony in NBA Documentaries," in Sarkar and Walker, eds., *Documentary Testimonies*, 59.

36 Ghosh, "We Shall Drown," 78.

37 Casey, *Remembering*, 193.

38 Casey, *Remembering*, 194.

39 Casey, *Remembering*, 180.

40 Duff argues in "On the Role of Affect" that Michel de Certeau's emphasis on the constant "doing" and "making" of the modern city "in the undulating contours of its built environments and in the routines and improvisations of practice" (881) is important but neglectful of the "*affective dimensions* of city life" (abstract; emphasis original). I do not agree.

41 Michel de Certeau, *The Practice of Everyday Life*, trans. Steven Rendall (Berkeley: University of California Press, 1984), 97–98. The title of this section is indebted to de Certeau's "Walking in the City" and to the popular song "Walking to New Orleans" (1960; written by Bobby Charles for, and recorded by, Fats Domino).

42 Here I am drawing on Duff's proposition that Edward Casey's distinction between "thick" and "thin" places is helpful for "restor[ing] the affective fecundity of place." ("On the Role of Affect," 882). The particular Casey work cited by Duff in this regard is "Between Geography and Philosophy: What Does It Mean to Be in the Place-World?" *Annals of the Association of American Geographers* 91 (2001): 683–93.

43 Thrift, "Intensities of Feeling," 58.

44 Katy Reckdahl, "Nagin OKs Demolition of Lafitte Housing Complex," *Times-Picayune*, 25 March 2008.

45 The proceedings epitomized Michael Renov's insight that the screening venue constitutes a major point of mediation in a documentary film's creation of meaning. Michael Renov, "Re-thinking Documentary: Toward a Taxonomy of Mediation," *Wide Angle* 8, nos. 3 and 4 (1986). The question of whether or how much the Lafitte complex flooded during the hurricane and flood remains subject to debate.

46 *Land of Opportunity* is available for purchase at www.landofopportunitymovie.com.

47 *Land of Opportunity* places peoples' struggles for public housing and the support to rebuild in owner-occupied African American neighbourhoods in relation to a broader geography of labour and mobility. Whereas Demme concentrates on African American residents fighting to stay in place, Dantas includes the affecting stories of two immigrants who came to New Orleans from Brazil seeking work in an anticipated building boom.

48 Thrift, "Intensities of Feeling," 68. Thrift exemplifies his argument through a reading of Bill Viola's experimental video works.

49 Félix Guattari, quoted by Thrift, "Intensities of Feeling," 68.

50 Thrift, "Intensities of Feeling," 58, 64.

51 Mike Davis's response, entitled "Gentrifying Disaster," alerted readers to government decisions that, less than two months after landfall, were already undermining minority homeowners' ability to return: turning down the state's request to support the voting rights of displaced minority residents, awarding construction contracts to out-of-state firms, and evicting tenants precipitously to demolish public housing. Mike Davis, "Gentrifying Disaster in New Orleans: Ethnic Cleansing, GOP-Style," *Mother Jones* online, 24 October 2005, http://www.motherjones.com/politics/2005/10/gentrifying-disaster.

52 Robert O. Zdenek, Ralph Scott, Jane Malone, and Brian Gumm, "Reclaiming New Orleans' Working-Class Communities," in Hartman and Squires, eds., *There Is No Such Thing*, 169.

53 John Taylor and Josh Silver, "From Poverty to Prosperity: The Critical Role of Financial Institutions," in Hartman and Squires, eds., *There Is No Such Thing*, 242. See also, Sheila Crowley, "Where Is Home? Housing for Low-Income People after the 2005 Hurricanes," in Hartman and Squires, eds., *There Is No Such Thing*, 121–66.

54 William W. Falk, Matthew O. Hunt, and Larry L. Hunt, "Hurricane Katrina and New Orleanians' Sense of Place: Return and Reconstitution or 'Gone with the Wind'?" *Du Bois Review* 3, no. 1 (2006), 115. In 2010, US Census Bureau figures revealed that the population of New Orleans had indeed shrunk by 29.1%, from 484,674 in the year 2000 to 343,929 people ten years later, and that the percent of the population identifying themselves as African American had dropped 7% from 67% in the year 2000 (while the Hispanic population size increased over the same period). Arlette Saenz, "New Orleans Population Shrinks by 1/3 in 10 Years," ABC News, 7 February 2011, http://abcnews.go.com/Politics/orleans-population-shrinks-10-years/story?id=12856256.

55 Thrift, "Intensities of Feeling," 75.

56 Park and Miller, "The Social Ecology," 10.

57 Park and Miller, "The Social Ecology," 17.

58 Park and Miller, "The Social Ecology," 17 (emphasis mine). Relative to the testimonial documentaries under discussion, the importance of story sharing to the mitigation of "high rates of poverty and ingrained patterns of racism in the U.S." is also foregrounded by Park and Miller (21). "If every clinician engaged in post-disaster response wrote a narrative to be shared with others—either in professional presentations, letters to the newspaper, op-ed pieces, poems, or other forms of public expression there would be many voices contesting the pre-disaster consensus of normalcy. Such narratives would keep crucial issues about human suffering and social inequality in the forefront of public consciousness" (21).

59 Thomas Waugh, ed., *"Show Us Life": Toward a History and Aesthetics of the Committed Documentary* (Metuchen, NJ: Scarecrow, 1984).

60 Population figures cited by The Greater New Orleans Data Center. The 2010 figure refers to the period after the 2005 hurricane and the demolition of the projects in 2008. "St. Bernard Statistical Area," Greater New Orleans Data Center, http://www.gnocdc.org/Neighborhood Data/4/StBernard/index.html.

61 See Katy Reckdahl, "St. Bernard Site Holds Potential for Holistic Redevelopment, Visitors Say," *Times-Picayune*, 2 March 2010, http://www.nola.com/news/index.ssf/2010/03/st_bernard_site_housing_holds.html.

62 Carolyn Parker: "I came to this meeting to find out what your *vision* [is] for the Lower 9th Ward. And I'm not surprised because the vision is not too clear. I'm speaking for the people that's out there, that's dispersed all over the United States. That cannot get back ... I'm asking you, all of you, the whole panel, because I heard *nothing* really for the Lower 9th Ward. Those are my family, my friends, my neighbours. I've been down there—yes I'm telling my age—59 years. And I know who been here, I know who came here, and who went. So I'm asking you, you named every part of New Orleans, but *you never named anything* really for the Lower 9th Ward. So I'm here for those persons who cannot get back."

63 See Kristen Buras, "Challenging the Master's Plan for Lower 9th Ward," *ZMagazine* 24, no. 5 (May 2011), http://www.zcommunications.org/challenging-the-masters-plan-for-lower -9th-by-kristen-l-buras.html.

64 Elizabeth Fussell, Narayan Sastry, and Mark VanLangingham, "Who Returned to New Orleans after Hurricane Katrina?" Population Reference Bureau, July 2010, http://www.prb.org/Publications/Articles/2010/katrina.aspx.

65 R.W. Kates et al., "Reconstruction of New Orleans after Hurricane Katrina: A Research Perspective," *Proceedings of the National Academy of Sciences* 103, no. 40 (3 October 2006), 14654.

66 Kates et al., "Reconstruction," 14658, 14653.

67 Kates et al., "Reconstruction," 14653.

68 Kates et al., "Reconstruction," 14653.

69 Kates et al., "Reconstruction," 14658, 14653.

70 Kates et al., "Reconstruction," 14657.

71 As a *New York Times* article reported, "Much of the Lower Ninth is 'two to three feet higher' than areas of the Lakeview neighborhood and the western side of Jefferson Parish, Dr. Mashriqui said. 'Nobody is talking about people having to move from there.'" John Schwartz, "Can the Lower Ninth Ward Be Saved?" *New York Times*, 25 April 2006.

72 Duff, "On the Role of Affect," 882.

73 Freudenburg et al., *Catastrophe in the Making*, 11.

BIBLIOGRAPHY

Buras, Kristen L. "Challenging the Master's Place for Lower 9th Ward." *ZMagazine* 24, no. 5 (May 2011). http://www.zcommunications.org/challenging-the-masters -plan-for-lower-9th-by-kristen-l-buras.html.

Carter, Sean, and Derek P. McCormack. "Film, Geopolitics and the Affective Logics of Intervention." *Political Geography* 25 (2006): 228–45.

Casey, Edward S. "Between Geography and Philosophy: What Does It Mean to Be in the Place-World?" *Annals of the Association of American Geographers* 91 (2001): 683–93.

———. *Remembering: A Phenomenological Study*. Bloomington: Indiana University Press, 2000.

Certeau, Michel de. *The Practice of Everyday Life*. Translated by Steven Rendall. Berkeley: University of California Press, 1984.

Crowley, Sheila. "Where Is Home? Housing for Low Income People after the 2005 Hurricanes." In *There Is No Such Thing as a Natural Disaster: Race, Class, and*

Hurricane Katrina, edited by Chester Hartman and Gregory D. Squires, 121–66. New York: Routledge, 2006.

Davis, Mike. "Gentrifying Disaster in New Orleans: Ethnic Cleansing, GOP-Style." *Mother Jones* online, 24 October 2005. http://motherjones.com/politics/2005/10/gentrifying-disaster.

Duff, Cameron. "On the Role of Affect and Practice in the Production of Place." *Environment and Planning D: Society and Space* 28 (2010): 881–95.

Falk, William W., Matthew O. Hunt, and Larry L. Hunt. "Hurricane Katrina and New Orleanians' Sense of Place: Return and Reconstitution or 'Gone with the Wind'?" *Du Bois Review* 3, no. 1 (2006): 115–28.

Freudenburg, William R., Robert Gramling, Shirley Laska, and Kai T. Erikson. *Catastrophe in the Making: The Engineering of Katrina and the Disasters of Tomorrow*. Washington, DC: Island Press, 2009.

Ghosh, Bishnupriya. "'We Shall Drown, But We Shall Not Move': The Ecologics of Testimony in NBA Documentaries." In *Documentary Testimonies: Global Archives of Suffering*, edited by Bhaskar Sarkar and Janet Walker, 59–81. New York: Routledge, 2010.

Hartman, Chester, and Gregory D. Squires, eds. *There Is No Such Thing as a Natural Disaster: Race, Class, and Hurricane Katrina*. New York: Routledge, 2006.

Kates, R.W., C.E. Colten, S. Laska, and S. P. Leatherman. "Reconstruction of New Orleans after Hurricane Katrina: A Research Perspective." *Proceedings of the National Academy of Sciences* 103, no. 40 (3 October 2006): 14653–60.

Land of Opportunity. Directed by Luisa Dantas. New Orleans: JoLu Productions, 2011. DVD.

Lefebvre, Henri. *The Production of Space*. Translated by Donald Nicholson-Smith. Malden, MA: Blackwell, 1991. Original French edition, 1974.

Massumi, Brian. "The Autonomy of Affect." *Cultural Critique* 31 (Autumn 1995): 83–109.

———. *Parables for the Virtual: Movement, Affect, Sensation*. Durham, NC: Duke University Press, 2002.

Park, Yoosun, and Joshua Miller. "The Social Ecology of Hurricane Katrina: Re-Writing the Discourse of 'Natural' Disasters." *Smith College Studies in Social Work* 76, no. 3 (2006): 9–24.

Reckdahl, Katy. "Nagin OKs Demolition of Lafitte Housing Complex," *Times-Picayune*, 25 March 2008.

Renov, Michael. "Re-thinking Documentary: Toward a Taxonomy of Mediation," *Wide Angle* 8, nos. 3 and 4 (1986): 71–77.

Right to Return: New Home Movies from the Lower 9th Ward. Directed by Jonathan Demme. Arlington, VA: Public Broadcasting Service, 2006. DVD.

Rutherford, Anne. "Cinema and Embodied Affect," *Senses of Cinema* 25 (2003), http://sensesofcinema.com/2003/feature-articles/embodied_affect.

Schwartz, John. "Can the Lower Ninth Ward Be Saved?" *New York Times*, 25 April 2006.

Taylor, John, and Josh Silver. "From Poverty to Prosperity: The Critical Role of Financial Institutions." In *There Is No Such Thing as a Natural Disaster: Race, Class, and*

Hurricane Katrina, edited by Chester Hartman and Gregory D. Squires, 233–54. New York: Routledge, 2006.

Thrift, Nigel. "Intensities of Feeling: Towards a Spatial Politics of Affect." Special issue: "The Political Challenge of Relational Space," *Human Geography* 86, no. 1 (2004): 57–78.

Trouble the Water. Directed by Carl Deal and Tia Lessin. New York: Zeitgeist Films, 2008. DVD.

Walker, Janet. "Rights and Return: Perils and Fantasies of Situated Testimony after Katrina." In *Documentary Testimonies: Global Archives of Suffering*, edited by Bhaskar Sarkar and Janet Walker, 83–113. New York: Routledge, 2010.

Waugh, Thomas, ed. *"Show Us Life": Toward a History and Aesthetics of the Committed Documentary*. Metuchen, NJ: Scarecrow Press, 1984.

When the Levees Broke: A Requiem in Four Acts. Directed by Spike Lee. New York: HBO, 2006. DVD.

Zdenek, Robert O., Ralph Scott, Jane Malone, and Brian Gumm. "Reclaiming New Orleans' Working-Class Communities." In *There Is No Such Thing as a Natural Disaster: Race, Class, and Hurricane Katrina*, edited by Chester Hartman and Gregory D. Squires, 167–84. New York: Routledge, 2006.

11

Evoking Sympathy and Empathy
The Ecological Indian and Indigenous Eco-activism

Salma Monani

> Few images are as ubiquitous and loaded as those of Native Americans
> in popular culture.
> —*Michelle Raheja*

Defying socio-cultural and economic hegemonies often seems impossible.
Yet it is precisely these hegemonies that many indigenous groups, faced
with both historical and ongoing marginalization, work to confront politically. In their various struggles for recognition, many indigenous groups have
employed visual media (photographs, film, video, or Internet platforms) to
make their presence felt and their concerns heard.[1] Cognitive film theory presents ideas of emotion that provide compelling ways to engage indigenous
films' activist possibilities. A film's political impact is based on its ability to
persuade, and as film theorist Carl Plantinga writes, "this persuasion relies
in large part on the emotional and affective qualities of the film text and the
experience it affords."[2] As many cognitive film scholars point out, "Affective
experience and meaning are neither parallel nor separable, but firmly intertwined."[3] That is, a film's persuasion is dependent both on rational appeals
and on emotional impact.

Integral to such persuasive appeals is the role of characters as emotive agents
in film. Characters evoke feelings associated with sympathy and/or empathy
(as well as their adverse, antipathy).[4] While there is some debate on whether
sympathy and empathy are necessarily different, scholars generally agree that

such feelings can and do motivate audience members to connect with the values and ideologies of key characters (the protagonists in particular), and often-times of the film.

In this chapter, I focus on the "ecological Indian," a historically prominent yet controversial symbol of environmental consciousness, as filmic character. I draw on post-colonial and indigenous concepts of strategic essentialism and anti-essentialism to highlight how the ecological Indian is an emotion-ally charged rendition of indigenous identity. I then turn to eco-activist films screened at the 2011 "Mother Earth in Crisis" Native American Film and Video Festival (NAFVF) to consider how it is both used and rejected by such indigenous media. I pay particular attention to two films, *A Message from Pandora* (2010), featuring celebrity director James Cameron, and *River of Renewal* (2009), featuring American Indian actor Jack Kohrer. In exploring these films, I follow the lead of film cognitivist Dan Flory and draw together theories of character engagement and critical race theory to suggest that how these films evoke sympathy versus empathy is racially layered. I further argue that distinc-tions between sympathy and empathy take on particular significance when we consider the potentially different ramifications each might have for indigenous activism and political agency.

SYMPATHY, EMPATHY, AND THE POLITICS OF RACE

Cognitive scholars recognize that characters are emotive agents with whom audience members can have feelings *with* or *for*. For example, as an audience member, I can feel happiness *with* a happy drunk on screen. I can also feel pity *for* the drunk instead of experiencing happiness. Some scholars seek to differ-entiate these types of feelings *for* and *with* as sympathetic versus empathetic respectively.[5] Others see these empathetic and sympathetic feelings as prob-lematically entwined.[6] Boundaries between the two become particularly blurry when feelings of sympathy and empathy occur simultaneously (for example, I can feel happiness with the drunk but also pity for him), or when one con-siders suggestions that empathy is a "precursor" to sympathy, where a sharing of emotions can prompt feelings for another.[7] In such cases, scholars such as Carl Plantinga suggest that empathy should be subsumed under sympathy, or vice versa, as both ultimately engage "a capacity or disposition to respond with concern to another's situation."[8]

However, despite the fact that sympathy and empathy are closely related, I am cautious about classifying them as one and the same. Instead, I draw from the work of Dan Flory to suggest that distinctions do matter, especially when thinking about racial dimensions.[9] As one of the first film cognitivists to consider race and character engagement together in his analysis of African Americans and film, Flory distinguishes empathy and sympathy because racial assumptions often impinge on how viewers feel concern *for* or *with* characters. Given that there are "largely unconscious ... cultural assumptions concerning what it is to be white,"[10] many white viewers can "have trouble imagining what it is like to be African American 'from the inside'—engaging black points of view empathetically."[11] Race can be a barrier to engaging empathetically with non-white characters. It can also allow viewers to be sympathetic and forgiving of the racism of white characters, as Flory argues quite convincingly in his analysis of Sal's character in Spike Lee's *Do the Right Thing*.[12]

White racial privilege, Flory points out, is "implicitly built into much Western visual media like film."[13] He argues for films that prompt viewers to question this privilege and unbalance the racial status quo. He writes, how a film "orchestrates audience emotions of sympathy and empathy" can "encourage viewers to think philosophically about the racialized dimensions of film perception, the human condition, and current circumstances of human equality."[14] Such emotional engagement, he indicates, in turn can be a foundation for activism.[15]

Despite this nod towards activism, Flory's primary focus is more on the ways in which films orchestrate sympathy and empathy and less on their possible outcomes. Such caution is well founded as the links between a film's intention, a viewer's interpretations, and a viewer's subsequent actions are anything but well determined. However, there are studies that link altruistic behaviour to sympathy and empathy.[16] Therefore, I advocate theoretically extending Flory's ideas in the direction of possible outcomes, which in turn I believe can have significant ramifications for race politics. This is because sympathy and empathy suggest very different motivations for activism. Specifically, one can argue that sympathy, as primarily a concern *for*, is motivated not necessarily by a sense of sharing but instead by a sense of charity. While altruistic, charity signals a sense of concern that is hierarchical in nature, and inherently patronizing. In contrast, empathy, which is tied to sharing feelings, hints at an altruism that is more grounded in a sense of equality. When acting from empathy, I do what I do because I've taken on your perspective; your pain is my pain; your joy is my joy. Because I find myself suffering and/or experiencing as I think you do, I have put myself on a similar plane as you.[17]

Acknowledging these motivating factors in sympathy and empathy becomes particularly important when considering how viewers might be inspired to act. In indigenous politics, where autonomous agency and self-politicization are significant, acting *for* might not be enough. This is particularly true when we put such gestures into historical context. Colonists often presented efforts to "civilize the native" (for example, via assimilation practices of boarding schools and missionaries) as gestures of sympathy when in reality these gestures were thinly veiled policies of subjugation and conquest.[18] Simply put, in the messy realm of indigenous race politics, acting *for* is often quite problematic.

To better make sense of these considerations of sympathy, empathy, and the politics of indigeneity in film, I focus on the "ecological Indian" as a character often evoked in eco-activism. Like Flory, I utilize Murray Smith's theory of character engagement to help us understand how films orchestrate sympathy and empathy through the use or rejection of this character.[19] Specifically, I draw from Smith's triad of recognition, alignment, and allegiance to help illuminate how films at the 2011 NAFVF work to orient indigenous agency and activism.

Recognition, Murray Smith writes, is a form of "mimetic" referencing prompted by both a film's textual characteristics and "knowledge of the real world."[20] In recognizing characters, such referencing is associative, sparking memories of past events and experiences. These associations are not carefully and rationally thought out but are often triggered subconsciously and involve both cognitive and affective processes.[21] As I discuss below, the "ecological Indian" is a well-recognized image with strong emotional resonance.

Unlike recognition, *alignment* arises from the text itself. Smith isolates two textual characteristics—"spatio-temporal attachment" and "subjective access"— that are essential to alignment.[22] While attachment "shows us what characters do," subjective access "reveals what characters desire, believe, think, and feel."[23] Through its cinematic choices, a film aligns us with some characters more than others, and whether these characters are indigenous or white becomes significant in the context of race politics.

Finally, distinguishing *allegiance* from recognition and alignment, Smith sees the latter two as simply requiring the viewer to comprehend the character, while "with allegiance we go beyond understanding, by evaluating and responding emotionally to the traits and emotions of the character, in the context of the narrative situation."[24] Narrative situation *and* extra-filmic context are important in how audiences evaluate a character. For example, allegiance can be prompted by audiences sharing similarities with specific characteristics, such as race or ethnicity.[25]

As Smith, Flory, and others who have used this triadic framework suggest, recognition, alignment, and allegiance work together (or sometimes at cross-purposes with each other) to prompt viewers to engage with characters; however, other factors also guide viewers' emotional responses as they watch a film. The narrative arc with its twists and turns can prompt "direct" emotions such as "curiosity, suspense, anticipation," while the responses of other viewers in a theatre can prompt various "meta-emotions."[26] While I allude to these other types of emotions since they work in concert with character-specific emotions to influence viewer responses, I focus primarily on emotions associated with the ecological Indian to highlight the relationships between sympathy, empathy, and the politics of race.

RECOGNITION: THE ECOLOGICAL INDIAN AS EMOTIVE SIGNIFIER

The ecological Indian can be termed a *prototypical* character.[27] Most viewers easily recognized its presence in James Cameron's recent 3-D blockbuster *Avatar* (2009). *Avatar*'s Na'vi are indigenous primitives who live in harmony with nature. When they are threatened by an invading colonial power, they respond with warnings about disrespecting nature but their worldview seems hopelessly outmanoeuvered by the technological power and capitalist greed of the colonists. *Avatar* is simply the latest popular rendition of ecological Indians. From early productions such as Robert Flaherty's 1922 documentary, *Nanook of the North*, to more recent Hollywood offerings such as Kevin Costner's Oscar-winning *Dances with Wolves* (1990) and Disney's *Pocahontas* (1994), *Avatar* has a number of popular precursors.[28] An iconic image of the ecological Indian is the "crying Indian" of the 1971 Keep America Beautiful Inc. public service announcement. Michelle Raheja describes this televised announcement: "Iron Eyes Cody [the actor], became for many people throughout the world, the quintessential symbol of the American Indian.... Each night in thousands of suburban homes, Cody's anachronistic ghostly Indian figure paddled swiftly across the screen against the backdrop of polluting factories, an image that foregrounds modern anxieties of autochthony and (im)migration, nature and technology, authenticity and imitation."[29] Raheja's discussion of the crying Indian is a reminder of the affective resonance of the Native American used as a popular symbol of eco-purity. In a period when environmental laws were being enacted in the United States, the commercial was immeasurably popular.[30] Her emphasis on the "anachronistic ghostly Indian figure" is also spotlighted by other scholarly critiques as the "vanishing Indian" or the "Taxidermic Indian"—that is, the primitive from the past.[31] Scholars note that this prototype functions mainly to feed Euro-American emotions of romantic and nostalgic escape from modernity, rather than as a real symbol for indigenous eco-justice.[32]

The culture wars sparked by environmental historian Shephard Krech's *The Ecological Indian: Myth and History* (1999) also demonstrate how the image is emotionally charged. Krech's treatise used historical evidence to debunk the idea of Native Americans as "ecologists and conservationists."[33] In their introduction to *Native Americans and the Environment* (2007), editors Michael Harkin and David Rich Lewis point out how Krech's assertions inflamed many in the Native American community who saw his arguments as both unreliable in the way they privileged Euro-American historical sources, and more importantly, as an affront to indigenous activism, where struggles for cultural recognition and sovereign rights embraced the ecological Indian as representing a crucial aspect of indigenous identity.[34] At the same time, many inside and outside Native American communities welcomed Krech for challenging a stereotypical way of representing Native Americans. Harkin and Lewis write that *The Ecological Indian* was "remarkable for the *strength of feeling* associated with both positive and negative readings of it."[35]

Darren Ranco's chapter in Harkin and Lewis's collection is eloquent in capturing the "strength of feeling" in these controversies. He writes that in the politics of recognition, "the fact that Indians have to use a stereotype rooted in colonial desires for this type of recognition is tragic, not only because these stereotypes are 'misleading' but because they potentially fulfill the colonial fantasies of disappearance." He continues, "In this logic, if you stop acting like 'real Indians,' your political authority (and your land) might just disappear, even though the settler state has tried to assimilate you."[36] He, and others such as Corinn Columpar, suggest that indigenous people use the ecological Indian strategically in ways that are complicated by legacies of colonial oppression.[37]

Columpar writes that such *strategic essentialism* is often a "means to an anti-essentialist end, the first step in a protracted process that culminates in an embrace of … the partial, fragmented, multiple, hybridized" and thus is usually "politically expedient."[38] However, Columpar, like Harkin and Lewis, also suggests that many, including within indigenous communities, see it as "theoretically impure" (after all, essentialism is a reductive presentation of identity), and consequently have favoured anti-essentialist strategies instead.[39]

Anti-essentialism that rejects the ecological Indian, however, is not without its risks, as suggested by the quote from Ranco above. Also, as various indigenous scholars write, because for many indigenous societies nature grounds not only material rights but also cultural worldviews fundamentally different from colonial conceptions, there is something "real" anchoring the idea of the ecological Indian.[40] Columpar captures the dilemma of anti-essentialism well when she writes, "since abandoning essence, then, entails abandoning claims to sovereignty [of land and culture], it is not hard to see why Indian scholars have, when pressed to choose, favored essentialism."[41]

Given these complicated dimensions, the ecological Indian remains controversial and emotionally charged. Its ubiquitous presence in popular culture
and the extensive discourse that encircles it suggests that encounters with the
image are invariably laden with mimetic referencing. Some viewers experience emotional responses of annoyance, derision, and dismissal, recognizing a
stereotype with which they are morally uncomfortable. Other viewers see the
prototype as an authentic portrayal of indigenous experience and are more
likely to embrace its presence on screen. This raises the potential for sympathetic allegiance as emotions such as sadness, guilt, and nostalgia colour the
viewers' experience. For films with goals of activism, such associative triggers
can both help and hinder their agendas. In considering films screened at the
2011 Native American Film and Video Festival whose explicit theme was an
eco-activist one, "Mother Earth in Crisis," I suggest how indigenous activism
both uses and rejects the prototypical character of the ecological Indian to
orchestrate viewer recognitions to further guide allegiance.

NAFVF ran in New York from 31 March to 3 April at the National
Museum of the American Indian's Film and Video Center.[42] The festival is
a transnational event, featuring films from all over the Americas. Since the
organizers do not send out a thematic call for submissions but use common
threads in the submissions to help guide festival themes, environmental issues
as presented in a number of submitted films became the primary theme for
the 2011 festival. On Friday, the second day of the festival, a special afternoon
symposium focused on eight films about indigenous struggles around rivers
across the Americas. The screenings were followed by a round-table discussion
that featured filmmakers and activists. While the symposium signalled dedicated time to an eco-activist agenda, films that explicitly addressed environmental concerns could be found throughout the festival; in fact, the festival was
inaugurated with the feature documentary *Qapirangajuq: Inuit Knowledge and
Climate Change* (2010) co-produced by Canadians Zacharias Kunuk and Ian
Munro. In addition to explicitly eco-activist films, the festival included films
highlighting themes such as language loss, violence against women, alcohol use,
and generational misunderstandings. Festival director Elizabeth Weatherford
acknowledges that an environmental consciousness is often simmering below
the surface of these films.[43] I focus on films from the Friday symposium (primarily James Cameron's *A Message from Pandora* and Jack Kohrer's *River of
Renewal*) as telling examples of the ways in which the ecological Indian enables
sympathetic and/or empathetic viewer engagement.

STRATEGIC ESSENTIALISM: WHITE MAN'S TROPE TO INDIGENOUS-OWNED

There's diegetic clapping. On the right and closest to the camera, in medium shot, is a middle-aged white man holding a spear. His pale face is painted with red streaks; he's standing tall, and his expression is serious. To the left, positioned further back but still in medium shot, is a slender Kayapo Indian youth, who appears to be waiting in line to speak with him. He is shirtless and his dark skin is painted with black lines; his face is also painted with red streaks. But unlike the white man, his posture is relaxed; he's looking straight at the camera, grinning. There are others in the shot, filling the background between him and the white man: a woman seated and clapping; behind her a man standing with arms akimbo, flash of teeth; beside her another sitting and watching; and still behind a scattering of people sitting and standing. None are white. The scene is outdoors. Sunshine in the background dapples the dirt ground. The clapping continues as the Kayapo puts a beaded necklace around the white man's neck, and shaking his hand. The white man maintains the same expression of solemn machismo. The shot cuts again, to an older Kayapo with elaborate body paint, a colourful armband, necklace, and crown, paying his respects to the white man. He speaks briefly, and we hear the words, "He wants to give you his crown" from off-camera as the Kayapo places his featured headdress on the white man's head.

One can imagine a number of associations being triggered by this scene of contact between white man and indigenous peoples. The presence of the indigene in traditional regalia, behaving with respect and friendliness toward the white man, conjures the prototypical noble savage, which in turn signals the ecological Indian. Underlining this recognition: the white man is James Cameron, and the scene is from his documentary *A Message from Pandora* (2010). Such recognition immediately serves to skew a viewer's allegiance. Whether derisive of the stereotype or awed by Cameron's environmental commitment, a viewer is already emotionally invested to engage with (or disengage from) the film and the film's alignment reinforces this engagement (or disengagement) through continuously reinforcing the prototype. In its spatio-temporal attachment and subjective access, the film presents the Kayapo Indians as ecologically connected in ways that are laden with Raheja's sense of the "anachronistic ghostly" Other and presents Cameron as the neo-liberal "saviour" speaking for white fantasies.

Produced in 2010 in collaboration with the US-based non-profit Amazon Watch, the twenty-minute documentary combines expository and participatory modes. Cameron narrates as participant in the action, as interviewee, and as voice-of-God over shots of the Brazilian rainforest, animation from *Avatar*, and technically rendered maps of the Xingu river and its proposed hydroelectric Bel Monte dam. The film is Cameron's attempt to highlight the destruction that the dam will do to the Brazilian rainforests and its indigenous Kayapo peoples. Yet, despite its focus on issues crucial to the Kayapo, the film uses Cameron as its protagonist.

From the opening scenes of the film—a grainy nondescript shot presented as a film negative that cuts sharply to its more recognizable positive, a close-up that zooms out to reveal an oil-slicked dead bird lying on sand and the voice-over that accompanies it stating "I was in high school ..."—the film aligns viewers with Cameron. Preceding the appearance of the title is a full minute of Cameron's narration about how he became interested in environmental issues, accompanying a montage of eco-apocalyptic images—the oil-slicked bird, archival sepia footage of an atomic explosion, shots of bridges swaying and palm trees assaulted by winds cut to a digital animation of an aerial view of the rainforest. Interspliced into this montage is Cameron's appearance at an in-studio interview. Cameron states his environmental anxieties explicitly: "There was this threat that the technological world was overwhelming the natural world, and destroying it." In contrast to this technological world, he highlights the "primeval, untouched world of the rain forest," "the last bastion of nature," which he explains he has always wanted to visit, and finally had good reason to.

Cameron sets up his central role as spokesperson early in the film by presenting his part in a sustainability conference held in Manaus, Brazil, where he speaks against the dam. Only in the documentary's sixth minute (of twenty) do we see substantial footage of the Kayapo. When we do, the camera's alignment generates both a sense of "Other" and of Cameron's privileged position among the "Other" through his access to a meeting of Kayapo leaders. In this scene, footage of Kayapo—many sporting traditional garb, alighting from a boat, then partaking in ritual singing—is accompanied by Cameron's words that suggest that the meeting for which these leaders were gathering was "not for the press, not for the government, but for their own planning." For the duration of the film, access to the Kayapo is filtered through Cameron. While Cameron points to language barriers (translations from Kayapo to Portugese to English and back), the effect is that the film literally drowns out the voices of the Kayapo with Cameron's narration. In the whole film, we hear just one Kayapo speak, a young woman, Sheyla Yakarepi Jurana, whose first words are translated to highlight Cameron as "our new and latest warrior."

In contrast, Cameron has a lot to say about the Kayapo. His statements, punctuating the entire narrative, like his demeanor, convey respect but in ways that mark these people as prototypical pre-modern ecological Indians:

> For these people in that place, it's the end of the world as they know it, and they are reacting accordingly, you know. They are there with their spears and bows and arrows saying they will fight....
>
> [In *Avatar*] I was thinking I was making an historical comment, if you will, on what had happened in North America, in recent history. But, you know, a hundred years ago, hundred and fifty years ago, and back through the colonial period ... I landed up going to Brazil and all of a sudden I was living in *Avatar*....
>
> And I'm not saying we have to abandon the cities to go and strip off our clothes and run out to the forest and live like the Kayapo; the Kayapo don't want us there.

Thus, Cameron renders the Kayapo as one-dimensional shadows, distinctly anachronistic in their ways of living. (Two of *Avatar*'s actors, Sigourney Weaver and Joel David Moore, accompany Cameron on his second trip to the Amazon and provide similar narration.) Because the film turns the Kayapo into background characters within their own story, it's hard for viewers to empathetically engage with them. We can sympathize with them, but the film guides empathy with Cameron.

The prototypical rendering of the ecological Indian coupled with aligning with Cameron suggest both potentials for, and limits to, eco-activism. *A Message from Pandora* is marketed to First World audiences, and as cognitivists such as Flory point out, empathy is often born from shared experiences. For a New York City viewer, seeing things through Cameron's "urbanized eyes"[44] might be more effective in striking a chord of shared emotion than seeing from the point of view of a Kayapo Indian. By including *A Message from Pandora* in their festival offerings, NAFVF could have been playing to the allegiance of viewers who are tuned into narratives of ecological primitivism versus technological hubris, and see Cameron's position as an analogous way to express their own positions of sympathy and agency. These allegiances, however, are problematic. In empathizing with Cameron and envisioning themselves as potential "saviours," one can argue that such gestures of concern *for*, rather than *with*, the Kayapo undermine indigenous agency by suggesting the need of a white sponsor. As Emma Mitchell writes, such representations of white privilege evade "the perhaps more threatening self-politicisation of Indigenous peoples and communities, as well as the institutionalised racism that perpetuates their structural oppression."[45] That is, these gestures play into insidious racism.

However, before we criticize Cameron too strongly, such critiques are complicated by how indigenous peoples use Cameron's film. Though *A Message from Pandora* is not an indigenous production, it is made in collaboration with Amazon Watch (which works in collaboration with the Kayapo) and it is shown at NAFVF (an indigenous collaboration). As indicated in my earlier discussions much has been written about the contradictions and compromises that indigenous people face when engaging in political activism. Faye Ginsberg has suggested that indigenous political negotiations can be likened to a Faustian contract. Focusing on media, she notes, on the one hand, indigenous communities are able to gain access to media to use for their own means, but on the other hand, they are constantly assaulted by the hegemonies of colonial power that conscribe these media.[46] This is certainly the case with indigenous use of *A Message from Pandora*. On the one hand, they use the clout of Hollywood's star and narrative power to move audiences; on the other hand, in doing so they are faced with an erasure of their own voices.

A Message to Pandora was the festival's only film to limit the voices of indigenous people. Other films took indigenous people as their protagonists, and some of these—such as *Los Derechos de la Pachamamma/The Rights of Mother Earth* (2010) from Peru, and the dual shorts *Elderly Words* (*Who's Threatening the Water?* and *How Did We Do Elderly Words?*) a 2009 Colombian indigenous tribes collaboration (Arhuaco, Wiwa, and Kogui)—also employ the language and imagery of primitivism though in different ways than *A Message from Pandora* and with different sympathetic and empathetic openings.

These films suggest a strategic essentialism that acknowledges Ginsburg's Faustian contract but also points to Harald Prins's notion of the "primitive perplex."[47] The prototype is not simply a stereotype deployed to engage white fantasies but holds emotive and rhetorical value for indigenous communities. As Prins describes, the imagery is powerful in capturing "a way of life utterly different" from that of colonial oppressors and can serve to help revive and preserve traditional practices.[48] He quotes his Mikmaq collaborator, Donald Sanipass, who elaborates on this point: "We wanted to make a film in which our voices can be heard and in which we show how we live, how we work, and where we have chosen to continue the life of our forefathers and mothers."[49] In essence, "primitivist" imagery is strategically used to speak directly to indigenous audiences to continue traditional ways of life. In doing so, it is rarely as ahistorically static as suggested by the white man's trope.

Both *Los Derechos de la Pachamamma/The Rights of Mother Earth* and *Elderly Words* are festival films that highlight elders as traditionally garbed and speaking wisely of the environment. However, they also draw attention to the fact that indigenous communities are in charge of the filming (this is the explicit theme of *How Did We Do Elderly Words?*). Such strategies illuminate the ways in which native communities are users of modernity's tools even as they respect traditional ways. As Terence Turner writes, "cultural forms, together with the capacity and motivation of social actors to produce them, are reinforced, rearticulated, and transformed in various ways through the use of new techniques of representation and new social forms of utilizing and circulating them."[50] The imagery might conjure references to the prototypical ecological Indian; however, these images speak both to the agency of indigenous protagonists and indigenous filmmaking. They are examples of "visual sovereignty." Coined by Michelle Raheja, visual sovereignty points to indigenous ownership of imagery, and how such self-representations often interact with popular stereotypes to reject and/or re-cast them.[51]

While the focus on indigenous identity through essentializing difference can constrain how a non-indigenous viewer engages with the film empathetically, alignment with indigenous voices nonetheless makes room for such allegiances, especially from indigenous audiences. These gestures are politically more empowering than those of *A Message from Pandora* as they literally give indigenous peoples more say. Other films at NAFVF employ visual sovereignty with different ecological Indian engagements to prompt empathy from both indigenous *and* non-indigenous audiences, as I discuss below.

STRATEGIC ANTI-ESSENTIALISM: VISUAL SOVEREIGNTY AND THE REJECTED ECOLOGICAL INDIAN

River of Renewal (2009), a feature documentary, also screened at the Mother Earth symposium. As with the pre-title sequence of *A Message from Pandora*, the start of *River of Renewal* establishes the environmental conflict that the film will focus on, and introduces the main character. The film opens with aerial and long-shot views of the West coast, and a tracking shot of a verdant river valley. Guitar strums and soft seabird calls dissolve to a male voice-over, which begins, "The Klamath basin, a land united by water and divided by people ..." We are introduced to the three divided groups—coastal fishermen in northern California and Oregon, tribal Indians along the rivers, and farmers in the upper Klamath basin. Each is presented briefly, engaged in a contemporary activity—fishermen unloading fish, a Native motoring down the river, a blond child holding up a protest sign displaying the words "Farmers First!" and a fish inscribed in a "no entry" circle. The shot of the child cuts to more protest scenes, and then to a camper along a mountain road, and then another cut, this time to a close-up profile of our narrator, driving the camper. His voice-over states: "I'm Jack Kohrer. I was raised in San Francisco. A sidewalk Indian." Kohrer is wearing a red baseball cap, with his long hair tied in a ponytail. A montage of shots establishes him as an urban Indian with Yurok/Karuk and Welsh ancestry. As a child, Kohrer explains, he was unclear about his Indian heritage. He became an engineering student at Stanford and then an actor who played "Indian leaders." A part in a play, *Watershed*, exposed him to water management policies on the Klamath river, which led to his interest in making *River of Renewal*.

Three points are salient during this pre-title sequence. First, we have subjective access to an indigenous person. Second, this narrator does not conform to the image of the prototypical ecological Indian. Third, there's an explicit rejection of such prototypes. Kohrer's voice-over explains over a 1950s poster image depicting Stanford's Indian mascot and archival video shots of the mascot whooping around a football field, "A few years before I went to Stanford, the mascot had been the stereotypical Indian ... who was dressed as a plains Indian." Kohrer continues, "In those years not many knew that California Indians still existed." The film's immediate rejection of the prototype serves as a useful narrative tool to guide direct emotions, for example, of curiosity: if not the prototypical ecological Indian, then what is Kohrer? The film's attachment and access to Kohrer invites viewers to embrace Kohrer's character, and in doing so, also sympathize *and* empathize with its indigenous characters and their environmental plight.

We spatio-temporally and subjectively follow Kohrer, quickly recognizing that he is no "anachronistic ghost" stuck in an anti-modernist time-warp. Urbanized and of mixed heritage, Kohrer presents himself in anti-essentialist terms. His positioning as educated (a Stanford engineering graduate) and therefore articulate, but also invested (it's his Indian heritage he's seeking to understand) opens the door to empathetic possibilities with his average First World viewer. Additionally, as a Native American interested in ecological matters, Kohrer presents himself as someone who is *not* immediately affected by the conflict, but as an outsider. This outsider identification sets up further grounds for empathetic connections as it adopts a modicum of distance from the conflict.

In investigating the conflict, Kohrer presents a "journey of self-discovery" that is grounded in evidentiary standards of proof. Interviewee voices, of which there are many, from various sides of the debate, take precedence over his own. At the same time, Kohrer builds credibility for what they say by presenting the viewer with visual evidence of various events—news photographs, archived live televised coverage, and footage captured by the filmmakers themselves.

For example, in depicting the 2001 conflicts, the film takes us into the crowds of protesters gathered with signs such as "phuck the sucker" (an endangered fish) and "depend on farmers, not fuzzy liberal ideas!" As diagetic noise of the crowd scene fills the background, a middle-aged white protestor denies vehemently to the filmmakers (who are off-screen) that the fish were here before the farmers. Confrontation brews as a filmmaker's voice states, "What about the tribal legends?" to which the protestor's angry response is, "Oh *screw* the tribal legends." While the film cuts away from this confrontation, it remains with the crowd scene, maintaining tension, as a uniformed policeman crosses in front of the camera, and his image momentarily fills the screen.

With such textual crafting, the film mediates fears of potential mob violence and racism. When juxtaposed with the quiet, reasonable voices of interviewees who are recalling these events, the film steers the viewer to empathetic engagement. After all, the interviewees seem anything but deviant miscreants of civil unrest. Instead, they are sensible, everyday people who got caught in threatening situations. Such alignment places commonality versus difference as a key aspect for character engagement.

In fact, commonality *is* the thread of *River of Renewal*, constantly prompting empathetic connections. In interviews we see members of the Yurok, Karuk, and Hupa tribes either indoors, in familiar home or office spaces, or outdoors, engaging in activities with a decidedly contemporary feel, such as fishing (with motor boats), camping (with nylon tents), or managing fisheries (with factory machinery). Even scenes devoted to cultural revival such as building fish platforms and pikaiwish ("fixing the world") rituals occur in the here-and-now as interviewees discuss their relevance to contemporary survival. Kohrer resembles the average American, and so do the other Native Americans.

While the first thirty minutes of the film focus on Native Americans, commonality is further strengthened by including other voices in the remainder of the film. At the mid-point of the film, we are introduced to farmers in the upper Klamath basin. Interviews with John and Bob Anderson, a son-and-father team, use the same format as interviews with Native stakeholders. Their words are juxtaposed with historical imagery that helps show how their survival, like that of the tribesmen, is also threatened by circumstances in complex socio-political systems larger than themselves. Like the commercial fishermen who also enter the narrative, all are driven to participate in emotionally charged political protests to preserve their livelihoods despite the danger of violence. In encountering their struggles, a viewer is invited to feel not only for, but *with* the characters. These are after all, not struggles for static primitivism, but potentially close-to-home struggles for jobs, livelihoods, and place-based identity.

Along with these empathetically relatable concerns, the film's spatio-temporal attachment and subjective access with indigenous voices first, followed by these other voices, are powerful in prompting emotional allegiance with indigenous peoples. Even as the viewer learns how "non-Indians have demonized Indians," they also see how the tribes welcome a chance to correct past settler wrongs in ways that will safeguard both their own interests and those of others. The film's ending highlights a move for a legislative solution to the conflict—the decommissioning of some of the rivers' hydroelectric dams—and, in doing so, heightens the appeal of such inclusive perspectives. While all parties had to compromise, the film's privileged alignment with Native Americans suggests a true tale of moral forgiveness and goodness on their part. As the film re-centres on Kohrer, coming full circle to the first profile shots of him in the van, his words conclude the film:

> I came here to make a movie and to find my roots. I found my roots growing in a tangle of connectedness. As an urban Indian by the river of my ancestors, the legacy is pikaiwish, responsibility for fixing the world. As a human being, as a citizen, as a consumer my use of water and electricity, my choice of who to vote for and what to invest in all impact natural places like the Klamath.

Once again, the empathetic connections between average First World viewer and indigenes are emphasized—"human being, citizen, consumer." For many suspicious of the prototypical ecological Indian, this more modern-day, technologically infused self-representation of ecological sensibilities is less problematic. By allowing access to indigenous voices and presenting indigenous peoples as average, everyday people trying to preserve their livelihoods, the film makes room for concern *with* rather than simply concern *for*. Such gestures recognize more equitable notions of self-politicization than in *A Message from Pandora*. Whereas the latter casts indigenes as the obviously disadvantaged "spear and bow-and-arrow"-toting primitives, *River of Renewal* positions them as independently capable of negotiating modern-day politics. This is an empowering message for indigenous agency.

CONCLUSIONS: VISUAL SOVEREIGNTY, EMPATHY, AND THE POTENTIAL OF THE ABSENT ECOLOGICAL INDIAN

In tying character engagement theories to critical race theory, I have tried to emphasize how visual sovereignty serves to prompt films to generate space for empathy with indigenous characters. Empathy, or a concern *with*, as opposed to sympathy, or a concern *for*, serves to ground emotional motives for activism that are not simply tokens of charity but also emblems of equality. In the messy realm of race politics, being recognized as an equal is of invaluable importance, signalling that traditionally disenfranchised people can be autonomous and fully capable partners in political endeavours. While *A Message from Pandora* is an activist film, Cameron's sympathetic gestures are rife with colonial racism. Such racist gestures are challenged, if not completely subverted by films such as *Los Derechos de la Pachamamma/The Rights of Mother Earth*, *Elderly Words*, and *River of Renewal* that align viewers with indigenous protagonists. When indigenous-owned, whether used or rejected, the ecological Indian generates space for empathetic engagement.

However, because the ecological Indian is so heavy with cultural baggage, even these films are not without their complications. Essentialist portrayals such as *Los Derechos de la Pachamamma/The Rights of Mother Earth* and *Elderly Words* can always turn the emotionally jaded viewer away from the nuances of how indigenous peoples appropriate the ecological Indian not simply to appeal to white audiences but also to speak of their own cultural traditions and heritage. Anti-essentialism as expressed in the *River of Renewal* also has its downsides, suggesting a different sort of instutionalized racism. While Kohrer rejects the ecological Indian prototype, his rejection is nonetheless heavy with colonial hierarchies. In adopting the evidentiary discourse of Western rationality, in repeatedly highlighting his educational credentials as a Stanford engineering graduate, and in stressing commonality over difference, *River of Renewal's* appeals seem to type indigenous worth by its adherence to colonial culture's standards of worth. Viewers aren't necessarily encouraged to question these standards of evaluation. An astute viewer may remain uncomfortable with the ways in such racism insidiously undermines indigenous agency and empowerment.

In highlighting this dimension of the film, I do not wish to undervalue ways in which *River of Renewal's* empathetic contours are more empowering to indigenous self-politicization than *A Message from Pandora's* purely sympathetic ones. However, I do wish to suggest that perhaps we can also look to other cinematic expressions of indigenous visual sovereignty that *altogether* absent the ecological Indian as a potential way around these dilemmas. The explicitly activist films of the symposium tend to presence the ecological Indian in some shape or form. However, NAFVF's extended programming with its many films that don't explicitly promote eco-activist messages usually steer clear of such immediately associative triggers. Instead, because natural environments figure as central in conceiving characters' emotions of ambivalence toward living in two worlds—traditional *and* colonized—viewers are prompted not only to recognize ecological connections as a significant factor in struggles for indigenous identity but also to question taken-for-granted standards of contemporary Western colonialism. Given the shortness of this chapter, such films cannot be explored here.[52] However, I mention them to point to the continued productivity of the melding of cognitivist film theory with critical race theory when engaging indigenous cine-eco-activism.

NOTES

I am especially grateful to Elizabeth Weatherford and others at the Smithsonian's Native Film and Video Center for providing me with access to the 2011 Native American Film and Video Festival's archives. Thanks to Gettysburg College for funding the project, to Matt Beehr for his editing, and to Alexa Weik von Mossner for her insightful comments and work on this collection.

1   A rich scholarship, particularly in visual anthropology and indigenous studies, points to this appropriation of media as a tool for political activism and cultural redress. While the research is extensive, the following works are useful starting points for scholarly exploration: Faye Ginsburg, "Indigenous Media: Faustian Contract or Global Village?" *Cultural Anthropology* 6, no. 1 (1991): 92–112; Steve Luethold, "Native Media's Communities," in *Contemporary Native American Cultural Issues*, ed. Duane Champagne (Walnut Creek, CA: AltaMira, 1999), 193–216; Fatimah Tobing-Rony, *The Third Eye: Race, Cinema, and Ethnographic Spectacle* (Durham, NC: Duke University Press, 2006); as well as the essays in Faye Ginsburg, Lila Abu-Lughod, and Brian Larkin's edited volume *Media Worlds* (Berkeley: University of California Press, 2002).

2   Carl Plantinga, *Moving Viewers: American Film and the Spectator's Experience* (Berkeley: University of California Press, 2009), 200.

3   Plantinga, *Moving Viewers*, 3. See also film cognitivist overviews such as David Bordwell and Noel Carroll, eds., *Post-Theory: Reconstructing Film Studies* (Madison: University of Wisconsin Press, 1996); Carl Plantinga and Greg Smith, eds., *Passionate Views: Film, Cognition, and Emotion* (Baltimore: Johns Hopkins University Press, 1999); and Daniel Shaw, *Film and Philosophy: Taking Movies Seriously* (London: Wallflower, 2008).

4   For key references in theories of character engagement, see, for example, Murray Smith, *Engaging Characters: Fiction, Emotion, and the Cinema* (Oxford: Clarendon, 1995); Berys Gaut, "Identification and Emotion in Narrative Film," in Plantinga and Smith, *Passionate Views*, 200–16; Carl Plantinga, "The Scene of Empathy and the Human Face on Film," in Plantinga and Smith, *Passionate Views*, 239–56; and Alex Neill, "Empathy and (Film) Fiction," in Bordwell and Carroll, *Post-Theory*, 175–94. Daniel Shaw's overviews of sympathy and empathy in *Film and Philosophy* (London: Wallflower, 2008) provide a helpful summary.

5   See, for example, Neill, "Empathy and (Film) Fiction"; Amy Coplan, "Empathetic Engagement with Narrative Fictions," *Journal of Aesthetics and Art Criticism* 62, no. 2 (2004): 141–52; and Dan Flory, *Philosophy, Black Film and Film Noir* (Philadelphia: Pennsylvania University Press, 2008).

6   Carl Plantinga is particularly wary of separating the two. See specifically his discussions in *Moving Viewers*, 97–101; and "Scene of Empathy."

7   In "Empathetic Engagement," Coplan draws on psychology research to distinguish empathy from sympathy but clearly acknowledges that they can occur simultaneously (143). In "A Theory of Narrative Empathy" (*Narrative* 14, no. 3, 2006), Suzanne Keen draws from psychologist Daniel Batson's *The Altruism Question: Toward a Social-Psychological Answer* (Hillsdale, NJ: Erlbaum, 1991) to point to the idea that empathy is a precursor to sympathy and even calls the latter empathic concern (see specifically Keen, "A Theory," 208). While I believe empathy

can lead to sympathy, as I suggest in this paper, we can also have sympathy without empathy; thus, I am cautious of Keen's relation of the two terms.

8 Plantinga, *Moving Viewers*, 98. In *Moving Viewers*, Plantinga places empathy within sympathy; in "Scene of Empathy," he places sympathy within empathy.

9 Dan Flory, "Spike Lee and the Sympathetic Racist," *Journal of Aesthetics and Art Criticism*, 64, no. 1 (2006): 67–79; and Dan Flory, *Philosophy*.

10 Flory, "Spike Lee," 71.

11 Flory, "Spike Lee," 68.

12 Flory, "Spike Lee," 68.

13 Flory, "Spike Lee," 71.

14 Flory, *Philosophy*, 2.

15 He writes, "These works of art goad viewers to concentrate reflectively on typical conceptions of race, equality, and knowledge that often form the foundation of their moral action and thought." Flory, *Philosophy*, 3.

16 See, for example, Coplan's and Keen's reviews of psychology research in this area.

17 Keen makes a distinction between empathy and personal distress, which I also acknowledge. She states that personal distress is "an aversive emotional response also characterized by apprehension of another's emotion." Unlike empathy, which involves concern projected towards another, personal distress "focuses on the self" and leads to "avoidance." Keen, "A Theory," 208.

18 Accounts such as Henry Fritz's *The Movement for Indian Assimilation* (Philadelphia: Pennsylvania University Press, 1963) point to how federal policies of assimilation were deemed "the only practical and humane answer to the Indian problem" (19). The language of "the Indian problem" highlights how insidiously political these sympathetic gestures were, as can be seen in this excerpt from Nelson Miles 1879 piece of the same name:

> The real issue in the question which is now before the American people is, whether we shall continue the vacillating and expensive policy that has marred our fair name as a nation and a Christian people, or devise some practical and judicious system by which we can govern one quarter of a million of our population, securing and maintaining their loyalty, raising them from the darkness of barbarism to the light of civilization, and put an end to these interminable and expensive Indian wars. (*North American Review* 128.268 [1897]: 304)

As George Tinker writes in his preface to Ward Churchill's excellently titled *Kill the Indian, Save the Man* (San Francisco: City Lights Books, 2004), Churchill puts to rest any ideas that the Indian schools "were the best attempt by the liberal colonizer to advance the state of Indian peoples in North America" (xiii).

19 Originally Smith had set empathy outside his theory of character engagement because he saw empathy as a state where viewers literally think they are the characters (*Engaging Characters*, 96). This type of "central imagining," he argued was not necessary to the ways in which we can engage with characters through recognition, alignment, and allegiance. Thus, he called his triadic framework, a "structure of sympathy." Since he originally devised this framework, these ways of defining empathy have been disapproved by psychology research (see for example, Coplan's "Empathetic Engagement" for further discussion). Flory productively extends Smith's framework beyond sympathy to include analysis of empathy (see particularly, his chapter "Noir Protagonists and Empathy in *Do the Right Thing*," in *Philosophy*, 65–99).

20 M. Smith, *Engaging Characters*, 53.

21 While a number of film cognitivists acknowledge this melding of affect and consciousness, Greg Smith's introduction to *Film Structure and the Emotion System* (Cambridge: Cambridge University Press, 2003) is particularly useful.

22 M. Smith, *Engaging Characters*, 83.

23 Plantinga provides this articulate distinction in *Moving Viewers*, 107.

24 M. Smith, *Engaging Characters*, 85.

25 M. Smith, *Engaging Characters*, 84. See also Plantinga, *Moving Viewers*, 108. Flory's analyses are grounded in the sense that race and ethnicity are morally loaded—see specifically, *Philosophy*, 14.

26 Plantinga provides an excellent schematic in "Table 1: Types of Spectator Emotions," in *Moving Viewers*, 69.

27 Greg Smith's definition of a prototype is helpful. He writes that prototypes "organize human experience by allowing us to categorize new data. They guide our expectations concerning what members of a category should look like and what they should do." G. Smith, *Film Structure*, 21.

28 Also, scholars such as Ann Fienup-Riordan point to how such stock imagery did not originate in film but "formed over the last five centuries from various sources" and "abound[s] in many domains of popular American culture, including paperback literature, television [etc.]." *Freeze Frame: Alaskan Eskimos in Movies* (Seattle: University of Washington Press, 2003), 7. There is a sizeable literature on Native American representations in film, which includes seminal work such as Ward Churchill, *Fantasies of a Master Race: Literature, Cinema and the Colonization of American Indians* (Monroe, ME: City Light Books, 1992) and Peter C. Rollins and John E. O'Connor, eds., *Hollywood's Indian: The Portrayal of the Native American in Film* (Lexington: University Press of Kentucky, 1998). More recent literature includes Michelle Raheja, *Reservation Reelism: Redfacing, Visual Sovereignty, and Representations of Native Americans in Film* (Lincoln: University of Nebraska Press, 2010); Salma Monani, "Environmental Justice in Extreme Oil: The Wilderness and Oil on Ice," *Environmental Communication: A Journal of Nature and Culture* 2, no. 1 (2008): 119–27; Salma Monani, "Wilderness Discourse in Adventure-Nature Films: The Potentials and Limitations of *Being Caribou*," *Interdisciplinary Studies in Literature and the Environment* 19, no. 1 (2012): 101–21; and Corinn Columpar, *Unsettling Sights: The Fourth World on Film* (Carbondale: Southern Illinois University Press, 2010).

29 Raheja, *Reservation Reelism*, 103–4.

30 Raheja's chapter "Tears and Trash" in *Reservation Reelism* delves into the socio-political and historical contexts surrounding the crying Indian. Others who have discussed the crying Indian include Edward Buscombe in *Injuns! Native Americans in the Movies* (London: Reaktion Books, 2006) and Shephard Krech III in *The Ecological Indian: Myth and History* (New York: W.W. Norton, 1999). As far as I am aware, no scholarship has specifically drawn on cognitive theories of emotion to explore the affect of this image.

31 See for example, Buscombe and Tobing-Rony respectively.

32 For example, Philip Deloria used the phrase "playing Indian" as the title of his seminal work on Indian-white relationships; *Playing Indian* is a historical examination of Euro-Americans donning native garb and mannerisms to express their own nationalistic and individual identities (New Haven, CT: Yale University Press, 1991). Shari Huhndorf uses the term "going native," seeing it as an even more problematic appropriation than "playing Indian" as she argues that it invariably provides "self-justifying fantasies that conceal the violence marking European American origins." *Going Native: Indians in the American Cultural Imagination* (Ithaca, NY: Cornell University Press, 2001), 5.

33 Krech, *Ecological Indian*, 22.

34 Michael Harkin and David Rich Lewis, eds., *Native Americans and the Environment* (Lincoln: University of Nebraska Press, 2007).

35 Harkin and Lewis, *Native Americans*, xix (my emphasis).

36 Darren J. Ranco, "Critiquing the Ecological Indian in the Age of Ecocide," in Harkin and Lewis, *Native Americans*, 45.

37 See also Raheja, *Reservation Reelism*; Steven Leuthold, "Native Media's Communities," in Champagne, *Contemporary Native*, 193–216; Harald Prins, "Visual Media and the Primitivist

Perplex: Colonial Fantasies, Indigenous Imagination, and Advocacy in North America," in *Media Worlds*, ed. Faye Ginsburg, Lila Abu-Lughod, and Brian Larkin (Berkeley: University of California Press, 2002), 58–74.

38 Columpar, *Unsettling Sights*, 13. The term "strategic essentialism" was coined by post-colonialist Gayatri Chakravorty Spivak—see Donna Laury and Gerald MacLeau, eds., *The Spivak Reader: Selected Works* (New York: Routledge, 1996), 214. While Spivak has not been fully satisfied with the term (see Michael Kilburn's discussion in *Glossary of Key Terms in The Work of Gayatri Spivak*, 1996; available at http://postcolonialstudies.emory.edu/gayatri-chakravorty -spivak), it has nonetheless been useful to scholars exploring the politics of marginalized communities. Suzanne Keen has applied Spivak's concept to cognitive theory but obtusely—not referencing Spivak in the first version of her essay "A Theory of Narrative Empathy" (2006) and mentioning her "in slant rhyme" in a revised version of the essay, "Narrative Empathy," in *Towards a Cognitive Theory of Narrative Acts*, ed. Frederick Luis Almada (University of Texas Press, 2010), 83. Keen suggests that writers strategically work to generate different types of empathy—bounded, ambassadorial, and broadcast—depending on who is the specific target group: an in-group, those of another group, or everyone ("A Theory," 215). While her triadic framework suggests similar categories of audiences that I point to in this chapter, I do not utilize her terms as she suggests that empathy is a precursor for sympathy, even calling the latter empathic concern ("A Theory," 208). In my analyses, I point to sympathy that can occur without empathy and thus am cautious about overlaying Keen's categories here.

39 Columpar, *Unsettling Sights*, 13.

40 Columpar, *Unsettling Sights*, 13–14.

41 Columpar, *Unsettling Sights*, 14.

42 I provide more details on the festival in a forthcoming article, "Environmental Themes in Indigenous Film Festivals: The case of the 2011 Native Film + Video Festival." For *NECSUS: The European Journal of Media Studies*. The festival website is http://www.nativenetworks .si.edu/eng/blue/nafvf_11.html.

43 Elizabeth Weatherford, personal communication, April 2012.

44 A phrase Cameron uses during his narration.

45 Emma Mitchell, "Seeing Blue: Negotiating the Politics of Avatar Media Activism" (unpublished honours thesis, University of Sydney, 2011), 24.

46 Ginsburg, "Indigenous Media," 96.

47 Prins, "Visual Media," 60.

48 Prins, "Visual Media," 62.

49 Prins, "Visual Media," 65.

50 Terence Turner, "Representation, Politics, and Cultural Imagination in Indigenous Video: General Points and Kayapo Examples," in *Media Worlds*, ed. Faye Ginsburg, Lila Abu-Lughod, and Brian Larkin (Berkeley: University of California Press, 2002), 80.

51 Michelle H. Raheja, "Reading Nanook's Smile: Visual Sovereignty, Indigenous Revisions of Ethnography, and Atanarjuat (The Fast Runner)," *American Quarterly* 59, no. 4 (2007): 1159–87. See also, Raheja, *Reservation Reelism*.

52 See Salma Monani, "*Kissed by Lightning* and Fourth Cinema's Natureculture Continuum," in *Ecoambiguity, Community, and Development: Towards a Politicized Ecocriticism*, ed. Scott Slovic, Swarnalathat Rangarajan, and Vidya Sarveswaran (New York: Lexington Books, 2014), 131–47; and Salma Monani and Miranda J. Brady, "ImagineNATIVE 2012: The Indigenous Film Festival as Ecocinematic Space," *Reconstruction: Studies in Contemporary Culture* 13, nos. 3/4 (forthcoming).

BIBLIOGRAPHY

Buscombe, Edward. *Injuns! Native Americans in the Movies*. London: Reaktion Books, 2006.

Churchill, Ward. *Fantasies of a Master Race: Literature, Cinema, and the Colonization of American Indians*. San Francisco: City Light Books, 1992.

———. *Kill the Indian, Save the Man*. San Francisco: City Lights Books, 2004.

Columpar, Corinn. *Unsettling Sights: The Fourth World on Film*. Carbondale: Southern Illinois University Press, 2010.

Coplan, Amy. "Empathetic Engagement with Narrative Fictions." *Journal of Aesthetics and Art Criticism* 62, no. 2 (2004): 141–52.

Deloria, Philip. *Playing Indian*. New Haven, CT: Yale University Press, 1991.

Elderly Words (Two parts: *Who's Threatening the Water?* and *How Did We Do Elderly Words?*). Directed by Amado Villafaña (Arhuaco), Saúl Gil (Wiwa), Silvestre Gil Zarabata (Kogui). Gonawindúa Tayrona Organization in co-production with TeleCaribe, 2009.

Fienup-Riordan, Ann. *Freeze Frame: Alaskan Eskimos in Movies*. Seattle: University of Washington Press, 2003.

Flory, Dan. *Philosophy, Black Film, and Film Noir*. Philadelphia: Pennsylvania University Press, 2008.

———. "Spike Lee and the Sympathetic Racist." *Journal of Aesthetics and Art Criticism* 64, no. 1 (2006): 67–79.

Fritz, Henry. *The Movement for Indian Assimilation*. Philadelphia: Pennsylvania University Press, 1963.

Gaut, Berys. "Identification and Emotion in Narrative Film." In *Passionate Views: Film, Cognition, and Emotion*, edited by Carl Plantinga and Greg M. Smith, 200–16. Baltimore: Johns Hopkins University Press, 1999.

Ginsburg, Faye. "Indigenous Media: Faustian Contract or Global Village?" *Cultural Anthropology* 6, no. 1 (1991): 92–112.

Harkin, Michael, and David Rich Lewis, eds. *Native Americans and the Environment*. Lincoln: University of Nebraska Press, 2007.

Huhndorf, Shari. *Going Native: Indians in the American Cultural Imagination*. Ithaca, NY: Cornell University Press, 2001.

Keen, Suzanne. "Narrative Empathy." In *Towards a Cognitive Theory of Narrative Acts*, edited by Frederick Luis Almada, 61–94. Austin: University of Texas Press, 2010.

———. "A Theory of Narrative Empathy." *Narrative* 14, no. 3 (2006): 207–36.

Krech III, Shepard. *The Ecological Indian: Myth and History*. New York: W.W. Norton, 1999.

Leuthold, Steven. "Native Media's Communities." In *Contemporary Native American Cultural Issues*, edited by Duane Champagne, 193–216. Walnut Creek, CA: AltaMira, 1999.

Los Derechos de la Pachamama/The Rights of Mother Earth. Produced by Sallqavideastas and InsightShare, 2010.

A Message from Pandora. Produced by James Cameron, Laurent Bouzereau, and Thomas C. Grane. Los Angeles: Twentieth Century Fox, 2010.

Miles, Nelson. "The Indian Problem." *North American Review* 128.268 (1897): 304–14.

Mitchell, Emma. "Seeing Blue: Negotiating the Politics of Avatar Media Activism." Unpublished honours thesis, University of Sydney, 2011.

Monani, Salma. "Environmental Justice in Extreme Oil: The Wilderness and Oil on Ice." *Environmental Communication: A Journal of Nature and Culture* 2, no. 1 (2008): 119–27.

———. "*Kissed by Lightning* and Fourth Cinema's Natureculture Continuum." In *Ecoambiguity, Community, and Development: Towards a Politicized Ecocriticism*, edited by Scott Slovic, Swarnalathat Rangarajan, and Vidya Sarveswaran, 131–47. New York: Lexington Books, 2014.

———. "Wilderness Discourse in Adventure-Nature Films: The Potentials and Limitations of *Being Caribou*." *Interdisciplinary Studies in Literature and the Environment* 19, no. 1 (2012): 101–21.

Monani, Salma, and Miranda J. Brady. "ImagineNATIVE 2012: The Indigenous Film Festival as Ecocinematic Space." *Reconstruction: Studies in Contemporary Culture* 13, nos. 3/4 (2013).

Neill, Alex. "Empathy and (Film) Fiction." In *Post-Theory: Reconstructing Film Studies*, edited by David Bordwell and Noel Carroll, 175–94. Madison: University of Wisconsin Press, 1996.

Plantinga, Carl. *Moving Viewers: American Film and the Spectator's Experience*. Berkeley: University of California Press, 2009.

———. "The Scene of Empathy and the Human Face on Film." In *Passionate Views: Film, Cognition, and Emotion*, edited by Carl Plantinga and Greg M. Smith, 239–56. Baltimore: Johns Hopkins University Press, 1999.

Prins, Harald. "Visual Media and the Primitivist Perplex: Colonial Fantasies, Indigenous Imagination, and Advocacy in North America." In *Media Worlds*, edited by Faye Ginsburg, Lila Abu-Lughod, and Brian Larkin, 58–74. Berkeley: University of California Press, 2002.

Raheja, Michelle H. "Reading Nanook's Smile: Visual Sovereignty, Indigenous Revisions of Ethnography, and Atanarjuat (The Fast Runner)." *American Quarterly* 59, no. 4 (2007): 1159–87.

———. *Reservation Reelism: Redfacing, Visual Sovereignty, and Representations of Native Americans in Film*. Lincoln: University of Nebraska Press, 2010.

Ranco, Darren J. "Critiquing the Ecological Indian in the Age of Ecocide." In *Native Americans and the Environment: Perspectives on the Ecological Indian*, edited by Michael Harkin and David Rich Lewis, 32–51. Lincoln: University of Nebraska Press, 2007.

River of Renewal. Directed by Carlos Bolado. Pikiawish Productions and Specialty Studios, 2009.

Rollins, Peter C., and John E. O'Connor, eds. *Hollywood's Indian: The Portrayal of the Native American in Film*. Lexington: University Press of Kentucky, 1998.

Shaw, Daniel. *Film and Philosophy: Taking Movies Seriously*. London: Wallflower, 2008.

Smith, Greg M. *Film Structure and the Emotion System*. Cambridge: Cambridge University Press, 2003.

Smith, Murray. *Engaging Characters: Fiction, Emotion, and the Cinema.* Oxford: Clarendon, 1995.

Turner, Terence. "Representation, Politics, and Cultural Imagination in Indigenous Video: General Points and Kayapo Examples." In *Media Worlds*, edited by Faye Ginsburg, Lila Abu-Lughod, and Brian Larkin, 75–89. Berkeley: University of California Press, 2002.

12

Affect and Environment in Two Artists' Films and a Video

Sean Cubitt

Of all that exists terribly near us
Like you, my love, and light
—*John Ashbery, "How Much Longer Will I Be Able to Inhabit the Divine Sepulcher ..."*

Discussions of affect and emotion in contemporary cultural criticism, including those of the most sophisticated commentators (for example, Ticinieto Clough [2000]), tend to build upon older strata of discourse that seem very frequently to lie upon a base of Nietzsche's distinction between Apollonian and Dionysiac.[1] It is going to be important to ask whether this opposition can be brought to equilibrium, whether it is a constant state of struggle (perhaps requiring that all humans must take sides), whether it comprises an endless oscillation between two states coming in and out of dominance, or whether it can be overcome.

Given the importance of affect to the history of environmental thinking since the Romantics, the question is relevant to discussions of ecology, and loosely to the orientation of ecology as science or as politics. Adam Curtis argues in the second episode of his documentary series *All Watched Over by Machines of Loving Grace* (2011) that scientific and political ecology emerged as an application of a specific mechanistic logic—systems theory—based on the metaphor of the computer.[2] To that extent, our environmentalism is premised on an Apollonian assessment of connectedness, and a call to efficient management of resources in a closed system. If on the other hand we want to understand the cultural allure of eco-apocalypse, or to analyze and arouse political passions, we need to understand and deploy a primal, affective connection with the world. This may appear in the post-Freudian surrealist guise of Georges Bataille's "general economy" of explosive expenditure and excess,[3] or it might appear as the Heideggerian privilege of Being,[4] in either case with profound political and ethical consequences.

Philosophically, the question of connection leads us to the recent history of phenomenology: of Edmund Husserl making the world present to the perceiving human, and Maurice Merleau-Ponty placing the perceiver in the world. The latter conception, the more sophisticated from an environmental perspective, belongs in a tradition that includes Wordsworth's nostalgic reconstructions of rural childhood, and his absorption into universal natural processes

> Roll'd round in earth's diurnal course,
> With rocks, and stones, and trees.[5]

The phenomenological connection that places the human in the world belongs also with the American Transcendentalist tradition out of Thoreau, a tradition very important in the American tradition of landscape arts, and especially to Stan Brakhage, whose *Dog Star Man* (1961–64), our first exemplar, is one of the key expressions of environmental affect in the canon of avant-garde film.[6]

Ranged against this subjectively oriented environmentalism, we find ranged the taxonomic tradition which, since Linnaeus, has sought to establish an order in the world, or more specifically in our relations with the world. Through Darwin to contemporary bioengineering, this tradition embraces the micro-scale of genetic modification and the macro-scale of the Anthropocene, with its massive disruptions of carbon, nitrogen, and water cycles, and the equally massive engineering solutions mooted to counter its potentially disastrous consequences. Taxonomy proposes a fundamentally formalist position, a goal-oriented practice stated in terms of problems and their solutions, but one which also has its own aesthetic, built on the formal structures of mathematics for which world and mind are isomorphic. This formalism, and especially the ecological systems theoretic perspective, informs one of the most influential of vanguard landscape artists working in the moving image, Chris Welsby, who provides our second exemplar.[7] It is unkind and unjust to make these works stand for oversimplified models of environmental thought. The formal concerns—especially with rhythm—of Brakhage's films are highly apparent; and Welsby's film *Sky Light* addressed here is especially emotionally loaded—he mentions in interview that the film was in part inspired by the birth of his daughter shortly before the shoot, as well as by political anger. In that sense this essay risks setting up a non-viable binary opposition, and can only score an unimpressive victory over it. But there are thematic threads in these films that can help us understand the role of affect in cinema, the specificity of time as the native dimension of affect, and the relation between affect and environment which the moving image, the audiovisual moving image as the art of time par excellence, is uniquely fitted to express.

STAN BRAKHAGE

Dog Star Man comprises a Prelude of twenty-four minutes, and four Parts varying between thirty and five and a half minutes. According to Brakhage, the Prelude is the nocturnal dream from which his epic character, the Dog Star Man, awakes. In Part 1, he is the woodsman, accompanied by his dog, who wrestles the world tree Yggdrasil which, however, is in this age of the world dead and withered. Part 2, according to one of his closest commentators Fred Camper, is a family history, centred on the birth of Brakhage's child; Part 3 is a sexual daydream; and in Part 4 the world falls apart, the world tree condemned to be no more than firewood. Emerging from a lengthy stretch of black leader, the film begins with flashes of inchoate colour isolated in darkness. A journey seems to be being undertaken, by car at night. Gradually, at the end of the Prelude and especially in Part 1, photographic images get clearer: but throughout the film has been painted, scratched, coloured in optical printing, while time-lapse, anamorphosis, application of crystals, dirt, oil, and other materials to the film strip and microscope and telescopic images assemble, passing through varieties of monochrome to brilliant, even lurid fields and fragments of colour. Throughout, the film has been superimposed in camera or in printing, and intense montage, often of single frames, agitates the surface. Cinematographic images of bodies in the act of love, of the infant child, and of the artist in the role of the woodsman, labouring up and finally falling down a snowy slope give the film, if not a narrative, then a mythopoeic structure. The term "epic" is often applied to it: in reference to Homer, to the Norse myths, and to modernist takes on the epic in Pound, Joyce, and Olson. It is often difficult to descry what, if anything, has been in front of the lens: in some sequences, the lens seems to have been removed; in others smeared, loosely mounted, or otherwise tampered with; and often the film strip has clearly been worked on by hand rather than mechanically. But with the exception of the opening passage of the Prelude, machines are conspicuously absent, the only tools visible are the axe the Dog Star Man carries, and the cinematic apparatus which makes its presence viscerally felt.

During the time *Dog Star Man* was being composed, Brakhage wrote his most famous essay, first published in the launch issue of *Millennium Film Journal*. "Metaphors on Vision" opens with well-known paragraphs that commence: "Imagine an eye unruled by man-made laws of perspective, an eye unprejudiced by compositional logic, an eye which does not respond to the name of everything but which must know each object encountered in life through the adventure of perception. How many colours are there in a field of grass to the crawling baby unaware of 'Green'?"[8] Brakhage will go on to deny that it is possible to return to this Edenic state: we can only go forward, schooling the eye to Vision through disciplines of imagination, hallucination, and spiritual exercises. Here, Brakhage appears to be moving backwards from Husserl, who moved from the "pure consciousness" of phenomenal perception toward an intersubjectively shared "lifeworld," where what counts for "world" is always pre-given, not uniquely for "me" (the transcendental ego of Husserl's earlier philosophy) but as an artifact of the necessarily social formation which every individual undergoes. The lifeworld is always ours. For Brakhage then, the challenge is to burst through the habits of vision which supplant infantile pure consciousness; to restore, at a higher level, the once primal, now tertiary vision of the individual. His method in this film is on the one hand physical and intuitive (he describes, in an interview recorded by Colin Still in 1993 included on the first volume of the *By Brakhage* DVD compilation, nature as "the most beautiful, terrible enemy"), and on the other a quasi-Jungian reaching back into myth and poetry for a metaphoric language with which to renew his own vision and visual culture more broadly.

In the films *The Garden of Earthly Delights* (1961) and *Mothlight* (1965), just before and just after *Dog Star Man*, Brakhage avoided the camera altogether.[9] The former places foliage from the area around his Colorado home directly on the filmstrip; the latter adds moths' wings and other garden debris—the former on 35 mm, the latter on 16 mm film. In the original screenings, the found objects were mounted on adhesive tape the same width as the film strip, to which the tape was then affixed, so that the original items were directly projected on screen (later versions were prints taken from these reels). In those first screenings, the presence of the unperceived components of the perceptual landscape are promoted to the status of objects of vision, at the same time as they reveal the taxonomic apparatus of projection, which severs the real items into rectangular modules for projection. The result is a struggle between the natural and the artificial, a struggle not only over what but how we perceive, especially when it comes to perceiving both the natural world and the mediating procedures, of lifeworld and of mechanical media, through which we perceive. There is no doubt on which side of this argument Brakhage stands: in *Dog Star Man* we confront, in the recurring images of solar coronas lent to the artist by the University of Colorado's astronomers, a cosmic landscape of great beauty and fury, equalled by the beauty and fury of the microscopic *and* of the human universe as it is acted out in birth, in lovemaking, and in work. Dying is all part of the same cycle: it is not dying that is fearsome, but rather death, the deadness of the dead tree, the impossibility of communicating with what is no longer alive, or, as Brakhage has it in speaking of Yggdrasil, no longer alive to us.

Despite Brakhage's reputation for machismo, the vulnerability expressed in *Dog Star Man* constantly brings us back to the grounding relation of human and wilderness, in which the human survives by good luck and cunning, not by might or even by knowledge. The relationships that survive are human-to-human: sex, and birth, and by intimation and analogy (explored more explicitly in others of his films) death. At the same time, the heroism of this epic is quite real, but less physical: a heroic quest for a place in the world which is not determined by social mores, beyond habitual perception and particularly beyond regulation of vision by language, and capable not only of revealing the splendour of the world anew, but of releasing the hallucinatory powers of interior vision, seeing with eyes closed, the Goethean vision that explodes from darkness into light. The recurrent motif of ejaculation, like the wasted effort of climbing through forbidding snow up a too-steep slope, are Bataillean *gaspillage*, wastage, spilling, expenditure without meaning or purpose. There comes the powerful sense here that the mountain man, even when no longer the champion of older heroic American myths of the lone man surviving the wilderness, stands for a new compact derived from a move out of the cities into the mountains and the woods—indeed, the kind of journey described so vividly in the poetry of his contemporary, the ecological visionary and Buddhist Gary Snyder, who sought to "dig the / universe as playful, cool and infinitely blank"[10] in sequences like *Six Sections from Mountains and Rivers Without End* (1970), packed with fragmented incident, cross-cultural reference, and the ambition to construct a cosmic body from the mutual implication of everything, from cells to stars, in the porous, infinitely sympathetic human; and to unmake the narrow, conformist consumer of goods and services as cosmic visionary by a process which passes through immersion in the great outdoors.[11]

The "infinitely blank" universe is both a spiritual and a socio-political experience of otherness, and in Snyder grounds of a modest, vulnerable environmentalism. The backwoods return of commune cultures in the 1960s pioneered by the Beat poets and Brakhage belongs to the history of affect, not only for its ideal content but for its attention to the Rimbaldian methodology: "Le poète se fait voyant par une longue, immense et raisonnée dérèglement de tous les sens."[12] Though canonically the type of the anarchic auteur, Rimbaud's un-ruling demands not only discipline across time, but is "reasoned," and its goal is not to deregulate reason but the senses. For Snyder's Buddhism, and Brakhage's Romanticism and approximation to the American Transcendent-alist tradition, however, reason is to be overcome; in Snyder in favour of the blank void of the universe, in Brakhage of its solar energy, its explosive ecstasy, beyond prettiness (portrayed only to be exploded in Part 4 of *Dog Star Man* in the form of picture postcard landscapes).

CHRIS WELSBY

Studying painting at the Royal College of Art during the 1970s, Chris Welsby developed an interest in time and process that brought him into contact with both the moving image and the ideas of systems theory. Film theory in the 1970s in London was dominated by two discourses, one the political semiotics of the Society for Education in Film and Television (SEFT) and its house jour-nal *Screen*, the other the emerging language of structural materialism, a rigor-ous, equally political, equally semiotically inspired theme, but one aimed at and grounded in the radical practices associated with the London Film-Makers Co-op (LFMC). Though the art world, especially magazines like *Artforum*, which gave generous coverage to the moving image arts at a time when national collections were ignoring them, was flirting with systems theoretic criticism,[13] the film theorists were largely uninterested in systems theory. The interest for Welsby seems to have come from three aspects: the process, and especially the inclusion of time; landscape, the possibility of understanding landscape (and ocean) as ecologies; and an engineering orientation which may have come from his maritime background.[14] Most of all, however, it belongs with the Rimbaldian "reasoned deregulation of the senses."[15]

The banality of the observable lifeworld belongs to habits of seeing, but also to constraints on the human optic system. We see within a restricted spectrum, under limited conditions of illumination. As Brakhage observed of conven-tional realism in the *Metaphors*, "Realize the garden as you will—the growing is mostly underground."[16] We perceive time to a certain scale, not its granular speed, nor its epoch-spanning slowness. Where however the Americans—Jack-son Pollock in his drip paintings, John Cage in his I Ching compositions—had resorted to chance, Welsby wanted to construct machines that would perceive in modalities dictated not by human will but by the determining principles of the systems operating on the world he wanted to image. Thus where to Brakhage the call was to imagine, for Welsby it was to engineer systems capable of communicating, and communicating with, the spinning of the planet and revolutions of the sun.

For *Wind Vane* (1972) Welsby built two weathervanes that he attached to a pair of 16 mm cameras mounted on floating-head tripods and installed them a few metres apart on Hampstead Heath.[17] Both cameras' points of view were thus dictated by shifts in wind direction, both panning across the same area of the Heath. The small distance between them was sufficient, however, to ensure that the differences in microclimate, the gap between the arrival of gusts, and the slightly changed angles of thrust, produced asynchronous and rarely paired images in the final two-screen installation. The result is, among other things, a film record of something invisible: the wind. Its overall aesthetic is of course intentional, but the microdynamics of the system are dictated by a force outside the control of the artist. This sacrifice of control had been a tenet of the surrealists. Some of the major breakthroughs (decalcomania, grattage, dripping) had been pioneered by Max Ernst in the years since his personal manifesto *Au delà de la peinture* in the early 1930s,[18] passing into the New York avant-garde in the 1940s when Ernst, Picabia, and Duchamp were in exile. But the use of chance there was held as a gateway to the unconscious: for Welsby, it was a gateway first to the systems of the world, and second to the isomorphic systems governing the mind.

The inspiration is clearer still in *Seven Days* (1974), for which Welsby secured the use of an equatorial mount, a device used by astronomers to track the sun across the sky.[19] Taking a frame every ten seconds over a week, Welsby tilted the camera downwards when the sun was out, and upwards when it was obscured by clouds. The camera's shadow cast on the blown terrain of a Welsh mountain acts as a kind of sundial, and the film as a whole anticipates Christian Marclay's *The Clock* (2010–11) in the sense that it operates as a chronometer.[20] At the same time, unlike Marclay's piece, it records a patch of land and sky, switching brusquely between them, capturing step motion of clouds, taking the sky away from the Constable tradition of observation towards an abstraction which, however, succumbs neither to meteorology nor to the picturesque. Nor is the structure strictly random: it is accounted for by the tempos of natural processes; and like *Wind Vane* its loyalty is to a very specific piece of the world, not to the typifying strategies of Lukácsian realism. In one sense it may be read as one of those scientific instruments that give us a highly detailed account of an event or sequence of events, with no means to determine how typical they are of natural processes more generally: the greater the detail given by an instrument, the less we know about its place in the order of things.

The other kind of instrument typical of modern science is statistical in nature. Counting devices give us very little detail about each event, but a lot of knowledge about the typical sequences of event, the statistical likelihood of their recurrence. Such is the Geiger counter which figures prominently in one of Welsby's most personal films, Sky Light (1986). Peter Galison observes the disparity between these two forms of instrumentation and the forms of knowledge they produce: the unique analogical photogram, and the probabilistic calibration.[21] One informs us, we might say, of accidence, the phenomenal perception of the instant in which the operation of the laws of nature "happens" to converge on a singular conjuncture of light, shade, texture, and organic and physical processes. The other tells us of tendencies, of norms and divergence from norms. The norm in question, in 1986, was the background radiation that occurs in any landscape, and the divergence from it caused by the westward drift across Europe of fallout from the Chernobyl meltdown. Father of a newborn daughter in Thatcher's UK, at a time when government by public relations was coming into its own, Welsby's film is shot through with anger. The unseens that had been the subject of an innovative but nonetheless calm reflection in earlier works were now threats to the life of his child. The pastoral beauty that opens the piece, shots of sky glimpsed through branches reflected in flowing water, is no longer tenable as an image of the landscape.

Instead, Welsby moves into a process of starting and stopping the camera, a process that punctuates the cloudscapes with which much of the film is occupied with flash frames, where light flushes the film chamber as the shutter reopens, and as the pace of starting and stopping increases, the sharp diagonal of the film shutter becomes a powerful structural element in the composition of individual frames. On the soundtrack, we hear a clutter of radio noise. Welsby reports that during the nighttime sequences of an earlier film, the microphone shielding had not been enough to muffle wind noise or the reception of European radio stations, their messages carrying far further at night, recording onto the uncloaked microphone as the wind brought them in and out of range. Something similar occurs here: voices in various languages emerge from the white noise, itself a carrier of information on background radiation, usually solar, now mixed with passages of Geiger-counter clicks. As rain patters onto the Perspex protecting the lens, the possibility that any drop of drizzle might bear in it fatal doses of Ukrainian plutonium unpicks the bloom of sunlight and water cycle. Towards the end of the film's twenty-six minutes, around the twenty-minute mark, the image itself begins to be deranged, infected by colour fields splashing in from lower left, as the film is fogged by light seeping in through the deliberately loosened camera body. At last the film breaks down, from imaging the outer world to reckoning the un-lensed, incoherent light, itself a form of radiation, as the film moves to sheer fields of colour, paler colour, and finally to white as the Geiger counter chatters on.

As mentioned in the opening to this essay, it would be as unfair to *Sky Light* to describe it as a formalist film, as it is to *Dog Star Man* to describe it, as I have, without responding to the formal properties of its rhythms. Yet in bold these films parse two possible ways of engaging the ecological themes that began to gain a purchase on artistic, critical, and political life in the 1960s and '70s. Where Brakhage is explicit and Welsby coy about the spirituality of their films, both clearly seek a kind of accommodation between cosmic processes and mental. Both want to create articulations between the complex inweaving of specificity and generality in both ecological events and human perception of them. Both address the personal component of perception and the desire to alter the perceptual habits of wider communities, and in doing so to introduce the possibility of seeing with other eyes, other senses, that are not exclusively human: indeed *Mothlight* has frequently been interpreted as an account of the moth's perception of her habitat. Both films might be construed, in Welsby's terms, as being "not about nature but incorporated into the structures of nature."[22] It would be fair to say, however, that Brakhage's film is less easily thought of as about "structures," and more about processes, about some form of immanence, and about the mediation of the individual seer, where Welsby does address nature as system, and is concerned with the mediation of the technology as a third party in the communication, rather than as expressive vehicle for nature speaking through the artist.

VOYAGE D'HIVER

Robert Cahen's 1993 single-channel video *Voyage d'hiver*,[23] shot in the Chilean Antarctic, treats the captured images and sounds as data from which to compose a film (in this rather like DJ Spooky's more recent *Terra Nova: Sinfonia Antarctica* [2009])[24] incorporating sound and image. Cahen's score, self-composed, is a treatment of audio data, his image-track of visual. It is the latter that is most significant here, but it is important to note that Brakhage avoids sound in almost every one of his several thousand films, while Welsby integrates direct sound, only discovering by experiment that direct recording can also garner sounds arriving at the venue of the recording by non-traditional means not necessarily audible to human ears as they are to microphones. Cahen takes this only one step further, gathering wind, ice, and water and recombining them (he studied under Pierre Schaeffer with Michel Chion) as auditory material.

This practice of sampling and remixing, pioneered, again by Cage, in the 1930s, is still both radical vanguard technique and very familiar from dub, hip-hop, and electronica music scenes. It is easier to understand what happens aesthetically in the mix when the materials are sonic. Rather oddly, given the far more radical suspicion with which modernist music is regarded compared to modernist visual arts or literature, this postmodernist technique has been easily grasped in sound, but is regarded with suspicion in the visual arts. Data visualization takes over from photography as the key metaphor for the operation of visual data capture. We are moving from the image-based instruments towards the statistical, to use Peter Galison's terminology. But as Galison argues in his introduction to *Image and Logic*, the two traditions of measurement are now, in the field he studies most closely, subatomic physics, increasingly convergent.[25]

CCD and CMOS chips work by taking a sample of light over the area of a pixel array (a 35 mm CMOS chip, as used in RED One cameras, has over a million pixels on an area the size of a 35 mm frame) over the duration of an exposure: in video, somewhat less than one twenty-fifth of a second. Though tiny, each pixel has a finite area, and the quantum events it records—the number and wavelength of incoming photons—are averaged over that area and duration. Recall that photons are far, far smaller and far greater in number than the available pixels, even as those reach the molecular scale of silver halide salts in traditional 35 mm film. The effect is in fact very like traditional film, in which a latent image is only triggered by sufficient numbers of photons in the applicable range of wavelengths for each colour-sensitive layer of tri-pack film. There are two critical differences. Tri-pack film uses filters to ensure that the incoming light is allocated to the appropriate layer of the negative: the actual negative uses generic light-sensitive salts, exactly the same as in black and white film. It is only in printing from the negative that colour dyes are used. In digital imaging, the colour is recorded as charge, a direct physical effect of the wavelength as well as the quantity of light. The second difference is that while both technologies capture light across their whole area during the exposure, digital imaging has to use a clock-function to drain the charge off the chip in lockstep for conversion to voltage and thence to digitization.

It is these latter differences that provide Cahen with the raw materials for his treatment of the visual data he has captured. The challenge in all digital imaging is to capture and maintain the maximum amount of data through a production process that loses data at every step: in conversion from voltage to data; in compression and decompression when transferred from camera to storage; further compression-decompression in each step of editing, effects, rendering, transfer to playback media, transmission, and viewing. Data loss in the image parallels exactly data loss in older forms of scientific instrument, including photography, but takes a slightly different form, being premised on an unspoken but professionally recognized agreement to produce images good enough to fool the human eye. The "good enough" is however never good enough, because it will always decay further from the already lossy form in which it is broadcast or projected: the pitiful 40 percent of the humanly visible spectrum available to digital playback is just one example of the betrayal of vision conducted every day.

Cahen's *Voyage d'hiver*—the title hides a auditory pun, *Voyages divers*, diverse journeys—revisions his journey at multiple levels and from multiple perspectives, effectively multiplying the number of voyages—through a series of modulations of the data stream, engaging both the nature of the image as data, and the necessarily time-based structure not just of the succession of images, but of each scanned electronic video frame. Different horizontal zones of the image are treated differently: at one point the slow pan across the landscape is outstripped by racing waters in the bottom fifth of the screen; at another the luminance is reversed in the lower half, turning the black of open waters opalescent white, remaking the landscape out of texture (as in the famous passage of *Kontakte* [1959–60] when Stockhausen reduces a note to its tonal and rhythmic elements, and finally to pure timbre). A third passage, towards the end of the sixteen-minute piece, places an inverted close up of drifting snow in the sky, tinged with blue, and given the impression of rippling by the panning motion of the camera.

Two other devices are worthy of special mention in our context. As counter-point to the "negative" effect that makes water take on the same snowy colour as the distant shore, the saturated orange of the parkas worn by the two figures in the central passages of the video, the saturated red of the building they pass, and the saturated blue of the skies over them, articulate the alien quality of colour in these latitudes. They also point to the extremes of perception such colourlessness evokes; and the extreme incompetence of both digital media and the super-saturated hues of 3-strip Technicolor, which is humorously imitated here, in capturing either physical or psychological optics. The other device is the pixelation that affects the landscape in the pan that constitutes the second landscape passage of the tape. Here it is as if Cahen has used the edge-finding capabilities of the editing software to emphasize the construction of the image. Today, most cameras feature edge-finding algorithms, and many also have face-recognition, at least to the extent of being able to distinguish faces from other visual material. The edge-finder serves a similar function to face-finding: it instructs the camera on which areas of the image are likely to change, and where therefore mechanical "attention" should be focused. Since human eyelines typically gravitate towards faces, a greater density of information can be preserved in those areas of the image, while sacrificing detail in other areas.

Edge-finding served a similar function both in early digital cameras and in video codecs (compression-decompression algorithms used in broadcasting and recording to reduce the amount of information required during transit). They instructed the electronics where to concentrate data, and therefore where to sacrifice it. Areas of lesser data would then become "blocky," with large areas of undifferentiated colour. This not only instructs the viewer where to look (rather like the short focal length so radically criticized by André Bazin), so depriving them of the freedom to survey the whole frame in the manner of all-over composition; it also abstracts from and reduces the data associated with the crudely delineated areas, in a statistical sampling process which denies the actuality, as of course the particularity, of the area, of the world as well as of the image. To the extent that electronic image capture is a mode of scientific instrumentation, this is a betrayal of the data, even if it is a betrayal undertaken on the probabilistic principle on which the instrument functions in the first place.

Cahen's challenge in the *Voyage d'hiver* is then to maintain faith with a landscape that is at once the least human on our crowded world, and thus both utopia and heterotopia, and simultaneously the most fragile of environments, a continent that acts as a gigantic measuring-rod for climatological, oceanic, and species-specific change. The detail is where these sufferings lie. The struggle with data is not just to save it but to make it count: after all, a decade after this tape was completed, it was announced that our exponentially increasing production of data had finally, and terminally, outstripped the production of storage media.[26] The boost to the edge-finding in this passage of *Voyage d'hiver* is a formal expression of the frailty and vulnerability of data, including the data we require to measure and delay climate change and its Antarctic impacts. It is not a question of going back to some imaginarily pure cinematic realism, some privileged photographic indexicality, as promoted by "Death of Cinema" theorists (Rodowick [2007], Mulvey [2006]): no such purity existed historically, and binary oppositions between analog and digital are historically as well as philosophically flawed. It is a question of analyzing the probabilistic nature of all cinematography, photochemical or opto-electronic, its part in the governmentality implicit in image-making, and in the trade in images that makes of the endless succession of frames the model for an information economy in which any datum is exchangeable for any other, when the only value recognizable is economic, not semantic.

Containing as it does far more radically than the photochemical frame the ephemerality of its own existence as a structural principle of its working, the scanned image is far readier to hand as a medium for the analysis of time in visual culture. The multiple timescales operating within and between frames in Cahen's piece—like the different colour values (how the small group of people in silhouette to the right look archaic, impossibly indigenous even, compared to the brilliantly painted figures on the left)—construct incompatible spaces. We must remember that, like Welsby's fear of terror from the air, so deep-seated a night-fear in the twentieth century (Peter Sloterdijk traces the relation between aerial bombardment, poison gas, and nuclear pollution in his *Terror from the Air*),[27] Cahen filmed under the then recently discovered ozone hole, his blue-white landscapes bathed in an invisible rain of carcinogenic ultraviolet light. The incompossible spheres of extraterrestrial radiation and the landscape made almost exclusively from water—waves, snow, and ice—belong in different time zones. Only the digital image, carrying in itself the traces of its construction and coding as temporal being, can do such justice to the temporalities that coexist and intertwine in bulk—as abstracted measurements—and in detail. The boosted edge picks out the rocks among the ice, the punctuation that, along with visual rhythm, bears upon the geological time of Gondwana, the wanderings that brought this anti-Odysseus to its mirror Ultima Thule.

These rocks, effectively painted with these tools, are "mythical" not because they bear some ancient wisdom, but only in the sense of that myth exists in a time outside history, a time parallel to human historical passage. Not even astronomical time, the time of the calendar from Ur and Stonehenge to the Nazca desert, a time in some way tamed as it became the instrument of measuring and, in astrology, of destiny, has the mythic power of geological time, the time that made the mountains and stirred the seas. Such time cannot be revealed in film, even in an effect: it can only be indicated, shadowed, with a gesture that has the same shape as the time it gestures toward—it can, in fine, only be *drawn*. And that is how, in this tape, the digital functions: as a drawing of time. It is a graph then, but not the famous "hockey stick" that shows Earth's surface temperature swooping up since industrialization. Rather it has a certain freedom: we must ask where that lies.

Unlike Welsby, Cahen has rarely evoked systems or structure as the shaping aesthetic of even his most serial works. Here the tripod mount that keeps the pans level is one structuring device; the interlaced scan in capture and the raster array in display are structural elements of his images and their succession;

but they do not take the place of the observer, the artist Robert Cahen, whose motivating presence behind the camera we have no reason to doubt. There is instead the enigma of the young girl's face in the snow, a face that seems as much a drawing as a photograph, over which a veil appears to be superimposed that might however also be read as her own hair blowing in an unseen wind. This enigmatic face—she echoes the two-screen installation *Traverses* (2004) Cahen made a decade later, in which figures move towards the viewer out of a snowstorm—has no definitive position in the work: she is at once the observer of events, the spirit of place, and the ghost in the machine.

To reiterate an argument made in my *EcoMedia* (2005), environmentally responsible work: work which derives its aesthetics from its alertness to environmental factors, can neither separate human from natural, nor exclude the technological from the natural or the human.[28] Technologies, especially media technologies, mediate between the organic and physical processes of the world and us, who are in all cases anyway already physical and organic creatures, while our instruments are living partners. When Marx spoke of technology as "dead labour," he made a value judgment based on the nature of social relations in the factory system, pitching the machine against its minders. Today we are at a crossroads where we can recognize that technology is where we Westerners keep our ancestors. All the million hands whose skills compiled across millennia are ossified in our machines are so because we have lost the art of speaking with them, of inviting them to share with us the day's work and its rewards. In an information economy, the presence of the ancestors, of the little girl in the TV set, is not only not scary; in the information economy, we are no longer condemned to keep our ancestors in slavery, or to see and treat them as our enemies, more beautiful and terrible than nature herself. The rippling code effects interlacing with the landscape in Cahen's *Voyage* exposes a third reading of the title: it is Winter herself who is going on a voyage, and its vehicle is suitably metaphysical. In the Antarctic winter, hut, garments, and camera are technologies without which the scene would be fatal, and to that extent invisible.

Impossible visualizations of invisible entities are the stuff of environmental science, which addresses changes too slow for even the most patient of time-lapse cameras, and losses and absences which are by nature not recordable. The swiftness of affect, the rippling changes of the heart, are things we can only stereotype in narrative fiction, where we tend to ascribe to emotion and inner life a sluggish coherence over time we rarely experience in life (see Dryden Goodwin's portraits of faces in crowds in his *Wait* [2000]).[29] The awareness of time which avant-garde film and video gives us, by leaving aside the mechanisms feature films normally use to avoid noticing time passing, or to steal the time from us while substituting its action for our thoughts, that time of which we become aware, is time in which the perilously rapid passage of affect can be experienced; and in these works experienced as and in meditations on the relations between human and environment at the level, as here explored at least, of the transition from mythopoesis via perception and mediated perception into the gestural, a prototype for action. Emphasizing the excessive in Brakhage, the formal in Welsby, and mediation in Cahen helps understand these operations, and how, especially, the affective, which is so constrained by the formulae of classical storytelling and novelistic norms, can be liberated, technically, not only to experience wider and more mobile modes of emotional life—far beyond Nietzsche's rough face-off between gods—but to understand how that liberty is dependent on its implication in technology, and its articulations in and of the organic and physical world which are, as another of Brakhage's titles has it, "Commingled Containers."

NOTES

1 Patricia Ticinieto Clough, *Autoaffection: Unconscious Thought in the Age of Teletechnology* (Minneapolis: University of Minnesota Press, 2000).

2 *All Watched Over by Machines of Loving Grace*, directed by Adam Curtis (London: BBC, 2011).

3 Georges Bataille, *The Accursed Share*, vol. 1, *Consumption*, trans. Robert Hurley (New York: Zone Books, 1988).

4 See Adam Sharr, *Heidegger's Hut* (Cambridge, MA: MIT Press, 2006).

5 William Wordsworth, "She dwelt among the untrodden ways," *Wordsworth: Poetical Works*, ed. Thomas Hutchinson and Ernest de Selincourt (Oxford: Oxford University Press), 86.

6 *Dog Star Man*, directed by Stan Brakhage (USA, 1961–64).

7 *Sky Light*, directed by Chris Welsby (UK, 1986).

8 Stan Brakhage, "From Metaphors on Vision," in *The Avant-Garde Film: A Reader of Theory and Criticism*, ed. P. Adams Sitney (New York: Anthology Film Archives, 1978), 120.

9 *The Garden of Earthly Delights*, directed by Stan Brakhage (USA, 1961); *Mothlight*, directed by Stan Brakhage (USA, 1965).

10 Gary Snyder, "T-2 Tanker Blues," in *Riprap and Cold Mountain Poems* (Berkeley, CA: Counterpoint, 2009), 29.

11 Gary Snyder, *Six Sections from Mountains and Rivers without End* (San Francisco: Four Seasons Foundation, 1970).

12 Arthur Rimbaud, in a letter of 15 May 1871 to Paul Demeny, in Arthur Rimbaud, *Poésies, Une Saison en enfer, Illuminations*, ed. Louise Forestier, préface de René Char (Paris: Gallimard, 1999), 202.

13 See, for example, Jack Burnham, *The Structure of Art* (New York: Braziller, 1971) and *Great Western Salt Works: Essays on the Meaning of Post-Formalist Art* (New York: Braziller, 1974); see also Edward Shanken, "The House That Jack Built: Jack Burnham's Concept of Software as a Metaphor for Art," *Leonardo Electronic Almanac* 6, no. 10 (1998), available at http://leoalmanac.org/journal/Vol_6/lea_v6_n10.txt.

14 See interview in *The Frame: Chris Welsby*, Illuminations, included on the BFI DVD of Welsby's work.

15 Arthur Rimbaud, in a letter of 15 May 1871 to Paul Demeny, in Rimbaud, *Poésies*, 202.

16 Brakhage, "From Metaphors on Vision," 124

17 *Wind Vane*, directed by Chris Welsby (UK, 1972).

18 Max Ernst, "Au dela de la peinture," *Cahiers d'Art* 11, nos. 6–7 (1936): 149–84. Translated from French and published in *Max Ernst: 'Beyond Painting' and other Writings by the Artist and his Friends*, ed. Robert Motherwell (New York: Wittenborn, Schultz, 1948), 3–19.

19 *Seven Days*, directed by Chris Welsby (UK, 1974).

20 *The Clock*, directed by Christian Marclay (USA, 2010–11).

21 Peter Galison, *Image and Logic: A Material Culture of Microphysics* (Chicago: University of Chicago Press, 1997), 19–31.

22 See interview in *The Frame: Chris Welsby*, Illuminations.

23 *Voyage d'hiver*, directed by Robert Cahen (France, 1993).

24 *Terra Nova: Sinfonia Antarctica*, directed by DJ Spooky (USA, 2009).

25 Galison, *Image and Logic*, 31–45.

26 John F. Gantz et al., *The Diverse and Exploding Digital Universe*, IDC White Paper, Framingham, MA: IDC, March 2008, http://www.emc.com/collateral/analyst-reports/diverse-exploding-digital-universe.pdf.

27 Peter Sloterdijk, *Terror from the Air*, trans. Amy Patton and Steve Corcoran (Los Angeles: Semiotext(e), 2009).

28 Sean Cubitt, *EcoMedia* (Amsterdam: Rodopi, 2005).

29 *Wait*, directed by Dryden Goodwin (UK, 2000).

BIBLIOGRAPHY

Bataille, Georges. *The Accursed Share*. Vol. 1, *Consumption*. Translated by Robert Hurley. New York: Zone Books, 1988.

Brakhage, Stan. "From Metaphors on Vision." In *The Avant-Garde Film: A Reader of Theory and Criticism*, edited by P. Adams Sitney, 120–28. New York: Anthology Film Archives, 1978.

Burnham, Jack. *Great Western Salt Works: Essays on the Meaning of Post-Formalist Art*. New York: Braziller,1974.

———. *The Structure of Art*. Rev. ed. New York: Braziller, 1971.

Cubitt, Sean. *EcoMedia*. Amsterdam: Rodopi, 2005.

Ernst, Max. "Au dela de la peinture." *Cahiers d'Art* 11, no. 6–7 (1936): 149–84. Translated from French as *Max Ernst: Beyond Painting and Other Writings by the Artist and His Friends: The Documents of Modern Art*, edited by Robert Motherwell. New York: Wittenborn, Schultz, 1948.

Galison, Peter. *Image and Logic: A Material Culture of Microphysics*. Chicago: University of Chicago Press, 1997.

Gantz, John F., Christopher Chute, Alex Manfrediz, Stephen Minton, David Reinsel, Wolfgang Schlichting, and Anna Tonchev. *The Diverse and Exploding Digital Universe*. IDC White Paper. Framingham, MA: IDC, March 2008. http://www.emc.com/collateral/analyst-reports/diverse-exploding-digital-universe.pdf.

Mulvey, Laura. *Death 24x a Second: Stillness and the Moving Image*. London: Reaktion Books, 2006.

Rimbaud, Arthur. *Poésies, Une Saison en enfer, Illuminations*. Edited by Louise Forestier. Paris: Gallimard, 1999.

Rodowick, David Norman. *The Virtual Life of Film*. Cambridge, MA: Harvard University Press, 2007.

Shanken, Edward. "The House That Jack Built: Jack Burnham's Concept of Software as a Metaphor for Art." *Leonardo Electronic Almanac* 6, no. 10 (1998). http://leoalmanac.org/journal/Vol_6/lea_v6_n10.txt.

Sharr, Adam. *Heidegger's Hut*. Cambridge, MA: MIT Press, 2006.

Sloterdijk, Peter. *Terror from the Air*. Translated by Amy Patton and Steve Corcoran. Los Angeles: Semiotext(e), 2009.

Snyder, Gary. *Six Sections from Mountains and Rivers without End*. San Francisco: Four Seasons Foundation, 1970.

———. "T-2 Tanker Blues." In *Riprap and Cold Mountain Poems*. Berkeley, CA: Counterpoint, 2009.

Ticinieto Clough, Patricia. *Autoaffection: Unconscious Thought in the Age of Teletechnology*. Minneapolis: University of Minnesota Press, 2000.

Contributors

PAT BRERETON is currently Head of School of Communications at Dublin City University in Ireland. As a film and media scholar, he has published widely in ecology and environmental communication. His books include *Hollywood Utopia: Ecology in Contemporary American Cinema* (Intellect, 2005); *Continuum Guide to Media Education* (Continuum, 2001); and most recently *Smart Cinema: DVD Add-ons and New Audience Pleasures* (Palgrave Macmillan, 2012). He is currently working on a book for Routledge titled *Environmental Ethics and Cinema*.

SEAN CUBITT is Professor of Film and Television at Goldsmiths, University of London; Professorial Fellow of the University of Melbourne; and Honorary Professor of the University of Dundee. His publications include *Timeshift: On Video Culture* (Comedia/Routledge, 1991), *Videography: Video Media as Art and Culture* (Macmillan/St. Martin's Press, 1993), *Digital Aesthetics* (Sage, 1998), *Simulation and Social Theory* (Sage, 2001), *The Cinema Effect* (MIT Press, 2004) and EcoMedia (Rodopi, 2005). He is the series editor for Leonardo Books at MIT Press. Current research is on the history and philosophy of visual technologies, on media art history, and on ecocriticism and decolonization.

JOSEPH K. HEUMANN is Professor Emeritus of Communication Studies from Eastern Illinois University and still teaches various film courses. He and Robin L. Murray co-authored *Ecology and Popular Film: Cinema on the Edge* (SUNY Press, 2009), *That's All Folks?: The Ecology of the American Animated Feature* (University of Nebraska Press, 2011), *Gunfight at the Eco-Corral: Western Cinema and the Environment* (University of Oklahoma Press, 2012), the forthcoming *Film and Everyday Ecodisasters* (University of Nebraska Press, 2014), and are currently working on a manuscript exploring monstrous nature. They also maintain an ecocinema blog: http://ecocinema.blogspot.com.

DAVID INGRAM is a lecturer in Screen Media at Brunel University, London. He is the author of *Green Screen: Environmentalism and Hollywood Cinema* (University of Exeter Press, 2000) and *The Jukebox in the Garden: Ecocriticism and American Popular Music Since 1960* (Rodopi, 2010). His articles have been published in journals including *Green Letters*, the *European Journal of American Culture*, the *Journal of American Studies*, and *Scope*. He is a member of the Advisory Board of the Association for the Study of Literature and the Environment–UK and Ireland.

ADRIAN IVAKHIV is Professor of Environmental Thought and Culture at the Rubenstein School of Environment and Natural Resources, University of Vermont. His research focuses at the intersections of culture, ecology, identity, media, and religion. His publications include *Ecologies of the Moving Image: Cinema, Affect, Nature* (Wilfrid Laurier University Press, 2013) and *Claiming Sacred Ground: Pilgrims and Politics at Glastonbury and Sedona* (Indiana University Press, 2001). He edits the blog Immanence: Ecoculture, Geophilosophy, Mediapolitics (http://blog.uvm.edu/immanence).

SALMA MONANI is a tenured faculty member at Gettysburg College's Environmental Studies department. As a humanities scholar her research and teaching include explorations in literary ecocriticism and cine-ecocriticism. She is co-editor of *Ecocinema Theory and Practice* (AFI Film Series at Routledge, 2013); has published in a variety of journals including *Interdisciplinary Studies in Literature and Environment* and *Local Environments*; and co-edited a special collection devoted to ecomedia and just sustainability for Environmental Communication: *The Journal of Nature and Culture* (5.1, 2011). Current projects include a monograph examining contemporary indigenous media expressions in the Americas and the forthcoming co-edited *Ecomedia: Key Issues* (Routledge Earthscan).

ROBIN L. MURRAY is Professor of English at Eastern Illinois University, where she teaches film and literature courses and coordinates the film studies minor. She and Joseph K. Heumann co-authored *Ecology and Popular Film: Cinema on the Edge* (SUNY Press, 2009), *That's All Folks?: The Ecology of the American Animated Feature* (University of Nebraska Press, 2011), *Gunfight at the Eco-Corral: Western Cinema and the Environment* (University of Oklahoma Press, 2012), the forthcoming *Film and Everyday Ecodisasters* (University of

Nebraska Press, 2014), and are currently working on a manuscript exploring monstrous nature. They also maintain an ecocinema blog: http://ecocinema .blogspot.com.

NICOLE SEYMOUR is the author of *Strange Natures: Futurity, Empathy, and the Queer Ecological Imagination* (University of Illinois Press, 2013). Since July 2013 she has been a fellow at the Rachel Carson Center for Environment and Society in Munich, Germany, where she has been working on a new book project titled *Bad Environmentalism: Affective Dissent in the Ecological Age*. Previously, she was Visiting Assistant Professor of English at the University of Louisville and Assistant Professor of English at the University of Arkansas at Little Rock. As of August 2014, she is Assistant Professor in Literature and the Environment at California State University, Fullerton.

BELINDA SMAILL is a Senior Lecturer in Film and Television Studies at Monash University. She is the author of *The Documentary: Politics, Emotion, Culture* (2010) and co-author of *Transnational Australian Cinema: Ethics in the Asian Diasporas* (2013). Her essays have appeared in numerous journals including *Camera Obscura*, *Quarterly Review of Film and Video*, *Continuum: Journal of Media and Cultural Studies*, and *Feminist Media Studies*.

JANET WALKER is Professor of Film and Media Studies at the University of California, Santa Barbara, where she is also affiliated with the Environmental Media Initiative of the Carsey-Wolf Center. A specialist in documentary film, trauma and memory, and media and environment, her books include *Trauma Cinema: Documenting Incest and the Holocaust* (University of California Press, 2005); and *Documentary Testimonies: Global Archives of Suffering* (co-edited with Bhaskar Sarkar, Routledge, 2010). Moving to spatial media studies, Walker co-led the interdisciplinary project, "Figuring Sea Level Rise," and has been engaging in site-specific research locally and in Israel-Palestine and post-Katrina New Orleans for a book on geomedia and environment.

ALEXA WEIK VON MOSSNER is Assistant Professor of American Studies at the University of Klagenfurt in Austria and an Affiliate at the Rachel Carson Center for Environment and Society at the University of Munich. Her writings have been published in journals including *Interdisciplinary Studies in Literature and Environment* and *Environmental Communication*. She is the author of *Cosmopolitan Minds: Literature, Emotion, and the Transnational Imagination* (University of Texas Press, 2014) and co-editor of *The Anticipation of Catastrophe: Environmental Risk in North American Literature and Culture* (with

Sylvia Mayer, Winter 2014). She is currently working on a book project that explores the emotional and cognitive dimensions of our engagement with environmental literature and visual culture.

BART H. WELLING is an Associate Professor of English and an Environmental Center fellow at the University of North Florida in Jacksonville, where he has been teaching courses in environmental literature and film, ecocriticism, and animal studies (in addition to general literature classes) since 2003. His work has been published in journals including the *Mississippi Quarterly* and *Green Letters* and in such essay collections as *Teaching Ecocriticism and Green Cultural Studies* (Palgrave Macmillan, 2012) and *The Bioregional Imagination: Literature, Ecology, and Place* (University of Georgia Press, 2012). He has recently published essays on anthropomorphism in animal photography and the role of animals in religion, and he is currently working on a book about the rise of "petroleum discourse" in literature, film, and everyday life.

DAVID WHITLEY is a lecturer in the Faculty of Education at Cambridge University, where he teaches film, poetry, and children's literature. He is particularly interested in the way the arts, especially poetry and film, offer different forms of understanding and engagement with the natural world. In addition to numerous articles and chapters, he has edited *Poetry and Childhood* (with Morag Styles and Louise Joy, Trentham, 2010). His most recent book is *The Idea of Nature in Disney Animation: from Snow White to WALL·E* (Ashgate, 2012).

Index

actors, 51

Adventure Is Out There bonus feature, 190. See also *UP*

affect(ive): Anne Rutherford on film studies and, 24; in avant-garde film, 262–63; as central to understanding how films work, 155; cognitive effect of, 35; David Ingram view of, 23; definition of, 1; dimensions of city life, 219n40; eco-, 160; in ecocritical film studies, 1; and emotion in contemporary cultural criticism, 249; engineering of, 212; Greg Smith view of, 23; in history of environmental thinking, 249; human geographers and social scientists on, 203–4; importance of in viewing eco-cinema, 14; Nigel Thrift on four major definitions of, 218n21; and phenomenological approaches, 26; relationships developed and mediated by virtual technologies, 6; serious modes of, 10, 61, 62; stereotyped in narrative fiction, 262; studies, 4; theory, 6, 13; unserious modes of, 61, 73–74

Age of Stupid, The: approach to, 42, 49; Archivist in, 50, 51; cartoons in, 54; as discourse of consequence, 55; documentary strands of, 50–51, 51–54; emotional impact of, 8; first scenes of, 50; inspiration for, 50–51; Rachel Howell's study on impact of, 8, 54–55, 57n41, 58n46; rhetorical form in, 45

Ahmed, Sara, 7–8, 110

Alaskan conservation method, 126

alignment, in character engagement, 33, 228

Allee, Warder C., 123

allegiance: in character engagement, 33, 228; perverse, 25. See also identification

allegory, 166

Allison, Leanne: *Being Caribou* projects, 88–91, 98n37

All Watched Over by Machines of Loving Grace, 249

Altman, Rick, 154

Altruism Question, The (Batson), 241n7

Amazon Watch: *A Message from Pandora*, 232, 235

American Transcendentalism, 250, 254

Anderson, John and Bob, 238

And Tango Makes Three (Parnell, Richardson, and Cole), 75n20

animal consciousness, 118n14

animal emotions, 83, 85

animal liberation, 122, 128, 131, 136, 137

Animal Liberation (Singer), 131

animal presence, 95

animal rights: vs. animal welfare, 132; basis for, 131–32; and biotic community, 132, 137; combined with organismic ecology, 123; in *The Cove*, 116, 117, 121, 123, 133, 135, 136, 137; and *Darwin's Nightmare*, 127; effect of in documentaries, 131, 132; lack of in *The End*

271

ENVIRONMENTAL HUMANITIES SERIES

Environmental thought pursues with renewed urgency the grand concerns of the humanities: who we think we are, how we relate to others, and how we live in the world. Scholarship in the environmental humanities explores these questions by crossing the lines that separate human from animal, social from material, and objects and bodies from techno-ecological networks. Humanistic accounts of political representation and ethical recognition are re-examined in consideration of other species. Social identities are studied in relation to conceptions of the natural, the animal, the bodily, place, space, landscape, risk, and technology, and in relation to the material distribution and contestation of environmental hazards and pleasures.

The Environmental Humanities Series features research that adopts and adapts the methods of the humanities to clarify the cultural meanings associated with environmental debate. The scope of the series is broad. Film, literature, television, Web-based media, visual art, and physical landscape—all are crucial sites for exploring how ecological relationships and identities are lived and imagined. The Environmental Humanities Series publishes scholarly monographs and essay collections in environmental cultural studies, including popular culture, film, media, and visual cultures; environmental literary criticism; cultural geography; environmental philosophy, ethics, and religious studies; and other cross-disciplinary research that probes what it means to be human, animal, and technological in an ecological world.

Gathering research and writing in environmental philosophy, ethics, cultural studies, and literature under a single umbrella, the series aims to make visible the contributions of humanities research to environmental studies, and to foster discussion that challenges and reconceptualizes the humanities.

Series editor:
Cheryl Lousley, English and Film Studies, Wilfrid Laurier University

Editorial committee:
Adrian J. Ivakhiv, Environmental Studies, University of Vermont
Catriona Mortimer-Sandilands, Tier 1 CRC in Sustainability and Culture,
    Environmental Studies, York University
Susie O'Brien, English and Cultural Studies, McMaster University
Laurie Ricou, English, University of British Columbia
Rob Shields, Henry Marshall Tory Chair and Professor, Department of Sociology,
    University of Alberta

For more information, contact:
Lisa Quinn
Acquisitions Editor
Wilfrid Laurier University Press
75 University Avenue West
Waterloo, ON N2L 3C5
(519) 884-0710 ext. 2843
Email: quinn@press.wlu.ca

Books in the Environmental Humanities Series
Published by Wilfrid Laurier University Press

Animal Subjects: An Ethical Reader in a Posthuman World, Jodey Castricano, editor / 2008 / 324 pp. / ISBN 978-0-88920-512-3

Open Wide a Wilderness: Canadian Nature Poems, Nancy Holmes, editor / 2009 / 534 pp. / ISBN 978-1-55458-033-0

Technonatures: Environments, Technologies, Spaces, and Places in the Twenty-first Century, Damian F. White and Chris Wilbert, editors / 2009 / 282 pp. / ISBN 978-1-55458-150-4

Writing in Dust: Reading the Prairie Environmentally, Jenny Kerber / 2010 / 276 pp. / ISBN 978-1-55458-218-1 (hardcover), ISBN 978-1-55458-306-5 (paper)

Ecologies of Affect: Placing Nostalgia, Desire, and Hope, Tonya K. Davidson, Ondine Park, and Rob Shields, editors / 2011 / 360 pp. / illus. / ISBN 978-1-55458-258-7

Ornithologies of Desire: Ecocritical Essays, Avian Poetics, and Don McKay, Travis V. Mason / 2013 / 306 pp. / ISBN 978-1-55458-630-1

Ecologies of the Moving Image: Cinema, Affect, Nature, Adrian J. Ivakhiv / 2013 / 432 pp. / ISBN 978-1-55458-905-0

Avatar and Nature Spirituality, Bron Taylor, editor / 2013 / 378 pp. / ISBN 978-1-55458-843-5

Moving Environments: Affect, Emotion, Ecology, and Film, Alexa Weik von Mossner, editor / 2014 / vi + 290 pp. / ISBN 978-1-77112-002-9

Sustaining the West: Cultural Responses to Western Environments, Past and Present, Liza Piper and Lisa Szabo-Jones, editors / forthcoming 2015 / ISBN 978-1-55458-923-4